VALUES AND DISORDER IN MENTAL CAPACITY LAW

This book draws on the disciplines of law, philosophy, and psychiatry to interrogate whether the Mental Capacity Act 2005 meets the challenges posed by mental disorder to decision-making. It is often assumed that to allow space for individuality, any test for capacity must focus only on decision-making processes and not on the substance of the values that underpin decisions. Auckland challenges this assumption, arguing that the current law serves merely as a façade, behind which judgements can be made about the nature of a person's values, free from proper scrutiny. This book provides an in-depth analysis of when and how a person's disordered values should be relevant to the determination of their capacity, offering novel suggestions for reforming the capacity test to better reflect the impact of disorder on decision-making. It also explores the implications of this analysis for people found to lack capacity, concluding that reforms to the best interest provisions are urgently needed. This title is part of the Flip it Open Programme and may also be available Open Access. Check our website Cambridge Core for details.

CRESSIDA AUCKLAND is Assistant Professor in Law at the Law School, London School of Economics and Political Science. Auckland's research focuses on mental capacity and end-of-life decision-making. She has published extensively on the topic of medical decision-making for minors, with her publications featuring in the *Law Quarterly Review*, *Modern Law Review*, *Cambridge Law Journal*, and *Medical Law Review*. She is also an associate editor of the *Journal of Medical Ethics*, and an academic fellow of the Middle Temple.

CAMBRIDGE BIOETHICS AND LAW

This series of books – formerly called Cambridge Law, Medicine and Ethics – was founded by Cambridge University Press with Alexander McCall Smith as its first editor in 2003. It focuses on the law's complex and troubled relationship with medicine across both the developed and the developing world. In the past twenty years, we have seen in many countries increasing resort to the courts by dissatisfied patients and a growing use of the courts to attempt to resolve intractable ethical dilemmas. At the same time, legislatures across the world have struggled to address the questions posed by both the successes and the failures of modern medicine, while international organisations such as the WHO and UNESCO now regularly address issues of medical law. It follows that we would expect ethical and policy questions to be integral to the analysis of the legal issues discussed in this series. The series responds to the high profile of medical law in universities, in legal and medical practice, as well as in public and political affairs. We seek to reflect the evidence that many major health-related policy and bioethics debates in the UK, Europe and the international community over the past two decades have involved a strong medical law dimension. With that in mind, we seek to address how legal analysis might have a trans-jurisdictional and international relevance. Organ retention, embryonic stem cell research, physician-assisted suicide and the allocation of resources to fund health care are but a few examples among many. The emphasis of this series is thus on matters of public concern and/or practical significance. We look for books that could make a difference to the development of medical law and enhance the role of medico-legal debate in policy circles. That is not to say that we lack interest in the important theoretical dimensions of the subject, but we aim to ensure that theoretical debate is grounded in the realities of how the law does and should interact with medicine and health care.

Series Editors

VALUES AND DISORDER IN MENTAL CAPACITY LAW

CRESSIDA AUCKLAND

London School of Economics and Political Science

CAMBRIDGE
UNIVERSITY PRESS

CAMBRIDGE UNIVERSITY PRESS

Shaftesbury Road, Cambridge CB2 8EA, United Kingdom

One Liberty Plaza, 20th Floor, New York, NY 10006, USA

477 Williamstown Road, Port Melbourne, VIC 3207, Australia

314–321, 3rd Floor, Plot 3, Splendor Forum, Jasola District Centre, New Delhi – 110025, India

103 Penang Road, #05–06/07, Visioncrest Commercial, Singapore 238467

Cambridge University Press is part of Cambridge University Press & Assessment, a department of the University of Cambridge.

We share the University's mission to contribute to society through the pursuit of education, learning and research at the highest international levels of excellence.

www.cambridge.org
Information on this title: www.cambridge.org/9781009482066

DOI: 10.1017/9781009482080

When citing this work, please include a reference to the DOI 10.1017/9781009482080

First published 2024
First paperback edition 2025

A catalogue record for this publication is available from the British Library

Library of Congress Cataloging-in-Publication data
Names: Auckland, Cressida, 1992- author.
Title: Values and disorder in mental capacity law / Cressida Auckland, London School of Economics and Political Science.
Description: Cambridge, United Kingdom ; New York, NY : Cambridge University Press, 2024. | Series: Cambridge bioethics and law | Includes bibliographical references and index.
Identifiers: LCCN 2023058915 (print) | LCCN 2023058916 (ebook) | ISBN 9781009482073 (hardback) | ISBN 9781009482066 (paperback) | ISBN 9781009482080 (ebook)
Subjects: LCSH: Great Britain. Mental Capacity Act 2005. | Capacity and disability–Great Britain. | Mental health laws–Great Britain. | Insanity (Law)–Great Britain.
Classification: LCC KD737.A3282005 A53 2024 (print) | LCC KD737.A3282005 (ebook) | DDC 346.4101/30874–dc23/eng/20240117
LC record available at https://lccn.loc.gov/2023058915
LC ebook record available at https://lccn.loc.gov/2023058916

ISBN 978-1-009-48207-3 Hardback
ISBN 978-1-009-48206-6 Paperback

For my father, Keith, who never got to see the finished product, and my mother, Ambra, who had to read it more times than she would have cared for.

CONTENTS

ACKNOWLEDGEMENTS

There are a number of people I would like to thank for their help in completing this monograph. First, special thanks go to Emily Jackson, whose guidance and support has been invaluable, not just in the writing of this book but also throughout my early career. This book originated from the work of my PhD, which I could not have completed without my fantastic PhD supervisor, mentor, and friend, Imogen Goold. I am also grateful to my wonderful colleagues at the LSE Law School, whose scholarly and other support has been essential over the years, in particular Sarah Trotter and Tatiana Cutts for their constant friendship. And thanks to my fantastic research assistant Allegra Enefer, for her careful editing and thoughtful comments on the final draft.

Finally, this book would not have been possible without the immense support of my friends and family over the best part of a decade. For most people, this support is limited to the emotional, and I certainly owe a huge debt of gratitude to them for keeping me sane during the highs and lows of this process. But my family were required to provide more than merely moral support, and so a special thanks is owed to my mother, Ambra Edwards, whose reading (and re-reading) of my PhD thesis and early chapters went well beyond the call of motherly love, and to my husband, Max Marenbon, who dutifully took a draft manuscript as 'holiday reading' and provided endless invaluable comments without complaint!

CASES

Dudgeon *v.* United Kingdom 7525/76 (1983) 5 EHRR 573
X and Y *v.* Netherlands (1986) 8 EHRR 235
Re T (Adult: Refusal of Medical Treatment) [1992] 4 All ER 649
Re C (Adult: Refusal of Treatment) [1994] 1WLR 290 (Fam)
B *v.* Croydon HA [1995] Fam 133
Norfolk and Norwich HealthCare (NHS) Trust *v.* W [1996] 2 FLR 613
Rochdale Healthcare (NHS) Trust *v.* C [3 July 1996] (unreported)
Tameside and Glossip Acute Services Trust *v.* CH [1996] 1 FLR 762 (QBD)
Re MB [1997] EWCA Civ 3093
St George's Healthcare NHS Trust *v.* S [1998] 3 All ER 673
R *v.* Collins and Ashworth Hospital Authority ex parte Brady [2001] 58 BMLR 173
R (Wilkinson) *v.* Broadmoor Special Hospital Authority [2002] 1 WLR 419
Re B (Adult: Refusal of Medical Treatment) [2002] 2 All England Reports 449
Jepson *v.* The Chief Constable of West Mercia Police Constabulary [2003] EWHC 3318
The NHS Trust *v.* Mrs T [2004] EWHC 1279 (Fam)
Y.F. *v.* Turkey (2004) 39 EHRR 34
Re SA (Vulnerable Adult with Capacity: Marriage) [2006] 1 FLR 867
Re MM (An Adult) [2007] EWHC 2003 (Fam)
Re M (Statutory Will), ITW *v.* Z and Others [2009] EWHC 2525 (Fam)
Re P [2009] EWHC 163 (Ch)
Re S and S (Protected Persons) [2009] WTLR 315
G *v.* E [2010] EWHC 621 (Fam)
Jehovah's Witnesses of Moscow and Others *v.* Russia 302/02 [2010] ECHR
Re G(TJ) [2010] EWHC 3005
VAC *v.* JAD and Others [2010] EWHC 2159 (Ch)
Hillingdon LBC *v.* Neary [2011] EWHC 1377 (COP)
PH *v.* A Local Authority and Others [2011] EWHC 1704 (Fam)
W *v.* M and Others [2011] EWHC 2443 (Fam)
A Local Authority *v.* E [2012] EWCOP 1639 (COP)
DL *v.* A Local Authority [2012] EWCA 253
Re D [2012] EWHC 885 (COP)
Re SA (Vulnerable Adult with Capacity: Marriage) [2012] EWCA 253

XCC *v.* AA and Others [2012] EWHC 2183 (COP)
ZH *v.* Commissioner of Police for the Metropolis [2012] EWHC 604 (QB)
A Local Authority *v.* WMA & Ors [2013] EWHC 2580 (COP)
Aintree University Hospitals NHS Foundation Trust *v.* James [2013] UKSC 67
An NHS Trust *v.* Dr A [2013] EWHC 2442 (COP), [2013] MHLO 4
NHS *v.* VT and Another [2013] EWHC B26 (Fam)
NT *v.* FS and Another [2013] EWHC 684
PC & NC *v.* City of York Council [2013] EWCA 478 (Civ)
Re M (Best Interests: Deprivation of Liberty) [2013] EWHC 3456 (COP), [2013] MHLO 97
Re SB (A Patient; Capacity to Consent to Termination) [2013] EWHC 1417 (COP)
An NHS Foundation Trust *v.* Ms X [2014] EWCOP 35, [2014] MHLO 96
Heart of England NHS Foundation Trust *v.* JB [2014] EWHC 342 (COP)
IM *v.* LM [2014] EWCA Civ 37
Newcastle upon Tyne Hospitals Foundation Trust *v.* LM [2014] EWHC 454 (COP), [2014] MHLO 14
Northamptonshire Healthcare NHS Foundation Trust *v.* ML [2014] EWCOP 2, [2014] MHLO 31
Northamptonshire Healthcare NHS Foundation Trust *v.* ML (Rev 1) [2014] EWCOP 2
Nottinghamshire Healthcare NHS Trust *v.* RC [2014] EWCOP 1317
RB *v.* Brighton and Hove CC [2014] EWCA Civ 561, [2014] MHLO 25
Re TZ (No 2) [2014] EWHC 973 (COP)
Sheffield Teaching Hospitals NHS Foundation Trust *v.* TH and Another [2014] EWCOP 4
The Mental Health Trust/The Acute Trust & The Council *v.* DD and VC (Number 2) [2014] EWCOP 13
United Lincolnshire Hospitals NHS Trust *v.* N [2014] EWCOP 16
Westminster City Council *v.* Sykes [2014] EWHC B9 (COP), [2014] MHLO 11
Essex County Council *v.* RF [2015] EWCOP 1, [2015] MHLO 2
Kings College Hospital NHS Foundation Trust *v.* C & Anor [2015] EWCOP 80
M *v.* N [2015] EWCOP 76
Montgomery *v.* Lanarkshire Health Board [2015] UKSC 11
Re CD [2015] EWCOP 74
Re LC [2015] EWCOP 25
Wye Valley NHS Trust *v.* Mr B [2015] EWCOP 60
NHS Foundation Trust *v.* QZ (A Patient) [2017] EWCOP 11
An NHS Trust and Others (Respondents) *v.* Y (By His Litigation Friend) [2018] UKSC 46
An NHS Foundation Trust *v.* AB & Ors [2019] EWCOP 26
East Lancashire Hospitals NHS Trust *v.* PW [2019] EWCOP 10
Guys and St Thomas' NHS Foundation Trust *v.* X [2019] EWCOP 35
Leicester City Council *v.* MPZ [2019] EWCOP 64

Manchester University NHS Foundation Trust *v.* DE [2019] EWCOP 19
Re AB (Termination of Pregnancy) [2019] EWCA Civ 1215
United Lincolnshire Hospitals NHS Trust *v.* CD [2019] EWCOP 24
Avon and Wiltshire Mental Health Partnership *v.* WA & Anor [2020] EWCOP 37
Guys and St Thomas' NHS Foundation Trust (GSTT), South London and Maudsley NHS Foundation Trust (SLAM) *v.* R [2020] EWCOP 4
Hull University Teaching Hospitals NHS Trust *v.* KD [2020] EWCOP 35
Northamptonshire Healthcare NHS Foundation Trust *v.* AB [2020] EWCOP 40
Sherwood Forest Hospitals NHS Foundation Trust *v.* C [2020] EWCOP 10
University Hospitals Bristol NHS Foundation Trust *v.* ED [2020] EWCOP 18
University Hospitals of Leicester NHS Trust *v.* TC (By Her Litigation Friend, the Official Solicitor), AC, BC, DC [2020] EWCOP 53
A Local Authority *v.* JB [2021] UKSC 52
An NHS Foundation Trust *v.* An Expectant Mother [2021] EWCOP 33
East Lancashire Hospitals NHS Trust *v.* GH [2021] EWCOP 18
NHS Trust *v.* X [2021] EWHC 65 (Fam)
Pennine Acute Hospitals NHS Trust *v.* TM [2021] EWCOP 8
R (SC) *v.* Secretary of State for Work and Pensions [2021] UKSC 26
SS *v.* London Borough of Richmond upon Thames [2021] EWCOP 31
University Hospital Birmingham NHS Foundation Trust *v.* AI & K [2021] EWCOP 37
X NHS Foundation Trust & Anor *v.* Ms A [2021] EWCOP 17
London Borough of X *v.* MR & Ors [2022] EWCOP 1

STATUTES

Abortion Act 1967
Children Act 1989
Human Rights Act 1998
Mental Capacity Act 2005
Mental Health Act 1983 (as amended by Mental Health Act 2007)
Assisted Decision-Making (Ireland) Act 2015
The Court of Protection (Amendment) Rules 2015
Mental Capacity Act (Northern Ireland) 2016

Introduction

> It is a terrible thing to be assessed as lacking capacity when you do not – to have others make decisions on your behalf and set aside your own wishes based on what they think is in your best interests. You lose control over your life. You are no longer in charge of your destiny.
>
> It is a terrible thing to be said to have capacity when you do not – to be left to cause yourself and those you love great harm on the basis that you know what you are doing and you are making your own choices, when in fact your decisions are not really yours. To have others harm you and to be told no protection is offered because you have chosen this harm, even though it is against your deepest values, is horrific.[1]
>
> *Jonathan Herring and Jesse Wall*

The law draws a sharp line between those who have capacity and those who do not. People deemed to have capacity to make autonomous decisions are free to make their own decisions, for good or for ill.[2] A finding of incapacity, however, provides the justification for depriving a person of their right to determine what will happen to them, even in the most intimate of decisions.

This approach, premised on Enlightenment ideas about the bounds of legitimate state authority, depends heavily on the test for capacity, as a means of accurately distinguishing those who are capable of autonomous decision-making from those who are not. This has given rise to two concerns which have dominated the academic literature in recent years. The first – inspired in large part by the United Nations Convention on

[1] J. Herring and J. Wall, 'Autonomy, Capacity and Vulnerable Adults: Filling the Gaps in the Mental Capacity Act' (2015) 35(4) *Legal Studies* 698, 1.

[2] This is qualified only by the provisions contained in the Mental Health Act (1983) and the powers of the courts under the Inherent Jurisdiction, both of which will be considered in Chapter 1.

the Rights of Persons with Disabilities (the CRPD) and its mandate to move towards a system of supported (as opposed to substitute) decision-making – is critical of the cliff-edge approach to capacity adopted, which fails to reflect the fact that capacity is not binary but exists on a spectrum.[3] The second – influenced by the rise of relational and feminist theories of autonomy – has been critical of the individualistic and rational 'liberal subject' which this liberal framework relies upon, arguing for the need for greater recognition in the law of the numerous social, cultural, and relational influences on our decision-making.[4] While the conclusions in this book lend support to these critiques (particularly the former), its focus is on a different consequence of the liberal underpinnings of the law, namely that in order to perform its role in delineating the autonomous decision from the non-autonomous decision, the Mental Capacity Act 2005 (MCA) subscribes to a form of value neutrality in its test for capacity, which is neither possible nor desirable.

That a person's capacity does not depend on the substance of a person's values or beliefs is considered central to the Act's legitimacy in defining when the state will defer to individual subjective choice and when it will not. Consequently, the test contained in sections 2 and 3 of the MCA proceeds on the assumption that a person subject to a capacity assessment (who I will refer to in this book as the 'agent') either possesses the capacity to make decisions or they do not, and that this can be objectively determined through a test for capacity which assesses various cognitive capacities a person may have (understanding, retention,

[3] See, for example, B. Clough, *The Spaces of Mental Capacity Law: Moving beyond Binaries* (Routledge, 2022); W. Martin *et al.*, *Achieving CRPD Compliance: Is the Mental Capacity Act of England and Wales Compatible with the UN Convention on the Rights of Persons with Disabilities? If Not, What Next?* (2014) Essex Autonomy Project, 22 September 2014; G. Richardson, 'Mental disabilities and the law: From substitute to supported decision making' (2012) 65(1) *Current Legal Problems* 333–354.

[4] See, for example, C. Kong, *Mental Capacity in Relationship: Decision-Making, Dialogue and Autonomy* (Cambridge University Press, 2017); C. Mackenzie and N. Stoljar, *Relational Autonomy: Feminist Essays on Autonomy, Agency and Social Self* (Oxford University Press, 2000); C. MacKinnon, *Toward a Feminist Theory of the State* (Cambridge: Harvard University Press, 1989); M. Sandel, *Liberalism and the Limits of Justice* (2nd edn., Cambridge: Cambridge University Press, 1997); P. Wolpe, 'The Triumph of Autonomy in American Bioethics: A Sociological View' in R. de Vries and H. Subedi (eds.) *Bioethics and Society: Constructing the Ethical Enterprise* (Upper Saddle River, NJ: Prentice Hall, 1988); C. Mackenzie, 'Relational Autonomy, Normative Authority and Perfectionism' (2008) 39 *Journal of Social Philosophy* 512, 51; J. Christman, 'Relational Autonomy, Liberal Individualism, and the Social Constitution of Selves' (2004) 117(1/2) *Philosophical Studies* 143–164.

weighting of information), without engaging with the substance or origins of the values, beliefs, or desires that underpin any given decision – that is, with the agent's evaluative judgements or their motivations for acting. While this approach is widely assumed to be more conducive to maintaining a sphere of independence in which people are free to pursue their own conception of what is good or valuable, the reality, as this book will explore, is that a value-free understanding of (and test for) capacity in fact does precisely the opposite, indeed that it provides a façade behind which judgements can be made about the origins of an agent's values, free from proper scrutiny or challenge. It will be argued that in practice, it is impossible to assess decision-making capacity without reference to the values that underpin a decision, since the parameters of what decision a person could reasonably have made, had they 'used' and 'weighed' the relevant information, must be set by that person's own values, beliefs, and commitments. Moreover, this is not merely a problem with the way in which the MCA (and specifically, the 'use or weigh' criterion) is framed. No test can assess the decision-making process without taking account of the values, priorities, and beliefs that drive that decision. Nor should it seek to do so if it is to capture the complex ways in which a person's autonomy in taking that decision may be undermined, particularly in the psychiatric context.

In fact, the failure of the Act to engage with the role that values are playing in assessments of capacity does not insulate such assessments from value judgements by assessors, but rather creates space for such judgements to be made without meaningful scrutiny or challenge. When one examines the case law[5] (supplemented with evidence from interviews conducted with doctors[6]), it is clear that assessors *are* invoking values in

[5] Given the unusually fact-sensitive nature of the case law on the MCA, it is used in this book simply to illustrate how the courts approach assessments of capacity and best interests and what factors seem to influence their judgments.

[6] A full methodology for these interviews is contained in Appendices A–E. The purpose of these interviews was to gain a better understanding of how the provisions in the MCA are being understood and applied in practice. They consist of a series of semi-structured interviews with medical consultants from a range of specialisms, in order to explore how they conducted capacity and best interests assessments. These include Liaison Psychiatry, Old Age Psychiatry, Psychiatry (emergency medicine), Psychiatry (general), Emergency Medicine, Geriatric Medicine, Intensive Care, and General Practice (see Appendix C for further details of the participants). Each interview followed the same format, which began with a series of general questions (Appendix A), asking participants what they thought they were testing for when assessing whether a person has capacity, whether they often came across hard or borderline cases and what it was that made those cases difficult, and what factors they weighed up when deciding what was in the best interests of someone who lacked capacity. They were also asked for their provisional thoughts on recent

the determination of capacity. Often these will be the agent's own values (does the putative decision appear broadly consistent with those things that the agent states that they value and believe in?) but this is not always the case, and there are many examples in which both judges and doctors appear to be judging the coherence or rationality of a decision by reference to values other than the agent's own. Sometimes this may be driven by straightforward paternalistic concerns about the harmful outcome of the decision, but, more often, underpinning these cases can be discerned concerns about the 'authenticity' of the agent's stated values, that is, whether the values or beliefs being expressed by that person are really 'authentically held' or they are in fact attributable to some mental disorder or impairment. The implicit suggestion is often that if the agent were *not* suffering from that particular disorder or impairment, they would have decided in a different, less self-destructive way.

While this problem is not exclusive to cases involving mental disorder, it is particularly evident in that context. This is because certain disorders may distort the agent's value or belief systems without substantially undermining their ability to understand, retain, and reason abstractly about information, unlike some other types of impairment that are more likely to affect their cognitive abilities as well. Since such concerns about the authenticity of the agent's decision cannot be addressed explicitly within the current framework of the MCA, they are instead being shoehorned into the 'use or weigh' limb of the Act, with judges and doctors inferring from the fact that an agent holds certain disordered values or beliefs that they cannot properly weigh up the information

proposals put forward by the Law Commission. The participants were then presented with a number of short vignettes in which someone with questionable or uncertain capacity required treatment (Appendix B). The participants were asked to decide in relation to each of the scenarios whether they thought the person in question had capacity or not, what factors or pieces of information were important when making that assessment, and whether there was any other information they would have needed or wanted in order to make that assessment. They were subsequently asked whether, if the person was found to lack capacity, the treatment in question would be in the best interests of the patient, as well as what factors were important when making this assessment and why they were weighing the factors in that particular way. This research is qualitative and not quantitative, and given the relatively small sample size, it cannot be extrapolated to the medical body at large, as robust evidence about the way in which capacity assessments are made in general. However, it does demonstrate some common themes or factors which appear to be influencing the decisions of doctors, and some shared concerns amongst the medical profession about the difficulties inherent in making these assessments. It also highlighted that, even within the relatively small numbers of participants interviewed, there were clear differences of opinion when it came to interpreting and applying the test.

relevant to the decision in question. This not only conflates questions about *whether* the agent can weigh information with those of *how much weight* they are giving to information (which is difficult to reconcile with the liberal framework on which the MCA is based), but it also means that such determinations are not subjected to proper scrutiny, and the normative assumptions that underpin them are left unchallenged.

Determining that a mental disorder or impairment has compromised a person's *cognitive* capacities in a way that makes them unable to make a decision is, of course, already an explicit element of the MCA, with s2(1) requiring that the agent's inability to make a decision must be caused by an impairment in the functioning of the mind or brain.[7] While at times this can be difficult to assess, it does not raise the same issues as the determination that an agent's values or belief systems derive from disorder or impairment, and so any decision resting on them is taken without capacity. The effect of the latter is to essentially prevent people from acting on the basis of *certain* values and beliefs, thus implicitly imposing substantive conditions on when a decision will be deemed autonomous or not.

This is especially so given that mental disorder is itself diagnosed by reference to an agent's behaviour or stated beliefs or values, such that the very same behaviour which gives rise to a diagnosis of a disorder may also be the basis on which the person's decision is deemed incapacitous. This creates the risk of a status-based approach to capacity being introduced through the back door, whereby when one suffers from certain psychiatric illnesses, one is automatically deemed to lack the capacity to take certain decisions.

Given these concerns, it is important to interrogate the empirical and normative claims underpinning the determination in some of these cases that a person's (impaired) values indicate that they lack capacity. The book will focus on claims relating to values affected by mental disorder, since this is the context in which such concerns most commonly arise. This includes examining the core assumption that mental disorder is capable of being distinguished – both practically and conceptually – from non-disorder, and that it undermines the person's capacity for autonomous decision-making in some meaningful way. Whether these claims are correct depends in part on how mental disorder is conceptualised and

[7] Mental Capacity Act 2005, section 2(1). For more discussion of the 'causative nexus' between the inability to make a decision and the impairment in the functioning of the mind or brain, see *PC v. York CC* [2013] EWCA 478 (Civ).

whether there is any 'natural' or scientific fact about disorder, which can be determined without recourse to social or cultural norms. After all, if disorder is based *merely* on judgements about the normality (or abnormality) of certain behaviours or beliefs, then it might legitimately be asked why so-called disordered values or beliefs ought to be treated any differently from any others.

Through an examination of the wide-ranging literature on the nature of mental disorder, it will become clear that it is not possible to identify disorder without making reference to personal or social norms. The notion of disorder requires that a person's thought processes, beliefs, or behaviour are dysfunctional in some way, and this cannot be ascertained without judging it against some implicit standard of what is 'normal' thinking. Once this is accepted, it becomes clear that the line between disordered and 'ordered' values or beliefs is not categorical but rather blurred, being socially and culturally contingent.

However, the fact that determining the boundary between order and disorder will not always be easy (either theoretically or empirically) does not mean we should abandon altogether the notion of disorder and, with it, any attempt to distinguish disordered from non-disordered values or behaviours. While rejecting disorder as a basis for intervention may well be a 'neat' conceptual solution, it will not always be a compassionate one: too puritanical a commitment to liberal ideals of freedom and value neutrality risks ignoring the very real suffering experienced by a large number of people who would be left unprotected from the serious risk of harm they may pose to themselves. While negotiating the exact boundaries of disorder is difficult,[8] there are nonetheless observable features of 'disorder' which distinguish it from simply 'abnormal' or 'deviant' behaviour, namely that the behaviour in question is caused by some dysfunctional psychological mechanism or 'abnormality of the mind' as opposed to being a deliberate act of agency, and that it results in the person experiencing distress or impairment in the conduct of everyday activities, such as holding down a job or forming successful relationships.

If it is possible to distinguish disordered values in this way, the question then becomes whether (and how) the fact that a person's values are disordered affects or undermines their capacity for autonomous decision-making. Does the mere fact that a person acts on the basis of disordered values *always* mean they are unable to make an autonomous

[8] Although this problem also afflicts the application of the Mental Health Act 1983, the focus of this book is on the Mental Capacity Act 2005.

decision, or are there some instances in which such a decision can still be autonomous? Drawing on the philosophical literature on the concept of autonomy, it will be argued that autonomous decision-making requires more than merely an expression of choice if it is to be valuable. It requires the decision to be in some way authentic to the agent, that is, to reflect the values, beliefs, and priorities that the agent holds to be valuable to them. Where this is not the case, their decision cannot be truly autonomous. So, if the capacity threshold is intended to distinguish those who are capable of autonomous decision-making from those who are not, and (as most modern liberal understandings accept) an essential ingredient of an autonomous decision is its authenticity, then it would seem right in principle to find an agent to lack capacity if their decision lacks that authenticity.

The question, then, is how mental disorder affects authenticity. This is difficult to answer given the many different interpretations of authenticity in the philosophical literature, which point to different factors as being important to establishing whether a desire is authentic or not: the causal origins of a desire, the agent's attitude towards that desire, or the coherence of that desire with the agent's character system. These different accounts of authenticity and their implications for mental disorder will be explored in detail in Chapter 3. Suffice to say for now, however, that while there will often be overlap between these accounts (an agent may not endorse a desire precisely because they understand it to be disordered in origins and otherwise incoherent with their character system), the mere fact that a value or desire might be disordered in origin is not alone sufficient to render it inauthentic, if the agent would otherwise endorse or sanction that desire as part of their cohering character system or identity. Consequently, while an agent acting on the basis of disordered beliefs or values will often be acting inauthentically (since they would not endorse that belief or value system otherwise), this will not always be the case, and situations could arise (in theory at least) in which there is reason to believe that the agent would endorse or sanction their belief, even knowing it derived from illness. Mr B in *Wye Valley* might be a potential example of this from the case law: his religious beliefs were deeply meaningful to him, even though they stemmed from hallucination.[9] In such cases, it would be difficult to justify finding that person to lack capacity, since it is not clear that their

[9] *Wye Valley NHS Trust v. B* [2015] EWCOP 60, [43].

capacity for autonomous decision-making has been undermined by their disorder or impairment.

In cases such as this, capacity assessors must navigate a difficult course between respect for autonomy and protecting vulnerable people from non-autonomous and deeply harmful choices. While I argue in this book that there will be occasions in which it is right to find the agent to lack capacity where the decision they wish to make is being based on disordered values or beliefs, once the shaky conceptual ground on which such judgements are made is acknowledged (depending as they do both on judgements at a societal level about what amounts to socially or culturally 'normal' behaviour, and at an individual level about whether the agent's behaviour is sufficient to fall into the categories of disorder), it becomes essential that these judgements should be brought out into the open, where they can be subject to appropriate scrutiny. This book therefore explores ways in which the law could seek to address concerns about authenticity, how it might identify when a person's disordered values or beliefs ought to be considered as part of their authentic value-system, and when they should be regarded as undermining a person's capacity for autonomy. Ultimately, I conclude that while philosophically it may be difficult to justify intervening where the agent would endorse certain values or beliefs, the difficulty in translating this into a workable legal test leans in favour of adopting a more pragmatic proxy, which focuses on the origins of the values or beliefs that the agent applies to the information in their decision-making. (The agent's attitude toward that desire should then be reflected in the weight accorded to it in the best interests assessment.) A new limb of the MCA is therefore proposed, which focuses on whether the person is unable to make a decision because the values or beliefs by which they are evaluating the relevant information have been caused by or altered as a consequence of the person suffering from a disorder, illness, or impairment. This would negate the need to shoehorn such cases within the 'use or weigh' criterion.

This is not held out as a perfect solution: there simply is no perfectly 'tidy' solution to such a messy conceptual and practical problem. One concern with such an approach may be that in practice, given the way that mental disorder is diagnosed (via observation of the agent's behaviour or belief systems), the provision might effectively impose substantive conditions on capacity: holding certain value systems (for example, that avoiding calories is more important than anything else, including life) will, in reality, always give rise to a diagnosis of disorder, and so decisions based on them will always be deemed incapacitously taken. However, despite the threat this poses to liberal ideals of value neutrality, it will be argued that in practice, the greater scrutiny allowed for by this limb will result in less unwarranted intrusion into the private sphere than currently occurs. For this reason, this solution will also be preferred to two alternatives that have been suggested in the literature: an 'appreciation' limb of the capacity test (as seen in other jurisdictions, including Northern Ireland) and an 'ability to value' limb, sometimes advocated as a less direct challenge to liberalism.

However, acknowledging the complexity and fragility of capacity assessments on the margins, especially where concerns relate to the 'authenticity' of decisions, has implications beyond how we test for capacity. It ought also to affect how we approach best interests decision-making.

Highlighting the inevitable grey area that exists on the cusp of capacity calls into question the 'cliff-edge' approach we currently adopt whereby the agent either has capacity – in which case they may decide as they wish, without any fetters and no matter how harmful the decision may be – or they lack it, in which case a decision will be taken for them, which 'takes account' of their wishes but does not necessarily follow them. It suggests the need to 'soften' this cliff edge, to dilute the current all-or-nothing approach to capacity, by according greater weight to the agent's wishes, values, and beliefs in the assessment of their best interests, in a way that better aligns with the vision of the CRPD.

It also casts a light on the way in which the impairment of cognitive capacities, and the disruption of values, may not always go hand in hand. A person's values and beliefs may have been affected by disorder without any impairment of the person's cognitive processes, just as a person's cognitive capacities may be impaired while their values remain intact. This is important for determining a person's best interests, since it implies that a person may retain authentic values even if they have lost their ability to act on them – values which *ought* to be respected in any decisions taken for them. Similarly, as noted earlier, a person might endorse values or beliefs even knowing that they originate in mental disorder, and so may be acting autonomously, even if under the proposed changes to the test for capacity, they would be found to lack capacity. This also ought to be reflected in the weight accorded to them in the best interests assessment.

Chapters 5 and 6 will therefore consider what changes need to be introduced to the way in which best interests assessments are taken in order to reflect these points. It will begin by examining how best interests decisions are currently being taken, concluding that despite a number of empowering court decisions, the lack of direction on how to apply the MCA has still resulted in different weight being attributed to the agent's wishes, based on a variety of (sometimes implicit) factors. Meanwhile, this trend towards greater empowerment has not yet trickled down to decisions being taken on the ground by doctors and care workers, which still remain characterised largely by paternalism and risk aversion. A new approach to best interests is therefore necessary if assessors are to feel able to prioritise the wishes of the individual, even where that will put the agent at risk of harm.

Accordingly, it will be suggested that there ought to be a presumption that the agent's wishes and feelings will be determinative of what is in their best interests, which may only be rebutted where giving effect to them will expose the person to a risk of significant harm. This reflects the clear psychological and emotional harm done to a person when their wishes are frustrated and when treatment or care interventions (which often involve incursions into their liberty or bodily integrity) are imposed on them against their will. However, as the foregoing discussion has highlighted, even where the harms *are* significant, there will still be occasions where the agent's wishes and feelings should nonetheless take precedence; where to do otherwise would involve frustrating their deeply and authentically held beliefs, values, or commitments. Assessors should therefore be provided with a list of factors that they *must* take into account when determining how much weight to give to the agent's wishes in this context, which will ensure greater consistency of approach, through providing a framework for assessors to work through the relevant issues. This should be supplemented to an amendment to the defence to battery contained in section 5 of MCA so that it applies only where the intervention was necessary to prevent the agent from suffering serious harm.

The concept of decision-making capacity lies at the confluence of law, philosophy, and psychiatry. Yet as the foregoing discussion has highlighted, a fundamental tension exists between the liberal ideal underpinning legal and philosophical notions of capacity – that all people ought to be free to pursue their own conception of a good life, according to those values that are important to them – and the intuition that lies at the heart of psychiatry, that there are certain values or beliefs, deriving from mental illnesses, which do not demand respect and from which the agent ought to be protected. When determining how the law ought to conceptualise and test for capacity, therefore, a balance must be struck between philosophical or jurisprudential purity on the one hand, and the state's important duty to protect its most vulnerable citizens on the other. This book has attempted to strike this balance, yet in doing so, it recognises the challenge posed by cases on the cusp of capacity, which are, by definition, complex and messy. Given this, the importance of ensuring sensitive yet empowering best interests decisions is paramount, and it is hoped that through the changes proposed to section 4 of the MCA here, the law will strike a better balance between empowering people to make decisions which reflect and promote their values and beliefs, and protecting them from making harmful decisions which they cannot understand and would not ultimately wish for themselves.

This issue is of increasing importance in the wake of the CRPD. Fundamental to the CRPD is the notion that in order to treat people with disabilities with dignity and respect, we must empower them in decisions which affect them, supporting them to take their own decisions wherever possible, in accordance with what matters to them. This is embodied in the directive in Article 12(4) CRPD that signatories (including the UK) must undertake to 'ensure that measures relating to the exercise of legal capacity respect the rights, will and preferences of the person',[10] irrespective of their disability or legal capacity. Yet despite the absolutist language of the CRPD, no one would plausibly contend that we ought to respect *any* expressed preference, irrespective of its content, cause, or consequences. To use an extreme example, few would seriously argue that if a sufferer of Schizophrenic Affective Disorder held a delusional belief that he could fly, and sought to jump off a multi-storey building, we ought to respect this decision and allow him to fall to his death. As a result, the question of how we determine *which* expressions of will or preferences to give effect to is crucially important: we must understand how and when a person's mental disorder is undermining their ability to make authentic, and so autonomous, decisions, if we are to know how best to support them in decisions about their treatment and care. Without this, we risk throwing those who suffer from mental illness 'into the fires of libertarian ideology'.[11]

[10] UN General Assembly, *Convention on the Rights of Persons with Disabilities: Resolution Adopted by the General Assembly*, 24 January 2007, A/RES/61/106, Article 12.

[11] A. Plumb, 'UN Convention on the Rights of Persons with Disabilities: Out of the Frying Pan and into the Fire? Mental Health Service Users and Survivors Aligning with the Disability Movement' in H. Spandler, J. Anderson, and B. Sapey (eds), *Madness, Distress*

Navigating the tension between respect for (and deference to) idiosyncratic values and protection from disorder or impairment must, therefore, be a precondition for adopting any CRPD-compliant model. However, it is also crucial to understanding how any 'fused' mental capacity and mental health legislation ought to be framed; an issue that has gained salience since the passing of Northern Ireland's (fused) Mental Capacity Act in 2016. Clearly, if calls to adopt fused legislation prove successful, the treatment and detention of those suffering from mental illness will become contingent on the person's mental capacity. Ensuring that the test for capacity is able to adequately accommodate the impact of disorder on decision-making capacity would thus be essential.

It should be noted that while the argument put forward in this book lends support for embracing a less-severe all-or-nothing approach to capacity, it does not argue in favour of adopting a supported decision-making scheme in this jurisdiction at this time. In addition to the concern expressed earlier that properly accounting for mental disorder is a precondition for any ethically acceptable supported decision-making scheme, there are also pragmatic reasons for this. As Gavin Davidson *et al.* have argued, implementing a scheme of supported decision-making 'takes time and resources, and may require a shift in attitudes of some care providers and in some service users themselves'.[12] It is doubtful that there is the time, resources, or appetite for this at present, particularly in a political climate grappling with the fallout from Brexit, the Covid-19 pandemic, and the Ukraine war. Even before any of these events, the Law Commission was clear when considering avenues for reform of the Mental Capacity Act in 2015 that the abandonment of substituted decision-making would be 'highly politically and ethically contentious at this stage' and fell outside of the remit of their review.[13] Given that the prospect of such a scheme being implemented imminently is, as Genevra

and the Politics of Disablement (Bristol: Bristol University Press 2015). Quoted in A. Ruck Keene, N. Kane, S. Kim, and G. Owen, 'Mental Capacity – Why Look for a Paradigm Shift?' (2023) *Medical Law Review* (January), p. 9 (advanced availability online). Available at: https://academic.oup.com/medlaw/advance-article/doi/10.1093/medlaw/fwac052/6987005.

[12] G. Davidson et al., 'Supported Decision Making: A Review of the International Literature' (2015) 38 *International Journal of Law and Psychiatry* 61, 73.

[13] Law Commission Consultation Paper No. 222, 'Mental Capacity and Deprivation of Liberty' (2015). Available at: www.lawcom.gov.uk/wp-content/uploads/2015/07/cp222_mental_capacity.pdf, 12.44.

Richardson describes, 'vanishingly slim',[14] this book instead seeks to posit a more immediate and workable solution, which takes account of and seeks to remedy some of the difficulties generated by a threshold approach to capacity, without abandoning the concept altogether.

Nor does the book seek to argue explicitly for reforming (or abandoning) the Mental Health Act (MHA), although its findings undoubtedly lend support for those who seek to do so. As this book is concerned with the impact of disorder on autonomous decision-making, its critique is less directly relevant to a framework which is based on risk avoidance rather than respect for autonomy. However, given that its findings clearly imply that at least some people suffering from mental disorders *can* decide autonomously, this may buttress criticisms of the MHA for permitting the detention and treatment of those with disorders against their capacitous wishes. It thus lends broad support for those favouring a move to fused mental health and capacity legislation, albeit only with changes to the test for capacity proposed previously.

Before going on to consider the law's current approach to these issues, it is helpful to briefly elaborate on some of the concepts which this book will draw upon. Although not defined in the Act, the term 'values' is being used here to denote principles or ideals that guide and motivate our attitudes and actions. Through helping us to determine what matters to us (what is valuable or important), they enable us to evaluate actions, persons, or situations and, from that, to guide our decisions and actions. They may be personal values, in the sense of things the individual views as personally important to them (such as the importance of family, of religion, of independence, of loyalty, etc.), or moral values, in the sense of principles which help them to assess what is morally right or wrong (such as principles of equality, fairness, honesty, etc.). Beliefs, meanwhile, are convictions that something is true about the world. These will often shape and inform those values: a person attaches great importance to spirituality because of their belief in God's salvation, for example. By contrast, desires (or wishes) are hopes that some particular thing (or set of things) will happen. This may be a reflection of their values or beliefs (a person wishes to live at home *because* they deeply value independence above all else, for example), but this will not always be the case, and people often wish for things in the short term which are incompatible with their long-term values (for instance, a person may deeply value their

[14] Richardson, 'Mental Disabilities and the Law'.

religious convictions while also wishing to skip Mass one sunny Sunday so as to go to the beach instead).

Agnieszka Jaworska distinguishes valuing from mere desiring by identifying three features which are essential to, or strongly indicative of, valuing. First, 'a person could contemplate being free from a desire with a sense of relief, but one would always view the possibility of not valuing something that one currently values as an impoverishment, loss or mistake.'[15] Consequently, 'we think it would be a mistake to lose our current values – we hold our values to be correct, or at least correct for us',[16] whereas we do not always think the same of a desire, which we may (as in the case of certain unconventional sexual desires) desperately wish to lose. Secondly, 'a person's values are usually entangled with her sense of self-worth in a way which is not true of desires: a person values herself in terms of how well she lives up to her values.'[17] Finally, values 'express the person's concern with something fully independent of his or herself. By contrast, in merely desiring something, part of the person's aim is usually the pleasure or the agreeable state of mind that will result from achieving or contemplating the object of desire.'[18] This is not necessarily the case for all values, since sometimes people come to value some of their pleasures (Jaworska gives the example of a food connoisseur). Nonetheless, where something matters to a person irrespective of how it would affect their own experience, 'this is very likely not a mere desire, but a value'.[19]

The importance of this distinction for the agent's capacity and best interests will depend, in part, on the nature of the impairment from which they suffer. While the MCA applies to all those whose capacity is in doubt, the nature, extent, and longevity of that incapacity varies. For some such as those with learning disabilities or someone who has sustained a brain injury – their impairment may be relatively stable. For others – such as those in acute pain or suffering from a mental illness – incapacity might fluctuate. Meanwhile, for those with a degenerative cognitive illness such as dementia, incapacity is progressive, with the individual gradually losing capacity as their cognitive functions

[15] A. Jaworska, 'Respecting the Margins of Agency: Alzheimer's Patients and the Capacity to Value' (1999) 28(2) *Philosophy & Public Affairs* 105–138, 114.

[16] Ibid, 115.

[17] Ibid.

[18] Ibid, 116.

[19] Ibid.

decline. Depending on the type of impairment, the relationship between the agent's values and desires, and the role and significance of these in the assessment of their capacity and their best interests, will vary. The agent may have values that predate their loss of capacity, for example, or they may not. Their loss of capacity may coincide with a distortion of their values; or their values may remain constant, but their ability to formulate desires which reflect those values may have become impaired. While the question of how the law should respond to these different scenarios will be explored in Chapters 1–6, it is worth noting at the outset a fundamental limitation of the MCA: that in attempting to apply a single test for capacity to such a diverse range of clinical presentations and impairments, it is perhaps inevitable that it will apply less aptly to some circumstances or impairments than to others. It is the contention of this book that reforms to the test for capacity are necessary if it is to properly accommodate the impact of mental disorders on decision-making autonomy.

1

A Value-Neutral Understanding of Capacity

1.1 A Cliff-Edge Approach to Capacity

In law, a bright line is drawn between those who are deemed to have the capacity to make a decision and those who are not. For those found to have capacity (or, more accurately, those not found to lack it, given the law's starting point is that people are presumed to have capacity[1]), that decision is determined by their autonomous choices. Consent must be sought for any treatment or care intervention, and the agent's right to bodily integrity permits them to refuse any treatment, regardless of whether the reasons are 'rational, irrational, unknown or even non-existent',[2] and even where the refusal will result in their death.[3] Treating a capacitous person without their consent will amount to a battery (a form of the tort of trespass to the person, which is committed whenever a person intentionally and directly inflicts force on another[4]), as well as a breach of article 8 of the European Convention on Human Rights (ECHR), which protects the agent's right to 'private and family life' and has been held to encompass both their 'physical' and 'psychological' integrity.[5] Public bodies, including public hospitals and courts, are obliged to act in accordance with this Convention[6] and, while article

1 Mental Capacity Act 2005, s1(3).

2 *Re T (Adult: Refusal of Medical Treatment)* [1992] 4 All ER 649, 664.

3 *Re B (Adult: Refusal of Medical Treatment)* [2002] 2 All England Reports 449.

4 A battery has been defined by Clerk and Lindsell on Torts (22nd edition) as 'the direct imposition of any unwanted physical contact on another person' (at 15-09).

5 *X and Y v. Netherlands* (1986) 8 E.H.R.R. 235, [22]; *Y.F. v. Turkey* (2004) 39 EHRR 34, [33].

6 Human Rights Act 1998, Section 6.

8 is qualified[7] and subject to restrictions made 'in accordance with law' where 'necessary in a democratic society . . . for the protection of health or morals',[8] in the absence of consent, any interference would not be in accordance with the law, and thus not justified by article 8(2). In extreme cases, treating a person without their consent might even amount to 'inhuman and degrading treatment', protected under article 3 ECHR, which has been held, for example, to apply in the context of forcible feeding.[9] The result is that those who have capacity within the terms of the MCA are accorded extensive powers to govern their lives according to their own values and priorities, with serious ramifications for anyone who seeks to interfere with this without the person's consent.

This is qualified only by the courts' powers under the Inherent Jurisdiction of the High Court, and the Mental Health Act 1983. The former, as Mr Justice Munby has explained, plugs the 'gap' in the MCA's coverage, offering vital protections for vulnerable non-autonomous adults where

> on a strict mental health appraisal, such an individual does not lack capacity in the terms of the MCA 2005 and therefore falls outside the statutory scheme, but other factors, for example coercion and undue influence, may combine with his borderline capacity to remove his autonomy to make an important decision, why, one may ask, should that individual not be able to access the protection now afforded to adults whose mental capacity puts them on the other side of that borderline?[10]

Although he felt it would be 'unwise, and indeed inappropriate'[11] to attempt to define *all* those who might fall under the jurisdiction, he has indicated that it would include a vulnerable adult who,

> even if not incapacitated by mental disorder or mental illness, is, or is reasonably believed to be, either (i) under constraint or (ii) subject to coercion or undue influence or (iii) for some other reason deprived of the capacity to make the relevant decision, or disabled from making a free

[7] Convention for the Protection of Human Rights and Fundamental Freedoms (European Convention on Human Rights, as amended (ECHR)), article 8(2).

[8] Ibid.

[9] *A Local Authority v. E* [2012] EWCOP 1639 [126].

[10] *DL v. A Local Authority* [2012] EWCA 253, [65].

[11] *Re SA* (*vulnerable adult with capacity: marriage*) [2006] 1 FLR 867, [77].

> choice, or incapacitated or disabled from giving or expressing a real and genuine consent.[12]

Crucially, as with those found to lack capacity under the MCA, the justification for intervening in such cases is that the agent's capacity for autonomous decision-making has to some extent been undermined by the influence of others, thereby calling into question whether their decision should be upheld.

The same is not necessarily true of those who fall within the remit of the Mental Health Act (MHA), which, justified by reference to risk prevention rather than capacity, covers the detention, care, and treatment of those with a mental disorder. This permits the detention of a person for twenty-eight days for assessment, irrespective of their consent, if it can be shown that they are suffering from a 'mental disorder of a nature or degree' which warrants detention[13] and that detention is necessary for the person's own safety or the safety of others.[14] While detained, the person may be treated for his or her mental disorder, or for any symptom or manifestation of this, and for the first three months, the consent of the patient to this treatment is not required.[15] While a large proportion of people falling within the remit of the MHA will lack the capacity to take treatment decisions, this is not invariably the case. Evidence from Gareth Owen *et al.* suggests that around 86 per cent of people detained under the MHA in general adult acute inpatient units lack capacity to make decisions about their treatment (the figure is around 60 per cent for those on an acute psychiatric ward who are not detained under the MHA).[16] There will be some people detained under the Act then, who do have

[12] Ibid [79]. Subsequently, it has also been held to capture people who lack capacity under the terms of the MCA, providing that they do *not* have a remedy available under the Act: *XCC v. AA & Others* [2012] EWHC 2183 (COP), [54].

[13] MHA, s2(2)(a).

[14] Ibid, s2(2)(b).

[15] MHA, s63. There are two exceptions to this. Where the treatment is Electric Convulsive Therapy, if the agent has capacity, they must consent to the treatment. If they do not have capacity, a second opinion must be provided by a registered medical practitioner that the treatment is appropriate (s58A). Where the treatment is psychosurgery, the agent must both consent to the treatment, and a second opinion must be provided by a registered medical practitioner that the treatment is appropriate (s57). After the initial three months, the administration of medicine can occur only if either the patient has capacity and consents to it or if they lack capacity but a second opinion confirms that continued treatment is appropriate. Other forms of treatment, including psychotherapy, and even force-feeding, can continue regardless of their consent.

[16] Ibid.

the capacity to consent to treatment – or, of course, to refuse it – yet they may be treated regardless.

While this would seem to be a substantial interference with rights and freedoms of at least some people with capacity, and there is good reason to question its legitimacy,[17] two points must be borne in mind. First, the MHA applies only to those with mental illness, defined as 'any disorder or disability of the mind'.[18] It does not apply to those with alcohol or drug dependency,[19] most learning disabilities (unless associated with abnormally aggressive behaviour),[20] or brain injuries or other cognitive impairments. Secondly, the MHA only permits treatments for the agent's mental disorder, or for symptoms or manifestations of *that* disorder. While this has been broadly interpreted to include treatment for a physical disorder where this might affect the agent's mental health,[21] it will not apply to treatment for a physical illness or condition which is *not* a symptom or manifestation of that mental disorder.[22] The result is that except in two categories of cases (namely, where the agent has a mental disorder and requires treatment for that disorder; and where the agent is deemed especially vulnerable and is subject to the coercion or undue influence of others), an agent's capacitous refusal of treatment will be determinative.

For those who lack capacity, meanwhile, their decisions are not treated as legally authoritative, and a decision must instead be made on the basis of what is in their 'best interests'.[23] Although the term 'best interests' is not defined in the Act, the case law is clear that it captures 'welfare in the widest sense, not just medical but social and psychological'.[24] The Act sets out a number of relevant factors that must (or must not) be taken

[17] It should be noted that there is currently a Draft Mental Health Bill 2022, which would seek to alter the grounds for detention. For a critique of the MHA, see, for example: Department of Health and Social Care, *Modernising the Mental Health Act: Increasing Choice, Reducing Compulsion: Final Report of the Independent Review of the Mental Health Act 1983* (London: TSO, 2018), see in particular pp. 49–64.

[18] Mental Health Act as amended by Mental Health Act 2007, s1(2).

[19] Ibid, s1(3).

[20] Ibid, s1(2A).

[21] For example, in *Tameside and Glossip Acute Services Trust v. CH* [1996] 1 FLR 762 (QBD), this provision was relied upon to authorise the caesarean section of a pregnant woman suffering from schizophrenia, on the basis that a stillbirth would cause a deterioration in her mental state and interrupt the treatment of her schizophrenia.

[22] For a detailed discussion of this, see *A NHS Trust v. Dr A* [2013] EWHC 2442 (COP).

[23] MCA ss1(5) and (4).

[24] *Aintree University Hospitals NHS Foundation Trust v. James* [2013] UKSC 67, [39] per Lady Hale.

into account by the assessor when making this assessment. The decision cannot be made merely on the basis of the age or appearance of the person;[25] the likelihood of the person regaining capacity must be considered[26] and the assessor is required to 'permit and encourage the person to participate' in the decision.[27] They must take into account, 'if it is practicable and appropriate to consult them', the views of others engaged in the care of the person, or interested in their welfare.[28] Importantly, the assessor must also, 'so far as is reasonably ascertainable', consider

(a) the person's past and present wishes and feelings (and, in particular, any relevant written statement made by [them] when [they] had capacity),
(b) the beliefs and values that would be likely to influence [their] decision if [they] had capacity, and
(c) the other factors that [they] would be likely to consider if [they] were able to do so.[29]

Finally, the assessor must also never be motivated by a desire to bring about death.[30]

Crucially, the framing of section 4 makes clear that none of the factors it outlines is to take priority in the best interests assessment.[31] It is thus left to each individual assessor to decide on the weight to be accorded to each, with the result that an individual's wishes and feelings may frequently be outweighed by other factors, where the perceived need to protect them (or a fear of the legal consequences if the assessors fail to do so) is thought to take precedence over the desire to empower them. While the way in which the provisions are being applied will be considered in Chapter 5, suffice for now to say that the way the provision in section 4 is framed gives doctors very little incentive to make empowering decisions.

The law thus adopts a cliff-edge approach to capacity: for those safely on the clifftop, autonomy and self-determination dominate; but those

[25] MCA s4(1).
[26] Ibid, s4(3).
[27] Ibid, s4(4).
[28] Ibid, s4(7).
[29] Ibid, s4(6).
[30] Ibid, s4(5).
[31] See, for example, *Re M* [2009] EWHC 2525 (Fam), [32] per Mr Justice Munby.

who fall over the edge are powerless – someone else's view of what is 'best' for them is imposed upon them. This approach has been widely criticised in the academic literature,[32] and it is not my intention to rehearse this here.[33] It need only be said that, under the current legal framework, only those deemed to have capacity have the right to decide what will happen to them, both in the treatment and care context (which is the subject of this book), and in a range of other financial and administrative matters.

1.2 The Role of the Capacity Threshold in Defining the Limits of Legitimate State Authority

This approach to capacity reflects Enlightenment ideas about the limits of legitimate state authority, as encapsulated in John Stuart Mill's conception of liberty.[34] According to this, considerable justification is required before the state may interfere with the autonomous choices of its citizens;[35] justification, in his view, is found only where the actions of an individual will cause harm to another person.[36] To understand how Mill's conception of liberty operates, it is necessary to put it in the context of his wider philosophy. In his view, 'happiness is desirable, and the only thing desirable, as an end, all other things being desired as a means to an end.'[37] As a proponent of utilitarianism, Mill argued that actions are right if they result in producing the greatest sum of human happiness. It is not therefore that people have a 'right' to liberty, but rather that respecting it will result in the best outcome for society and

32 See, for example, Clough, *The Spaces of Mental Capacity Law*; Martin *et al.*, *Achieving CRPD Compliance*; Richardson, 'Mental Disabilities and the Law'.

33 See Conclusion for more discussion of this.

34 J. S. Mill, *On Liberty* (Cosimo Classicz, 2005 [1859]); for a more detailed discussion of this, see J. Feinberg, *Harm to Self* (Oxford: Oxford University Press, 1986).

35 As J. Coggon and J. Miola 'Autonomy, liberty, and medical decision-making' (2011) 70(3) *Cambridge Law Journal* 523–543, there are many other theories in political philosophy which state that a person should be free to act autonomously, 'provided they do not breach well-grounded external laws which legitimately limit their actions' (p. 528). While Mill's harm principle represents the simplest and most widely accepted basis for these laws, other examples cited by them include 'positive obligations derived directly from the receipt of benefits inherent in membership of a stable political system, and in being part of a system of civic republicanism' (p. 528).

36 Mill, *On Liberty*, 68.

37 J. S. Mill, *Utilitarianism* (Oxford Philosophical Text Series edn, Oxford: Oxford University Press 1998), 81.

its citizens, 'utility in the largest sense, grounded on the permanent interests of man as a progressive being'.[38] Achieving happiness demands that a person be free to pursue '[their] own good in [their] own way',[39] providing this does not interfere with the interests of others. As Mill asserts:

> In the part which merely concerns himself, his independence is, of right, absolute. Over himself, over his own body and mind, the individual is sovereign.[40]

For Mill, a sphere of independence from state intervention was essential for human individuality to develop. It was also necessary if people were to have the freedom to pursue those things which they enjoyed, or deemed morally appropriate, and thus was an essential part of ensuring the happiness and morality of individuals.[41] Other commentators have similarly seen respect for autonomy as important because it leads to greater well-being – although often this is intended to apply to individual 'welfare' rather than collective 'happiness' in the Millian sense. As David Molyneux observes, this might occur instrumentally and intrinsically.[42] Regarding the former, it is argued that respecting autonomous choice is the best way of determining what is best for the individual: as Mill explains it, individuals are best placed to make choices that are good for them.[43] Others, by contrast, are often not very good at assessing what may be in someone else's interests,[44] inevitably facing limitations in their attempts to do so. As Kim Atkins observes, respect for autonomy is therefore

> an acknowledgment of the limitations of our knowledge of other people and a willingness to incorporate that understanding into our world-views. When we respect autonomy we do not simply observe another's freedom from a distance, as it were; we accede to our fundamental fallibility and epistemological humility. It is in recognition of the fact that we cannot

[38] Mill, *On Liberty*, 70.
[39] Mill, *Utilitarianism*, 56, 142.
[40] Mill, *On Liberty*, 14.
[41] Ibid, 75–76.
[42] D. Molyneux, 'Should Healthcare Professionals Respect Autonomy Just Because It Promotes Welfare?' (2009) 35 *Journal of Medical Ethics* 245.
[43] Mill, *On Liberty*.
[44] For a discussion of this, see Herring and Wall, 'Autonomy, Capacity and Vulnerable Adults', 698, 702.

> experience from another's perspective that we normally refrain from judging what will make another's life good for them.[45]

But it may also be the case that autonomy is a fundamental (or intrinsic) part of well-being. As Ronald Dworkin explains, it is essential for our fulfilment that we lead our life by our own beliefs:

> Autonomy makes each of us responsible for shaping his own life according to some coherent and distinctive sense of character, conviction, and interest. It allows us to lead our own lives rather than be led along by them, so that each of us can be, to the extent such a scheme of rights can make this possible, what he has made himself.[46]

In a similar vein, Will Kymlicka argues that an authentic life is one that is lived from the inside, pursuing values and objectives that the *individual* considers important;[47] while Joseph Raz notes that an autonomous person's well-being consists in 'the successful pursuit of *self-chosen* goals and relationships'.[48] John Stuart Mill further observes that the capacity to choose, and the exercise of this choice, is in itself fulfilling, enabling us to use our 'human faculties of perception, judgement, discriminative feeling, mental activity, and even moral preference' to come to a reasoned decision.[49] James Griffin captures this inherent value of autonomy when he makes the point that 'even if you convince me that, as my personal despot, you would produce more desirable consciousness for me than I do myself, I shall want to go on being my own master'.[50] This intuition, as Jonathan Pugh observes, suggests that 'we value autonomy for its own sake, and not just because we believe that being autonomous will lead to our attaining other prudentially valuable ends'.[51] Autonomy is thus 'partly *constitutive* of (rather than merely instrumental to) well-being'.[52]Accordingly,

[45] Atkins, 'Autonomy and the Subjective Character of Experience' (2000) 17 *Journal of Applied Philosophy* 71, 75.

[46] R. Dworkin, 'Autonomy and the Demented Self' (1986) *The Millbank Quarterly* 4, 5.

[47] W. Kymlicka, *Liberalism, Community, and Culture* (USA: Clarendon Press, 1991), 12.

[48] J. Raz, *The Morality of Freedom* (Oxford: Clarendon Paperbacks, Oxford University Press, 1988).

[49] Mill, *On Liberty*, 122.

[50] J. Griffin, *Well-Being: Its Meaning, Measurement and Moral Importance* (USA: Oxford University Press, 1988), 9.

[51] J. Pugh, *Autonomy, Rationality, and Contemporary Bioethics* (Oxford: Oxford University Press, 2020), 237–238.

[52] Ibid.

> as long as an individual's choice is autonomous, that should give us at least a *pro tanto* reason to believe that respecting that choice will benefit that person, not because the choice is likely to lead to greater happiness (as the explanatory hedonist might claim), but rather because on this view there is prudential value to directing the course of one's life in accordance with one's own beliefs about what is of value, and with one's own beliefs about which values should take precedence.[53]

While the role of autonomy in promoting individual well-being is the most convincing rationale for why it should be respected, it should be noted that not all philosophers who advocate the importance of it regard its value as deriving from its contribution to (and constituent importance of) well-being.[54] Molyneux draws on Darwall's theory of demand autonomy, for example, which involves an essentially Kantian argument that there is something fundamentally important about being a person that demands our respect for the person's autonomous choices,[55] 'not because the choices are respect-inducing in themselves, but because respect for choices is what one person can reasonably demand of another person'.[56] In other words, respect for a person and their capacity for self-rule demands that we respect their autonomy, even when to do so would not promote their individual (or collective) welfare.

This, for reasons aptly explained by Jennifer Hawkins, is less compelling than explanations tied to well-being:

> [I]t is an argument that makes *no appeal whatsoever* to what it might be like for the subject to be interfered with. It does not appeal to the *value* of free choice for the person who has it. It ultimately locates the wrongness of paternalism in a kind of irrationality on the part of the would-be paternalist.[57]

53 Ibid, 256.

54 It is important to be clear at the outset that for the present discussion, I am concerned with autonomy only in the sense of a quality, trait, or characteristic that individuals can exhibit throughout their lives, not in a Kantian sense, which concerns the person's capacity to impose moral law on themselves (E. Kant, *Groundwork of the Metaphysics of Morals* (Cambridge Texts in the History of Philosophy ed, 2nd edn, Cambridge University Press 2012)), or as a source of political legitimacy, according to which political power and authority can be justified only if it is acceptable to all the citizens who are bound by it (see, for example, J. Rawls, *Political Liberalism* (New York: Columbia University Press, 1993), 144–150).

55 S. Darwall, 'The Value of Autonomy and Autonomy of the Will' (2006) 116(2) *Ethics* 263.

56 Molyneux (n61), 248.

57 J. Hawkins, 'Why Even a Liberal Can Justify Limited Paternalistic Intervention in Anorexia Nervosa' (2021) 28(2) *Philosophy, Psychiatry & Psychology* 155–158.

Hawkins is therefore right to suggest that 'if paternalism is wrong, it must be because of how it affects those who are treated paternalistically'[58]: it imposes something onto them which does not contribute to their well-being, in the way that respect for autonomy would. But whatever one's reasons for respecting autonomy, given the normative importance that is attached to people being free to make autonomous choices, it is widely accepted that this sphere of independence should not be too readily interfered with by the state.

One circumstance in which most accept that the state has jurisdiction to intervene, is where in exercising their autonomy, a person causes (or is likely to cause) harm to another, thereby interfering with that person's autonomy. Mill captured it thus: 'the only purpose for which power can be rightfully exercised over any member of a civilised community, against his will, is *to prevent harm to others.*'[59] Of course this must be subject to qualifications. Mill himself set out a number: he differentiated harm (an action that was injurious or set back important interests of others) from 'mere offence' (which did not warrant protection),[60] excluded consensual harms,[61] and reiterated that harm prevention should be seen as a necessary, but not a sufficient condition for restricting individual liberties (which will depend on a utilitarian calculation of whether the benefits of regulation outweigh its disadvantages[62]). While it is not necessary to examine these in detail for the purposes of this discussion, it is clear that the law has a legitimate utilitarian goal of promoting the welfare of its citizens, such that when a person's welfare is infringed by another, the law is sometimes justified in encroaching on the liberty of the infringer in order to prevent this from occurring.

Much more contentious, however, is the role of the state in protecting its citizens from *themselves*. Mill's stance on this issue was clear: paternalistic interference of the state is not deemed acceptable where a person understands the decision they are making and is capable of freely

58 Ibid.

59 Mill, *On Liberty*, 68.

60 Mill, *Utilitarianism*, 141. This distinction was reiterated by Joseph Feinberg, who likewise distinguishes hurt and offence – which, while undesirable, does not thwart our interests – from harm, which he defines as a setback to interests (see J. Feinberg, *Harm to Others: The Moral Limits of the Criminal Law* Volume 1 (Oxford Scholarship Online, November 2003), 45–51). For a more in-depth discussion of the nature of 'harm', see Chapter 6 (Section 6.2) of this book.

61 Ibid, 142.

62 Mill, *Utilitarianism*, 70.

exercising their autonomy. However, even for later liberal philosophers who have been vociferous in their objections to paternalism, intervention in self-regarding decisions is acceptable only in very limited cases, and certainly would not be accepted in the kinds of treatment and care decisions being contemplated in this book. Joseph Raz, for example, contemplates some intervention where it is necessary to protect the person from making decisions which will severely limit their future autonomy.[63] While he does not set out in detail when these circumstances will arise, he notes in particular that

> paternalism affecting matters which are regarded by all as of merely instrumental value does not interfere with autonomy if its effect is to improve safety, thus making the activities affected more likely to realize their aim.[64]

Regulations directed at the safety and efficacy of products or mandating the use of seat belts in cars may therefore be justifiable: they do not greatly violate the person's autonomy, since the behaviour which they constrain is not a central purpose of the person's reason for acting. However, a distinction can be drawn between this and, for example, a risky sport, 'where the risk is part of the point of the activity or an inevitable by-product of its point and purpose'.[65]

It is the latter kind of choice which aligns more closely with the sorts of treatment and care decisions which are being contemplated in this book. Where an agent makes a decision to either have or to refuse treatment or care, they are usually deliberately seeking a certain outcome or, at the very least, are aware of (and accept) the risks inherent in making the choice that they do. The risks are therefore rarely unforeseeable or inadvertently taken; rather, the agent has weighed up the advantages and disadvantages of different courses of action and formed a judgement about which they would rather pursue, based on their values and

[63] Central to his theory is the idea that the government has a positive duty to protect and promote the autonomy of its citizens. The use of coercion thus violates their autonomy in two ways: 'it violates the condition of independence and expresses a relationship of domination and an attitude of disrespect for the coerced individual', and it 'is a global and indiscriminate invasion of autonomy': Raz, *The Morality of Freedom*, 418. Its use is therefore a way of causing harm to the person, depriving them of opportunities which they would otherwise have. However, it may be justified where it is necessary to prevent one's actions diminishing the autonomy of others, 'even of that person himself in the future' (Ibid, 413).

[64] Ibid, 422.

[65] Ibid.

priorities. To interfere with this decision would thus constitute a very large invasion of their autonomy, even more so given that imposing treatment or protective care measures on an agent will likely necessitate the infringement of either their bodily integrity or their liberty, causing potentially substantial psychological or emotional harm.[66] Therefore, while Raz and others have taken a less robust stance against paternalism than Mill, their views do not undermine the importance attached to people being able to exercise their autonomy in decisions about their treatment and care. Indeed, elsewhere Raz explicitly distinguishes 'decisions about the safety of pharmaceutical products' (which are *not* the sort of decisions which a person ought to decide for themselves, rather than following authority), from 'decisions about undergoing a course of medication or treatment where we may well feel that I should decide for myself, rather than be dictated to by authority'.[67] This may be especially important when seen in the context of medical practice, where widespread paternalism provoked a powerful movement in favour of greater protections for patient autonomy in the latter part of the twentieth century.[68] As Jos and Sander Welie explain:

> The history of medicine, health care and biomedical research is marked by silence, disregard of patients' wishes, and at times coercion. In order to protect patients against medical paternalism, patients have been granted the right to respect of their autonomy. First explored in the late 19th and early 20th century, by the end of the second millennium patient autonomy had become an undisputed staple of all codes of ethics in health care and a legally protected and enforceable right. This right is operationalized first and foremost through the phenomenon of informed consent. If the patient withholds consent, medical treatment, including life-saving treatment, may not be provided.[69]

Yet, crucially, this proscription against interfering with an individual's choices does not extend to those who are incapable of autonomous

[66] This is especially so given that, unlike for health and safety regulations or the mandatory wearing of seat belts, such interventions do not entail the removal of 'bad' options at a legislative level, but rather involve an individual doctor or carer taking a view of what is best for the specific person in the future and overriding individual choices accordingly.

[67] J. Raz, 'The Problem of Authority: Revisiting the Service Conception' (2005) 90 *Minnesota Law Review*1003.

[68] Beverley Clough identifies a similar trajectory in the social care context, where increasing importance has been attached to choice and independence: see Clough, *The Spaces of Mental Capacity Law*, 46–49.

[69] J. V. M. Welie and S. P. K. Welie, 'Patient Decision-Making Competence: Outlines of a Conceptual Analysis' (2001) 4(2) *Medicine, Healthcare and Philosophy* 127–138.

decision-making. Immediately following the harm principle, Mill notes that 'it is perhaps hardly necessary to say that this doctrine is meant to apply only to human beings *in the maturity of their faculties* ... Those who are still in a state to require being taken care of by others must be protected against their own actions as well as against external injury'.[70] Later this is made even more explicit: the principle of liberty has no application to people incapable of 'free and equal discussion',[71] those without an 'ordinary amount of understanding',[72] or to someone who is 'a child, or delirious, or in some state of excitement or absorption incompatible with the full use of the reflecting faculty'.[73] Mill also gives an example of someone about to cross a bridge that is unsafe. If there is no time to warn him, then it is acceptable to grab him and pull him back, as this does not interfere with his liberty, as liberty is only the freedom to do what one voluntarily desires, and in this instance, he does not desire to fall into the river below. If, however, he determines, with knowledge of the risk, to proceed over the bridge, we must accept his autonomous choice.[74] While in this instance the lack of autonomy is attributable to a lack of information rather than an inherent vulnerability caused by an impairment or illness, it is demonstrative of the fact that Mill permits a degree of paternalistic interference where it does not interfere with the *autonomous* choices of people. Similarly, H. L. A. Hart argues that paternalism can be justified if a person's capacity to make free and informed choices is diminished by factors such as 'inner psychological compulsion' or 'pressure from others', or where they have an inadequate appreciation of the consequences of their choices.[75]

Although neither Mill nor Hart engaged in detail with why the principle of non-interference ought not to apply to people incapable of making autonomous choices, the justification for this differential treatment lies in the reasons we have for respecting autonomy in the first place. Generally the decisions people make will reflect their values and desires, enabling them to live according to their own conception of the 'good life'. Respecting a person's autonomous choices is therefore most likely to maximize their welfare, both because people are best placed to

[70] Ibid, 69.
[71] Ibid.
[72] Ibid, 142.
[73] Ibid, 166.
[74] Mill, *On Liberty*, Ch 5.
[75] H. L. A. Hart, *Law, Liberty and Morality* (Stanford, CA: Stanford University Press, 1963), 32–33.

determine what is good for them and because there is value in itself to governing one's life. There will be some people, however, who are incapable of making autonomous decisions which reflect and further their priorities and goals and whose decisions may therefore not be welfare-enhancing, even according to their own subjective standards. In these cases, the law is justified in intervening to ensure that the decision that is made is one which promotes the person's interests, and to prevent them from harming themselves through making decisions, the consequences of which they do not fully appreciate. As Jonathan Herring observes, enabling people to flourish 'may be possible with little intervention by the state' for some people, but for others, some degree of intervention may be necessary 'to enable a person (or a group of people) to live their lives fully'.[76] This 'right and duty to care for those not able to care for themselves'[77] has been recognised in England since feudal times, with the *parens patriae* doctrine originally bestowing the power to do so on the monarch, before this was transferred to the courts in the sixteenth century.[78]

For those who regard autonomy as having independent normative importance beyond its connection to welfare, it may also be said that decisions made by people incapable of autonomy do not warrant the same respect. According to Kant, it is their capacity for rational action that distinguishes humans from other animals, and makes them worthy of respect.[79] As Simon Lee suggests, respect for autonomy thus rests on an assumption: that people are rational beings, capable of assessing the information and weighing the options available to them.[80] The value in recognising people as rational agents capable of making choices may therefore be deemed less pertinent for people who lack that decision-making ability.

According to the liberal framework which underpins the MCA, therefore, while people capable of autonomy ought to have the liberty to make decisions free from state interference, for those who are incapable, the law has a legitimate role in intervening to ensure that the decision made best reflects the agent's values and beliefs and protects their interests. As

[76] J. Herring, *Caring and the Law* (Oxford: Hart Publishing 2013), (n74), 304.

[77] G. Laurie, 'Parens Patriae Jurisdiction in the Medico-Legal Context: The Vagaries of Judicial Activism' (1999) 3 *Edinburgh Law Review* 95, 95.

[78] Ibid.

[79] Kant, *Groundwork of the Metaphysics of Morals.*

[80] S. Lee, *Law and Morals: Warnock, Gillick, and Beyond* (Oxford: Oxford University Press, 1986), 64.

Beverley Clough observes, 'this distinction between the public sphere of interference and the private sphere of non-interference has been challenged by many feministic legal theorists', as has the Enlightenment 'ideal of an individualistic, rationalistic, and masculine legal subject' on which such legal frameworks are built.[81] It is not my intention to rehearse such criticisms here (though they will be picked up on again in the Conclusion).[82] Rather, I aim simply to acknowledge the political and jurisprudential framework which underpins the current law with a view to analysing the extent to which it does – and indeed can – live up to the liberal ideals it seeks to promulgate. According to this framework, it is essential that the law can reliably distinguish those who are capable of making autonomous choices from those who are not. This is the role of capacity in law, which, as Jonathan Herring and Jesse Wall note, seeks to determine 'the minimum necessary for autonomy and treats the person as autonomous once they cross that threshold'.[83] Capacity is thus generally understood as a condition for the exercise of autonomy: if a person has capacity, then absent other ways in which their autonomy may be being undermined (such as the coercion or undue influence of others), they are deemed to be capable of acting autonomously. If they do not, they are thought not to be able to take autonomous decisions. The test for capacity contained in the MCA thus plays a crucial role in determining when the state will defer to the 'individual's subjective choices, protecting individual's autonomy from outside intrusion',[84] and when it will not.

1.3 The Test for Capacity

Given its role in determining the limits of legitimate state authority, it is generally assumed that the test for capacity must be neutral as to the

81 Clough, *The Spaces of Mental Capacity Law*, 45. See, for example, Mackenzie and Stoljar, *Relational Autonomy: Feminist Essays on Autonomy, Agency and Social Self*, 2000; MacKinnon, *Toward a Feminist Theory of the State*; Sandel, *Liberalism and the Limits of Justice*; Wolpe, 'The Triumph of Autonomy in American Bioethics'; Mackenzie, 'Relational Autonomy, Normative Authority and Perfectionism', 512, 51; Christman, 'Relational Autonomy, Liberal Individualism, and the Social Constitution of Selves', 143–164; Kong, *Mental Capacity in Relationship*.

82 For a good discussion of deconstructing the normative assumptions on which our legal framework is based, see Clough, *The Spaces of Mental Capacity Law*.

83 Herring and Wall, 'Autonomy, Capacity and Vulnerable Adults', 698, 703.

84 Kong, 'Mental Capacity in Relationship'.

substance of the values, beliefs, or reasons underpinning any given decision. After all, to place any substantive limits on the types of decision that a person can capacitously take, or the reasons or values that a person may choose to act upon, would seem to directly contradict the objective of creating a protected space for individual autonomy. As a result, the Mental Capacity Act 2005 adopts a process-orientated account of capacity, which focuses on whether certain of the agent's cognitive capacities are intact, and not on the outcome of the decision, or on the substance or origins of values or beliefs which underpin it.

Although the MCA imposes a presumption in favour of an agent having capacity,[85] whether they are deemed capable of making a decision depends on whether they meet the test for capacity set out in sections 2 and 3 of the MCA. Under section 2(1) of the MCA, an agent 'lacks capacity in relation to a matter if at the material time [they are] unable to make a decision for [themselves] in relation to the matter because of an impairment of, or a disturbance in the functioning of, the mind or brain'. Section 3(1) further explains that 'for the purposes of section 2', an agent is 'unable to make a decision' if they are unable'

(a) to understand the information relevant to the decision,
(b) to retain that information,
(c) to use or weigh that information as part of the process of making the decision, or
(d) to communicate [their] decision (whether by talking, using sign language, or any other means).

Further guidance on these limbs of the test for capacity can be found in the Code of Practice accompanying the MCA.[86] This makes clear that the information 'relevant' to the decision includes 'the nature of the decision, the reasons why the decision is needed, and the likely effects of deciding one way or another, or making no decision at all',[87] while the agent must only retain the information 'long enough to use it to make an effective

85 MCA, s1(2).

86 Department for Constitutional Affairs, Mental Capacity Act 2005 Code of Practice (London: TSO, 2007). NB: there has recently been a consultation on a new Code of Practice, with the final version expected soon. See www.gov.uk/government/consultations/changes-to-the-mca-code-of-practice-and-implementation-of-the-lps. Accessed 21 September 2022.

87 Ibid, 4.16.

decision'.[88] It also elaborates on what is meant by the ambiguous 'use or weigh' limb of the test (explored in more detail in Chapter 2), explaining that

> sometimes people can understand information but an impairment or disturbance stops them using it. In other cases, the impairment or disturbance leads to a person making a specific decision without understanding or using the information they have been given.[89]

The MCA thus proceeds on the assumption that an agent either possesses the capacity to make decisions or they do not, and that this can be objectively determined through a test for capacity which assesses various cognitive capacities an agent may have (understanding, retention, weighting of information). As Natalie Banner explains, according to this approach,

> capacity can be operationalized through measuring its constituent psychological processes, which are taken to be, in principle, amenable to observation and measurement via the construction of behavioural indices.[90]

That the MCA focuses on *cognitive* processes is perhaps unsurprising given its conceptual origins in liberal thinking. As Robin Mackenzie and John Watts have observed, the criteria for capacity have inevitably been shaped 'by liberal views of the person who expresses free will and agency in rational, self-determining decisions' which makes 'it is logical enough that competence tests would center upon measuring cognitive abilities'.[91]

However, defining competence in these 'exclusively cognitive terms' is, as Louis Charland observes, also essential to maintaining an air of objectivity in the test: 'so defined, competence has little or nothing to do with value ... [making] it easier to view it as an objective commodity'.[92] Given the role played by the test for capacity in defining when an agent may make decisions for themselves, this objectivity is perceived as crucial. Whether or not an agent is able to decide for themselves ought to

[88] Ibid, 4.20.

[89] Ibid, 4.21.

[90] N. Banner, 'Unreasonable Reasons: Normative Judgements in the Assessment of Mental Capacity' (2012) 18(5) *Journal of Evaluation in Clinical Practice* 1038–1044, 1039.

[91] R. Mackenzie and J. Watts, 'Including Emotionality in Tests of Competence: How Does Neurodiversity Affect Measures of Free Will and Agency in Medical Decision Making?' (2011) 2(3) *AJOB Neuroscience* 27–36, 28.

[92] L. Charland, 'Mental Competence and Value: The Problem of Normativity in the Assessment of Decision-Making Capacity' (2001) 8(2) *Psychology and Law* 135–145, 136.

hinge on whether they have, or do not have, certain cognitive capacities, and should not depend on the idiosyncrasies of either the assessor or the agent themselves. As Charland observes:

> Similar tests should yield similar judgements in like cases. The standards employed should be sufficiently objective to be replicable in a manner that yields consistent results across like cases. Anything less would be unjust to those whose competence is at issue.[93]

Since a person's values and beliefs are inherently subjective and idiosyncratic, any reliance on them when assessing capacity may risk introducing subjectivity into the test. It was for this reason that the Law Commission cautioned against any approach which focused on the *content* of a person's decision, given the risk inherent in it, that 'any decision which is inconsistent with conventional values, or with which the assessor disagrees, may be classified as incompetent', which 'penalises individuality and demands conformity at the expense of personal autonomy'.[94] In a similar vein, the Law Commission recommended including a further provision in the Mental Capacity Draft Bill to reiterate that 'a person is not to be treated as unable to make a decision merely because he or she makes a decision which would not be made by a person of ordinary prudence'.[95] This now embodies one of the key statutory principles underpinning the Act, contained in section 1(4) of the MCA (albeit the notion that a person of 'ordinary prudence' has been replaced with simply 'an unwise decision'[96]), and the accompanying Code of Practice further emphasises that when testing for capacity, 'what matters is [the agent's] ability to carry out the processes involved in making the decision – and not the outcome'.[97]

The test for capacity thus adheres to a form of 'value-agnosticism'.[98] As Richard Huxtable explains, the test 'purports to focus upon functioning (and thus process and rationality) rather than on the substance of, or the reasons (and values) underpinning, the decision'.[99] Indeed, as Lord

93 Ibid.
94 Law Commission Consultation Paper, *Mental Incapacity*, Law Com No 231 (HMSO, 1995), 3.4.
95 Ibid, 3.19.
96 MCA 2005, s1(4).
97 Department for Constitutional Affairs, 4.2.
98 Coggon and Miola, 'Autonomy, Liberty, and Medical Decision-Making', 523–543.
99 R. Huxtable, 'Autonomy, Best Interests and the Public Interest: Treatment, Non-Treatment and the Values of Medical Law' (2014) 22(4) *Medical Law Review* 459–493, 463.

Donaldson set out in *Re T*, a person who has capacity is entitled to refuse treatment or care interventions whether the reasons are 'rational, irrational, unknown or even non-existent'.[100] This, as John Coggon observes, would seem to suggest that 'as long as the patient's thought processes are not in doubt, his underlying reasons are not open to question',[101] a view reinforced by Lady Justice Butler-Sloss's powerful assertion in *Re MB* that even a decision 'which is so outrageous in its defiance of logic or of accepted moral standards that no sensible person who had applied his mind to the question to be decided could have arrived at it'[102] should not be taken to be illustrative of incapacity.

At first sight, this approach has much to commend it. It helps to ensure certainty and consistency in the application of the law, which is essential if people are to be able to plan their lives accordingly and not have their freedom arbitrarily interfered with. More importantly, it is essential to protecting a sphere of independence for people to pursue their own values, in accordance with the principles of a liberal society set out earlier. As Charland explains, 'the right of an individual to make his or her own medical treatment decisions goes to the heart of what it means to be an autonomous individual'.[103] The decision of whether to accept treatment or care is not merely a medical question – it engages the agent's priorities and aims in life, their familial and relational circumstances, and sometimes even their belief system. The agent must balance a number of different factors and interests against one another to determine what course of action will be best for them, the weight or importance being attached to each inevitably depending on how they value and prioritise different aspects of their life, or death. Given this, there is no one objectively verifiable answer to the question of what is best for a person in any given treatment and care decision: people may legitimately reach different conclusions, as perspectives diverge on the sanctity of human life, on what chances are worth taking at what cost, on what

[100] *Re T (Adult: Refusal of Medical Treatment)* [1992] 4 All ER 649, 664. See also Lady Justice Butler-Sloss in *Re MB (Medical Treatment)* [1997] EWCA Civ 3093: 'A mentally competent patient has an absolute right to refuse to consent to medical treatment for any reason, rational or irrational, or for no reason at all, even where that decision may lead to his or her own death.' [17].

[101] J. Coggon, 'Varied and Principled Understandings of Autonomy in English Law: Justifiable Inconsistency or Blinkered Moralism?' (2007) *15 Health Care Analysis* 235, 239.

[102] *Re MB (Medical Treatment)* [1997] EWCA Civ 3093, [30].

[103] Charland, 'Mental Competence and Value', 135–145.

makes for a 'good' life and a 'good' death. Nowhere is this more true than in decisions at the end of life. As Alexander Kon observes, 'deciding when the outcome of care will be a fate worse than death' is a deeply personal matter: 'there is no right or wrong answer'.[104] A finding that someone lacks capacity in this context, denying them the right to make decisions according to their own values and beliefs merely because these contravene 'conventional values',[105] would seem wrong: it would be to force objective conceptions of what is valuable on a person, denying them the opportunity to pursue values and commitments that *they* consider important. This, as Kymlicka explained, does not benefit a person,[106] and it might even harm them. In Ronald Dworkin's powerful words, 'making someone die in a way that others approve, but he believes a horrifying contradiction to his life, is a devastating, odious form of tyranny'.[107]

Maintaining value neutrality and objectivity in the test for capacity is thus considered essential for it to perform its role in demarcating the appropriate boundaries of state interference. In a liberal democracy committed to value pluralism and tolerance of different beliefs and perspectives, a person ought, in principle, to be able to live – or die – according to their own values, beliefs, and commitments, providing that in doing so, they do not cause harm to others. And as Rob Heywood notes,

> if the law is to take seriously views about freedom of religion, expression, and the right to respect for private and family life, it must attach genuine significance to medical decisions which are underpinned by those values.[108]

Yet, as Chapter 2 will make clear, the picture is, in reality, far more complex. Given the way the current test for capacity is framed, it cannot be applied in practice without reference to the values that underpin the decision. This is not merely a problem with its current framing in the MCA; rather, as Charland captures, 'there is no such thing as mental

[104] A. Kon, 'When Parents Refuse Treatment for Their Child' (2006) 8(1) *JONA'S Healthcare Law, Ethics, and Regulation* 5–9.

[105] Law Commission Consultation Paper, 3.4.

[106] Kymlicka, *Liberalism, Community, and Culture*, 12.

[107] R. Dworkin, *Life's Dominion: An Argument about Abortion, Euthanasia, and Individual Freedom* (New York: Alfred A Knopf, 1993), 217.

[108] R. Heywood, 'Parents and Medical Professionals: Conflict, Cooperation, and Best Interests' (2012) 20(1) *Medical Law Review* 29, 33.

competence without value, and normative considerations associated with value cannot be eliminated from the assessment of decision-making capacity'.[109] An agent's decision-making processes cannot be assessed in isolation from the substance of the values, priorities, or beliefs driving that decision. In practice, the current approach, with its ostensible value agnosticism, gives assessors considerable latitude to determine how they wish to use values in their assessments and whose values they wish to use. The result is not only subjectivity and inconsistency in the application of the test for capacity but also the obscuring of heavily value-laden judgements, which are insulated from scrutiny and challenge, allowing potentially unwarranted paternalism to go unchecked.

In Chapters 2–6, changes to the test for capacity will therefore be suggested, which articulate a more explicit role for values. In doing so, they will be required to engage head-on with the tension this raises between the liberal ideals espoused in this chapter, and the complex realities of decision-making on the ground, where, especially in the psychiatry context, too puritanical a commitment to value neutrality may result in a failure to protect highly vulnerable and non-autonomous individuals.

[109] Charland, 'Mental Competence and Value', 135–145.

2

An Essential Role for Values in Assessments of Capacity

Inherent in the approach of the MCA is the assumption that a person either possesses the capacity to make a decision or they do not, and that this can be objectively determined through a test which measures its 'constituent psychological processes',[1] independently of the values or beliefs that underpin any given decision. The adoption of this 'procedural notion of capacity' has, as Natalie Banner explains, 'a very clear purpose in the law':

> [T]o avoid as far as possible the threat of medical paternalism, which would lead to a patient's right to autonomy being overruled if a clinician does not agree that the patient has made the right or best decision.[2]

This chapter will begin by exploring a key problem with this approach, namely that it is impossible to assess a person's capacity to 'use or weigh' the information relevant to a decision without engaging with the values that underpin their decision. This is because, while in principle it may be possible to assess whether a person has the *capacity* to use or weigh information independently of the weight they in fact attribute to that information, in practice the assessor must look at the content of the decision to discern what impact, if any, the information appears to be having on the decision-making process. Yet this is impossible without knowing what the values or beliefs underpinning the decision are, since the parameters of the decision that a person could reasonably have made, had they used the relevant information, is set by the person's own values. By failing to engage openly with the role that values are playing in capacity assessments, the current law allows assessors to evaluate capacity

[1] Banner, 'Unreasonable Reasons', 1038–1044.

[2] N. Banner, 'Can Procedural and Substantive Elements of Decision-Making be Reconciled in Assessments of Mental Capacity?' (2013) 9(1) *International Journal of Law in Context* 71–86.

by reference to values that are not the person's own, resulting in a potentially illiberal application of the MCA.

However, not all instances of this are necessarily instances of unwarranted paternalism. In fact, underpinning a number of cases appears to be a concern that an illness or impairment is affecting the nature of the beliefs or values that motivate a decision, such that the decision reached is not one that the person would have made, but for the disorder. An example might be a person refusing a surgical intervention on the basis of a delusional belief that the surgeon has sinister intentions; or a person with depression refusing life-saving treatment because they see no value to continued life. Given its exclusive focus on cognitive processes rather than on the substance of the values or beliefs underpinning a decision, there is no mechanism within the MCA to capture such situations directly. Consequently, capacity assessors are forced to manipulate the test for capacity by finding the person to be unable to use or weigh information, if they are to prevent people from making harmful decisions which the assessor does not consider to be truly autonomous. While this may prevent harm in certain cases, the result of conflating different types of impairments under the nebulous 'use or weigh' criterion is to obscure the value-laden and highly controversial claims that may underpin such decisions, which remain insulated from scrutiny or challenge.

2.1 Deconstructing 'Use or Weigh'

According to section 3(1)(c) of the MCA, a person lacks capacity if he or she is unable to use or weigh the information that is relevant to a decision (namely, its nature and consequences) as 'part of the process of making the decision'.[3] This has been fairly described as the limb of the capacity test which is both the 'most conceptually difficult to understand' and the most 'empirically difficult to test or measure'.[4] Yet, as Banner has noted, 'there is surprisingly little discussion in the theoretical and empirical

[3] Mental Capacity Act 2005, s3(1)(c).

[4] Banner, 'Unreasonable Reasons', 1038–1044. Two exceptions to this is exploring how the courts have understood the 'use or weigh' criteria: N. Kane, A. Ruck-Keene, G. Owen, S. Kim, 'Applying Decision-Making Capacity Criteria in Practice: A Content Analysis of Court Judgments' *PLOS ONE*, Published: 5 February 2021, https://doi.org/10.1371/journal.pone.0246521; S. Kim, N. Kane, A. Ruck-Keene, G. Owen, 'Broad Concepts and Messy Realities: Optimising the Application of Mental Capacity Criteria' (2021) 2021 *Journal of Medical Ethics* 1–7.

literature on capacity detailing either what is meant by using or weighing information, or what constitutes fulfilment of this criterion'.[5] The MCA and its 'Explanatory Notes' do little to elucidate its precise meaning or explain how it should be tested, stating simply that a person 'must be able to use and weigh [the relevant information] to arrive at a choice'.[6] The Code of Practice (which gives guidance on how to apply the MCA) goes a little further, explaining that:

> [f]or someone to have capacity, they must have the ability to weigh up information and use it to arrive at a decision. Sometimes people can understand information but an impairment or disturbance stops them using it. In other cases, the impairment or disturbance leads to a person making a specific decision without understanding or using the information they have been given.[7]

Two examples are provided. The first is of a person suffering from anorexia nervosa, who 'may understand information about the consequences of not eating. But their compulsion not to eat might be too strong for them to ignore'.[8] The second is of someone with serious brain damage, who 'might make impulsive decisions regardless of information they have been given or their understanding of it'.[9] These examples are instructive. In the case of a person with anorexia, the suggestion is that although they understand the relevant information (namely that without food they may die), they cannot use this to form a decision to accept food, because they are compelled by their illness to act in a certain way. For the person with brain damage, meanwhile, the implication is that he or she lacks the cognitive ability to project into the future and apply the consequences of their decision to their own life, with the result that the decision is not informed in any way by the information they have been provided with. In both these illustrations, the 'use or weigh' limb is clearly grappling with the question of whether information about the nature and consequences of a decision has really informed or affected the decision-making process in any way.

Certainly, this reading accords with the origins of this limb of the capacity test. In the original proposals put forward by the Law

[5] Banner, 'Can Procedural and Substantive Elements of Decision-Making Be Reconciled in Assessments of Mental Capacity?', 71–86.
[6] Explanatory Notes to the Mental Capacity Act 2005, [26].
[7] Department for Constitutional Affairs, 4.21.
[8] Ibid, 4.22.
[9] Ibid.

Commission, the phrase 'use or weigh' did not feature at all. The Law Commission advocated that

> a person should be regarded as unable to make a decision by reason of mental disability if the disability is such that, at the time when the decision needs to be made, he or she is *unable to make a decision based on the information relevant to the decision*, including information about the reasonably foreseeable consequences of deciding one way or another or failing to make the decision.
>
> (Draft Bill, clause 2(2)(b) [emphasis added])

This provision was intended to capture decisions 'based on a compulsion, the overpowering will of a third party or any other inability to act on the relevant information as a result of mental disability'.[10] The report highlighted certain 'compulsive conditions' which caused people 'to arrive, inevitably, at decisions which are unconnected to the information or their understanding of it', such as a person with anorexia who 'always decides not to eat'.[11] This formulation was then picked up on in a Government Green Paper published in 1997,[12] and then again in a Government White Paper in 1999,[13] which provided that

> a person will be unable to make a decision by reason of mental disability if the disability is such that, at the time when the decision needs to be made, the person is *"unable to understand or retain the information relevant to the decision, or is unable to make a decision based on that information"*.[14]

Yet in the Draft Mental Incapacity Bill (2003) that followed this, this terminology was changed from an inability to make a decision *based* on that information, to an inability 'to *use* the information relevant to the decision as part of the process of making the decision'.[15] Although no explanation can be found for this alteration, it may be that it was designed to reinforce the idea that a person's capacity was not dependent

[10] Law Commission Consultation Paper, 3.17.

[11] Ibid, 3.17.

[12] Lord Chancellor's Department, 'Who Decides? Making Decisions on Behalf of Mentally Incapacitated Adults; a consultation paper issued by the Lord Chancellor's Department' (Stationery Office, December 1997), 3.14.

[13] Making Decisions, October 1999, Cm 4465. Available at www.mentalhealth.org.uk/sites/default/files/making_decisions.pdf. Accessed 17 September 2020.

[14] Lord Chancellor's Department, *Making decisions: The Government's proposals for making decisions on behalf of mentally incapacitated adults – A report issued in the light of responses to the consultation paper 'Who decides?'* (Cm 4465) October 1999, 1.6.

[15] Draft Incapacity Bill (introduced 23 June 2003), Clause 2.

on the expected outcome of their decision, since the new provision examined whether the person was using the information to *make* a decision, and not how much the eventual decision reached appeared to be based on the information given. It also better captures situations where a decision may be informed by knowledge of its likely consequences, but not 'based' exclusively on such information, being influenced also by other factors or beliefs. This new terminology was then carried forward into the Mental Capacity Bill, but with the addition of the 'weigh' provision that we now see in the Act.[16] In accordance with the statutory wording ('use *or* weigh'), the courts have (largely) been clear that an impairment in *either* the person's ability to use the information or to weigh it would render a person lacking in capacity.[17] Yet it is difficult to conceive of a situation in which a person could be unable to 'use' information when making a decision but able to 'weigh' it up, so 'use' would seem to encompass 'weigh' as well. In any event, the two elements are rarely distinguished in capacity assessments.

Examining the pre-legislative material casts some light on how 'use or weigh' ought to be interpreted, suggesting that the origins of the provision lie in testing whether the information has any effect on the decision-making process or, to put it another way, whether the decision reached has been informed or affected by the relevant information. In doing so, it captures situations where a person understands the information but is unable to attribute any weight to it in the decision-making process, because, for example, a powerful affective attitude (such as an addiction or phobia) compels them to choose a certain option.

Importantly, the question is whether a person is *able* to use information about the nature and consequences of a decision in order to decide which course of action to take. This limb is not concerned with *how* they have used the information, or whether they have attributed the '*correct*' weight to different pieces of information. An agent should

[16] MCA 2005, s3(1)(c).

[17] See, for example, *IM v. LM* [2014] EWCA Civ 37, where it was said: 's3(1)(c) of the Act refers to the ability to use or weigh information as part of the process of making the decision. In some circumstances, having understood and retained relevant information, an ability to use it will be what is critical; in others, it will be necessary to be able to weigh competing considerations' [52]. While MacDonald J. suggested in *Kings College NHS Foundation Trust v. C* [2015] EWCOP 80 that both must be present for the agent to be found to lack capacity, this has been criticised by some commentators: see, for example, the commentary of 39 Essex Chambers. Available at: www.39essex.com/cop_cases/kings-college-nhs-foundation-trust-v-c-and-v/. Accessed 11 November 2018.

therefore only be deemed unable to use or weigh the information if their disorder or impairment has rendered them incapable of putting weight on certain pieces of information, not merely where their value commitments or beliefs lead them to choose not to, or to give such information only limited weight. MacDonald J. captured this point in *King's College Hospital NHS Foundation Trust v. C & V*:[18]

> Where a court is satisfied that a person is able to use and weigh the relevant information, the weight to be attached to that information in the decision making process is a matter for the decision maker. Thus, where a person is able to use and weigh the relevant information but chooses to give that information no weight when reaching the decision in question, the element of the functional test comprised by s 3(1)(c) will not be satisfied. Within this context, a person cannot be considered to be unable to use and weigh information simply on the basis that he or she has applied his or her own values or outlook to that information in making the decision in question and chosen to attach no weight to that information in the decision making process.[19]

Maintaining a distinction between having the capacity to weigh and how the agent in fact weighs is essential to the MCA retaining its value neutrality. As Charland explains, ranking or weighing alternatives necessarily involves values, as without these, an individual would be unable to 'evaluate the nature and personal meaning of the alternatives he or she faces'.[20] If assessments of capacity hinged on whether or not the assessor deems the agent to have attached the 'appropriate' weight to certain pieces of information, therefore, then for the reasons given in Chapter 1, this would severely constrain people's liberty to act in accordance with their own values and priorities. As a matter of principle, then, whether someone is *able* to attach any weight to information and what weight they in fact choose to give to it must remain distinct.

Yet, unable to see into the agent's mind, the assessor inevitably faces a problem when determining if they are really *unable* to use or weigh information in practice. The assessor, as Banner explains, is 'operating from an epistemically limited position, and many of the factors that influence a patient's decision making are likely to be opaque from a third person perspective'.[21] While the assessor can discuss the reasons for a

[18] [2015] EWCOP 80.
[19] Ibid, [38].
[20] Ibid, 139.
[21] Banner, 'Unreasonable Reasons', 1038–1044.

decision with the agent, this will not always elicit all the necessary information: people often find it difficult to identify all the factors or reasons that influence their decisions, and even if they can, they may not always be entirely honest about the basis of their choices. This is particularly the case with people suffering from a mental disorder, since they may lack insight into their illness and thus may not appreciate or accept how their illness is affecting their decision-making processes. Where a person does not believe they are suffering from an eating disorder, for example, it will be impossible for them to identify and articulate the role that their disorder is playing in their decision to refuse food, and even if they do have insight into their illness, a desire for others to accede to their wishes may lead them to justify their decisions in certain ways that they think may appear more rational or acceptable to others.[22] For a person suffering from depression, meanwhile, their illness may affect their whole sense of agency in relation to the decision and its consequences. As Jesse Wall observes, 'individuals with major depression may employ a reflective attitude that is informed by a sense of worthlessness or excessive pessimism',[23] as depression tends to impair their 'concern for self and appreciation of future possibilities'.[24] Matthew Ratcliffe describes the depressive person as undergoing 'existential change'[25] in which 'she gradually loses the sense that the world could offer happiness; she ceases to experience its possibility'.[26] The effect is that the person loses their sense of agency, and in losing any conviction that they may be able to alter their circumstances, they lose the will to do so. Mary Donnelly explains how depression might affect a person's decision-making in the treatment context:

> In decisions about treatment for the depressive condition, if there is no possibility of improvement/recovery, then treatment is either a hopeless, or where the person experiences existential guilt, a wrongful waste.

[22] This will be discussed in more detail later at the text to fn327, drawing on the account of T. Hope *et al.*, 'Agency, Ambivalence and Authenticity: The Many Ways in Which Anorexia Nervosa Can Affect Autonomy' (2013) 9(1) *International Journal of Law in Context* 20–36.

[23] J. Wall, 'Being Yourself: Authentic Decision-making and Depression' in C. Foster and J. Herring (eds), Depression: Law and Ethics (Oxford: Oxford University Press, 2017), 134–144.

[24] Ibid, 134.

[25] M. Ratcliffe, *Experiences of Depression: A Study in Phenomenology* (Oxford: Oxford University Press, 2015), 14.

[26] Ibid, 66.

> A similar issue arises with treatment for other illnesses or conditions. Although such conditions may have other biological bases, the interlinkage between bodily feelings and existential feelings, means that the experience of a loss of possibility of recovery may well extend to these. Thus, in both respects, a person may have a perfectly accurate cognitive understanding of the proposed treatment, its side-effects, risks and benefits, but may be unable to conceive that the treatment would succeed. It is not simply that s/he does not believe that the treatment will be effective in his or her case; rather, the scope of his or her 'possibility space' is so reduced that such a possibility does not even arise.[27]

Donnelly draws further on evidence from Owen *et al.*, which suggests that depression has an effect on what they termed the person's 'temporal agility'.[28] Part of that includes the person's ability to see their future as open and to imagine the impact of their choices on that future, or to conceive of different possible futures.[29] For people with severe depression,

> the future was not experienced as open or as able to be shaped by their actions. Alternatively, some seemed to be able to see a future but not a future that made a difference or one which was normatively differentiated. For people in this situation, decisions lack significance; they make no difference and offer no possibility for the future.[30]

Within this context, clearly the capacity assessor cannot rely exclusively on the agent's own view of the effect of their illness or impairment on their decision-making processes. So when assessing if they are able to use and weigh the relevant information when forming a decision, the assessor is in reality making an educated guess. Unable to rely solely on the evidence provided by the agent themselves, the assessor must instead look at the content of the decision that they wish to make, to try and discern what impact, if any, the 'relevant' information has on the decision-making process. This, as Section 2.2 will make clear, is impossible without some engagement with what those values and beliefs underpinning the decision may be.

[27] M. Donnelly, 'Depression and Consent to Treatment: The Limits of a Capacity-Based Approach' in C. Foster and J. Herring (eds), *Depression: Law and Ethics* (Oxford: Oxford University Press, 2017), 200–210.

[28] G. Owen *et al.*, 'Temporal Inabilities and Decision-making Capacity in Depression' (2015) 14 *Phenomenology and the Cognitive Sciences* 163, 165.

[29] Ibid, 170.

[30] Donnelly, 'Depression and Consent to Treatment', 200–210.

2.2 The Role of the Agent's Values in Assessments of Their Capacity

To understand how the decision-maker's values are an inextricable part of capacity assessments, it is helpful to divide the inquiry into whether a person can 'use or weigh the relevant information' into two consecutive stages: first, has the person *in fact* used the information when making their decision; and second, if it appears they have not, is this owing to an inability to do so (due to an impairment in the functioning of the mind or brain), or rather a decision not to in light of their beliefs. These two stages will be considered in turn.

2.2.1 Did the Agent 'Use or Weigh' the Information When Making Their Decision?

For an agent to be deemed *unable* to use or weigh the relevant information, clearly they must be neither using nor weighing it when formulating their putative decision. After all, if the agent attaches weight to certain pieces of relevant information, the assessor cannot contend that they are unable to do so. The assessor must therefore start by examining the content of the decision, to see whether the decision-maker has used the information in their deliberations or attached any weight to the information. Yet ascertaining whether or not the agent has done so is impossible without the assessor having a sense of the values or beliefs which are being applied to that information, since the parameters of the range of decisions which the agent could reasonably make, if using the information, is set by the agent's own values. The assessor thus needs to know something of the values or beliefs that underpin a decision in order to tell whether that decision suggests the use of information or not.

Banner uses the following example, which is helpful to illustrate this point:

> [S]ay I were to tell a person standing at a set of traffic lights that a lorry was hurtling along the road ignoring red lights, and I have every reason to believe he understands my utterances. He then proceeds to step directly into the lorry's oncoming path. Without being able to delve into his reasoning, I would judge that this person had failed to use or weigh the information I had given him, because he did not respond to that information in the way that he ought to (taken with the assumption that he had an interest in preserving his own life).[31]

[31] Banner, 'Unreasonable Reasons', 1038–1044.

This assumption (that the person had an interest in preserving his life) is, however, crucial. *Assuming* the person wishes to live, then he ought not to have stepped on the road; doing so indicates that he had not used the relevant information when forming his decision. If, however, we knew that the person was suicidal and wished to end his life, we would form a very different conclusion. In this case, he would have used the information that the lorry was coming to further his own end of killing himself. So whether or not the person failed to use or weigh the information in this example thus inevitably hinges on what their priorities or motivations might be: the outcome of the decision-making process alone cannot determine this.

A particular area of difficulty which has arisen in the case law is the refusal of blood transfusions. Such refusals aptly illustrate the point. Two pieces of information appear to be particularly germane to this decision – first, that the procedure involves the transfer of blood or blood products into one's circulation, and second, that the consequences of refusing the transfusion will (in some cases, at least) likely be death from a shortage of blood. Whether these factors have been 'used' or 'weighed' by a person who wishes to refuse a transfusion will depend entirely on their beliefs. For a Jehovah's Witness who believes that accepting blood products will result in eternal damnation, the information may well have been most carefully weighed, since their decision to refuse is entirely coherent with that belief. If, by contrast, the patient has no principled objections to the use of blood products and demonstrates a strong desire to live, this would imply a failure to understand or to use the information as part of the process of making that decision. The assessor must therefore have some sense of the end that the person is seeking, in order to know if they have used the information in pursuit of that end.

This is not only conceptually true, but is evidenced in the way that the MCA is being applied in practice. In order to understand how the provisions were being received and applied by doctors on the ground, interviews were conducted with consultants from a range of specialisms. These showed that at least some doctors understood the 'use or weigh' provisions in this way, with one suggesting that the criterion was about 'how much they are factoring in the relevant information about that decision against their background, beliefs and values and wishes' (Tatiana, p. 1). In the case law too, there have been many examples of capacity assessors appealing to the decision-maker's values in order to determine their capacity to use or weigh the information. In *Re MB*,[32] for

[32] [1997] EWCA Civ 3093.

example (which was decided before the MCA came into force but using a very similar test for capacity),[33] despite repeatedly consenting to a caesarean section (and even requesting it on two occasions), at the point of having the anaesthetic, the patient withdrew her consent as a result of a needle phobia. In finding her to lack capacity, her doctor made it clear that while she undoubtedly understood and accepted the need for the caesarean section, 'at the moment of panic . . . her fear dominated all'.[34] He explained that the nature of phobias was such that, typically, on encountering the object of the phobia, it 'triggers a panic and the patient's sole thought is to distance themselves from the object which threatens them'.[35] As a result, despite her clear wish to undergo the procedure (and thereby to ensure the safety of her baby), 'at that moment the needle or mask dominated her thinking and made her quite unable to consider anything else'.[36] So although she was thought able to reason in accordance with her priorities when away from the needle, when faced with the object of her phobia, the effect distorted her reasoning so far that she could no longer weigh the information in such a way as to make the decision that achieved her main goal – the healthy birth of her child. Accordingly, Lady Justice Butler-Sloss concluded that MB was unable to use and weigh the information, and so lacked capacity.[37]

Similar concerns underpinned the decision in *Guys and St Thomas' NHS Foundation Trust v. X*[38] to authorise a caesarean section for a woman with a history of mental health problems, who was deemed unable to 'balance the pros and cons' of treatment,[39] evidenced by the fact that X's 'wishes are that her unborn baby's health and wellbeing is the most important consideration, yet she still refuses the options as to

[33] This test derived from Mr Justice Thorpe's judgment in *Re C (Adult: Refusal of Treatment)* [1994] 1WLR 290 (Fam), in which he drew on the Law Commission's suggestions for reforming the law in this area, creating a common law test for capacity, which formed the basis of the statutory test under the MCA.

[34] Ibid, [11].

[35] Ibid, [10].

[36] Ibid, [12].

[37] A similar conclusion was reached in *Re L* [5 December 1996] (*unreported*), a case which also involved an urgent application in respect of a patient with a needle phobia who required an emergency caesarean. In this case, Kirkwood J. held 'that her extreme needle phobia amounted to an involuntary compulsion that disabled "L" from weighing treatment information in the balance to make a choice. Indeed it was an affliction of a psychological nature that compelled "L" against medical advice with such force that her own life would be in serious peril'.

[38] [2019] EWCOP 35.

[39] Ibid [27].

medical intervention'.[40] The case of *Tameside and Glossip Acute Services Trust v. CH*[41] also concerned whether to authorise in advance an emergency caesarean section for a heavily pregnant woman with schizophrenia. Although the woman had agreed to be induced, the doctors were concerned that her 'psychotic and delusional' beliefs that 'the staff are a threat to her child'[42] might lead her to change her mind in the future.[43] The doctors were clear that the woman wanted her baby to be born alive, and that it was in her interests for that to happen, even if that required restraining her in order to perform a caesarean section against her wishes.[44] Accordingly, Mr Justice Ward authorised the caesarean section, accepting the evidence of the doctors that the patient was unable to understand or accept the advice she had been given,[45] perceiving 'it as malicious and harmful to her child'[46] (it was not specified whether 'acceptance' of information fell within the person's understanding or their 'use' of it[47]). Given the doctor was left with 'no doubt in his mind that the [woman] wanted the baby',[48] any refusal to have an emergency caesarean section must be attributable to her delusional paranoid beliefs about the medical professionals, thereby signifying that she lacked capacity to make such a decision.[49]

40 Ibid [20].
41 [1996] 1 FLR 762 (QBD).
42 Ibid, 766.
43 Ibid, 764.
44 Ibid, 767. Given her already paranoid beliefs about the intentions of the staff involved in her care, it was felt that the death of her child, which she would perceive as being the fault of the medical professionals, could erode trust further, severely harming her prospects of recovery in the future.
45 Ibid, 771.
46 Ibid, 766.
47 In fact, in a review of Court of Protection case law, Alex Ruck Keene *et al.* found that in 42 per cent of cases, the rationales offered by judges for the person being found to lack capacity was not explicitly linked to any MCA criterion, making this far from unusual: see A. Ruck Keene *et al.*, Taking Capacity Seriously? Ten Years of Mental Capacity Disputes before England's Court of Protection' (2019) 62 *International Journal of Law and Psychiatry* 56–76.
48 Ibid, 765.
49 Similar decisions were reached in *United Lincolnshire Hospitals NHS Trust v. CD* [2019] EWCOP 24; *Guys and St Thomas' NHS Foundation Trust (GSTT), South London and Maudsley NHS Foundation Trust (SLAM) v. R* [2020] EWCOP 4, where the courts also authorised caesarean sections in the event the person lacked capacity and they became necessary in the future.

By contrast, the refusal of a woman in *St George's Healthcare NHS Trust v. S*[50] to be treated for pre-eclampsia was found (after the event) to have been made with capacity. Despite being told that both her own life and that of her baby were at risk, she refused treatment for the condition, saying that she believed that nature should take its course. When asked to explain her reasons for refusing treatment, S did so with extreme clarity and articulacy, writing:

> (i) I am a qualified veterinary nurse, and am therefore quite able to comprehend the medical terminology used, and feel happy to ask for clarification if an unfamiliar term is used. (ii) I fully understand that pre-eclampsia is a potentially life-threatening condition, i.e. that the raised blood pressure may lead to haemorrhage, shock and, if untreated, death; or alternatively death due to total organ failure resulting from inability to compensate. (iii) I have always held very strong views with regard to medical and surgical treatments for myself, and particularly wish to allow nature to 'take its course,' without intervention. I fully understand that, in certain circumstances this may endanger my life. I see death as a natural and inevitable end point to certain conditions, and that natural events should not be interfered with. It is not a belief attached to the fact of my being pregnant, but would apply equally to any condition arising.[51]

Taken at face value, this suggests a well-thought-out decision which reflects long-standing and deeply held beliefs about not interfering with nature – beliefs which, while unusual, are no more or less rational than letting God determine one's fate. This is supported by the fact that S chose not to attend any antenatal appointments until she was thirty-six weeks pregnant, consistent with her stated desire to minimise medical involvement. The judge in this case found S to have had capacity (albeit the case was only heard after the healthy birth of the child): as her decision was consistent with her stated beliefs, there was nothing to indicate she had been incapable of using or weighing the information when formulating her decision. The medical team then, in treating her without her consent, had committed a battery for which she could seek damages.

There is good reason to question this specific decision, given the treating clinicians' view that she was suffering from an acute depressive episode. This will be explored in more detail later. However, what all these cases have in common is that what determined whether the women

[50] [1998] 3 All ER 673.
[51] Ibid, 681 [E-G].

were able to use and weigh the relevant information was their stated values and beliefs. In the first set of cases, the women clearly deeply wished for their children to be born healthy, so their decision implied that they had not used the information given to them in making their decision. The decisions they reached were not based on a true appreciation that refusal would result in the death of their babies, but on a phobia or delusional belief. In the latter case, by contrast, the woman clearly expressed that nature should take its course even if that resulted in her death, or that of her child, so the decision was entirely consistent with having using and weighed-up information about the consequences of the decision. In practice, then, capacity assessors must look to the individual's values or beliefs in order to determine whether their decision is within a reasonable range of options had they applied *those* values to the relevant information.

2.2.2 Is the Agent's Failure to Attribute Weight Due to an Inability to Do So?

Having decided that the person did *not* use certain pieces of information or attach any weight to them, the assessor must then determine whether this is a deliberate choice, made in the light of a value or belief system, or indicative of an inability to act on that information, caused by an impairment in the functioning of the mind or brain. Indeed in a study examining what led liaison psychiatrists to find capacity assessments especially difficult, Nuala Kane and others found this to be one of the key sources of challenge for psychiatrists, noting that

> [s]everal hard cases hinged on the nature of the beliefs driving the patients treatment refusal, where there was difficulty distinguishing whether these were due to a delusion or whether they were religious, cultural, or political beliefs. This was because (a) the relevant delusion was hidden or subtle, or (b) it was hard to tell if beliefs (unusual or unfamiliar to the psychiatrist) were congruent with the person's own personal or cultural belief systems.[52]

Clearly, the values underpinning any given decision are crucial to assessing this. For example, given that most people prioritise continued life over almost all other considerations, any failure to use information in a

[52] N. Kane, A. Ruck Keene, G. Owen, and K. Scott, 'Difficult Capacity Cases – the Experience of Liaison Psychiatrists. An Interview Study across Three Jurisdictions' (2022) 13 *Front Psychiatry* 946234. doi: 10.3389/fpsyt.2022.946234, 3.

way which furthers that aim might be considered indicative of impairment in their decision-making processes. But this would not be the case for a Jehovah's Witness refusing a blood transfusion, whose belief system requires them to prioritise the refusal of blood products over continued life. *Nottingham Healthcare NHS Trust v. RC*[53] provides an apt illustration of this. This case concerned whether a Jehovah's Witness, diagnosed with antisocial and emotionally unstable personality disorder, had capacity to refuse a blood transfusion. Despite the clinical evidence that 'his religious beliefs effectively create, in his mind (and others) an absolute prohibition on blood products and so there is relatively little "weighing" when it comes to this decision',[54] Mr Justice Mostyn found him to have capacity. He noted that the 'use or weigh' aspect of the test ought to be applied 'cautiously' in this context, explaining:

> In his essay John Stuart Mill speaks of the prohibition in Islam on the eating of pork. He describes how Muslims regard the practice with "unaffected disgust"; it is "an instinctive antipathy". There can be no circumstances where a Muslim could "weigh" the merit of eating pork. It is simply beyond the pale. So too, it would appear, when it comes to Jehovah's Witnesses and blood transfusions. But it would be an extreme example of the application of the law of unintended consequences were an iron tenet of an accepted religion to give rise to questions of capacity under the MCA. I therefore place little emphasis on the fact that a tenet of RC's religious faith prevents him from weighing the advantages of a blood transfusion should his medical circumstances indicate that one is necessary.[55]

That his belief system led him to not engage in any real weighing exercise, since there was no possibility of him accepting a blood transfusion, was not therefore deemed by the judge to be evidence of an inability to perform that weighing exercise. By contrast, in many of the cases that will be looked at later in this chapter, a person's belief was held to effectively prevent them from engaging in a weighing exercise. The refusal of *Mrs T*[56] to accept a blood transfusion, for example, in the belief that her blood was 'evil' was deemed evidence of an inability to weigh up the relevant information in the process of making a decision; as was the refusal of a leg amputation by Mr B in *Wye Valley*, based on his

[53] [2014] EWCOP 1317.
[54] Ibid, [33].
[55] Ibid, [34]–[35].
[56] [2004] EWHC 1279 (Fam).

belief that this was God's will;[57] or C's refusal of a hysterectomy in *Sherwood Forest Hospitals NHS Foundation Trust v. C*[58] on the basis that 'only God could cure [her] cancer'.[59]

Perhaps most pertinently for the current discussion, in *A Local Authority v. E*,[60] a woman with chronic anorexia was found to be unable to use or weigh the information because of her compulsion to not allow calories into her body. E was a thirty-two-year-old woman who had been controlling her eating since the age of eleven. She had spent over half her time between the ages of twenty-six and thirty in placements at specialist eating disorder units, and by the time the case came to court, she had not eaten any solid food for a year. Her problems with eating were compounded by her alcohol dependency and borderline personality disorder. Although Mr Justice Peter Jackson was clear that E could 'understand and retain the information relevant to the treatment decision and communicate her decision',[61] he found that

> for E, the compulsion to prevent calories entering her system has become the card that trumps all others. The need not to gain weight overpowers all other thoughts.[62]

Accordingly, he found her to be unable to use and weigh the information: her 'obsessive fear of weight gain'[63] meant that even if the result was that she would die, she was still unable to countenance any outcome which would involve her taking in calories. A very similar conclusion was reached in *NHS Foundation Trust v. X*, involving another woman with chronic anorexia.[64] In this sense, anorexia ought to be distinguished from a person merely on a diet who *is* able to use the information to further

[57] *Wye Valley* [2015] EWCOP 60.
[58] [2020] EWCOP 10.
[59] Ibid, [15].
[60] *E* [2012] EWHC 1639.
[61] Ibid, [48].
[62] Ibid, [49].
[63] *E* [2012] EWHC 1639, [49].
[64] [2014] EWCOP 35. In this case, Cobb J. approved the finding of her treating clinician that 'due to ongoing severe body dysmorphia, false beliefs about her weight, shape and nutritional state and absolute fear of weight gain from her anorexia, she was and is unable to apply the information to herself or believe in the need for it. In addition the absolute fear of weight gain and anxiety induced around the same overrides any loose connection she might have to the information pertaining to herself. The reality and importance of the associated risks including death in her malnourished state are therefore not truly appraised which means she is unable to weigh up the information provided in the decision-making process' ([27]–[29]).

their priority, namely losing weight. Indeed, in *Northamptonshire Healthcare NHS Foundation Trust v. AB*,[65] Mrs Justice Roberts expressly thought to distinguish anorexia from other situations where a person simply applies their subjective values to the decision-making process, explaining:

> Dr B's evidence speaks to the existence of 'an overvalued idea' or fixation which arises as a direct result of AB's illness and which overwhelms her thought processes so as to *prevent*, or disable, her from conducting the sort of weighing and balancing exercise required by s. 3(1)(c). This seems to me to go beyond the application of her individual subjective 'values or outlook' which she is perfectly entitled to bring to that decision making process.[66]

So while for a Jehovah's Witness, the 'effective block' that their beliefs create in their mind preventing them from accepting blood products was not evidence of an *inability* to attach weight to different outcomes, the compulsion among those with anorexia nervosa to not accept calories *was* seen as such. Assessors must therefore draw on the agent's values as part of the process of determining whether they are *unable* to use and weigh the information.

Crucially, under section 2(1) of the MCA, this inability must be caused by an impairment in the functioning of the mind or brain as opposed to other influences.[67] Therefore, it is not merely the way that a belief operates on a person's mind that is important to whether they are deemed to have capacity, but the nature or origins of that belief. This is perhaps best illustrated by *Kings College Hospital NHS Foundation Trust v. C & V*.[68] In this case, a woman had refused dialysis following a suicide attempt, on the grounds, amongst others, that her life had 'lost its sparkle' and she did not, therefore, wish to prolong it or to get old. The key question for the court in this case was whether she was *unable* to weigh up the information in order to make a decision because of a personality disorder, or whether she merely had eccentric and idiosyncratic views which led her to use and weigh information in an unconventional manner. After hearing evidence from the woman's daughters, who felt the decision to be in keeping with the values that their mother had

65 [2020] EWCOP 40.

66 Ibid, [26].

67 For a detailed discussion of how the causative nexus operates, see *PC & NC v. City of York Council* [2013] EWCA 478 (Civ).

68 *C & V* [2015] EWCOP 80.

exhibited throughout her life, the judge produced the following, illuminating description of C:

> C is a person to whom the epithet 'conventional' will never be applied … C has led a life characterised by impulsive and self-centred decision-making without guilt or regret. C has had four marriages and a number of affairs and has, it is said, spent the money of her husbands and lovers recklessly before moving on when things got difficult or the money ran out. She has, by their account, been an entirely reluctant and at times completely indifferent mother to her three caring daughters. Her consumption of alcohol has been excessive and, at times, out of control. C is, as all who know her and C herself appears to agree, a person who seeks to live life entirely and unapologetically on her own terms; that life revolving largely around her looks, men, material possessions and 'living the high life'. In particular, it is clear that during her life C has placed a significant premium on youth and beauty and on living a life that, in C's words, 'sparkles'.[69]

Against this background, the psychiatrists explained that while her symptoms were in keeping with a personality disorder, 'the question of whether a particular person has a histrionic or narcissistic personality disorder, as opposed to simply a very strong or difficult personality can be an area of some controversy'.[70] After considering the information available to him, Mr Justice Macdonald found C to have capacity to make the decision to refuse treatment, the evidence being 'equivocal' as to whether

> what was being seen might be the operation of a personality disorder or simply the thought processes of a strong willed, stubborn individual with unpalatable and highly egocentric views.[71]

Evidence about the values and priorities that underpinned her decision were thus essential to determining her capacity to make it. Her failure to attribute weight to certain factors was consistent with the beliefs and characteristics she had displayed throughout her life, leading the judge to conclude she was capacitous, at least in light of the presumption of capacity in the MCA.

The opposite conclusion was reached in *Avon and Wiltshire Mental Health Partnership v. WA & Anor*,[72] where the person's inability to weigh

[69] Ibid, [8].
[70] Ibid, [44].
[71] Ibid, [94].
[72] [2020] EWCOP 37.

information was deemed to be attributable to a mental illness rather than to his values. WA was a refugee from Palestine, who, following abuse at the hands of Hamas, had escaped and gained asylum in Italy. There he had been put into care, where he was physically and sexually abused by his foster carer, sustaining stab wounds and the amputation of his index finger. On the discovery of this, he was moved to the UK, where he was cared for by a family with whom he formed a strong bond. Perhaps unsurprisingly given all he had suffered, WA was diagnosed with PTSD and depression. While by the time of this hearing, it was common ground that there was no evidence of those diagnoses, it was nonetheless clear that he continued 'to suffer significant psychological distress from the awful traumas that he [had] endured'.[73]

On leaving Palestine, WA's grandmother (to whom he was close) informed him that his date of birth was 29 December 1994. This was initially accepted, however doubts were later raised, and two further age assessments were commissioned. These found WA to be five years older than he believed himself to be, leading the Home Office to determine his date of birth as 19 April 1989.[74] WA deeply objected to this. As Mr Justice Hayden explained:

> For WA the removal of his date of birth is perceived as a fundamental violation of his own rights and an assault on his identity. As a prisoner in Palestine and a victim of physical and sexual abuse in Italy, WA experienced the complete negation of his autonomy at a stage in his childhood and adolescence where he might otherwise have started to explore it. Having listened to him, his parents, the psychiatrists and psychologists, during the course of this hearing, it is clear that WA experienced the change of his date of birth as effectively abusive. It triggered, I have been told, the vivid memory of his powerlessness in the instances of childhood trauma that I have summarised above.[75]

After receiving advice that judicial proceedings were unlikely to result in any change to his official date of birth, WA started to refuse food and drink. WA's BMI was by now just 14.7, and although he was accepting some minimal nutrition through an NG tube, this was not enough to help him recover, and those around him feared that he might refuse nutrition altogether.

73 Ibid, [4].
74 Ibid, [5].
75 Ibid, [6].

When asked, WA was explicit that he wished to die, because the Home Office had 'taken away his identity'.[76] After the death of his parents, his date of birth was 'all he had of himself', and 'he could not ignore it'.[77] While he admitted to feeling low and tired, he explained that this was not depression, but lowness as a result of his situation and the actions of the Home Office. While there was much about his life that he loved, he did not feel he could continue to live without his identity and wished to have the right to die.

The question for Mr Justice Hayden was whether he suffered from an impairment which *prevented* him from weighing up information about whether to accept artificial nutrition and hydration or whether his subjective values, informed by his traumatic history, simply led him to place far greater weight on the importance of his date of birth than most others might do. There was substantial disagreement between the experts on this question. The view of the treating team was that:

> WA is so fixated with this perceived injustice that it overwhelms his ability to weigh CANH as a global decision. Though he can comprehend individual facets of the decision very clearly, the ultimate balancing of the key facts is compromised by the weight WA gives to his assigned date of birth, which he perceives to be the only way that his identity is validated.[78]

Dr C, a consultant psychiatrist, found his belief in his age to be 'unshakeable' and 'rigid' but not 'delusional as it is related to his personal cultural belief'.[79] Notwithstanding this, she concluded (albeit 'on a knife edge'[80]) that 'the rigidity of thinking and preoccupation in relation to his date of birth occluded WA's capacity to weigh and use the overall information relevant to a decision to accept nutrition and hydration',[81] and that this constituted an impairment of the mind as he displaced thoughts of his trauma by focusing entirely on his date of birth.[82]

Dr Wild, a specialist in trauma-related disorders, disagreed. In her view, WA was capable of using or weighing the relevant information; he simply gave

76 Ibid, [56].
77 Ibid, [56].
78 Ibid, [82].
79 Ibid, [62].
80 Ibid, [63].
81 Ibid.
82 Ibid, [62].

> the return to full health little or no weight when it is weighed against other information. That is, the suffering he would endure in living with the Home Office assigned date of birth, which extends his loss of dignity and identity.[83]

She further explained that while the reassigned age did remind WA of past trauma,

> in my opinion this does not constitute an impairment of mind (it is a reminder of trauma; he does not disassociate in response to reminders of his past trauma) and has no bearing on his ability to weigh relevant information to arrive at his decision.[84]

Dr Cahill, a consultant psychiatrist, described this case as 'up there' amongst the hardest cases he had encountered in ten years. Despite initially thinking he had capacity, Dr Cahill concluded that WA 'has become fixated with the assigned date of birth to a degree which overwhelms him and to a point where it dominates his thinking and becomes a conductor for past trauma' and that this prevented him from being able to use or weigh the relevant information. Mr Justice Hayden agreed with this analysis; determining that this was not an instance of someone merely choosing to place no weight on information because of strongly held values, but an example of an impairment which prevented them from attributing weight to any outcome that involved accepting the assigned date of birth. Clearly, however, thoughtful engagement with the beliefs and values motivating WA's decision was essential to reaching this conclusion.

A similar conclusion was reached in *Leicester City Council v. MPZ*,[85] which concerned whether Mary, a thirty-one-year-old woman with a learning disability, emotionally unstable personality disorder (EUPD), and dependent personality disorder (DPD), had the capacity to make decisions in respect of her residence, care, contact, and sexual relations. Mary had suffered abuse at an early age and frequently became involved in abusive and coercive relationships. Because of her personality disorders, she was taken to be unable to assess the validity of information provided by her abusers 'as a result of her emotional dependence on them', while at the same time minimising or dismissing information provided by third parties, especially professionals involved in her care.[86]

[83] Ibid, [69].
[84] Ibid, [71].
[85] [2019] EWCOP 64.
[86] Ibid, [18].

According to the consultant psychiatrist, Dr Lawson, it was not that she did not understand the information given to her, but that she did not believe that information, even when it was objectively true. Conversely, she would sometimes believe information provided by others (including those with whom she was in an abusive relationship) even when it was objectively untrue.

Her Honour Judge George concluded that the distinction drawn by Dr Lawson between 'understanding' and 'believing' was a difference in terminology rather than substance as the 'case law makes it clear that a failure to believe is a failure to understand and use or weigh in the context of the specific decision-making exercise engaged'.[87] She rejected the argument of the Official Solicitor, that while the personality disorder did always affect Mary, whether or not her capacity was vitiated depended on the circumstances, specifically whether she was subject to the coercive control of someone,[88] concluding that Mary's personality disorder so distorts her 'perception of the world, that she lacks MCA capacity in all domains'.[89] In other words (in reasoning that is in some ways analogous to that in the anorexia nervosa cases), although the 'perception of the world' that she applied to the information (and which caused her to discount the truth of certain information) was a long-standing feature of her personality, this was itself so heavily distorted by her disorder that she was incapable of believing anything different.

There is certainly logic to thinking that a failure to believe relevant information undermines a person's capacity to use or weigh it. After all, if the person does not believe a piece of information to be true, they are unlikely to use it or give it any weight in the decision-making process. However, whether this is indicative of incapacity hinges on whether the person is actually *incapable* of believing the information because of an impairment, or rather chooses not to believe it – as people frequently do – because they hold competing beliefs or are simply mistaken. A person might understand the weight of scientific evidence in support of having a Covid-19 vaccination, for example, while not truly believing that information, because they consider it to be the product of collusion by pharmaceutical companies to line their pockets; or simply because they think it is too early for that information to be reliable. Or someone may understand the prognosis given to them by their doctor, yet believe

[87] [2019] EWCOP 64, [34].
[88] Ibid, [35].
[89] Ibid, [36].

that they remain fit and healthy and so are likely to outlive it. As the counsel for Mary put it, the fact that the person in these kinds of cases is mistaken 'does not make his decision incapacitous'.[90]

People in abusive relationships whose capacity is not in doubt may also be prone to minimise or dismiss information by third parties that conflicts with that of their abuser. What distinguished Mary, and thus justified the finding that she was unable to use or weigh information, was that her failure to believe certain information could (in the view of the judge) be attributed to her personality disorder, as opposed to being merely a facet of her personality, developed over years of toxic relationships. Clearly, this once again required detailed engagement with Mary's belief systems. A decision could not be made about her ability to use and weigh the information purely on the basis of the outcome of the decision, since that would not be sufficient to distinguish the impact of her disorder from the effect of her abusive relationship.

Yet this also aptly demonstrates the potential circularity of such a determination. According to the DSM-5, a person may be diagnosed as having DPD if they have 'an excessive and pervasive need to be taken care of, submissive, clinging, needy behaviour due to fear of abandonment'. This may be expressed by:

(1) Difficulty making routine decisions without input, reassurance, and advice from others.
(2) Requires others to assume responsibilities which they should be attending to.
(3) Fear of disagreeing with others and risking disapproval.
(4) Difficulty starting projects without support from others.
(5) Excessive need to obtain nurturance and support from others, even allowing others to impose themselves rather than risk rejection or disapproval.
(6) Feels vulnerable and helpless when alone.
(7) Desperately seeks another relationship when one ends.
(8) Unrealistic preoccupation with being left alone and unable to care for themselves. (American Psychiatric Association, 2013)[91]

[90] Ibid, [24].

[91] Dependent Personality Disorder 301.6 (F60.7), in American Psychiatric Association, *Diagnostic and Statistical Manual of Mental Disorders: DSM-5*, 5th edn. (Washington, DC: American Psychiatric Publishing, 2013).

The result is that Mary's personality and behaviour, in particular her fear of abandonment and dependence on men, was both the evidence on which she was diagnosed as having a personality disorder (and thus an impairment within the terms of the MCA) and the cause of her inability to assess the validity of information which left her to be deemed unable to use or weigh it[92] and, therefore, to lack capacity.

These cases demonstrate the extent to which assessors must take account of the substance or content of the decision-maker's values when determining whether they suffer from an impairment which precludes them from using or weighing information. While they represent just a handful of examples from the case law, Kane *et al.*'s content analysis of Court of Protection case law also lends support for this conclusion. This found that rationales commonly cited by judges for finding a person to lack capacity included (a) the agent's inability to 'value or care' and (b) the agent being unable to provide a consistent or stable preference,[93] both of which necessarily demand engagement with the agent's values. The agent's perceived inability to value or care was often a basis for finding them unable to use or weigh information.[94] This was also acknowledged by the liaison psychiatrists interviewed as part of Kane *et al.*'s study on complex capacity assessments in practice, who noted that in resolving difficult questions over whether a decision was the person's 'own' or driven by mental illness, attention was paid both to psychopathology and 'to the patients' personal history and culture (often through involving others from the same culture)'.[95] One particularly challenging context was that of 'seemingly erratic or unusual decision-making in patients with unusual personalities',[96] where it could be important to consult 'families about whether a decision was in keeping with a patient's character'.[97] The authors gave an example of a case in which a patient suffering from chronic pain and loss of function due to a leg injury requested an amputation, when his surgeon preferred a more conservative treatment. Although an unusual choice, the psychiatrist ultimately found him to have capacity, as the patient's weighing 'was in keeping

[92] *Leicester City Council v. MPZ* [2019] EWCOP 64, [28].
[93] Kane *et al.*, 'Applying Decision-Making Capacity Criteria in Practice', e0246521.
[94] Ibid. It should be noted, however, that both rationales were sometimes put forward without linking them to specific capacity criterion.
[95] Kane *et al.*, 'Difficult Capacity Cases,946234. doi: 10.3389/fpsyt.2022.946234, 3.
[96] Ibid, 4.
[97] Ibid, 5.

with his personality, values, and world view'.[98] Clearly then, some consideration of the substance of the patient's values and beliefs will often be crucial to assessing capacity under the MCA.

2.3 An Unavoidable Role for Values in Assessments of Capacity

While the analysis has hitherto focused on the MCA, and specifically its 'use or weigh' criterion, this is not merely a problem with the way in which the MCA has been drafted. Rather, it is a problem that afflicts all process-orientated accounts of decision-making capacity, since one simply cannot assess the robustness of a person's cognitive processes in practice, without some reference to their motivations and beliefs about the world and whether these are broadly consistent with the decision that the person has reached. Banner likens capacity assessments to an 'information-processing black box', a common metaphor in cognitive psychology:

> On this model, various factors serve as inputs to decision-making, including the information given, along with a person's known beliefs, values, desires, fears, and so on. These are weighed up in a process whereby various cognitive mechanisms operate upon the information received, and subsequently an output emerges in the form of a decision about what the person wishes to do.[99]

If a person's cognitive processes are intact, then they ought to be able to evaluate information about the potential consequences of deciding one way or the other in light of their motivating values, beliefs, and priorities, reaching a decision which reflects or furthers these in some way. Establishing whether this is the case requires the assessor to ascertain whether there is any rational connection between the 'input' factors and the 'output', that is, between the outcome of the putative decision and the values, beliefs, and priorities which inform or motivate it. In other words, they must seek to determine whether the decision 'follows in light of the person's beliefs and values (whatever they may be)'.[100]

But the relationship between a person's values and the decision reached is not *merely* the best practical means of establishing the state of their understanding and reasoning abilities. Rather it goes to the heart

[98] Ibid.

[99] Banner, 'Can Procedural and Substantive Elements of Decision-Making be Reconciled in Assessments of Mental Capacity?', 71–86.

[100] Ibid.

of whether a decision can really be said to be autonomous at all, with the ability to draw appropriate conclusions from one's motivating beliefs being an essential component of having the capacity to take autonomous decisions. We will consider what it means for a decision to be autonomous in more detail in Chapter 3 and, in particular, what role notions of authenticity and rationality play in the autonomous quality of decisions. Suffice to say for now, however, that most modern liberal conceptions of autonomy demand some authenticity component, that is, that the person's desire must reflect or be justified by reference to values, beliefs, or priorities that the person holds in some way. Indeed it is this which is often thought to make autonomy valuable: as Chapter 1 explained, autonomy is valuable because it is an essential component of well-being, enabling people to live according to their own conception of what is good or meaningful. If a decision is not motivated by or coherent with a person's conception of what is good or valuable in any way, then it is at least questionable whether there is the same value in respecting it. Accordingly, while different philosophers have stated the requirements for decision-making capacity slightly differently, there is much support for the idea that assessing it requires some evaluation of whether the putative decision is internally consistent with the values or beliefs that are believed to motivate it.

Charland, for example, draws a helpful distinction between the external and internal rationality of decisions. External rationality 'has to do with the outcome of actual decisions' and its apparent rationality.[101] Internal rationality, by contrast, 'has to do with the coherence of putative decisions within a set of values and beliefs'.[102] It is the latter which is the preserve of capacity assessments, which involve 'assessing the internal rationality of a putative decision against a background set of values and beliefs'.[103] As he explains:

> A putative decision is rational in the internal sense if: (a) it coheres with an individual's enduring aims and values; (b) it is justified in light of those values and their associated beliefs; and (c) the proposed justification is deemed appropriate by the third party responsible for assessing competence. Again, the reasons offered do not have to entail the proposed decision. It is sufficient that they be recognised as an appropriate justification for selecting that option by the assessors. The reasons do not even

[101] Charland, 'Mental Competence and Value', 135–145.

[102] Ibid.

[103] Ibid.

> have to be true, nor do the assessors have to believe they are true. All that is required is that the individual in question believes them to be true.[104]

In so arguing, Charland builds on the work of Benjamin Freedman, and also of Allen Buchanan and Dan Brock. Benjamin Freedman was one of the first philosophers to claim that while understanding and appreciation are necessary for competence, they are not sufficient.[105] He argued that to be competent, an individual not only must understand and appreciate the nature and consequences of the decision at hand but also must be able to provide 'recognisable reasons' for it. By 'recognisable reasons', he meant that reasons 'must contain acceptable premises and a conclusion related to those premises'.[106] The conclusion need not follow logically from the premises, but the premises must be able to provide a strong justification for the conclusion reached. Importantly, the reasons must also be relevant in light of the individual's *own value system*. Although Freedman did not set out in detail what exactly was meant by this, it seems there must be some internal coherence between the underlying premises on which a decision is based – the values or beliefs which motivate it – and the conclusion which the person reached. As Charland has explained, internal rationality on Freedman's view thus 'has to do with whether the putative decision an individual is entertaining coheres with his or her system of values in a manner that satisfies the recognisable reasons criterion'.[107]

Buchanan and Brock, by contrast, were more explicit about the role that values played in competence. They considered there to be three essential components of competence: understanding and communication; reasoning and deliberation; and a set of values or conception of what is good.[108] Understanding involves 'the capacities to receive, process, and make available for use the information relevant to particular decisions', as well as the 'ability to appreciate the nature and meaning of potential alternatives – what it would be like and "feel" like to be in possible future states and to undergo various experiences – and to integrate this appreciation into one's decision making'.[109] Reasoning

[104] Ibid, 142.
[105] B. Freedman, 'Competence, Marginal and Otherwise' (1981) 55 *International Journal of Law and Psychiatry A* 53–72.
[106] Ibid, 61.
[107] Charland, 'Mental Competence and Value', 135–145.
[108] A. Buchanan and D. Brock, *Deciding for Others: The Ethics of Surrogate Decision Making* (Cambridge: Cambridge University Press, 1989), 23–25.
[109] Ibid, 24.

and deliberation, meanwhile, 'require the capacity to draw inferences about the consequences of making a certain choice and to compare alternative outcomes based on how they further one's good or promote one's ends'. Both of these necessarily involve values. In order to decide which course of action you wish to pursue, you must have a set of values by which to evaluate the choices available and their expected outcomes. Otherwise, you would remain paralysed in the face of choice. Therefore, some 'set or values or conception of what is good'[110] is necessary, as Buchanan and Brock have suggested, 'in order to be able to evaluate particular outcomes as benefits or harms, goods or evils, and to assign different relative weight or importance to them'.[111] Given the essential role played by values in decision-making capacity, they explain the function of a capacity assessor thus:

> A crude but perhaps helpful way of characterising the proper aim of the evaluator of the competence of a seemingly harmful or bad patient choice is to think of him or her addressing the patient in this fashion: 'Help me try to understand and make sense of your choice. Help me to see whether your choice is reasonable, not in the sense that it is what I or most people would choose, but that it is reasonable for you in light of your underlying and enduring aims and values.' This is the proper focus of a *process* account of competence.

Of course, there may be reason to question whether a purely 'process-orientated' or 'procedural' account of decision-making capacity is adequate and desirable – something that will be considered in detail in Chapter 4. However, this does not undermine the key point, that any procedural account of capacity requires some consideration of the relationship, or rational connection between the decision and the motivating beliefs or values.

In his recent work examining whether autonomy entails rationality, for example, Jonathan Pugh distinguishes between 'theoretical rationality', which relates to 'the set of norms that govern how we come to form and sustain our beliefs' (i.e., the rationality of the beliefs themselves), and 'practical rationality', which concerns the relationship (or rational connection) between the object of a desire and the content of the belief that motivates it.[112] He gives the following example to illustrate the differences between these two types of rationality:

110 Buchanan and Brock, *Deciding for Others*, 25.
111 Ibid.
112 Pugh, *Autonomy, Rationality, and Contemporary Bioethics*, 21.

> Suppose that Alice holds the irrational belief that smoking will improve her health, and that she forms a desire to smoke on the basis of this belief . . . we may say that Alice is theoretically irrational here because she holds the belief that smoking will improve her health, despite the overwhelming evidence she has against the veracity of this claim. However, her desire to smoke *given that she has that belief* can plausibly be described as practically rational.[113]

Decisional autonomy could thus be undermined *either* by theoretically irrational beliefs about information that is material to one's decisions or by the person holding a desire which cannot be justified by the content of the belief motivating it.

It is not necessary for the purposes of this discussion to consider the bounds of theoretical rationality in depth here. The crucial point is that Pugh too sees the rational connection between the object of a desire (or decision) and the content of the motivating beliefs or values as an important facet of decision-making capacity: a person is not deciding autonomously if they are motivated by desires which are inexplicable on the basis of his or her beliefs. He contrasts the example of Alice with that of Rosie, who holds the belief that smoking will damage her health and yet forms a desire to smoke on the basis of this belief. In his view, she lacks practical rationality because her desire to want to smoke is not a rational response to the belief that smoking is bad for her health. In Pugh's view, it is this practical rationality which

> grounds the moral significance of all the other abilities that we typically accept are necessary to autonomous decision-making. Understanding information, retaining it, and 'weighing' it only matters for autonomy if we assume that agents have the ability to link that information (and how much weight it is given) to their own values.[114]

Accordingly, he has been (rightly) critical of accounts of decision-making capacity (which must include the MCA, amongst many other legislative provisions) which could find someone to have capacity despite their choice being 'unconnected to what they themselves believe they have a reason to do in light of their own values'.[115]

Process-orientated accounts of decision-making capacity therefore cannot exist in a value vacuum but demand some engagement with the substance or content of the values or beliefs that underpin and motivate a

[113] Ibid, 24.
[114] Ibid, 210.
[115] Ibid, 203.

decision. This means that, as Charland observes, 'there is no such thing as mental competence without value, and normative considerations associated with value cannot be eliminated from the assessment of decision-making capacity'.[116] Accordingly,

> the idea that competence can be entirely objective is misguided, and an attempt to downplay or ignore the role of value in competence is wrong-headed. So is the strategy of restricting competence and its standards to what is purely cognitive and mechanistic.[117]

2.4 Whose Values? Problems with Relying on a 'Value-Neutral' Test for Capacity

While some recourse to the decision-maker's values is thus unavoidable in assessments of process-orientated accounts of capacity, the difficulty with the current legislative approach lies in its opacity. The 'use or weigh' limb ought to be testing the internal or procedural rationality of the decision: can the person use or weigh the information in order to reach a decision which is broadly consistent with their values, beliefs, and priorities? But as this section will demonstrate, because the assessor is not required to engage explicitly with this question, they are instead given room to invoke other values when assessing the person's capacity to use or weigh information, thus enabling them to find the person to lack capacity where their decision is inconsistent with them. In other words, far from preventing unwarranted paternalism, the façade of value neutrality may in fact be creating space for paternalistic judgements to go unchecked.

Given the empowering ethos at the heart of the MCA and the clear indictment not to find people to lack capacity merely on the basis of unwise decisions,[118] judges are naturally cautious about seeming to be influenced by the rationality or acceptability of a given outcome, and often stress empathically that their assessments has not been based on the expected outcome of the decision.[119] In *Pennine Acute Hospitals NHS*

[116] Charland, 'Mental Competence and Value', 135–145.

[117] Ibid.

[118] Mental Capacity Act 2005, s1(4).

[119] See, for example, *PH v. A Local Authority and Others* [2011] EWHC 1704 (Fam) [16, xiii], per Justice Baker; *Heart of England NHS Foundation Trust v. JB* [2014] EWHC 342 (COP) [7] per Justice Peter Jackson; *Northamptonshire Healthcare NHS Foundation Trust v. AB* [2020] EWCOP 40 [22] per Justice Roberts.

Trust v. TM, for example, Mr Justice Hayden was clear that 'it is the ability to take the decision, not the outcome of the decision, which is the focus', even where the outcome 'is an untimely and unpleasant death'.[120] Nonetheless, there are examples where, whether driven by concerns about the nature of the person's beliefs or about the outcome of the decision, judges appear to be invoking values other than the person's own in determinations of their capacity.

One example of this is the *NHS Trust v. Mrs T*[121] which, though decided before the MCA came into force, adopted a very similar test for capacity,[122] namely whether the person could comprehend and retain the information material to a decision, and use that information and weigh it in the balance as part of the process of arriving at the decision.[123] In this case, a woman suffered from borderline personality disorder. She had, on a number of occasions, self-harmed through blood-letting, with the result that her haemoglobin level was life-threateningly low, and she required a blood transfusion. Despite understanding that the consequence of refusing it were that she would die, she was nonetheless resistant to a transfusion and, accordingly, wrote an advance directive setting out her intentions and giving the grounds for her decision:

> I believe my blood is evil, carrying evil around my body. Although the blood given in transfusions is perfectly healthy/clean, once given to me it mixes with my own and also becomes evil. Contaminated by my own. Therefore, the volume of evil blood in my body will have increased and likewise the danger of my committing acts of evil.[124]

She also felt that she was in a vicious cycle of cutting herself and then requiring a transfusion which was 'too difficult for [her] to continue enduring'.[125] The judge in this case found her to lack capacity on the basis that her belief, which he described as a 'misconception of reality' notwithstanding its metaphysical nature, evidenced a 'disorder of the mind',[126] which meant she was 'unable to use and weigh the relevant information'.[127]

[120] *Pennine Acute Hospitals NHS Trust v. TM* [2021] EWCOP 8, [29].
[121] [2004] EWHC 1279 (Fam).
[122] This test similarly derived from Mr Justice Thorpe's judgment in *Re C* (*Adult: Refusal of Treatment*) [1994] 1WLR 290 (Fam).
[123] Ibid, [53]–[61].
[124] Ibid, [9].
[125] Ibid, [8].
[126] Ibid, [61].
[127] Ibid, [62].

Yet arguably Mrs T *did* 'use' the relevant information to form her decision to refuse a blood transfusion. She understood that the nature of the treatment involved introducing blood into her body and, on precisely that basis, rejected the treatment, not wishing for more blood to enter her body and mix with her 'evil' blood. She also understood that she would die without the transfusion but, weighing this against the alternative, rejected the transfusion, both to avoid committing evil acts and to break the vicious cycle of cutting herself and then requiring a transfusion which she found 'too difficult for [her] to continue enduring'.[128] In finding her to be unable to use and weigh the information, the judge was thus assessing her ability to use or weigh information not relative to her own (undoubtedly eccentric) beliefs, but to some objective conception of what her beliefs might have been had they not been disordered.

Similarly in *Wye Valley*[129] (examined in more detail in Section 2.5), a man with schizoaffective disorder was found to be unable to use or weigh the information relevant to the decision to refuse a leg amputation, even though his choice was entirely consistent with his belief that the Virgin Mary opposed the amputation;[130] as was a woman in *Sherwood Forest Hospitals NHS Foundation Trust v. C*,[131] who refused a hysterectomy on the grounds that only God could cure her cancer. In *Rochdale Healthcare (NHS) Trust v. C*, meanwhile[132] (again decided according to the pre-MCA common law test for capacity), a woman refused a caesarean section on the grounds that she had had one before and would rather die than have another. Although the treating obstetrician considered her to have capacity and it was not possible to obtain specialist psychiatric evidence in the time available, Johnson J. found, on 'the scantiest information' available, that the woman lacked the capacity to refuse a caesarean section, explaining:

> The patient was in the throes of labour with all that is involved in terms of pain and emotional stress. I concluded that a patient who could, in those circumstances speak in terms which seemed to accept the inevitability of her own death, was not a patient who was able properly to weigh-up the considerations that arose so as to make any valid decision, about anything of even the most trivial kind, still one which involved her own life.[133]

128 Ibid, [8].
129 *Wye Valley NHS Trust v. B* [2015] EWCOP 60.
130 Ibid, [35].
131 [2020] EWCOP 10.
132 *Rochdale Healthcare (NHS) Trust v. C* [3 July 1996] (unreported). See a discussion of the case in *Re MB* [1997] EWCA Civ 3093.
133 Ibid. Quoted in *Re MB* [1997] EWCA Civ 3093, [24].

It seems that underpinning this conclusion was the assumption that a patient *ought* to wish to preserve her own life and that of her child, and to have made a decision which reflected that. The very fact of her making a decision which accepted the possibility of her death was thus deemed to illustrate her lack of capacity.

It is notable in this regard that in *Pennine Acute Hospitals NHS Trust v. TM*,[134] Mr Justice MacDonald distinguished the case at hand from one in which

> a patient who, having understood that refusing treatment would very likely lead to their death, nevertheless considers this preferable to the consequences of receiving the treatment.[135]

In his view, the fact that the patient in this case, TM, did not understand that without treatment he would die, put him 'in a fundamentally different position'[136] from those other cases, justifying the determination that he was 'unable to weigh and sift important factors' and so lacked capacity.[137] Yet both C and Mrs T had understood and accepted the possibility of their deaths but were still found to lack capacity. Patients have therefore been found to lack capacity both because they failed to 'acknowledge the consequences of refusing treatment'[138] and because they 'seemed to accept the inevitability of [their] own death'.[139]

Not having to justify capacity assessments by reference to any particular set of values or beliefs (including the person's own) thus makes it far easier for assessors to deem a person unable to use or weigh information where they doubt the prudence of a given decision. This might be because they consider the decision to be harmful or ill-advised, and in interviews, some doctors were explicit that the way they conducted capacity assessments would be affected by the expected outcome of the decision. One clinician said, for example:

> [T]he thing that is not in the test but which I think will be the overriding thing in clinicians' mind is the pragmatic end results of this. If I say they lack capacity, it means I can do this, and this, and this. If I say they have capacity, then this and this and this is the likely outcome. And actually,

134 [2021] EWCOP 8.
135 Ibid, [32].
136 Ibid.
137 Ibid, [38].
138 Ibid, [32].
139 *Rochdale Healthcare (NHS) Trust v. C* [3 July 1996] (unreported). See a discussion of the case in *Re MB* [1997] EWCA Civ 3093.

> which is the outcome I want? Which is the least harmful? Which is the best for the patient? So I think all of those things are going through your mind as you are making that judgement and I think it's the harm or the outcome of the test which actually probably predominates. (Jonathan, p. 7)

Another suggested:

> I think the nature of the decision that the caregivers are going to make, or an imagined best interest decision, affects capacity ... Even if it should not, of course it affects capacity. So if somebody is making a decision – terribly unwise – then even if they have a right to do that ... it makes it easier to say that they lack capacity. (Oliver, p. 27)

This was borne out more widely in a study by Julie McVey into how healthcare staff from a specialist learning disability service were applying the MCA,[140] where she found staff would 'pre-empt risks' to service users by deeming them to lack capacity.[141] It was also reflected in Kane *et al.*'s study into how liaison psychiatrists applied the MCA, with psychiatrists 'willing to admit their own biases in assessing capacity, including emotional responses to suffering and risk, professional fears and values, and personal political views'.[142] In fact, it is a risk that some judges working within the Court of Protection have themselves acknowledged. Mr Justice Baker noted in *Re TZ (No 2)*, for example, that

> in a case involving a vulnerable adult, there is a risk that all professionals involved with treating and helping that person – including, of course, a judge in the Court of Protection – may feel drawn towards an outcome that is more protective of the adult and thus, in certain circumstances, fail to carry out an assessment of capacity that is detached and objective.[143]

140 J. McVey, 'The Experiences of Healthcare Staff in using the Mental Capacity Act (2005) when working with people with a learning disability' (2013). Available at https://livrepository.liverpool.ac.uk/10673/4/McVeyJul_Jan2013_10673.pdf.

141 Ibid, 81. There was also evidence in the interviews that where the doctor placed the threshold for capacity would be influenced by the outcome of the decision. One doctor gave the example of a man with schizophrenia who had been stabbed in his abdomen but refused surgery out of a fear that the surgeon would insert a chip into him. Given the grave consequences, their 'threshold to determine that he lacked capacity was very low' (Lucy, p. 11). Meanwhile, in considering the vignette of Isobel, a woman with mild dementia refusing a hip replacement, the same doctor suggested that they would place their 'threshold for capacity at a completely different level' if she was suffering from a life-threatening heart condition rather than pain and stiffness (Lucy, p. 11). Another doctor similarly felt that 'the higher the risk... the higher the bar' (Oliver, p. 8).

142 Kane *et al.*, 'Difficult Capacity Cases', 946234. doi: 10.3389/fpsyt.2022.946234, 6.

143 *Re TZ (No 2)* [2014] EWHC 973 (COP), [2014] COPLR 159 at [28].

If this is true, and at least some of those conducting capacity assessments are doing so on the basis of the external or substantive rationality of a decision, as opposed to its internal rationality, then not only is this at odds with s1(4) MCA and the clear principle that a person's capacity should not be contingent on whether their decision is regarded as wise or unwise, but it also raises concerns that capacity assessments may be susceptible to value-laden judgements by assessors. After all, there is no single verifiable answer to what is best for the person, and people may legitimately disagree over this. Whether the assessor perceives the outcome of a decision to be rational or irrational, wise or unwise, beneficial or harmful inevitably depends on *their own* value systems and how *they* weigh the different factors or interests in the balance. To the extent that this then affects the way the capacity assessment is conducted, the test cannot be said to have been value neutral or objective: it is both subjective and heavily dependent on the values of the assessor.

In fact, there is some evidence that the extent to which doctors make outcome-orientated decisions may itself be influenced by their personal values. In a survey study in Switzerland, for example, 72.6 per cent of physicians said that the severity of the consequences of a medical decision was 'rather' or 'very much' relevant to their assessment of capacity.[144] Interestingly, however, a connection was found between the doctor's likelihood of subscribing to a risk-relative view of capacity and their own values (including the importance they attached to power and achievement). The study found there to be a high prevalence of risk-relative evaluations for physicians 'who strive for maintenance and protection of their own prestige and for control over events, through their social and material resources'.[145] By contrast, physicians 'who strongly emphasise equal opportunity and equal treatment for all – a highly self-transcending value – tend to refrain from risk-relative standards',[146] as did those who valued 'conformity to laws, rules and authority'.[147] This led the authors of the study to suggest that it lent support for the claim 'that risk-relativity is being used to introduce unjustified medical paternalism through the back door'.[148]

144 H. Hermann, M. Trachsel, and N. Biller-Andorno, 'Physicians' Personal Values in Determining Medical Decision-Making Capacity: A Survey Study' (2015) 41 *Journal of Medical Ethics* 739–744. Notably, however, this was not then entirely reflected in their attitude towards specific case vignettes.

145 Ibid, 743.

146 Ibid.

147 Ibid.

148 Ibid.

This was acknowledged by liaison psychiatrists in Kane *et al.*'s study, who accepted their personal political views might impact capacity assessments. For example, one stated explicitly:

> I know that I have a much lower threshold for saying somebody's capable than many of my colleagues, and a much higher threshold for saying they are incapable [. . .] I think it's because I personally value autonomy as an ethical principle possibly more than my colleagues.[149]

Another self-identified as 'fairly-libertarian'.[150]

This tension was also acknowledged by retired judges and legal practitioners working within the Court of Protection, with Camillia Kong *et al.* finding professionals to recognise a 'tension'

> between a commitment to personal values and motivations underpinning their account of good practice in mental capacity law and the legal requirement placed upon them to undertake a detached and objective assessment of reasons in context.[151]

They quoted from one participant, a retired judge, who acknowledged:

> Nobody is objective . . . I think the best that you can say is that you try to be aware of your own prejudices and try not to let those suddenly become as if that's a given. If somebody says they are completely objective, I think they are fooling themselves. (RJ4)[152]

Another legal practitioner noted:

> I think that we kid ourselves if we think that we are simply undertaking some kind of – I do not know – scientific, objective, cold-hearted analysis. I think values are enormously influential in the way these things are determined. (LP 25)[153]

A third raised a concern that 'different judges bring very different values of their own to proceedings' with some 'more objective' and others less so,[154] creating problems with unpredictability.

149 Kane *et al.*, 'Difficult Capacity Cases', 946234. doi: 10.3389/fpsyt.2022.946234, 6, quoting P13.

150 Ibid.

151 C. Kong, R. Stickler, P. Cooper, M. Watkins, and M. Dunn, 'The 'Human Element' in the Social Space of the Courtroom: Framing and Shaping the Deliberative Process in Mental Capacity Law' (2022) 42 *Legal Studies* 715–734.

152 Ibid, 730.

153 Ibid.

154 Ibid, LP11.

These concerns are exacerbated when one recognizes that how the assessor perceives the outcome of a decision might depend not only on the effect that the agent's decision has on themselves but also on how it affects third parties. In *Rochdale*, for example, the woman's decision endangered not only herself but also her foetus. It may be, therefore, that in finding her to lack capacity, the judge was influenced not only by a consideration of what was best for the individual patient but also by a sense of responsibility towards the child. It is notable in this regard that in all the cases involving childbirth decisions considered in this book,[155] the courts have found the woman to lack capacity and authorised the caesarean sections or other interventions necessary to save the child's life.[156] The only exception is *St George's Healthcare NHS Trust v. S*,[157] where the appellant successfully appealed the judge's authorisation of a caesarean section against her wishes, though in this case, the child had been safely delivered long before the appeal was heard by the Court of Appeal.[158]

This concern for others also manifested itself in other ways. In interviews, one doctor openly acknowledged that the effect of the decision on themselves would have a bearing on the capacity assessment (Claire, p. 15); a finding borne out in Kane *et al.*'s study on liaison psychiatrists, who also 'spoke frankly about their fear of litigation or of being criticized in the event of the patient coming to harm', as a factor that might bias assessments of capacity.[159] Another doctor in interview expressed concern for the wider healthcare team, explaining that the 'easiest option' is always to find the person to lack capacity and treat them, because 'if you go down the pathway that other people do not agree

155 See, for example, *Rochdale Healthcare (NHS) Trust v. C* [3 July 1996] (unreported); *Norfolk and Norwich HealthCare (NHS) Trust v. W* [1996] 2 FLR 613; *Re MB* [1997] EWCA Civ 3093; *Tameside and Glossip Acute Services Trust v. CH* [1997] EWCA Civ 3093; *United Lincolnshire Hospitals NHS Trust v. CD* [2019] EWCOP 24; *Guys and St Thomas' NHS Foundation Trust (GSTT), South London and Maudsley NHS Foundation Trust (SLAM) v. R* [2020] EWCOP 4; *X NHS Foundation Trust & Anor v. Ms A* [2021] EWCOP 17; *East Lancashire Hospitals NHS Trust v. GH* [2021] EWCOP 18.

156 See Section 2.2.

157 [1998] 3 All ER 673.

158 One doctor was explicit when interviewed, that when faced with a situation in which a woman refused emergency caesarean section, they would advise intervening 'and deal [ing] with the consequences afterwards', notwithstanding the fact 'she probably has capacity', 'because at least the baby's life is saved' (Tatiana, p. 10).

159 Kane *et al.*, 'Difficult Capacity Cases', 946234. doi: 10.3389/fpsyt.2022.946234, 6.

with then you are making everyone involved in that patient's care complicit in your decision' (Conor, p. 9). Therefore, when evaluating the outcome of a decision, it is not just the decision-makers' own interests which may be taken into account, but also the implications of that decision for others. Drawing on a number of cases involving prisoners, John Coggan has even suggested that the social utility of the outcome might have affected the capacity assessment in certain cases.[160]

However, concerns about the outcome of the decision are not the only reason why assessors may seek to invoke values other than the person's own when assessing their capacity. In at least some of those cases identified previously, there may in fact have been good reason, given the suspected influence of disorder on the decision-maker's belief systems or set of values, for the assessor to have questioned whether their decision was truly autonomous and thus worthy of respect. As Section 2.5 will make clear, far from simply being instances of unwarranted paternalism, these cases in fact demonstrate a fundamental problem with the test for capacity: by focusing only on whether the person possesses certain cognitive abilities, and not on the substance of the beliefs or values underpinning the decision, the test cannot accurately explain and capture precisely why the decision-maker's capacity for autonomous decision-making is undermined in these cases and, accordingly, why some degree of paternalistic interference may in fact be warranted.

[160] Coggon, 'Varied and Principled Understandings of Autonomy in English Law', 235, 249–251. He compares the decision in *The NHS Trust v. Mrs T* [2004] EWHC 1279 (Fam) with that of *Re C (Adult: Refusal of Treatment)* [1994] 1 WLR 290, concluding, 'I see no convincing reason for the distinct judicial other than the judge's distinct evaluation *of the person*' (p. 249). Similarly, *B v. Croydon HA* [1995] Fam. 133 was found to be hard to reconcile with *R v. Collins* and another, ex parte *Brady* [2000] EWHC 639 (Admin). *B v. Croydon HA* concerned a twenty-four-year-old woman who suffered from borderline personality disorder, following extensive sexual abuse as a child. The symptoms of this included a compulsion to self-harm, which, following her detention under the Mental Health Act (which made cutting and burning herself impossible), manifested through the refusal of food. Although force-feeding was authorised under the Mental Health Act, Thorpe J. nonetheless found B to have the capacity to make the decision to refuse food. In *Brady*, by contrast, the infamous 'Moors murderer' Ian Brady was deemed unable to weigh up the risks of engaging in a hunger strike because of his intense dislike of Ashworth Hospital. John Coggon suggests (not without basis in the judgement) that such decisions display 'a different attitude [by the judge] towards the patient', noting that 'it does not seem too cynical to submit that the judge had no intention of allowing Brady to achieve his ends' (p. 250) of manipulating the criminal justice system.

2.5 Interrogating the Values Behind the Decisions

In many of those cases discussed previously in which people were deemed, sometimes rather dubiously, to be unable to 'use or weigh' the information, the real concern appeared to lie not with their cognitive processes but with the disordered nature of the values or beliefs that they were applying to that information. In *Mrs T*, for example,[161] the difficulty lay not in Mrs T's reasoning process, but in her disordered belief about her blood being evil, which she then applied to the information to reach a decision that she ought to refuse a transfusion. As John Coggon and José Miola explain, 'here, the rationality of the patient's decision-making is not to be doubted; it is the rationality of her *starting point* that is questionable'.[162]

The same is true of *Wye Valley*,[163] where Mr B refused a leg amputation on the basis of delusional beliefs, prompted by his hallucinations, that the Virgin Mary and angels were talking to him and telling him to refuse it. If the judge in this case had been concerned only with Mr B's decision-making *processes* and not with the rationality of the beliefs underpinning it, then it might at least be arguable that Mr B had capacity: he appeared (albeit somewhat inconsistently[164]) to understand that without the amputation he might die, and balanced this risk against his strong (if disordered) belief that it would be contrary to God's wish to have the operation. Nonetheless, Peter Jackson J. found him to lack the capacity to use or weigh the information, prompted by the (disordered) nature of the belief on which he was basing his decision.

The same can be seen in other cases. In *Sherwood Forest Hospitals NHS Foundation Trust v. C*,[165] for example, the court had to decide whether to authorise a hysterectomy in order to treat the endometrial cancer of a woman with paranoid schizophrenia. Although C had initially been engaged with investigating her illness, on discovering her diagnosis, she became increasingly withdrawn and later refused treatment on the basis that 'only God could cure [her] cancer'.[166] Mr Justice

161 [2004] EWHC 1279 (Fam).

162 Coggon and Miola, 'Autonomy, Liberty, and Medical Decision-Making', 523–543.

163 [2015] EWCOP 60.

164 At other points, Mr B professed the mistaken belief that his foot would get better on its own if he was allowed to walk on it [34].

165 [2020] EWCOP 10.

166 Ibid, [15].

Hayden found that 'her interest in religion began only after her mental health problems developed'.[167] He explained that

> her expressed religious beliefs have become a facet of her mental health problems and a channel for delusional thoughts. For example, she has in the past believed herself to be pregnant, carrying the child of God. This has been a delusion of such vibrancy for her that she has carried it through to purchasing baby clothes for the child she believed she was carrying. It is important therefore to disentangle capacitously held religious beliefs from the delusional views here. It requires some sensitivity.[168]

Consequently, he concluded that her rejection of the treatment was 'predicated on a delusional belief structure which manifests itself in the language of religion' and so she 'clearly lacked capacity'.[169] It was not her ability to use the information to come to a decision that was broadly coherent with her beliefs that was at issue, therefore, but that the belief she was applying to the information was itself delusional.

As noted previously, this concern was also evident from Kane *et al.*'s study on liaison psychiatrists, who identified determining when a decision was being driven by illness (as opposed to authentic beliefs) as a key challenge in capacity assessments, in particular deciding whether refusals were 'due to a delusion or whether they were religious, cultural, or political beliefs'.[170] The clear implication is that they *are* taking the disordered nature of the beliefs or values underpinning a decision into account when deciding whether the agent has capacity or not.

Although this point is demonstrated most clearly in the context of delusional or hallucinatory beliefs,[171] concerns about the disordered nature of beliefs and values underpinning a decision have also been raised in other contexts, most notably those involving depressive illnesses or eating disorders. This might, for example, explain the initial capacity assessment made by the doctors in *St George's Healthcare NHS Trust*

[167] Ibid, [18].
[168] Ibid, [18].
[169] Ibid, [19].
[170] Kane *et al.*, 'Applying Decision-Making Capacity Criteria in Practice', e0246521. https://doi.org/10.1371/journal.pone.0246521.
[171] Natalie Banner also makes the point that, in the context of a delusion, 'on a procedural account, no deficit or impairment in decision-making may be identifiable': Banner, 'Can Procedural and Substantive Elements of Decision-Making be Reconciled in Assessments of Mental Capacity?', 71–86.

v. S.[172] They considered S to be severely depressed, having experienced a number of recent difficulties with 'relationships, housing, changing jobs and indeed being pregnant with a child that she says she does not want and would give to the father as soon as it is born'.[173] Dr Jeffreys explained:

> She appears to be significantly depressed with low self-esteem and a profound indifference to the consequences of refusing treatment for her serious physical condition. She is pregnant and her behaviour is putting her own life and the life of her unborn baby at risk.[174]

At times she appeared 'tearful' and said that she 'would not be bothered if she dies and it would be better for the baby to be dead'.[175] When it was suggested to her that the baby might die, she responded that she was not interested in the pregnancy or the baby[176] and demonstrated complete indifference to 'the fact that she could die or be severely brain damaged if the pre-eclampsia is not treated'.[177] Dr Jeffreys found she could not adequately explain why she cared so little about what happened to her, but merely reasserted her belief that pregnancy was 'a natural process and any intervention was to be avoided'.[178] Consequently, the doctors took the view that her severe depression had resulted in her no longer attaching the same value to her life, or that of her foetus, as she would have done if she had not been suffering from the illness and, on this basis, found her to lack capacity. She was also detained under the Mental Health Act for assessment. The judge nonetheless found her (retrospectively) to have had the capacity to refuse treatment for her pre-eclampsia.

Similarly in *Re TC (Urgent Medical Treatment)*,[179] concerning an application to authorise urgent medical care to treat a woman's laryngeal cancer, the consultant forensic psychiatrist (with whom the judge agreed) found that although the woman was able to understand and retain the relevant information, as a result of her depressive illness,

172 [1998] 3 All ER 673.
173 Ibid, 678 [J].
174 Ibid, 679 [J].
175 Ibid, 680 [B].
176 Ibid, [G].
177 Ibid, 681 [B].
178 Ibid, 681 [C].
179 *University Hospitals of Leicester NHS Trust v. TC* (by her litigation friend, the Official Solicitor), AC, BC, DC [2020] EWCOP 53.

> she is experiencing symptoms of hopelessness and does not consider that she has a future. As is typical in severe depression she is experiencing catastrophic thinking. As a result, she is unable to weigh up the information she has been given in order to make a capacitous decision.[180]

In these cases, the concern lies not with the person's cognitive processes per se: S (and to a lesser extent TC) appeared perfectly able to understand the information and reason abstractly about it. Rather, as explained previously, there is a concern that the depressive illness may distort the values that the person is applying to that information, causing them to place very little weight on the significance of continued life, and the possibility of future improvement. Helena Hermann and others explain how depression might affect a person's decision-making:

> Depression is an affective disorder characterised by hopelessness, helplessness, deeply entrenched feelings of guilt and worthlessness, anhedonia, and other symptoms. These feelings are likely to affect the value assigned by patients to themselves, to their lives, and more specifically to the treatment options and outcomes they face. One likely consequence of such feelings is that a patient will become largely insensitive to their own welfare, perhaps to the point of not caring about risk, or even positively valuing negative consequences such as death.[181]

Although the person may therefore be *able* to weigh up information about the consequences of deciding one way or the other in the abstract, their illness may result in them failing to attach significance at an emotional level to an outcome that leads, for example, to their death. This has led Abraham Rudnick to argue that the standard criteria for capacity are insufficient, as they fail to capture the ways in which major depression disrupts the coherence of personal preferences, by altering those preferences.[182]

Although judges have tended not to do so explicitly, anorexia nervosa may be characterised in a similar way. In a study conducted by Jacinta Tan *et al.*, for example, it was found that participants with anorexia nervosa exhibited 'excellent understanding, reasoning, and ability to express choice', with scores on the MacCAT-T competence test

180 Ibid, [37].

181 H. Hermann, M. Trachsel, B.S. Elger, and N. Biller-Andorno, 'Emotion and Value in the Evaluation of Medical Decision-Making Capacity: A Narrative Review of Arguments' (2016) 7 *Frontiers in Psychology* Article 765, 6.

182 A. Rudnick, 'Depression and Competence to Refuse Psychiatric Treatment' (2002) 28 *Journal of Medical Ethics* 151–155.

comparable to a control group of 'healthy' participants.[183] However, participants' values were found to change in various ways as they developed anorexia, in ways that affected their decision-making. These included developing the strong belief that being fat was highly undesirable and diminished their worth; attaching little value to life and to the risk of death; and seeing weight loss as the thing of paramount importance in their lives which took precedence over most or all other things (including relationships, health, and academic achievement).[184] Of course, these altered values will inevitably affect the weight that a person then attributes to certain pieces of information: if one places little value on their health and continued life, and a great deal of value on not putting on any weight, then it is unsurprising that when faced with a decision over whether to prioritise their health or their weight loss, they feel compelled to opt for the latter.

This idea of distorted or pathological values has also been picked up on in the case law. In their content analysis of Court of Protection case law, for example, Kane *et al.* found that in respect of eating disorders, the second most commonly cited rationale for finding the person to lack capacity (after a failure to appreciate) was that the disorder caused the individual to be unable to value or care about relevant issues,[185] such as continued life or health. Avoidance of calories, by contrast, could take on undue importance. In *Northamptonshire Healthcare NHS Foundation Trust v. AB*,[186] for example, expert evidence described a woman's fixation on reducing calorific intake as an 'overvalued idea',[187] clearly denoting the idea that the disorder had affected her evaluative judgement. Mrs Justice Roberts neither accepted nor refuted this analysis, but she explained:

> Whether one calls this an "overvalued idea" or the fundamental manifestation of an illness which renders a sufferer powerless to resist a compulsion which, in this case, has proved incompatible with a normal life expectancy seems to me to matter not.. . . Her judgement in relation to [gaining weight] is critically impaired by an intense and irrational fear of weight gain.[188]

[183] J. Tan, A. Stewart, R. Fitzpatrick, and R.A. Hope, 'Competence to Make Treatment Decisions in Anorexia Nervosa: Thinking Processes and Values' (2006) 13(4) *Philosophy, Psychiatry & Psychology* 267–282.

[184] Ibid, 273–274.

[185] Kane *et al.*, 'Applying Decision-Making Capacity Criteria in Practice'.

[186] [2020] EWCOP 40.

[187] Ibid, [25].

[188] Ibid, [64].

The notion of an 'overvalued idea' was also used to describe a person's apparently obsessive belief that they had been given the wrong date of birth in *Avon and Wiltshire Mental Health Partnership v. WA & Anor* (discussed previously).[189] These cases therefore lend support to the idea that, in certain cases, health professionals and judges may be less concerned with the person's cognitive processes and more with the way in which an illness is affecting the values and beliefs they hold, which in turn affects the weight that is then ascribed to certain pieces of information and thus the evaluative judgements they make about alternative treatment options. In other words, their concern related to the *authenticity* of the decision: how might the decision have been different if they were not operating under the influence of a mental disorder? Similar concerns might also arise in the context of those suffering from dementia, whose decisions may be underpinned by new values that they did not hold prior to them developing their illness (a new religious belief, for example, or a resistance to 'modern medicine'), or by false beliefs (for example that their spouse is still alive, when they are not). However, given that changes in values will often occur alongside decline in cognitive functions, there may well be other bases on which the assessor can find the person to lack capacity, without requiring recourse to their disordered values, thus perhaps explaining the lack of case law on this.

In all such cases, the basis on which the person was found to lack legal capacity was an inability to 'use or weigh' the relevant information as part of the process of making a decision. While this 'rather amorphous standard' is, as Peter Bartlett has observed, frequently the basis on which courts make 'controversial findings of incapacity'[190] (in an analysis of forty Court of Protection cases, Ruck Keene *et al.* found that the inability to use or weigh information was 'cited in all but 2 cases in which P was determined to lack capacity and inabilities were cited'[191]), doing so in such cases nonetheless involves some straining of the statutory language. This is clearest in the context of delusional or hallucinatory beliefs, where, as explained in relation to Mrs T, the person *can* weigh up the consequences of deciding one way or another *and* use that information to reach a decision which reflects their beliefs; it is simply that those beliefs are themselves thought to be delusional or erroneous. In the case of

[189] [2020] EWCOP 37, [82].

[190] P. Bartlett, *Blackstone's Guide to the Mental Capacity Act 2005*, 2nd ed. (New York: Oxford University Press, 2008), 51.

[191] Ruck Keene *et al.*, 'Taking Capacity Seriously', 56–76.

depressive illnesses or anorexia nervosa, the position is more complex, as the illness may be characterised as operating a person in different ways, and the same illness might affect different people differently. However, questions may still be raised about how far the MCA truly captures the nature of the impairment precipitated by these illnesses.

In the context of anorexia nervosa, it might be said, for example, that a person cannot 'use or weigh' information, because the outcome of the decision is compelled by their illness, irrespective of the information they receive. In other words, they are not 'using' the relevant information to come to a decision or engaging in any meaningful weighing-up task; rather, their decision is based on other factors, namely the overwhelming anxiety that surrounds the idea of taking in calories. Certainly, the case law has portrayed anorexia nervosa as operating in this way. In *A Local Authority v. E*,[192] it was suggested that her 'need not to gain weight overpowers all other thoughts';[193] in *NHS Foundation Trust v. X*,[194] that it 'overrides any loose connection she might have to the information pertaining to herself',[195] and in *Northamptonshire Healthcare NHS Foundation Trust v. AB*[196] that it 'overwhelms her thought processes so as to *prevent*, or disable, her from conducting the sort of weighing and balancing exercise required by s. 3(1)(c)'.[197] Clearly, when analysed in this way, the effects of the illness can be adequately captured within the use or weigh criterion: the illness precludes any meaningful weighing task from being conducted.

However, evidence such as that of Tan *et al.*'s indicates that this is an overly simplistic understanding of how the disease affects people.[198] They found that people with anorexia nervosa *can* conduct some kind of balancing act in the abstract, and accordingly frequently score highly in tests of competence, but their distorted values lead certain pieces of information to lack salience to them, which causes them to not attribute weight to it. In other words, the person may well be able to perform the cognitive tasks associated with weighing up the information and using it to make a decision, and they likely are able to understand at a rational level that the effect of, for example, refusing food is to place them in grave

192 *E* [2012] EWHC 1639.
193 Ibid, [49].
194 [2014] EWCOP 35.
195 Ibid, [28].
196 [2020] EWCOP 40.
197 Ibid, [26].
198 Tan *et al.*, 'Competence to Make Treatment Decisions in Anorexia Nervosa', 267–282.

physical danger of dying, but their 'pathological values' lead them not to attach the same importance to that as a consequence, as they otherwise would.

This should not, as Tony Hope *et al.* note,[199] be constructed as a straightforward preference. They explain that people with anorexia nervosa typically experience very high levels of anxiety around the idea of gaining weight, which is often triggered when they see their body. It is not that they 'misperceive' their body as being fat, but that they have a strong emotional response telling them they are fat, even in the face of objective evidence to the contrary. These emotional responses are 'are so powerful that together with the lack of salience of the contradictory evidence she is led to believe that she is fat'[200] and on this basis, along with 'the lack of salience of the dangers of self-starvation',[201] refuses treatment. But when questioned by a doctor emphasising the objective evidence that they are in fact severely underweight, the person cannot rationally deny this. And so they must justify their refusal, and the only logical argument they can put forward is that they would rather risk death than put on weight. As Hope *et al.* explain, this might look like a 'preference', but it was not one that was held before the discussion with the physician; rather, 'it was constructed to create a rational argument for refusing treatment that can satisfy her physician'.[202]

Yet, even if not conceived of as a simple 'preference', this latter way of analysing the effect of anorexia nervosa on decision-making is hard to reconcile with the cognitive, process-orientated, and value-neutral account of capacity in the MCA. If the assessor's concern in fact relates to the weight that the person is attributing to certain pieces of information, then this clearly blurs the line drawn by Mr Justice MacDonald in *V & C*, between a person's 'ability' to use or weigh information – which *is* the preserve of the capacity assessment – and the weight they attach to that information, which is a product of their values and should not be relevant to their capacity.[203]

The same problems emerge in the context of depressive illnesses such as in *St George* or *Re TC* (*Urgent Medical Treatment*).[204] There are ways

199 Hope *et al.*, 'Agency, Ambivalence and Authenticity', 20–36.
200 Ibid, 29.
201 Ibid, 30.
202 Ibid.
203 Ibid, [38].
204 *University Hospitals of Leicester NHS Trust v. TC* (by her litigation friend, the Official Solicitor), AC, BC, DC [2020] EWCOP 53.

in which such illnesses may affect the person's weighing up of information. As Harold Bursztajn *et al.* have explained, affective disorders such as depression are likely to lead patients to suffer from the 'false premise of fixity' (the erroneous prediction that one's mood or situation will never change),[205] which, as Jodi Halpern explains, can impair the person's capacity to deliberate meaningfully, as the rigidity with which one sees their future may make them unresponsive to evidence and thus unable to think through alternatives. Moreover, Bursztajn *et al.* note that it is common for patients with bipolar disorder to develop 'an emotionally involving, self-convincing preoccupation with the risks of treatment coupled with denial of the benefits',[206] which affects their ability to weigh up information. Yet basing a capacity assessment on the fact that someone attaches no weight to information, because their illness leads them to believe that their position will not change or improve in any way (as occurred in *Re TC* (*Urgent Medical Treatment*)[207]), would once again seem to involve a blurring of the line between the weight or salience one attaches to the information, and their ability to conduct a weighing task at all.

And herein lies the challenge for the law. Either capacity assessors must seek to maintain complete value neutrality by not engaging with the substance and origins of the values that underpin a decision. In doing so, however, it becomes hard to meaningfully differentiate instances in which a person fails to attach weight to certain outcomes because of a disorder such as anorexia nervosa or depression, from those in which a person chooses not to attach weight because of their belief system (such as a Jehovah's Witness refusing blood products). Or they must engage with the way in which disorder or impairment affects evaluative judgements, but since there is no way of doing so explicitly within the Act, they can do so only by attempting (more or less convincingly) to crowbar these concerns within the 'use and weigh' criteria.

The lack of mechanisms in the Act through which assessors can directly question the nature or origins of a person's beliefs leaves assessors in an unenviable position in situations like these. If they apply the letter of the law and find the person to have capacity, on the basis that

205 H. Bursztajn, H.P. Harding, T.G. Gutheil, and A. Brodsky, 'Beyond Cognition: The Role of Disordered Affective States in Impairing Competence to Consent to Treatment' (1991) 19(4) *Bulletin of the American Academy of Psychiatry & the Law* 383–388.

206 Ibid.

207 *University Hospitals of Leicester NHS Trust v. TC* (by her litigation friend, the Official Solicitor), AC, BC, DC [2020] EWCOP 53.

they cannot identify any impairments in the person's cognitive processes (it is simply that their depressive attitude or eating disorder causes them to prioritise values differently, or their psychotic illness causes them to have certain metaphysical beliefs that they might not otherwise have), then the patient has complete freedom to act as they choose, even to do something that may be profoundly harmful to themselves. If, however, they find the person to lack capacity through deeming them unable to 'use or weigh' the information, they will be able to prevent this harm and to act in a way which they regard as best for the patient. It is no surprise, then, that many assessors opt for the latter.

St George's aptly illustrates this point. Although her actions later, in seeking to give the child up for adoption and then changing her mind, might lend some weight to the doctors' argument that her decision was the result of an acute depressive episode, we can never know for sure whether the doctors, or the judge, were right in this case. As it was, the judge was not called upon to determine the question of S's capacity until after the child had been safely delivered. Had this assessment been made at the time, however, it might well have resulted in the death of S, and of the child. Given this, the doctor's reluctance to respect a decision which they believed was the result of an acute depressive episode is understandable.

It is not the case, then, that assessments of capacity are neutral as to the decision-maker's values. Assessors do evaluate the substance or origins of their values or beliefs, but they do so under the pretence that they are interrogating the decision-making *process*, through assessing the decision-maker's ability to use or weigh information by reference to the values or beliefs which they would have held were it not for their disorder. Indeed, one doctor stated explicitly in interviews that where they have genuine concerns about the substance of the beliefs or values being applied to the information, 'usually, [we] just shove it under "weighing up" because that's the broadest, most nebulous aspect of the test' (Tatiana, p. 1).

While this might produce good (and humane) outcomes in certain cases, ensuring that those who are unable to make autonomous choices are not left unprotected by the law (as might have been the case in *St George's*),[208] the result is to conflate instances where the issue with an agent's capacity lies in their failure to process information (that is, they are not using the information to produce a decision which reflects their

[208] [1998] 3 All ER 673.

underlying values) and those situations where the concern lies in fact with the agent's values themselves, and the disordered nature of the beliefs or values underpinning a decision. This gives rise to a number of concerns.

From a practical perspective, by treating both of these different types of impairment as instances of a failure to 'use and weigh' the information, this creates a lack of transparency over exactly what the nature of the impairment is in any given case, which makes it extremely difficult for any patient to challenge the assessment or to know what evidence they must adduce in order to dispute it. Must they seek to demonstrate the authenticity of the decision, for example, or the internal rationality of their decision-making process?

The reason why a person has been found to lack capacity is also crucial when it comes to determining their best interests. How exactly best interests decisions should be made will be set out in more detail in Chapter 6. However, at a basic level, where a person suffers from an impairment which prevents them from acting in accordance with their values and beliefs (as where they have a compulsion to act in a certain way, or a phobia preventing them from doing so), then when making a decision on their behalf, the aim of the decision-maker is to overcome this difficulty, essentially acting as a facilitator to enable them to choose something that reflects their values, beliefs, and priorities. Where, however, the person is operating on the basis of disordered values and beliefs, the aim will very often not be to make a decision which reflects these beliefs or to facilitate the person in making a decision premised on harmful misconceptions about the world. Rather, the best interests inquiry will be directed towards discovering what they would have wanted if they did not have disordered beliefs, and to giving effect to this.

More fundamentally, however, by encompassing concerns both about the person's decision-making process *and* about the content or origins of their values within the 'use and weigh' criterion, the reach of the law (and thus the state) becomes obscured. While the law ostensibly subscribes to a process-orientated, value-neutral account of capacity, this discussion suggests that there are in fact substantive limits being placed on the kinds of decisions that a person can make – or, more specifically, on the kinds of beliefs and values which a person can act upon – which are not being subjected to scrutiny. Where the real basis for finding someone to lack capacity is that you consider the beliefs or values that are motivating their decision to be distorted by a mental illness, with the result that the decision is not authentically desired and so is unworthy of respect, this entails a number of empirical and normative claims which warrant interrogation. From an empirical perspective, it involves the claim that the specific values or beliefs which drive any particular decision do *in fact* originate in a mental disorder. Ascertaining this is, as Chapter 3 will elucidate, far from clear cut, since disorders in diagnostic manuals are not characterised in absolute terms, or capable of scientific testing, but are instead subject to complex clinical judgement. Assessment is not therefore merely a matter of observation, but of judgement – judgement which may be subject to legitimate disagreement between professionals.

From a normative perspective, meanwhile, this approach implicitly suggests that if they can be identified, disordered values are worthy of less respect than non-disordered values. Whether this is true depends on two further questions. First, can mental disorder be, in principle, distinguished from other non-disordered states, in the sense that there is something different and distinct about disorder that means it can be carved out as a separate category? Second, even if there is something distinct about disorder, does the nature of that distinction justify differential treatment? In other words, does disorder undermine the person's capacity for autonomous decision-making in a way that makes decisions that are motivated by it less worthy of respect?

These questions go to the heart of what mental disorder is and what autonomy demands, and they must be tackled head-on if we are to justify intervening on the basis of disorder, given the inherent tension between this and the liberal framework that underpins the Act. On the one hand, liberal ideals demand respect for and tolerance of different values and belief systems, whatever they may be. On the other, most people share a strong intuition that there are certain belief or value systems caused by mental disorders, which should not be respected, and which are so harmful that people ought to be protected from them. Examples include the refusal of those with eating disorders to accept food because of an overvaluing of thinness vis-à-vis their health; the rejection of life-saving treatment by someone with depression due to an undervaluing of their life; or, perhaps even more obviously, the refusal of treatment because of a belief born out of a hallucination or delusion.

Through focusing on the decision-making *process* and not the substance of the beliefs or values, legal tests for capacity, both here and elsewhere, have sought to avoid confronting this tension directly. But as this discussion has highlighted, in doing so, they fail to account for why intervention may be legitimate in certain cases, even where a person's cognitive processes are not fatally undermined by their condition. If in reality assessors *are* making assessments about the substance of beliefs and values and whether they are symptomatic of a disorder, and on that basis deeming people to lack capacity, then we need to find a compelling justification for *why* this ought to make a difference. Why, in other words, *should* Mrs T be treated any differently from a Jehovah's Witness?

These questions, which will be explored in the following chapter, are especially important given recent widespread support for abandoning the Mental Health Act 1983 and moving instead towards fused legislation,[209] where the treatment of mental disorders would rest on a person's capacity to consent. If the test for capacity were to become the touchstone for intervention, it would be essential that the test was capable of dealing appropriately and coherently with mental disorders. Indeed, as will be discussed later, it is notable that when Northern Ireland moved to fused legislation,[210] they introduced additional criteria to the MCA test for capacity with the explicit aim of allowing 'for things, such as lack of insight, delusional or distorted thinking, to be taken into account when assessing someone's ability to make a decision'.[211] This is therefore an issue which could become increasingly important if reform proposals are taken forward, and which must be resolved before any attempts are made to fuse capacity and mental health legislation. As alluded to in the Introduction, addressing it is also a necessary precursor to adopting a more CRPD-compliant model of decision-making, here or elsewhere, since understanding how mental disorder affects a person's ability to make autonomous decisions is crucial to determining how best to support them in decisions being taken about them.

209 For a discussion of this, see J. Dawson and G. Schmukler, 'Fusion of Mental Health and Incapacity Legislation' (2006) 1088 *British Journal of Psychiatry* 504–509; N. Rees, 'The Fusion Proposal: A Next Step' in B. McSherry and P. Weller (eds), *Rethinking Rights-Based Mental Health Laws* (Oxford: Hart Publishing 2010); Richardson, 'Mental Disabilities and the Law', 333–354. This is discussed in detail in 'Special Issue: A Model Law Fusing Incapacity and Mental Health Legislation – Is It Viable; Is It Advisable?' (2010) 20 *Journal of Mental Health Law*. In the final report of the Independent Review of the Mental Health Act 1983 ('Modernising the Mental Health Act: Increasing Choice, Reducing Coercion'. Available at https://assets.publishing.service.gov.uk/government/uploads/system/uploads/attachment_data/file/778897/Modernising_the_Mental_Health_Act_-_increasing_choice__reducing_compulsion.pdf), published in December 2018, the authors recognised the many benefits of fused legislation, but ultimately decided not to recommend it because of the time it would take in order to do so.

210 Mental Capacity Act (Northern Ireland) 2016.

211 Mental Capacity Act (Northern Ireland) 2016 Explanatory Notes: Part 1 Section 4: 'Meaning of "unable to make a decision"'.

3

Why Disorder Matters

In order to unpick whether the fact that a value or belief derives from a mental disorder is relevant to the determination of the agent's capacity (and if so, how), it is necessary to address two separate questions. The first is whether values that derive from a disorder can be distinguished from other, non-disordered values that guide an agent's life and decision-making, both practically and conceptually. If it is possible to distinguish disordered from non-disordered values, at least conceptually, the second question is whether the fact that a person's values are disordered affects or undermines their capacity for autonomous decision-making (and if so, how). Does the fact that a person is acting on the basis of disordered values *always* mean they are unable to make an autonomous decision, or are there some instances in which such a decision can still be autonomous? And what are the implications of this for when it is justifiable to find someone to lack capacity on the basis of disordered values?

3.1 What Is Different about Disorder?

The question of what, if anything, distinguishes mental disorder from other beliefs, behaviours, or values is not new. As Derek Bolton and Natalie Banner explain, it 'has long vexed philosophers and psychiatrists keen to distinguish conditions warranting healthcare from those variations and eccentricities of human experience that, whilst negative, are considered normal and not illness'.[1] A vast literature is devoted to this question, spanning philosophy, psychology, psychiatry, and wider medicine.[2]

[1] D. Bolton and N. Banner, 'Does Mental Disorder Involve Loss of Personal Autonomy?' in L. Radoilska (ed), *Autonomy and Mental Disorder* (Oxford: Oxford University Press, 2012), 78.

[2] This literature is helpfully summarised in J. Wakefield, 'The Concept of Mental Disorder: On the Boundary between Biological Facts and Social Values' (1992) 47(3) *America*

Within this, a series of tensions exist between different disciplines, each advocating different approaches to the question of how to conceptualise and characterise mental disorder, and advancing different perspectives on the question of whether disorders have some kind of 'objective', factual, and scientific basis or not. As Robert Kendell puts it, the key debate in this literature is over

> whether disease and illness are normative concepts based on value judgements, or whether they are value-free scientific terms; in other words, whether they are biomedical terms or sociopolitical ones.[3]

This is important for our current discussion because if disorder is based merely on value judgements about the normality (or abnormality) of certain behaviours or beliefs, then it might legitimately be asked why so-called disordered values or beliefs ought to be treated differently from any others. According to liberal frameworks, provided that a person's behaviour does not cause others harm, they ought to be free to make decisions according to their own values, whether or not these are acceptable to the majority. This creates an obvious tension: if the reason for finding someone to lack capacity is that their beliefs or values are thought to be affected (or distorted) by a disorder, and yet disorder is itself merely a sociopolitical label for certain (unusual) behaviours, then it is not clear how disorder negatively affects autonomy in a way that justifies paternalistic intervention. Given this, it is important to consider the nature of mental disorder, and the role that judgements about social norms play in the determination of disorder, both conceptually and when applied in practice. Doing so requires an account of a vast body of literature which has shaped modern-day psychiatry, and so the inevitable brevity of the overview that follows must be excused.

Heavily influenced by paradigms of nineteenth-century medicine and the rise of the 'disease model' (whereby disease was observable as a lesion or cellular pathology in the body),[4] the traditional medical approach to this issue typically saw disorder in terms of the disruption of normal bodily function. Applied to the psychiatric context, disorder was viewed as the product of some dysfunctional organic process in the person's body or

Psychologist 373–388, 374. See also D. Bolton, *What Is Mental Disorder? An Essay in Philosophy, Science and Values* (New York: Oxford University Press, 2008).

3 R. E. Kendell, 'What Are Mental Disorders?' in A. M. Freedman, R. Brotman, I. Silverman, and D. Hutson (eds), *Issues in Psychiatric Classification: Science, Practice and Social Policy* (New York: Human Sciences Press, 1986), 23–45, 25.

4 Bolton and Banner, 'Does Mental Disorder Involve Loss of Personal Autonomy?', 77.

neural system, which manifested in certain observable symptoms.[5] Since these dysfunctional processes relate to traditional categories of faculty psychology (perception, affection, cognition, memory), the disorder was classified as mental as opposed to physical; however, its cause was fundamentally a physical one: a lesion or disease which causes a breakdown in meaningful processes.

This 'medical' approach ran into conflict with psychological models of psychopathology (whether behavioural, psychoanalytic, or cognitive), which typically sought to minimise the supposed difference between 'normal' and 'abnormal' functioning through emphasising how allegedly abnormal behaviour may in fact be more understandable when seen in the context of the individual's background or through the lens of coping strategies. Derek Bolton highlights four ways in which this might be so.[6] First, through looking at a statistical variation of traits, psychology has shown how supposedly abnormal conditions are rather extremes of normal variation. There is no binary distinction between the two; instead, an evaluative judgement must be made about where, along the spectrum of traits, something is sufficiently extreme or outlying as to be deemed 'abnormal'. Secondly, it has sought to unearth the unrecognised meaning in emotional responses, either through examining the person's past experiences (for example, childhood trauma) or through specific conditioning episodes, or some other element of the context which might affect the person's interpretation of events. By way of example, suffering from major depressive disorder as a result of losing one's job might be more explicable if that job is linked to the person's sense of themselves and their identity or status. Thirdly, even in those instances where behaviour looks abnormal, it may be borne out of an attempt to problem-solve, either consciously or subconsciously (for example, avoiding an unmanageable task). Finally, psychological approaches have considered how abnormal behaviour might result from learnt patterns of behaviour being transferred from the original 'learning' environment to a different, inappropriate one. Normal and abnormal behaviour cannot therefore be neatly delineated, nor does mental disorder represent a total absence of order, since some responses might represent meaningful responses to challenging circumstances.

[5] Samuel Guze, for example, defines psychopathology as representing 'the manifestations of disturbed function within a part of the body': S. Guze, *Why Psychiatry Is a Branch of Medicine* (New York: Oxford University Press, 1992), 44.

[6] Bolton, *What Is Mental Disorder?*, 52–57.

This tension between medical and psychological approaches to disorder was to some extent mitigated in the 1960s by the introduction of cognitive or information-processing theories. Influenced by the invention of the computer, these theories focused on the way in which an individual's 'processing systems' (their perception, short-term memory, attention etc.) process (store, transform, retrieve, use) information that they derive from the environment, and regulate activity based on those processes. Such theories collapsed previous ideas of a separation between the biological (the brain) and the psychological, incorporating both in the analysis and in the understanding of mental disorder. With the help of advances in neuroimaging and genetics, this approach radically enhanced our understanding of the aetiology of mental disorder. Disorder was no longer seen in reductionist physical terms (as a lesion or pathology), or as simply a poorly adapted response to the environment; rather, it was recognised that the causes of disorder were multifactorial and complex. There were many different potential cases, which interacted with one another to influence the development of disorder. As Bolton succinctly summarises, these include

> genetic influences on traits, physical and interpersonal environmental impacts on early neural development, pre-, during and post-birth, subsequent adverse life events and chronic stressors, with effects through time evident in psychic life and the underlying neurochemistry, functioning abnormalities of the brain, lesions to the brain, by disease processes or injury, styles of information processing evident in neuropsychological experimental paradigms, the operation of meanings drawn from the surrounding culture and subculture, and personal meanings deriving from individual learning histories and modes of interpretation.[7]

There is now ample evidence, for example, that genes influence a person's susceptibility to developing certain conditions or patterns of behaviour which are generally regarded as disordered. As Steven Hyman observes in *Bulletin of the World Health Organization*:

> It is well established that the risk of mental illness runs in families. Family, twin and adoption studies have shown that, for schizophrenia, autism, manic depressive illness, major depression, attention deficit hyperactivity disorder, panic disorder and other mental illnesses, the transmission of risk is due to heredity.[8]

[7] Ibid, 73–74.

[8] S. E. Hyman, 'The Genetics of Mental Illness: Implications for Practice' (2000) 78(4) *Bulletin of the World Health Organization* 455–463 www.ncbi.nlm.nih.gov/pmc/articles/PMC2560734/.

This might be because genes and their protein products affect the synaptic structure of the brain, which in turn affects the way neurons operate.[9]

There is also substantial evidence that differences in the brain's neurological structure or chemical content might affect social function and result in the development of certain patterns of behaviour commonly associated with certain disorders, such as schizophrenia and bipolar disorder.[10] Meanwhile, the expression of both genetic and neurostructural differences may be influenced (or triggered: post-traumatic shock syndrome being the clearest example) by environmental factors, such that people with the same susceptibility may or may not develop a disorder depending on their environment or context. Indeed, as Jennifer Radden explains, the evidence suggests that

> even those [conditions] with more claim to idiopathic genetic, neurological, or biological causes or predisposing factors are recognized to exhibit a course more strongly influenced by environmental than (hypothesized) inherent factors . . . Solely internal, organic states and processes, and genes, cannot alone explain all, and probably any, diagnostic disorders.[11]

9 As Hyman explains, 'with respect to neural development, proteins form guidance cues or control their synthesis; these direct the migration of neurons to their correct places in the brain, leading to the establishment of appropriate connections. Other proteins are required if the brain is to adapt in response to environmental inputs associated, for example, with drugs, injury or disease . . . Variations in the DNA sequence of genes may lead to the expression of an altered protein with loss of function or with a new function that might be adaptive, neutral or toxic to cells. Variations in DNA sequences that regulate gene expression might alter the timing, cell type or spatial location in which a protein is expressed. Variations in either protein coding regions or regulatory regions of DNA might also result in a complete failure to express a protein. Sequence variants that affect behaviour, including the risk of mental illness, must affect neurons in such a way as to change the architecture, function or adaptability of neural circuits in the brain'. And genes are not 'the only factors involved in establishing and consolidating the synaptic structure of the brain; the activity of synapses themselves, partly resulting from experience, also plays a vital role': see Hyman, 'The Genetics of Mental Illness', 455–463.

10 See, for example, S. Lincoln and C. Hooker, 'Neural Structure and Social Dysfunction in Individuals at Clinical High Risk for Psychosis' (2014) 224(3) *Psychiatry Research: Neuroimaging* 152–158; E. Fuller Torrey *et al.*, 'Neurochemical Markers for Schizophrenia, Bipolar Disorder, and Major Depression in Postmortem Brains' (2005) 57(3) *Biological Psychiatry* 252–260; A. Yildiz-Yesiloglu and D. Pauler Ankerst, 'Neurochemical Alterations of the Brain in Bipolar Disorder and Their Implications for Pathophysiology: A Systematic Review of the In Vivo Proton Magnetic Resonance Spectroscopy Findings' (2006) 30(6) *Progress in Neuro-Psychopharmacology and Biological Psychiatry* 969–995; B. Amann and H. Grunze, 'Neurochemical Underpinnings in Bipolar Disorder and Epilepsy' (2005) 46(4) *Epilepsia* 26–30.

11 J. Radden, 'Mental Disorder (Illness)', *The Stanford Encyclopedia of Philosophy* (Stanford, CA: Stanford University Press, Summer 2023 edition) https://plato.stanford.edu/archives/sum2023/entries/mental-disorder/ accessed 23 May 2023.

Yet while most, if not all, behaviours may be caused by a combination of biological and social factors, the 'dominant' cause may vary depending on the behaviour in question. Evidence suggests, for example, that while those symptoms we associate with major depressive disorder or post-traumatic stress disorder may be more reactive to adverse life events or stressors, structural or functional neural abnormalities may play a greater role in the development of schizophrenia, while neurochemical abnormalities may do so for behaviours labelled bipolar disorder.[12]

We can also observe that symptoms have a tendency to coalesce, that is, that many people who suffer from certain symptoms or patterns of behaviour also suffer from other symptoms, such that the development of certain symptoms is a good predictor of the development of other symptoms. Opinion differs on whether this is because all such symptoms can be traced back to some underlying pathology, or whether they are in fact causally connected to one another. A new approach, coined the 'network analysis', conceptualises disorders as 'systems of causally connected symptoms rather than as effects of a latent disorder'.[13] Working from the starting point that people who have mental disorders suffer from symptoms, and that these symptoms appear to form clusters, this analyses disorders as follows:

> Instead of interpreting symptoms as a function of a set of underlying/latent disorders, the net-work approach conceptualizes symptoms as mutually interacting, often reciprocally reinforcing, elements of a complex network. Thus, rather than interpreting symptoms as measurements of a latent disorder ... symptoms are viewed as part of a causal system (Borsboom 2008a). As such, the relation between symptoms and disorder becomes one of mereology (a part–whole relation) rather than measurement (a causal relation; Reise and Waller 2009). In that respect, psychopathology symptoms are not symptoms in the strict sense of the word. Instead of passive receptors of the causal influence of a medical condition, symptoms are causally active ingredients of the mental disorders themselves.[14]

The reason why there is a grouping of similar 'symptoms' is not, therefore, because they are all manifestations of the same underlying pathology, but because they causally influence one another.[15] Accordingly,

12 Bolton, *What Is Mental Disorder?*, 74.

13 D. Borsboom and A. O. J. Cramer, 'Network Analysis: An Integrative Approach to the Structure of Psychopathology' (2013) 9(1) *Annual Review of Clinical Psychology* 91–121, 93.

14 Ibid, 96.

15 To use a very clear example, the fact that depressed appetite and weight loss often present together in those suffering from major depressive disorder is not because the disorder

treatment must seek to target the symptoms, or the relations between symptoms, rather than some amorphous underlying 'disorder'. This is not to suggest that there cannot be a role – for example, for genetics – in the development of disorders. Genetic differences may predispose certain people to develop disorders; however, 'persistent symptomatology (e.g., insomnia or loss of appetite) may cause differential gene expression just as well'.[16]

These developments enable us to understand the causal origins of different patterns of behaviour or 'symptoms'. Yet while medical and neuroscientific advances can help to establish what may cause us to act or think in certain ways, it does not tell us whether those behaviours amount to 'disorder' – that is, whether that behaviour is adaptive or maladaptive, functional or dysfunctional. It is over *that* question that debate has arisen, between those who argue that whether behaviour is 'disordered' must be judged relative to some conception of social norms of behaviour within our environment; and those that claim there is a scientific, factual, and value-free way of identifying dysfunctional behaviour which is irrespective of social norms.

This debate came to a head in the 1960s, with the rise of sociological critiques of mental disorder which challenged the entire discipline of psychiatry. Sometimes referred to as the 'anti-psychiatry movement', writers such as Thomas Szasz, Ronald David Laing, and Michel Foucault questioned the very basis of mental disorder, regarding it as little more than an evaluatory label attached to 'socially deviant' behaviours, in order to justify the use of coercive powers.[17] While criticisms varied between commentators, broadly such critiques shared the idea that 'disorders' were defined ultimately by reference to social values or norms, and not any natural fact. Mental disorder was not, in other words, rightly described as a 'disorder' at all, and certainly should not be pathologised in the way that physical ailments were. Rather the term simply denoted that the person had deviated from social or cultural norms and, as such, was mere social construction. Szasz, for example, regarded difficulties attaching to people's thoughts, feelings, behaviours,

causes them but because a depressed appetite results in the person eating less and thus losing weight.

[16] Borsboom and Cramer, 'Network Analysis', 91–121, 117.

[17] See, for example, M. Foucault, *Madness and Civilization: A History of Insanity in the Age of Reason* (*Folie et Déraison: Histoire de la folie à l'âge classique*), Richard Howard, trans. (New York: Vintage, 1965).

and relationships not as *pathological* but as moral issues, or 'problems with living'.[18] To apply the medical model to them was not only misconceived (as he did not regard the lesion concept of physical disorders applicable to mental disorders) but an overreach by the medical establishment.[19]

These criticisms have remained influential. Even for those who support the notion of psychiatric disorder, they continue to cast an important light on the extent to which the classification of mental disorders is merely an expression of culturally contingent social values or norms. This has resulted in broader support for the notion that disorder is fundamentally a value- rather than a fact-based concept. One of the clearest advocates of this view is Peter Sedgwick, who has argued that all mental illness 'is essentially deviancy [from] some alternative state of affairs which is considered more desirable', with 'the attribution of illness always proceed[ing] from the computation of a gap between presented behaviour (or feeling) and some social norm'.[20] If this is true, and the characterisation of behaviour as a mental disorder reflects scarcely more than the fact it deviates from socially accepted norms, then there would seem little basis on which we could justify intervening in decisions based on so-called disordered values. After all, committing to abnormal, even socially reprehensible, values does not in itself denote that a person's capacity for autonomous decision-making is undermined. If we wish to explain and justify our current approach to disorder therefore (indeed the whole approach of the Mental Capacity Act and the Mental Health Act), either we must reject the view that it is pure construction, through establishing some factual basis or 'core' to disorder, or we must seek to justify why it is still legitimate to intervene in the case of mental disorders, even if we recognise that the characterisation of behaviours or

[18] T. Szasz, *The Myth of Mental Illness* (London: Paladin, 1972).

[19] T. Szasz, *The Medicalization of Everyday Life* (New York: Syracuse University Press, 2007). He invoked the metaphor of a TV to illustrate his point: if we are unhappy with the quality of a TV programme we are watching, we cannot address this by adjusting the wiring of the TV set or summoning a TV engineer to fix it; rather, one must address things *outside* of the TV set itself (the scriptwriting, direction, casting, or production value of the programme), which involves very different considerations and discourses to that of engineering. In a similar vein, we cannot hope to treat or cure psychological difficulties with living by interfering with the body of the person suffering from them, nor should we use the language of medical pathology to frame problems inherent in psychiatry, which will lead only to confusion and oppression.

[20] P. Sedgwick, *Psycho Politics* (New York: Harper & Row, 1982), 32–34. See other examples of advocates of this view in Wakefield, 'The Concept of Mental Disorder', 373–388, 376.

values as disordered rests fundamentally on social and cultural norms, making disorder inherently contingent on the social, political, religious, and cultural context.

3.1.1 A Factual Component to Disorders?

It was in response to sociological critiques of psychiatry that a number of writers sought to establish some 'natural fact' underlying the conceptualisation of disorder, which could distinguish disorders from non-disorders in some objective fashion. This has primarily taken two forms: that disorder represents a biological statistical abnormality and that it entails a harmful evolutionary dysfunction. The key proponent of the first of these has been Christopher Boorse, who analysed diseases (including mental disorder) as 'internal states that depress a functional ability below species-typical levels (relative to age and sex)'.[21] His aim in doing so was to show that disorder could be conceptualised in an entirely value-free way. He defined health as the complete absence of pathological phenomena at every level of physiological function. Any part-dysfunction or pathology was thus evidence of ill health, and so part-dysfunction (defined in biostatistical terms) was both necessary and sufficient for disorder to be present.

Boorse's biostatistical theory has generated much criticism, both by those questioning whether this is a truly value-free definition[22] and by those pointing out that by treating part-dysfunction as sufficient in itself, this definition risks being over-inclusive. While we can establish the statistical distribution of certain traits (and this is a matter of fact), there must be a point along the bell curve of continuous distribution that we decide represents 'sub-normal' or atypical function (as opposed to the extreme end of 'normal' function) and where this point will be a matter of judgement, not fact. Moreover, as Lennie Nordernfelt has argued, the effect of Boorse's definition is that it would include within the term 'disorder' countless dysfunctions which are both trivial and harmless. Nordernfelt gives the example of a single dead cell. If the biostatistical

[21] C. Boorse, 'A Rebuttal on Health' in J. M. Humber and R. F. Almeder (eds), *What Is Disease?* (Totowa, NJ: Humana Press, 1997), 1–134.

[22] See, for example, K. W. M. Fulford, '"What Is (Mental) Disease?": An Open Letter to Christopher Boorse' (2001) 27 *Journal of Medical Ethics* 80–85; Bolton, *What Is Mental Disorder?*, 114. For example, value-laden judgements may permeate the assessment of how we define 'function', what level of function is typical for one's species, and the selection of the reference class against which this ought to be assessed.

theory classifies any part-dysfunction as a disorder, then it follows that any single dead cell renders someone disordered, even if it has no effect on one's overall functioning.[23] Or, to use another example put forward by Wakefield, a malfunctioning tail in a sperm cell that limited motility would, on this understanding, count as a reproductive disorder, even though this is a frequent occurrence which generally occurs at a level that has no effect on the person's overall reproductive potential. To classify such conditions as 'disorders' would, as Wakefield argues, seem highly counterintuitive, not least because the effect would be to render everyone disordered, making it impossible to distinguish disorder from non-disorder in any meaningful (that is, clinically useful) way.[24]

It was partly in response to concerns about the over-inclusivity of Boorse's definition that Wakefield put forward his highly influential 'hybrid' account of mental disorder. This recognised that values played some role in the determination that something was a disorder, but also that there was a factual component to disorders, which distinguished them from the 'myriad of other disvalued conditions'.[25] In other words, it sought to conceptualise disorder in a way which reconciled criticisms of the social-construction approach discussed previously (which could not explain why very many conditions that we recognise societally as undesirable are not classified as disorders), with those of the biostatistical approach (that any dysfunction, however minimal, resulted in disorder). According to his conception, disorder exists 'when the failure of a person's internal mechanisms to perform their functions as designed by nature impinges harmfully on the person's well-being as defined by social values and meanings'.[26] Internal functions encompassed both physical structures and organs, and mental structures and dispositions (e.g., motivations, and cognitive, affective, and perceptual mechanisms). Dysfunction is thus a necessary but not sufficient condition of disorder.

A person's 'natural functions' were defined in evolutionary terms and could be ascertained through looking at what effect a mechanism had, how that effect explained the existence and structure of the mechanism, and how, in turn, it contributed to evolutionary success. For example, the

[23] L. Nordernfelt, *On the Nature of Health: An Action-Theoretic Approach* (Dordrecht, The Netherlands: D. Reidel, 1987), 28.

[24] J. Wakefield, 'The Biostatistical Theory versus the Harmful Dysfunction Analysis, Part 1: Is Part-Dysfunction a Sufficient Condition for Medical Disorder?' (2014) 39 *Journal of Medicine and Philosophy* 648–682.

[25] Wakefield, 'The Concept of Mental Disorder', 373–388, 381.

[26] Ibid, 373.

fact that the heart pumps blood around the body, and that without blood being pumped around the body, the person cannot live (which is obviously a prerequisite for reproduction), indicates that a key natural function of the heart is to pump blood around the body. This also explains the structure of the heart, which was (in evolutionary terms) designed to perform that role. If, therefore, a person is born with a heart that is structured differently and so is unable to pump blood around the body, this would indicate a failure to perform its natural function. While this may seem more easily applicable to physical rather than psychological mechanisms, Wakefield gives the examples of perception and cognition:

> A natural function of the perceptual apparatus is to convey roughly accurate information about the immediate environment, and that is why gross hallucinations indicate dysfunctions. Some cognitive mechanisms have the function of providing a person with the capacity for a degree of rationality as expressed in deductive, inductive, and means-end reasoning (I am referring not to ideal rationality as represented by theoretical models, but to simply the degree of rationality that people manifest in everyday inferences), and that is why it is a dysfunction when the capacity for such reasoning breaks down, as in severe psychotic states.[27]

Dysfunction, then, according to Wakefield, can be defined in exclusively factual or scientific terms and does not depend on value judgements or social norms.

This does not mean judgements about dysfunction are unambiguous. Wakefield recognised that we currently lack the ability to identify dysfunction with certainty, and in 1992, he likened our level of understanding about dysfunctions within mental mechanisms to 'ancient physicians who had to rely on similar inferences in judging physical disorder'.[28] He hoped, however, that 'as we learn more about the naturally selected functions of mental mechanisms, our judgements about dysfunction will become correspondingly more confident'.[29]

For something to be a disorder, it must therefore entail some mental or behavioural mechanism 'not functioning as designed, selected for, in evolution'.[30] Not all dysfunctions are, however, disorders. As Wakefield acknowledges, there are a number of ways in which a mechanism or

[27] Ibid, 382.

[28] Ibid, 383.

[29] Ibid.

[30] D. Bolton, 'Conceptualisation of Mental Disorder and Its Personal Meanings' (2010) 19 (4) *Journal of Mental Health* 328–336.

organ may function abnormally, or indeed fail to function, which we do not consider to be disorder. He gives a number of examples of harmless abnormalities or anatomical variations (the heart being positioned on the right-hand side of the body, albinism and fused toes) which he would not consider disorders. Similarly, if one donates a kidney, there will certainly be a dysfunction, but it does not necessarily have an overall effect on the person's well-being or long-term health. Rather, to be a disorder, 'the dysfunction must also cause significant harm to the person under present environmental circumstances and according to present cultural standards'.[31] Consequently, Wakefield makes clear:

> A condition is a mental disorder if and only if (a) the condition causes some harm or deprivation of benefit to the person as judged by the standards of the person's culture (the value criterion), and (b) the condition results from the inability of some mental mechanism to perform its natural function, wherein a natural function is an effect that is part of the evolutionary explanation of the existence and structure of the mental mechanism (the explanatory criterion).[32]

As Derek Bolton explains,

> According to this approach, negative social evaluation is necessary for a condition to be a disorder. This has the consequence that conditions can change from being (considered as) disorders to being (considered as) normal, and vice versa, depending on the prevailing social norms. In this sense, its inclusion in the definition is consistent with the social constructionist anti-psychiatry critiques of the 1960s. On the other hand, Wakefield emphasizes that his approach puts a definite limitation on what legitimately counts as a mental disorder, namely that it has to involve, as a necessary condition, a failure of a natural psychological/behavioural function.[33]

His concept of disorder is therefore able to explain changing attitudes to mental illness (including, for example, the removal of homosexuality from the diagnostic manuals in the seventies), while retaining some factual basis on which to distinguish disordered from non-disordered behaviour. As Boorse explains, the latter is necessary to 'block the subversion of medicine by political rhetoric or normative eccentricity'[34]:

[31] Ibid, 383–384.
[32] Ibid, 385.
[33] D. Bolton, 'What Is Mental Disorder?' (2009) 8(12) *Psychiatry* 468–470, 469.
[34] Boorse, 'A Rebuttal on Health', 1–134, 100.

> As soon as biological dysfunction is required for disorder, virtually all the BST's benefits accrue [to the harmful dysfunction analysis] in clarifying professional and social controversies and preventing political abuse of medical vocabulary.[35]

Yet notwithstanding these clear advantages, fundamental criticisms of this approach remain. While it is not necessary to explore all such criticisms here, it is important to consider those which relate to the validity of the 'factual' component of disorder identified by Wakefield. After all, if he is correct and the disorder entails a dysfunctional mental mechanism identifiable without recourse to social norms, then this would prima facie seem to be a clear basis on which to intervene in decisions that stem from that dysfunctional process and which cause harm to the individual. If, however, he is unsuccessful in establishing that disorder must entail some factual dimension that does not depend on social norms, then this casts doubt on whether there is a clearly definable and distinguishable category of mental disorder which warrants separate treatment.

3.1.2 Distinguishing the 'Natural' from the 'Social'

This section will focus on two criticisms of Wakefield's analysis. The first relates to the validity of his division between natural and social function and design. The second concerns the problems inherent in determining whether something constitutes a dysfunctional internal mechanism or not under his model of disorder. Collectively, these demonstrate that while defining disorder as a harmful psychological dysfunction has much appeal, it will generally not be possible to identify a dysfunctional psychological process purely in evolutionary terms, as Wakefield suggests, with some recourse to social or cultural norms.

Wakefield's analysis rests on the idea that a person suffers from a disorder where a mental mechanism does not function as it ought, naturally, to do, determined through evolutionary design. But while it is clear to see how 'natural function' can be ascertained in the evolutionary design of most physical mechanisms, it is far harder to do so when considering mental or psychological faculties. As Bolton explains, this is because we now know that psychological characteristics are almost always influenced by evolutionary design (i.e., genetics), by social design (i.e., the influence of education, training, and socialisation), and by

[35] Ibid.

individual differences. It is impossible to neatly separate out these different influences,[36] not least because the evolution of humans has taken place primarily in social groups, and many evolved functions are social in nature – for example, attachment, empathy, concern for others, aggression. Consequently, the evolutionary design of a psychological trait or mechanism is inextricably linked to its 'social' design.

While evolution may contribute to the development of certain traits at an abstract level, the concrete social expression of these is fundamentally shaped by cultural factors and social norms. For example, the anxiety response comprises an evolved mechanism and response pattern (perceive a threat, process this information, and decide on a fight-or-flight response), but the behavioural response to this is influenced by the values of one's social group, as well as by individual differences (it is readily apparent that individuals respond differently to perceived threats to their safety). So while we might reasonably think the anxiety system was not functioning if it failed to respond to the presence of a threat at all,

> determination of presence or absence of threat, of what is a reasonable threshold for anxiety, of when fear should be overcome, not acted upon, because of other priorities – all these matters are not settled by natural, genetic, evolved factors alone, since they are highly sensitive to cultural and personal norms and values.[37]

There will, of course, be some extreme instances in which there is universal agreement about how one ought, evolutionarily, to respond. A person's anxiety system is probably not working from an evolutionary perspective if they do not react when approached by an untamed sabre-toothed tiger, for example. But most cases will not be so clear cut, and so whether or not an evolutionary psychological mechanism is 'working' as it was designed to do will often depend in large part on whether the person's behaviour is a socially appropriate response: *should* that person have regarded something as a threat, for example, and was that person's response broadly proportionate to the nature of the threat posed? Kirmayer makes a similar point in respect of systems designed for attachment to others:

> When are these too strong, too weak, or inappropriately directed? Clearly the normal functioning of these more complex systems cannot be defined

[36] Bolton, 'Conceptualisation of Mental Disorder and Its Personal Meanings', 328–336, 329–330.

[37] Bolton, 'What Is Mental Disorder?, 153.

> without reference to a specific social environment with its attendant cultural values.[38]

A good example, used by Bolton, is conversing with spirits. While this *may* be a failure of an evolutionary-designed cognitive-sensory mechanism, depending on the culture (or subculture) in which the person inhabits, it may be normal, socially sanctioned behaviour. The cultural and social context is therefore highly relevant to the determination of whether the person's psychological mechanisms are dysfunctional, with social and cultural norms putting the 'flesh' on the bones of evolutionary design. Yet if we cannot separate out whether a psychological mechanism appears to be dysfunctional by evolutionary standards (at least in anything but the most extreme cases), from whether it is dysfunctional by some 'social' standard, then we cannot say confidently that there is any 'natural fact' to dysfunction (and so to mental disorder), discernible irrespective of social and cultural norms. Social norms thus permeate the determination of dysfunction, as well as the question of whether the dysfunction causes harm to the individual.

Moreover, the adoption of Wakefield's analysis turns mental disorder into a theoretical claim, which has limited practical utility. This is because it is often impossible to tell whether or not a particular mental or behavioural condition involves a failure of an evolutionarily designed 'mechanism', or a reasonable response to a problematic environment. As John Richters and Stephen Hinshaw explain:

> There are numerous ways in which evolutionarily intact mental and psychological processes, combined with striking discontinuities within and between evolutionary and contemporary social/cultural environments, may cause nondysfunction variants of many widely accepted major mental disorder.[39]

These are highlighted by both Richters and Hinshaw, and Leda Cosmides and John Tooby.[40] First, some behaviours or 'symptoms' may in fact be defensive or coping strategies in response to a psychological dysfunction. Bolton gives the example of an autistic child engaging in repetitive

[38] L. J. Kirmayer, 'Rejoinder to Professor Wakefield: Debate on "Is the Concept of Disorder Culturally Relative"', in S. A. Kirk and S. D. Einbinder (eds), *Controversial Issues in Mental Health* (Boston, MA and London: Allyn and Bacon, 1994), 17–20, 18–19.

[39] J. E. Richters and S. P. Hinshaw, 'The Abduction of Disorder in Psychiatry' (1999) 108(3) *Journal of Abnormal Psychology* 438–445, 438.

[40] L. Cosmides and J. Tooby, 'Toward an Evolutionary Taxonomy of Treatable Conditions' (1999) 108(3) *Journal of Abnormal Psychology* 453–464.

isolated play to avoid situations that require cooperative or pretend play, and of a person with schizophrenia experiencing delusions which function to reduce uncertainty associated with unpredictable sensory experience.[41] What appears to be a dysfunction may in fact be a means of mitigating the effects of another dysfunction. Indeed one common form of coping strategy is to sacrifice one function that matters less to the individual than another: what appears disorder may thus reflect some underlying order or hierarchy.

More importantly, what appears to be a dysfunction in an evolutionarily designed mechanism may in fact be a mismatch between the evolutionary design and the current environment. Our current environment has changed radically from that faced by humans for the vast majority of evolutionary history, who largely existed in hunter-gatherer societies, characterised, as Bolton observes, 'by small closely related nomadic groups, sparse population densities with relatively rare encounters with strangers, stable social ties, simple social hierarchies, cooperative ventures organised around basic physical survival needs, with heavy demands on physical endurance, agility and prowess'.[42] Needless to say, this is a world away from the society many people now live in today, raising the possibility that behaviour that was evolutionarily designed may fail to 'match up to' the current environment. One possible example could be those behaviours characteristic of attention deficit hyperactivity disorder (ADHD) (such as hyperactivity), or traits associated with sociopathic personality disorder (such as satisfying one's own needs without being held back by concern for others), both of which could potentially have been adaptive and advantageous in a different social environment, or one with different task demands.

The result is that many conditions we currently think of as mental disorders may not involve dysfunction in the evolutionary theoretic sense proposed by Wakefield at all. They may follow from a failure of evolution to 'catch up' with environmental changes, or from coping mechanisms, or they may in fact bring about evolutionary advantages, even if they may appear socially undesirable. If this is right, then conditions we currently classify as disorders in the psychiatric diagnostic manuals are, on Wakefield's analysis, non-disorders; or at the very least we cannot yet establish for sure whether they are 'true' disorders, and may not be able to for a very long time, if ever. In the meantime, the designation of

[41] Bolton, 'What Is Mental Disorder?', 78–79.
[42] Ibid, 80.

something as a disorder must rely on speculation about evolutionary theory rather than observable data, reducing it to little more than a hypothesis about how evolution *might* have affected psychological mechanisms and behavioural traits. Consequently, it is unable to provide any basis for reliable and consistent diagnosis, as is so clearly needed in clinical practice. Indeed even if this level of knowledge is achieved in the future, as Bolton explains, it is questionable whether it would be of much practical import:

> If we were to follow this tack we may eventually sort out what conditions or sub-types are "disorders" (in the sense required by Wakefield's evolutionary theoretic analysis) and which are not. The ones that are not – Wakefield concedes – may still be associated with harm and with risk of harm. They would therefore still be in need of treatment (in a general sense including watchful waiting). Indeed the harm or risk associated with the non-disorder variants may be as high as for the "genuine disorders" - we will not know this until the science has been done (it cannot be known from the armchair). We would have a manual of "mental disorders and related mental health problems" (somewhat like the relaxed full title of the ICD) in which the difference between the two is less important than the associated harm and risk and consequent need for clinical attention and research. The evolutionary theoretic definition would not have done much practical work, because actually what drives practice is harm and risk.[43]

That Wakefield's evolutionary approach cannot provide the wherewithal to demarcate mental disorder in concrete cases (even if it allows boundaries to be drawn in theory) is illustrated by his later work with Allan Horwitz on major depressive disorder.[44] In decrying the 'loss of sadness', which has been transformed in the diagnostic manuals into the depressive disorder, they set out three criteria for 'normal' sadness responses: that it emerges in response to specific environmental triggers – in particular, loss; that they are proportionate (broadly) in intensity of that loss; and that they end roughly when either the loss ends or coping strategies allow for adjustment to new circumstances.[45] Only where a person's response deviates from such 'normal responses', in their view, should a person be regarded as suffering from depressive disorder. The consequence is that the determination of depressive disorder hinges on a

[43] D. Bolton, 'The Usefulness of Wakefield's Definition for the Diagnostic Manuals' (2007) 6 (3) *World Psychiatry* 164–165, 164.

[44] A. Horwitz and J. Wakefield, *The Loss of Sadness: How Psychiatry Transformed Normal Sorrow into Depressive Disorder* (USA: Oxford University Press, 2007).

[45] Ibid, 16.

number of judgements (about the appropriateness of object of the loss, the intensity of their response, and the timeliness of their recovery), which will necessarily be informed by social and cultural values and approaches to loss, and by whether we can recognise meaning in apparently 'inappropriate' responses. It would seem, then, that when moved from the realm of theory to application to particular conditions, even Wakefield must acknowledge some role for social norms in determining whether there is a dysfunction. Bolton is right, therefore, in concluding:

> How can evolutionary naturalism demarcate between disorders and normality? In practice it seems the distinction is not drawn by means of complex evolutionary theoretic models related to brain/mind functioning, but on more available phenomena including apparent lack of appropriateness, purpose, rationality or meaning of mental states and associated behaviour. These are the kinds of criteria invoked in the psychiatric manuals, and like deviance from indeterminate population norms, they are apparently not matters of absolute fact but are flexible. These criteria are also subject to local norms and assumptions.[46]

It seems, then, that naturalist attempts to define psychological dysfunction in a way that does not require any recourse to social norms or value judgements fail. The consequences of this are twofold. First and most simply, the assessment of whether behaviour amounts to a dysfunction rests on social and personal norms as well as medical or scientific ones and, as such, is not 'objective' but is, in important respects, contingent on personal, social, or cultural norms. Secondly, this discussion has shown that the distinction between order and disorder is not categorical or absolute. The line between abnormal and normal traits or behaviours, influenced as they are by genetic, environmental, and personal factors, is not absolute: such traits exist on a bell curve, and the determination of when they constitute 'abnormal' functioning is a matter of judgement.

However, rejecting Wakefield's evolutionary analysis does not mean rejecting his conception of disorder – indeed the concept of disorder more generally – in its entirety. As Section 3.1.3 will make clear, to do so would be to 'throw the baby out with the bathwater', introducing conceptual clarity into this complex area only at the expense of a failure to protect people who are clearly acting in ways which cause them to suffer great distress or impairment and over which they lack an important sense of agency. Mental disorder may not be a value-free scientific term but is

[46] Bolton, *What Is Mental Disorder?*, 161.

nonetheless a medically and socially important one, which cannot and should not be abandoned.

3.1.3 Disorder and Social Norms

Section 3.1.2 highlighted the way in which judgements about disorder inevitably depend to some extent on implicit standards of 'normal' or 'adaptive' behaviour within a given context. For the purposes of conceptual coherence, the easiest course of action may therefore seem to be to reject the notion of disorder, or at least the idea that 'disordered' valuing provides a justification for the kinds of paternalistic intervention currently employed. After all, if a person suffering from a psychological dysfunction is judged relative to standards of 'normal' behaviour within their social and cultural context, there is a risk that disorder amounts to little more than a label to denote socially abnormal behaviour. To prevent people from acting in accordance with disordered beliefs or values would then seem difficult to reconcile with the fundamental tenet of liberal democracies that people should be free to decide as they wish, regardless of whether their reasons are unusual, ill advised, or even morally reprehensible, as long as they do not harm others.

However, the fact that we cannot identify psychological dysfunction in a value-free way and so the boundary between disordered and non-disordered states may be blurred, even porous at times, does not mean that attempts to define and distinguish disorder is fruitless, or that there is no good reason to intervene in decisions that derive from states we regard as disordered. When considering how to conceptualise and respond to mental disorder, we cannot do so in a theoretical vacuum. While it may well be desirable to define mental disorders by reference to natural facts, and for them to be clearly distinguishable from non-disordered states, the reality is vastly more complex. We must acknowledge and engage with the messy realities of this area of clinical practice, accepting that in doing so, theoretical purity may become diluted. As Bolton rightly argues,

> the problem of boundaries – of what conditions should and should not be in the psychiatric manuals, of where the threshold for diagnosis and treatment of various kinds should be – is real and cannot be conceptually analysed away.[47]

[47] Ibid, 224.

Despite inevitable problems at the boundaries, it is readily observable that people act, think, or feel in certain ways over which they often experience a lack of control or agency; that these symptoms or behaviours often cluster in predictable ways; and that they collectively cause them to suffer great distress or impairment in everyday living. Acknowledging a role for social norms in the determination of dysfunction does not therefore reduce mental disorder to simply a question of whether or not people behave or think normally or abnormally – after all, people often act in socially abnormal or deviant ways which we do not consider to be disordered. Rather, as Wakefield observed, there are two key features of disorder which help to differentiate it from non-disordered behaviour and which together may justify some degree of paternalism.

First, it is not simply that the person's behaviours or beliefs differ from – or fall below – some implicit standard of what is 'normal', judged relative to the individual or society's behaviour; rather, this abnormal functioning *must* be thought to stem from an abnormality of the mind or psychological dysfunction, whether that is brought about by genetic differences, a physiological dysfunction (such as neurostructural or neurochemical abnormalities), the person's past or present environment, or (most likely) some combination or interaction between these. Wakefield is thus right to suppose that disorder entails a person's psychological mechanism not functioning 'as it ought to', even if this cannot be reduced to its evolutionary design but encompasses social design and individual differences too. Establishing this will not always be easy. However, it may be indicated by behaviour which appears to be outside of the control of the individual (they lack a feeling of agency in respect of it), unintentional, irrational, or (when seen in context) lacking in meaning. It is this 'apparent lack of appropriateness, purpose, rationality or meaning of mental states and associated behaviour'[48] that distinguishes disorder from other socially deviant behaviour, which may be deliberate or chosen, exhibited only in particular contexts, or for which comprehensible reasons or insight (which do not in themselves reflect a dysfunction) can be provided.

Secondly, to be characterised as a disorder, this deviation from normal functioning must cause harm to the individual in the sense that it causes them to suffer distress or renders them disabled or impaired in aspects of ordinary life, such as being unable to maintain relationships with people

[48] Bolton, *What Is Mental Disorder?*, 161.

or to hold down a job. Mere psychological differences in function do not constitute disorder unless they impair the person in some way or cause them to suffer. This too reflects Wakefield's conceptualisation, as well as the approach of the diagnostic manuals, which focus not on unearthing the nature of the underlying psychological dysfunction, but on its presentation or manifestation in the person's life: the distress or disability that the person experiences as a consequence of that dysfunction. According to the DSM-V, for example, a mental disorder is a syndrome characterised by

> clinically significant disturbance in an individual's cognition, emotion regulation, or behaviour that reflects a dysfunction in the psychological, biological, or developmental processes underlying mental functioning. Mental disorders are usually associated with significant distress or disability in social, occupational, or other important activities. An expectable or culturally approved response to a common stressor or loss, such as the death of a loved one, is not a mental disorder. Socially deviant behavior (e.g., political, religious, or sexual) and conflicts that are primarily between the individual and society are not mental disorders unless the deviance or conflict results from a dysfunction in the individual.[49]

The ICD-10, meanwhile, recognises that mental disorder is not an exact term but is generally used to imply 'a clinically recognisable set of symptoms or behaviours associated in most cases with distress and with interference with personal functions'.[50]

Of course, these are not entirely objective metrics which provide for a hard-and-fast boundary between order and disorder. Determining whether behaviour derives from a psychological dysfunction or abnormality of the mind will inevitably depend on societal and cultural views about appropriate or meaningful responses to events or stimuli, as seen in the example of distinguishing normal sadness or grief from depression mentioned earlier. Nor are the concepts it relies upon (distress and disability) absolute: the extent to which someone experiences distress or disability as a consequence of differential functioning will clearly depend on their social, cultural, and economic context (including task demands) and on individual differences.

[49] American Psychiatric Association. (2013). *Diagnostic and Statistical Manual of Mental Disorders*, 5th ed. (Arlington, VA: American Psychiatric Publishing), 20.

[50] World Health Organization. *The ICD-10 Classification of Mental and Behavioural Disorders: Clinical Descriptions and Diagnostic Guidelines.* (Geneva: World Health Organization, 1992).

The consequences of accepting this understanding of disorder are twofold. At a conceptual level, when one recognises that social and cultural norms inevitably play a part in the determination of dysfunction, it follows that our understanding of mental disorder may be subject to change. It seems inconceivable to modern ears that slaves escaping from their masters was previously conceived of as a disorder (drapetomania), while much of the debate around the conceptualisation of mental disorder was prompted by disagreement over the appropriateness of the inclusion of homosexuality within diagnostic manuals for disorder. It was not until 1973 that the American Psychiatric Association chose to declassify homosexuality as a mental illness in the DSM. Even after this, it was replaced first with 'sexual orientation disturbance' (where an individual with same-sex attractions found them distressing and wanted to change) and later 'ego dystonic homosexuality', before it was removed entirely in 1987.[51] Transgenderism is following a similar trajectory, having originally been included as 'transexualism' in the DSM-III in 1980, before being renamed 'gender identity disorder' and later (in 2013) 'gender dysphoria', which no longer focuses on the person's gender identity but on the distress that transgender people may experience.[52] This distress is inevitably influenced to some extent by social attitudes to transgenderism: in the future, then, transgenderism could disappear altogether from psychiatry. Mental disorder is thus partly relative, and we should expect conceptions of disorder to change, occasioned by changing social and cultural norms of behaviour.

At a practical (or individual) level, this also means that different people may manifest the same or similar behaviour or beliefs, yet while for some this might be demonstrative of disorder (because it is caused by some dysfunctional process and results in distress or impairment), for others this will not be the case. There are many instances in which similar belief systems may be held by people both with and without a disorder. In *King's College Hospital NHS Foundation Trust v. C & V*,[53] for example, the evidence was 'equivocal' as to whether C's highly egocentric and impulsive decision-making was the product of a histrionic or narcissistic personality or simply a strong-willed and difficult personality.[54] This is

[51] J. Drescher, 'Out of DSM: Depathologizing Homosexuality' (2015) 5(4) *Behav Sci* (*Basel*) 565–575.

[52] American Psychiatric Association, *Diagnostic and Statistical Manual of Mental Disorders*.

[53] *C & V* [2015] EWCOP 80.

[54] Ibid, [44] and [94].

also very clearly the case in the context of delusional beliefs, especially where they involve religious or metaphysical beliefs. After all, many people profess to have had religious experiences, and it is far from uncommon for people to refuse medical treatment on the grounds of their religion.[55] For example, the Followers of Christ (a Pentecostal faith healing sect operating in the US) reject all medical interventions, as do some fundamentalist Mormons and Christian scientists. What appears to be the same value or belief might therefore be held differently by different people, with different levels of conviction or for different reasons – some disordered, others not.

Consequently, the determination that socially abnormal behaviour amounts to a disorder depends heavily on clinical judgement. Sometimes these clinical judgements will relate to the *source* of the belief and whether it is thought to stem from a psychological dysfunction. When confronted in the interviews with a vignette of Max (a schizophrenic who believed that his bladder stone was God's punishment for the sins he had committed throughout his life[56]), for example, many doctors were clear that the challenge lay in attempting to determine whether his beliefs were merely unusual religious beliefs or a reflection of psychosis[57] – a problem identified as a more general challenge for liaison psychiatrists in Kane *et al.*'s study discussed previously.[58] In other cases, judgement may also be required to determine whether the *intensity* of a belief is indicative of disorder. For example, while there is a clear conceptual difference between a person who is insecure about their weight who goes on a diet, and a person suffering from anorexia nervosa,

[55] For the similarities between spiritual experiences and psychosis, see M. Jackson and K. W. M. Fulford, 'Spiritual Experience and Psychopathology' (1997) 4(1) *Philosophy, Psychiatry & Psychology* 41–65.

[56] The vignette read: 'Max suffers from schizophrenia, and experiences persecutory delusions. He has a kidney stone, which is causing him some abdominal pain, and he requires an operation to remove it. He understands the medical evidence in favour of having the operation, and the consequences of not having it, because he believes the pain is God's punishment for the sins he has committed during his life. He thinks doctors should not interfere with the actions of God, and that it is only God that will decide his fate. As a devout Christian throughout his life, he believes God will not let him die.'

[57] One doctor suggested that a 'huge focus of the assessment' would be 'the boundary around his Christian beliefs and his psychosis' (Jo, p. 10). Another suggested that 'you'd have to explore whether you felt this view about God was a part of his psychotic illness at the moment, or whether that is consistent with his previous belief system' (David, p. 18); while another questioned 'whether or not as a devout Christian, his beliefs were actually a reflection of his persecutory delusions' (Niamh, p. 20).

[58] Kane *et al.*, 'Difficult Capacity Cases', 946234.

these positions sit on a spectrum, and there will inevitably be a grey area somewhere in-between. According to the DSM-5, the diagnostic criteria for anorexia nervosa are as follows:

(a) Refusal to maintain body weight at or above a minimally normal weight for age and height.
(b) Intense fear of gaining weight or becoming fat, even though underweight.
(c) Disturbance in the way in which one's body weight or shape is experienced, undue influence of body weight or shape on self-evaluation, or denial of the seriousness of the current low body weight.
(d) In postmenarcheal females, amenorrhoea, i.e., the absence of at least three consecutive menstrual cycles.

While the criteria in (a) and (d) might be objective, both (b) and (c) clearly introduce a large degree of subjectivity into the assessment, relying on an assessment of the 'intensity' of the person's fear of gaining weight and the 'undue influence' this has over their self-evaluation. Many people have a distorted view of their own bodies, and it is not uncommon for this to affect the person's self-evaluation. Determining whether or not a person has anorexia is not therefore a simple 'yes' or 'no' answer; rather the psychiatrist must make a judgement about whether or not the person's symptoms are *sufficiently* extreme as to render the person's thinking and values disordered.

Fabian Freyenhagen and Tom O'Shea make a similar point in respect of the ICD-10 criteria for anankastic personality disorder, which includes 'feelings of *excessive* doubt and caution', '*undue* preoccupation with productivity to the exclusion of pleasure and interpersonal relationships', and '*unreasonable* reluctance to allow others to do things'.[59] As they explain:

> Judging what is excessive, undue or unreasonable presupposes evaluative standards, yet it is characteristic of 'ego-syntonic' conditions, such as anankastic personality disorder, that persons diagnosed do not consider their feelings or behaviour to be awry ... Thus, the diagnostic criteria presumably refer to what the majority of psychiatric professionals, or

[59] ICD-10: International Statistical Classification of Diseases and Related Health Problems (tenth revision, 2nd ed, 2003), F60.5.

> people in general, would take to be excessive, undue or unreasonable (or perhaps to an objective standard for such normative judgements).[60]

In addition to assessing the source and intensity of the person's beliefs, psychiatrists must also consider the extent to which these disrupt or interfere with their ordinary functioning. In the DSM-5, for example, the disturbance in the individual's 'cognition, emotion regulation, or behaviour' must be 'clinically significant' for something to be characterised as a mental disorder.[61] However, when something will amount to being 'clinically significant' is not specified, and immediately after this paragraph, the DSM-5 acknowledges that 'in the absence of clear biological markers or clinically useful measurements of severity for many mental disorders, it has not been possible to completely separate normal and pathological symptom expressions contained in diagnostic criteria'.[62] As Devin Singh and Walter Sinnott-Armstrong point out, this would seem to be an acknowledgment that

> the phrase "clinically significant" is underspecified, and its application relies heavily on the judgement of the mental health provider. There is no specific set of objective, quantifiable measurements offered in DSM-5 that a doctor is supposed to use in making these decisions.[63]

Hard cases will therefore arise in which determining whether or not the person's beliefs or values can be said to be 'disordered' will be difficult. Faced with this uncertainty, the assessor must make a judgement, and there is a risk that in doing so, those beliefs that do not reflect established religions or accepted belief systems may be more likely to be regarded as disordered. This is aptly illustrated when one compares the outcome in *Nottingham Healthcare NHS Trust v. RC*[64] with that of *Mrs T*, both of which involved the refusal of a blood transfusion. While RC's decision, resting on a belief that accepting blood products would result in eternal damnation, was not evidence of a failure to use or weigh information, Mrs T's belief that blood was evil was disordered and thus unworthy of

60 F. Freyenhagen and T. O'Shea, 'Hidden Substance: Mental Disorder as a Challenge to Normatively Neutral Accounts of Autonomy' (2013) 9(1) *International Journal of Law in Context* 53–70, 58.

61 American Psychiatric Association. *Diagnostic and Statistical Manual of Mental Disorders*, 20.

62 Ibid, 21.

63 D. Singh and W. Sinnott-Armstrong, 'The DSM-5 Definition of Mental Disorder' (2015) 29(1) *Public Affairs Quarterly* 5–31, 12.

64 [2014] EWCOP 1317.

respect. Given that both claims are, at base, metaphysical in nature (and thus not susceptible to proof), it is difficult to deny that this position – which, as John Coggon succinctly sums up, means 'we can disregard the belief that blood is evil, but can only treat with suspicion the belief that receiving the blood of another prevents our chance of salvation'[65] – entails some value claims being made by the capacity assessor about the validity of the person's underlying beliefs and the extent to which they demand respect.

In this vein, Shimon Waldfogel and Stacey Meadows have argued that 'the determination by a psychiatrist that particular supernatural and religious beliefs are delusional may be more a matter of cultural conflict than dispassionate scientific examination'.[66] Since religious beliefs are based on faith and not on empirical evidence, they may well be treated with 'skepticism by scientifically oriented physicians who question the validity of patient decision-making based on such religious concepts'.[67] This may be especially so where 'his beliefs seem extreme to the physician, or are not part of a mainstream religious denomination with which the physician is familiar'.[68] Religious beliefs are also 'intensely personal' and may not fall within an accepted religious creed, making it extremely hard to distinguish between 'irrational thoughts that reflect diminished capacity, and those that reflect merely a different cultural or religious orientation'.[69] There is a risk, therefore, that clinical judgements about disorder will favour those who hold values or beliefs which are 'understandable' or 'acceptable' to the assessor or society more generally (such as established religious beliefs) at the expense of those who hold more unusual value or belief systems.

Yet for all its conceptual and practical slipperiness, there are – and will remain – huge numbers of people whose inability to function 'normally' causes them great distress and impairs their ability to participate fully in ordinary aspects of life. While rejecting mental disorder as an unruly category prone to abuse and paternalism – as the sociological critiques of the 1960s did – might have appeal from the perspective of conceptual coherence, it comes at a heavy cost: the failure to adequately help and

[65] Coggon, 'Varied and Principled Understandings of Autonomy in English Law, 235, 252.

[66] S. Waldfogel and S. Meadows, 'Religious Issues in the Capacity Evaluation' (1996) 18 *General Hospital Psychiatry* 173–182, 176.

[67] Ibid.

[68] Ibid.

[69] Ibid.

protect people in the face of extreme suffering, who may experience great harm as a result of decisions over which they lack meaningful agency. Too much concern about problems at the margins risks ignoring the real and readily observable phenomena, powerfully captured by Bolton, of

> unbearable psychotic anxiety, hallucinatory and delusional persecution that lead people to kill themselves; or despair and depression of an individual worn down by trauma or chronic stressors; or the unmanageable distress of the child with autism trying to cope with change that is – for him – too much.[70]

It was on this basis that Bolton rejected sociological critiques of disorder, whose 'non-individualistic, social-systemic gaze' failed to recognise the unquestionable suffering of individuals.[71] In doing so, he shines light on a tension which lies at the heart of regulating this difficult area of law, between a medical approach focused on alleviating the suffering of particular individuals and a broader jurisprudential or sociopolitical lens, which seeks to ensure that encroachment into private life occurs only in certain carefully circumscribed occasions. While ensuring that the state does not overstep its legitimate authority is of the upmost importance, this must be balanced against an arguably greater evil: leaving people helpless and unsupported in the face of a grave illness which threatens their health, well-being, and sometimes even their lives.

The notion of mental disorder rests on shaky foundations, both conceptually and when applied in individual cases. However, the complexity and fragility that such judgements will inevitably entail does not mean we should refrain from making them – we simply do not have the luxury of pursuing this path if we wish to protect vulnerable people from deeply self-destructive behaviour over which they may lack control. Rather, this discussion highlights the importance of bringing such judgements out into the open so they may be subjected to proper scrutiny and challenge. This is essential for the individual involved – so that they may challenge a decision where they feel their autonomy is being wrongly frustrated – but it is also important for society more generally to reflect on whether the implicit social standards against which behaviour is being judged continue to be socially and culturally relevant and appropriate.

At present, these judgements (and the normative claims that underpin them) are being concealed within the nebulous determination that a

[70] Bolton, *What Is Mental Disorder?*, 90.
[71] Ibid.

person is unable to 'use or weigh' information, which insulates them from proper scrutiny. Assessors simply cannot explain how exactly a mental disorder affects the agent's decision-making, because such explanation must be shoehorned within the 'use and weigh' limb if the assessor is to have any power (under the MCA) to intervene in the decision. There is a risk that an approach like this which does not demand proper explanation may see the law tacitly return to a status-based (rather than decision-specific) approach to capacity, whereby the diagnosis of a mental disorder is alone sufficient to render the person incapacitated. It is imperative, therefore, that changes are introduced into the MCA (and other comparable legislation in other jurisdictions) to enhance the transparency surrounding such determinations so as to ensure that it is only those cases in which disorder truly impairs the person's capacity for autonomous decision-making that are captured by the test for capacity. These will be considered in Chapter 4.

Yet even if we accept that mental disorders entail harmful psychological dysfunctions that should, and (in many cases) can, be distinguished from simply socially abnormal behaviour, it does not follow from this that the fact that a person suffers from a disorder is justification enough for intervening in or overriding *any* decisions they wish to take. As Jennifer Hawkins and Louis Charland observe,

> even if the values driving decision-making are a product of mental illness, this does not by itself license the conclusion that these values are problematic. An additional link between the values in question and decision-making is needed and it is not yet clear whether one can be provided.[72]

Many people make decisions which are harmful to them, decisions which impair their quality of life, cause them distress, and even sometimes bring about an end to their lives. They may do so on the basis of holding certain beliefs or values – beliefs which cannot be said to be false but which are doubtless self-destructive, as in the case of the Jehovah's Witnesses' belief on blood transfusions. If we are to differentiate these decisions (which we do not interfere with) from those flowing from disordered values, we need to be able to show how (and why) acting on the basis of disordered values or beliefs negatively affects a person's capacity to take autonomous decisions. This will be examined in Section 3.2.

[72] J. Hawkins and L. Charland, 'Decision-Making Capacity' in *Stanford Encyclopedia of Philosophy* (Stanford, CA: Stanford University, 14 August 2020). Available at: https://stanford.library.sydney.edu.au/entries/decision-capacity/#ChalFourAbilModeValuAuth.

3.2 Disorder and Decision-Making

Where a disorder affects a person's *cognitive* capacities, its impact on decision-making is clear. Most would accept that at a basic minimum, the ability to decide autonomously requires some level of understanding of the nature and consequences of a decision and ability to weigh up this information, such that if a disorder prevented this, the person could not be said to have the capacity for autonomous decision-making. However, the position is more complex where the disorder is not merely affecting a person's cognition, but their affective attitudes and evaluative judgements, which then dictate how they attribute weight to different outcomes. In these cases, it is less obvious why acting on disordered values would undermine autonomy; why, in other words, does the fact that the beliefs or values that motivate a person's decisions originate in an illness make them any less worthy of respect?

Jennifer Hawkins attempts to answer this question, on the basis that at least some disorders demonstrably make people more likely to make prudential mistakes – that is, decisions which result in less welfare than if they had chosen otherwise.[73] While people make prudential mistakes all the time, there are certain disorders (or, to use her terminology, 'psychological conditions') which radically alter a person's evaluative outlook in predictable ways and which are known to make people worse at making judgements about what is good for them.[74]

It is certainly the case that people with certain types of disorders, such as eating disorders or depressive illnesses, routinely have their decision-making affected in similar ways *and* that many people who do recover from such mental disorders are later clear that they regret their earlier choices and are pleased that coercive powers were used to protect them from whatever harmful decisions they had wished to take.[75] This may therefore seem like good evidence to ground the claim that they are liable

[73] J. Hawkins, 'Decision-Making Capacity and Value', in Daniel D. Mosely and Gary Gala (eds), *Philosophy and Psychiatry: Problems, Intersections and New Perspectives*, (New York: Routledge, 2016), 204–213.

[74] Ibid.

[75] People suffering from anorexia nervosa are perhaps the clearest examples of this, whose evaluative outlook is frequently affected in such a way that they prioritise calorie intake over health, academic and professional success, and relationships, and who, when recovered, may profess to be pleased they were treated against their will (however traumatic) and offered the chance to recover. For a more in-depth discussion of this, see Hawkins, 'Why Even a Liberal Can Justify Limited Paternalistic Intervention in Anorexia Nervosa', 155–158.

to making prudential mistakes and that where there is strong evidence to suggest that they are indeed making one (based on evidence of previously expressed wishes, or discussions with their family about their non-disordered preferences), there is good reason to intervene. However, the fact that a person may make a prudential mistake, or may live to regret their choice, does not in itself suggest that a decision is non-autonomous: many people regret their decisions even when autonomously taken. Nor does it explain why their possible future wishes ought to be prioritised over their currently expressed ones. More explanatory work is therefore needed to show how acting on the basis of disordered values or beliefs might render that decision non-autonomous and thus justify the decision to prioritise the person's future well-being in these circumstances. This requires greater engagement with what it means for a decision to be autonomous.

3.2.1 Autonomy without Authenticity?

How and to what extent mental disorder impairs autonomous decision-making will necessarily depend on how one conceptualises autonomy and what characteristics or features are a necessary component of a decision being autonomous. Innumerable competing conceptions of autonomy have been advanced in both moral and political philosophy, which vary both in their substantive demands and in what capabilities they regard as being essential to the exercise of autonomy.[76] While it is impossible to do justice to every account of autonomy, John Coggon's taxonomy of the three main understandings of personal (as opposed to moral) autonomy provides a useful starting point from which to focus our discussion.[77] He divides accounts of autonomy into those advocating:

(1) Ideal desire autonomy – Leads to an action decided upon because it reflects what a person *should* want, measured by reference to some purportedly universal or objective standard of values.

[76] For a helpful discussion of this, see G. Dworkin, *The Theory and Practice of Autonomy* (New York: Cambridge University Press 1988), 6. Given the many ways in which autonomy can be understood, it is important to be clear at the outset that for the present discussion, we are concerned with autonomy only in the sense of a quality, trait, or characteristic that individuals can exhibit throughout their lives, not in a Kantian sense (which concerns the person's capacity to impose moral law on themselves), or as a source of political legitimacy.

[77] Coggon, 'Varied and Principled Understandings of Autonomy in English Law', 235, 240.

(2) Best desire autonomy – Leads to an action decided upon because it reflects a person's overall desire given his own values, even if this runs contrary to his immediate desire.
(3) Current desire autonomy – Leads to an action decided upon because it reflects a person's immediate inclinations, i.e. what he thinks he wants in a given moment without further reflection.[78]

It is not my intention to list the advantages and disadvantages of each of these types of accounts in depth here. Suffice to say, however, that within contemporary bioethics, there is little support for an 'ideal desire' account of autonomy, which has the effect of placing substantive conditions on autonomy, whereby a decision has to conform to certain norms or values for it to be autonomous – values which the person may not themselves endorse. As Jonathan Pugh notes in respect of substantive theories more generally, autonomy

> should allow for the possibility that agents can reach different views about value, and that part of being autonomous is choosing to act in accordance with one's own beliefs about value, even if those beliefs are not universally shared.[79]

An ideal desire account would deny agents that possibility, requiring conformity with certain (contestably good) values.

Current desire autonomy deserves similarly short shrift. If autonomy were to boil down to little more than what a person wants at any given moment in time – to the mere expression of a choice or even of 'instinct' – then one might wonder whether there is any value in respecting it. The importance of respecting autonomy, as Chapter 1 explained, lies in its relationship with the person's well-being. Allowing people to determine what is best for them given their unique character and convictions is instrumentally valuable in the sense that it enhances the prospect of them attaining ends that they regard as valuable, and as Pugh explains, it might also be valuable in itself to direct 'the course of one's life in accordance with one's own beliefs about what is of value'.[80] Neither is realised if the person is not able to make the evaluative judgements necessary to further those values or beliefs they hold dear. The relationship with the person's underlying values is thus what grounds the claim that respecting

[78] Ibid.
[79] Pugh, *Autonomy, Rationality, and Contemporary Bioethics*, 6.
[80] Ibid, 256.

autonomy has the capacity to enhance and promote individual well-being, and thus explains why these evaluative judgements 'speak' for us.

Accordingly, most understandings of autonomy (both liberal and 'relational')[81] rightly demand that the decision reflects the person's underlying values and beliefs in some way (i.e., they embrace a 'best desire' form of autonomy).[82] Most notable among such accounts are those of Harry Frankfurt[83] and Gerald Dworkin.[84] They introduced hierarchical models of autonomy in which autonomy demanded not just the freedom to make choices but also that the person is capable of making choices which reflect their values, beliefs, and priorities. As Gerald Dworkin wrote, autonomy is

> a second-order capacity of persons to reflect critically upon their first-order preferences, desires, wishes, and so forth and the capacity to accept or attempt to change these in light of higher-order preferences and values.[85]

Building on the work of Dworkin, Frankfurt similarly felt that to exercise autonomy, a person must reflect upon and evaluate their first-order desires, deciding which they wish to endorse or promote.[86] In exercising this capacity, Gerald Dworkin argues that people will 'define their nature, give meaning and coherence to their lives, and take responsibility for the kind of person they are'.[87] In a similar vein, Ronald Dworkin considers that autonomy, at least when understood in this more demanding sense, 'makes each of us responsible for shaping his own life according to some coherent and distinctive sense of character,

[81] Relational autonomy is, as Catriona Mackenzie and Natalie Stoljar explain, an 'umbrella term', used to describe all views of autonomy that share the assumption that 'persons are socially embedded and that agents' identities are formed within the context of social relationships and shaped by a complex of intersecting social determinants, such as race, class, gender, and ethnicity': Mackenzie and Stoljar, *Relational Autonomy: Feminist Essays on Autonomy, Agency and Social Self*, 2000, 4.

[82] It should be noted that on its face, the MCA appears to adopt the least demanding of these three understandings, in that the test focuses only on the person's decision-making and not whether the decision reflects underlying values or beliefs.

[83] H. Frankfurt, *Freedom of the Will and the Concept of a Person* (The Importance of What We Care about Edition, Cambridge: Cambridge University Press 1987).

[84] Dworkin, *The Theory and Practice of Autonomy*, 15–17.

[85] Ibid, 20.

[86] Frankfurt, *Freedom of the Will and the Concept of a Person.*

[87] G. Dworkin, 'The Nature of Autonomy' (2015) 2 *Nordic Journal of Studies in Educational Policy* 28479, 14.

conviction, and interest', which allows us to be what we have made ourselves.[88]

Autonomy thus understood contains two essential components: an 'authenticity' component and a 'competency' component. The 'authenticity' component of autonomy demands that to be acting autonomously, the individual must be guided by the values, desires, and characteristics that are 'authentic' to them in some way. As John Christman puts it, autonomy means

> to be one's own person, to be directed by considerations, desires, conditions and characteristics that are not simply imposed externally upon one, but are part of what can somehow be considered one's authentic self.[89]

Catriona Mackenzie and Wendy Rogers similarly suggest that to have autonomy, one must be 'able to determine one's *own* beliefs, values, goals and wants, and to make choices regarding matters of practical import to one's life free from undue influence'.[90] The opposite of self-determination is, in their view, where one's views or actions are determined either by other people or by external forces or constraints.[91] Other commentators have expressed this idea in similar terms: the autonomous nature of a decision depends on whether it reflects the agent's endorsed beliefs or desires,[92] their underlying and enduring commitments,[93] or how genuinely it expresses 'the self or individuality of the person', however this may be understood.[94]

But as Meyers notes, 'autonomous people are acquainted with their true selves, *and* they act in accordance with their true selves'.[95] Competency conditions, therefore, involve those capacities that are required in order to be able to live in accordance with one's authentic

88 Dworkin, 'Autonomy and the Demented Self', 4, 5.

89 J. Christman, 'Autonomy in Moral and Political Philosophy' in E. Zalta (ed), *The Stanford Encyclopedia of Philosophy* (Stanford, CA: Stanford University, Spring 2018 edition). Available at https://stanford.library.sydney.edu.au/archives/win2015/entries/autonomy-moral/.

90 C. MacKenzie and W. Rogers, 'Autonomy, Vulnerability and Capacity: A Philosophical Appraisal of the Mental Capacity Act' (2013) 9 *International Journal of Law in Context* 37, 43.

91 Ibid.

92 Jaworska, 'Respecting the Margins of Agency', 105–138.

93 Buchanan and Brock, *Deciding for Others*, 41.

94 O. O'Neill, *Autonomy and Trust in Bioethics* (Cambridge: Cambridge University Press; 2002), 34.

95 D. Meyers, *Self, Society, and Personal Choice* (New York: Columbia University Press 1989), 44.

values and beliefs. According to Christman, this involves the capacities for 'rational thought, self-control, and freedom from debilitating pathologies, systematic self-deception and so on'.[96] Jillian Craigie, terming it 'self-expression', observes that there has been much dispute over what attributes this entails,[97] and some accounts are certainly more demanding than others. Aspects discussed have included: 'reasoning that enables the coherent pursuit of current desires; reflection on and endorsement and rejection of desires; an ability to project oneself imaginatively into the future; planning and policy making; impulse control; and the ability to conceive of one's life as a whole'.[98]

Few, if any accounts of autonomy, thus equate autonomous decision-making with the mere expression of choice. Rather they demand something else – something more – for a decision to be said to be autonomous. They require that it is *authentic* to the individual in some way, reflecting values, beliefs, and priorities which are part of the person's character system (encapsulating those mental or moral qualities distinctive to an individual) or practical identity. The question, then, to be explored in Section 3.2.2 is what effect mental disorder has on the authenticity of a decision, and whether it undermines it in a way that renders a person incapable of deciding autonomously.

3.2.2 How Does Mental Disorder Affect the Authenticity of Decisions?

Notwithstanding this extensive philosophical support for autonomous decision-making demanding some notion of authenticity, what exactly it means for a value or belief to be 'authentic' is subject to debate. Widely divergent interpretations are evident in the philosophical and psychiatry literature, which each have different implications for whether or not the fact that a person's value or belief may be the product of a mental

96 Christman, 'Autonomy in Moral and Political Philosophy'.

97 J. Craigie, 'A Fine Balance: Reconsidering Patient Autonomy in Light of the UN Convention on the Rights of Persons with Disabilities' (2015) 29 *Bioethics* 398–405, 401.

98 Ibid. Meyers, for example, requires a person to have competencies in the skills of self-knowledge, communication, and deliberation (Meyers, *Self, Society, and Personal Choice*, 44), while Kim Atkins, drawing on Meyers's work, argues that the person must have 'a minimal understanding of how one's motives, values, beliefs, emotional dispositions, desires, and foibles can be related together and how they might influence one's choices and attitudes'(K. Atkins, 'Autonomy and Autonomy Competencies: A Practical and Relational Approach' (2006) 7 *Nursing Philosophy* 205, 211).

disorder renders it inauthentic. This is compounded by the different contexts in which authenticity has been invoked: while this discussion is concerned with authenticity as a quality of autonomous decision-making, it has also been drawn on in discussions about moral responsibility and in the context of self-development for people suffering from mental disorders.[99] With this, ideas about what is meant by a person's true or 'authentic' self, and of what it means to act authentically, have diverged.

Jesper Ahlin provides a useful, if somewhat simplistic, taxonomy for engaging with these different accounts of authenticity, dividing them into 'sanctionist theories', 'coherentist theories', and 'originist theories'.[100] According to sanctionist theories such as those of Dworkin and Frankfurt, discussed previously, authenticity requires the person to be able to reflect upon and endorse (or identify with) their own values, desires, and priorities. Different theorists have expressed this slightly differently: Frankfurt, for example, asked whether the person 'endorses reflectively' their desires,[101] while Gerald Dworkin thought the person must be able to question whether they identify with or reject their reasons for acting (albeit that he later dropped the requirement of identification).[102] As Paul Benson has succinctly summarised, sanctionist theories

> vary along many dimensions. Some demand actual endorsement; others require only counterfactual endorsement. Some require merely absence of

[99] Alexander Erler and Tony Hope have examined the significance of authenticity for those suffering from mental disorders, for example, finding that they consistently regarded authenticity as important, 'although the accounts of the relationships between authenticity and mental disorder differ widely'. This, they explained, was because those suffering from mental disorder often experience substantial inner conflict which is not only confusing and disorientating but also 'a barrier to coherent self-development'. In order to resolve this conflict, the person may seek to introduce a level of psychological unity and stability to their life, for which the concept of authenticity may be helpful, in clarifying 'the sort of unity and stability that one should strive to achieve'. Accordingly, an idea of an authentic self that is evolving and contingent on one's evaluative judgements would 'lack practical value to those who wish to draw on the notion of authenticity to help guide their choices and commitments': rather, Charles Taylor's 'true self' view of authenticity – according to which 'there are certain aspects of our identity which are given, independent of whether we identify with them', and in order to be authentic the person must strive to be faithful to that true self – is a more helpful guide on how to act and how to feel about different aspects of one's self: see A. Erler and T. Hope, 'Mental Disorder and the Concept of Authenticity' (2014) 21(3) *Philosophy, Psychiatry and Psychology* 219–232.

[100] J. Ahlin, 'The Impossibility of Reliably Determining the Authenticity of Desires: Implications for Informed Consent' (2017) 21(1) *Med Health Care and Philos* 43–50, 43.

[101] Frankfurt, 'Freedom of the Will and the Concept of a Person', 5–20, 10.

[102] Dworkin, *The Theory and Practice of Autonomy*, 15.

> reflective rejection or feelings of alienation, instead of positive endorsement. Some focus on formal, structurally defined relations among motives; others consider the historical routes through which an agent's attitudes were formed.[103]

While it is not possible to do justice to all the many variations of sanctionist theories here, broadly, according to such theories, the authenticity of a desire depends on the person's attitude towards it: do they, after critical reflection, endorse that desire either actually or hypothetically?

Coherentist theories, by contrast, judge the authenticity of a desire by its coherence with the values, attitudes, characteristics, and life goals that make up the person's character system. Given that people's desires and values constantly change and evolve, this will generally be stated at quite a high level. Scott Kim, for example, demanded that the bar for authenticity must not be set too high: a desire must be 'patently inconsistent with the set of values and history that roughly constitute the person's identity'[104] to be deemed inauthentic.

Originist theories of authenticity, meanwhile, focus on the origins or source of the person's desires or beliefs. In this sense, they differ from both sanctionist and coherentist accounts in that they focus on the *cause* of the person's values rather than the substance of the values per se, and the extent to which they are either coherent with or would hypothetically be endorsed by the person. Usually such accounts require that, to be authentic, a desire has to originate in a cognitive process which is within the control of the person. Conversely, a decision will be 'inauthentic' if, as Elster puts it, it is 'shaped by irrelevant causal factors'.[105] These might include an illness or a disorder, or the overbearing influence of others. In Alfred Mele's account, for example, a necessary condition of authenticity is that an agent is not 'compelled' to hold a given desire (which will be the

[103] P. Benson, 'Feminist Intuitions and the Normative Substance of Autonomy' in J. S. Taylor (ed), *Personal Autonomy: New Essays on Personal Autonomy and Its Role in Contemporary Moral Philosophy* (Cambridge: Cambridge University Press, 2005), 124–142.

[104] S. Y. H. Kim, 'The Place of Ability to Value in the Evaluation of Decision-Making Capacity', in Daniel D. Mosely and Gary Gala (eds), *Philosophy and Psychiatry: Problems, Intersections and New Perspectives* (New York: Routledge, 2016), 189–203, 196.

[105] J. Elster, *Sour Grapes: Studies in the Subversion of Rationality* (Cambridge: Cambridge University Press, 1983), 15.

case if they are caused to hold a value or desire in a way which bypasses their capacities for control over their mental life), that bypassing results in the agent being practically unable to shed that desire or value, and that the bypassing was not itself arranged or performed by the agent.[106]

Ahler's taxonomy does not fully capture accounts of authenticity, which often contain aspects or dimensions of each of these three separate 'categories'. Nor does it fully account for how this authenticity component relates to the overarching theories of autonomy of which they are a part. However, through drawing attention to different features which might ground the authenticity of a desire (its causal history, its coherence with a person's wider character system, or the person's attitude towards it), this taxonomy is helpful in explaining how these different accounts interact with one another and what the key areas of overlap, and of disagreement, between them are. In this section, some of the most influential of these accounts will be outlined, which have often evolved in response to the perceived failings of the accounts that preceded them, before exploring the implications of these for when decisions motivated by disordered beliefs or evaluative judgements might be said to be non-autonomous.

Despite its influence on bioethical discourse, Frankfurt's aforementioned theory, whereby a desire is authentic when it is sanctioned by one's higher order volitions, has faced substantial criticism.[107] The crux of the problem, as Pugh observes, is this: 'Why should we trust that our second-order volitions should serve as the proxy for the 'true self' and as the seat of self-governance?'[108] After all, as Gary Watson has pointed out, higher-order desires are still desires, and 'nothing about their level gives them any special authority with respect to externality. If they have that authority they are given it by something else'.[109] Faced with this problem, Frankfurt is left with two options: either this authority derives from an '*even higher* order volition [that] authenticates one's second-order

[106] A. Mele, *Autonomous Agents: From Self-Control to Autonomy* (New York: Oxford University Press, 2001), 166–171.

[107] See, for example, G. Watson, 'Free agency' (1975) 72(8) *The Journal of Philosophy* 205–220; J. Christman, 'Autonomy and Personal History' (1991) 21(1) *Canadian Journal of Philosophy* 1–24; B. Berofsky, *Liberation from Self* (New York: Cambridge University Press, 1995).

[108] Pugh, *Autonomy, Rationality, and Contemporary Bioethics*, 46.

[109] G. Watson, 'Free Action and Free Will' (1987) 96(382)*Mind* 145–172, 159.

volitions as being one's own',[110] in which case there would seem to be a problem of infinite regress, or it must be that this higher order does not require authentication. But this then leads to John Christman's 'ab initio' problem: if desires are authenticated by higher-order desires which are not themselves authentically the agents, then how can that desire be said to be autonomous? As Christman explains,

> either the acts of critical reflection which convey authenticity onto the person's desires are autonomous, or they are not autonomous. If they are, then the account of autonomy simply goes back one step and the same question arises at this level. If they are not, then this gives rise to the ab initio problem; i.e., a desire cannot be autonomous if it was evaluated by a desire that was not itself autonomous. Now if it is required that the acts of critical reflection that convey autonomy are themselves autonomous, then either they are autonomous in the same way that LODs [lower order desires] are autonomous, which gives rise to the regress problem, or they are autonomous in a different way, in which case we are owed an account of this new way.[111]

Much of the literature that has followed has concerned different attempts to overcome this problem of regress, in order to better explain what it is that gives a certain desire the authority to 'speak for' the agent. In Christman's original account of authenticity, for example, he sought to vary the Frankfurtian model through introducing greater focus on the origins or source of the agent's beliefs, asking instead whether the agent would have resisted the process by which a preference was formed, if they had attended to the process of development.[112] This, he felt, cut the problem of regress off at the first level, since it was sufficient for the autonomy of a desire that 'the act of appraisal of the processes by which a desire developed in an agent is carried out with sufficient self-awareness and minimal rationality' – there was no need to rely on a second level of desire in order to evaluate whether they would resist the development of this.[113] This was in turn criticised for failing to account for the fact that one can reject the process by which one acquired a desire and yet still endorse it on other grounds, resulting in a shift of focus in later revisions to his theory, from the process by which a person came to hold certain values, back to the values themselves. In this revised account, he asks

[110] Pugh, *Autonomy, Rationality, and Contemporary Bioethics*, 46.
[111] Christman, 'Autonomy and Personal History', 1–24, 7.
[112] Ibid, 10–11.
[113] Ibid, 18–19.

whether the person would feel deeply alienated from the characteristic or value if they engaged in critical reflection about it, in a variety of conditions, and in light of the history of that characteristic's development. He clarifies that alienation is 'not simply the lack of identification' (as in Dworkin's theory of authenticity)[114]; rather, 'to be alienated is to experience negative affect, to feel repudiation and resistance'.[115] This, as he explains, allows for some affective component to the requirements of autonomous agency, while allowing for greater flexibility to accommodate how people may relate to 'their often conflicting and necessarily complex internal lives'.[116] Christman is clear that this reflective non-alienation cannot itself be the result of manipulating forces.[117] Moreover, when engaging in this process of critical reflection,

> the judgement in question is whether the factor being considered can be taken in as part of the person's overall self-narrative; whether the person can accept this part of herself (without alienation) as part of an autobiographical narrative she embodies and enacts. One is not simply asking whether this factor is best for a person to have in general, nor is one asking merely whether one in fact embodies it. Rather one is asking whether I can take this as part of my ongoing autobiography, looking at my past as well as projecting into the future, and avoid the feelings of resistance and rejection characteristic of alienation. Therefore, 'critical reflection' here refers to the consideration of the factor as an ongoing part of one's self-narrative.[118]

Consequently, the result of his revisions was to signal a shift away from the origins of a desire, towards greater focus on how the agent perceives that desire to relate to their self-narrative.

Such a move has been made more explicitly by later philosophers, who have sought to ground the authority of a desire in its coherence with the person's character system. According to Laura Ekstrom,[119] for example, an agent is autonomous in acting on a first-order desire if they have a 'personally authorized preference' for that desire to be effective.[120]

[114] J. Christman, *The Politics of Persons: Individual Autonomy and Socio-Historical Selves* (Cambridge, UK: Cambridge University Press, 2009), 143.

[115] Ibid, 144.

[116] Ibid.

[117] Ibid, 146.

[118] Ibid, 155.

[119] L. Ekstrom, 'A Coherence Theory of Autonomy' (1993) 53(3) *Philosophy and Phenomenological Research* 599–616, 603.

[120] Pugh, *Autonomy, Rationality, and Contemporary Bioethics*, 49.

A preference is a specific type of desire formed in the search for what is good. Unlike Frankfurt's second-order volitions, which may be formed for any reason, a preference can only be formed because the agent finds a certain first-level desire to be good either in itself or as a means of realising one's general conception of the good.[121] In her view, a preference will be 'personally authorized' if it 'coheres' with the agent's 'character system', that is, with 'the agent's set of preferences at time *t*, in conjunction with the set of propositions that the agent accepts at *t*'.[122] It will cohere with an agent's character system if it is either

> (i) more valuable for the agent to prefer that desire than it is for her to prefer a competing desire, on the basis of their character system, or (ii) as valuable for the agent to prefer the conjunction of that desire and another neutralizing desire *n*, as it is for her to prefer a competing desire.[123]

The problem of infinite regress is thus overcome as the desire is evaluated relative to the agent's character system rather than some other 'higher order' desire, and 'a preference for that desire to be effective in action has authority if and only if it coheres with that system'.[124]

In his recent work, Jonathan Pugh defends a modified version of this coherence theory in his rationalistic account of decisional autonomy.[125] Such an approach was, in his view, best able to explain why 'those of an agent's preferences that cohere with her character system have agential authority, in so far as the agent's coherent preferences and acceptances may plausibly be understood as representing the agent's "true self"'.[126] As Chapter 1 explained, according to Pugh's theory, autonomy requires both theoretical rationality (i.e., that they are motivated by beliefs that were formed in theoretically rational ways) and practical rationality. The latter requires *both* that the person's motivating desires be endorsed by preferences that are held on the basis of beliefs which, 'if true, would give the agent reason to pursue the object of the desire'[127] *and* that these preferences cohere with their character system. In respect of the latter, he puts forward an alternative view to Ekstrom. While, on Ekstrom's view, this occurs where it is more valuable for an agent to prefer the object of one

[121] Ekstrom, 'A Coherence Theory of Autonomy', 599–616, 604.
[122] Pugh, *Autonomy, Rationality, and Contemporary Bioethics*, 49–50.
[123] Ibid, 50.
[124] Ekstrom, 'A Coherence Theory of Autonomy', 599–616, 615.
[125] Pugh, *Autonomy, Rationality, and Contemporary Bioethics.*
[126] Ibid, 50.
[127] Ibid, 142.

desire over another, Pugh only requires autonomous agents to choose 'in accordance with preferences that they have a sufficient reason to adopt'.[128] This accommodates the idea that they can make suboptimal choices which still reflect central elements of their character, particularly, as he observes, given the 'imprecise truths governing the strength of our competing practical reasons'.[129]

There is much that can be said about these different theories of autonomy and authenticity.[130] Here, however, the focus will be on what the implications of these are for how mental disorder (or other impairments affecting values) might undermine the person's capacity for autonomy. Clearly on a straightforward originist view akin to that of Mele, the fact that a person's desire is *caused* by a mental disorder may itself be enough to render it inauthentic: the person has been caused to hold a value in a way that bypasses their capacities for control over their mental life and the person is unable to shed that value.[131] In his original theory, Christman sought to refine this, focusing not on the causal origins (or process of development) of a value per se but the person's attitude towards that process: would they resist the process of development? Again, in many cases concerning mental illness, this is likely to be answered affirmatively. As the foregoing discussion has made clear, mental disorder typically involves some level of distress or inability to function, and thus few would be amenable to having the values that caused that imposed upon them beyond their control.

However, it remains unclear why the origins of a value or belief (or indeed the person's attitude towards those origins) ought to matter when determining whether that value is a reflection of the person's 'true self'. After all, no values arise ab initio; they are developed as a feature of (or response to) our upbringing, relationships, and environment, and constantly subject to influence. Given this, we generally think that their source (which will often be the teachings of one's parents or culture)

[128] Ibid, 54.

[129] Ibid.

[130] For example, for an examination of their implications in the context of adolescent treatment decisions, see C. Auckland, 'Authenticity and Identity in Adolescent Decision-Making' (2023) *Modern Law Review* (published online first: https://doi.org/10.1111/1468-2230.12834).

[131] Mele likens his concept of 'shed-ability' to 'commonsense conceptions of irresistible desires' (Mele, *Autonomous Agents*, 154). It seems plausible that many values held on account of a mental disorder that the person wishes to resist might be described as 'irresistible' in a meaningful sense.

matters less than their later endorsement by the person when an adult. It would be odd, for example, to deny the authenticity of an Orthodox Jew's religious and cultural beliefs and values, merely because they had been inculcated in them by their parents and community as a child, if as an adult they had chosen to adopt and endorse those beliefs and way of life. What matters is not *why* a person came to hold a given belief in the first place, but whether with the necessary knowledge and abilities of open reflection, they would choose to continue to hold that belief – that is, they would adopt it as their own. Indeed, even Mele seemed to accept this, since he added a necessary condition that the agent will only be non-autonomous in respect of a value which he was compelled to have, if

> *S* neither presently possesses nor earlier possessed pro-attitudes that would support his identifying with *P*, with the exception of pro-attitudes that are themselves practically unsheddable products of unsolicited bypassing.[132]

Christman, meanwhile, revised his theory to focus on the agent's attitude towards the value *in light of* its causal history rather than focusing on its process of development per se; while Pugh notes that 'the fact that one has been initially manipulated into holding a desire (by emotional means or otherwise) does not entail that one must thereby *forever* lack autonomy with respect to it', the key question instead is whether the person has decided for themselves 'to *sustain* it in the light of one's preferences'.[133] These moves would seem to be an acknowledgement that a person *can* act autonomously if they identify with a value in some way, notwithstanding knowledge of its origins. To conclude otherwise would seem bizarre. After all, if the value of autonomy is in allowing people to live in accordance with those things which truly matter to *them*, this ought to apply equally to values or beliefs which, although disordered in origin, are nevertheless deeply meaningful and important to the individual such that they would want to continue to hold them even if they understood their origins. That a person's decision is motivated by values or beliefs which have been caused by a mental disorder is therefore not enough to straightforwardly deem it inauthentic (and thus to ground the claim that the person lacks capacity to take a given decision): the relationship between disorder and autonomy is more complex and must concern the person's attitude towards the values or beliefs in question in some form.

[132] Mele, *Autonomous Agents*, 172.
[133] Pugh, *Autonomy, Rationality and Contemporary Bioethics*, 66.

The difficult question is what that attitude need entail, and it is on this question that philosophers start to diverge. As noted earlier, for Frankfurt, this involved endorsement by a higher-order desire, yet commentators have been right to criticise this account for failing to satisfactorily explain why endorsement by a higher-order desire is sufficient to make it the true 'seat of self-governance'.[134] And, of course, the problem is particularly acute in the context of mental disorder, since the disorder might affect the process of identification or endorsement itself. Higher-order endorsement does not therefore seem enough in itself to mean a disordered value or desire is (or is not) authentic: we must be sure that it is not being endorsed solely as a consequence of disorder.

In his attempt to overcome this problem, Christman posited a slightly different question: after reflecting on that value or belief, in the knowledge that it stems from disorder, does the person feel alienated from that value in the sense that they resist it as incompatible with their biographical narrative? If they do not feel alienated (and that critical reflection is not influenced by the disorder itself), then the value will be authentic. Of course, it is likely that in the context of mental illness, people will very often feel alienated from those values. It is demonstrably the case that many people resent the debilitating feelings they experience as a consequence of their illness, and so as Manne Sjostrand and Niklas Juth explain,

> desires and values that are the result of . . . irrational beliefs. . . phobia and other psychological disorders are such that we typically would be inclined to disapprove of having them, if we were convinced that this is how they came about.[135]

But this will not always be so. In *Wye Valley*, for example, Mr B's religious beliefs were described as 'deeply meaningful' to him, and 'an intrinsic part of who he is',[136] affecting the whole ethical framework by which he lived his life. Meanwhile, Tan *et al.*'s research on the experiences of people with anorexia nervosa evidence the complex relationship some people have with their disorder:[137] while some see it as something

[134] Ibid, 44.

[135] M Sjöstrand and N. Juth, 'Authenticity and Psychiatric Disorder: Does Autonomy of Personal Preferences Matter?' (2014) 17(1) *Medicine, Health Care and Philosophy* 115–122, 121.

[136] [2015] EWCOP 60, [43].

[137] J. Tan, T. Hope, and A. Stewart, 'Competence to Refuse Treatment in Anorexia Nervosa' (2003) 26(6) *International Journal of Law and Psychiatry* 697–707; see also Hope et al, 'Agency, Ambivalence and Authenticity', 20–36.

separate from their 'real' or authentic self, others experience it as an integral part of their self or identity and so may not be straightforwardly alienated from the values it engenders.

On Christman's theory, it is at least possible, then, that a disordered desire or value may be authentic to the person if, on reflection, they are not alienated by it (or would not be if they hypothetically engaged in this reflective exercise). He thus advocates a modified sanctionist approach: the agent must critically reflect on their desire *in light of* its disordered origins, that reflection process must not itself be affected by the person's disorder, and the person need not fully endorse the desire as long as they are not alienated from it (as he later expresses it, the question is whether 'the person can accept this part of herself',[138] which would seem closer to sanctioning a desire than endorsing it).

While Christman's theory offers a compelling account of the minimum necessary for a value to be authentically held, Pugh is critical of Christman attaching too great a significance to the causal origins of the agent's desires. While the 'dubious causal history' may mean that 'we ought to critically assess the content of those desires to ensure that we endorse them', Pugh remains 'sceptical of the claim that the agent's own attitude towards that causal history itself should matter with respect to the authenticity of their psychological characteristics themselves'.[139] He gives the example of Alex, who, though rationally persuaded by Ben's argument for a particular policy, is nonetheless alienated from a policy because he detests Ben.[140] In this view, it is 'implausible' to regard Ben's as a form of controlling influence that undermines Alex's autonomy. This may be true of this example, but the context of mental disorder is importantly different. In the context of mental illness, a dysfunctional psychological process causes a person to act in certain (abnormal) ways which are harmful to them. Sometimes the operation of the psychological dysfunction will be such that the person also does not understand how it is affecting their decision-making processes, or value and belief systems: they lack insight into their illness. Consequently, they may also lack insight into how they may feel if their condition were successfully treated, and they recovered from that illness. In such circumstances, that the person may critically reflect on the values they are holding in light of

[138] Christman, *The Politics of Persons: Individual Autonomy and Socio-Historical Selves*, 2009, 155.

[139] Pugh, *Autonomy, Rationality, and Contemporary Bioethics*, 77.

[140] Ibid.

(and in full knowledge of) their causal origins would seem crucially important. Imagine, for example, a person experiencing auditory hallucinations that God is conversing with them, leading them to believe that they are the Messiah and so must sacrifice themselves. Their decision to refuse treatment surely cannot be deemed authentic in the absence of full understanding that such a belief derives from disorder and may (with anti-psychotic medication, for instance) subside. So too of a person with a depressive illness refusing life-saving treatment, if their illness causes them to feel that there is no further value in life and that their life is not going to change or improve. Knowledge and acceptance of the way in which one's values are shaped by a dysfunctional psychological process would thus seem an essential element to a disordered value being deemed authentic.

In fact, Pugh would likely regard neither of the people in these two examples as acting autonomously. But the authenticity of their desires would be discounted in one of two ways, neither of which require recourse to the person's subjective attitudes towards the origins of their desires. First, both Pugh and Ekstrom require that the person's motivating desire has been endorsed (or personally authorised) by a preference *that is coherent with the person's character system*. The person's character system – that is, those desires a person holds in pursuit of what is good and those propositions they accept as true – thus plays a far more direct role in constraining the kinds of choices that a person can authentically make. To be authentic, there must be 'sufficient reason' to want a desire to be effective in light of that person's character system. And so, if a person's disordered values are incoherent with their character system, in the sense that they contradict those things that a person accepts to be true or good, then they will be unlikely to have sufficient reason to endorse it. This will often be the case in the context of mental disorder and could be the case in either of the two examples given earlier. But it will not invariably be so, especially in the context of chronic mental illness. As noted previously, Mr B's persistent auditory hallucinations of angels and the Virgin Mary in *Wye Valley* had, over the many years he had experienced them, become 'an intrinsic part of who he is'.[141] It is at least plausible to claim that the beliefs engendered by them had become part of his character system, such that the decision to refuse treatment on the basis that it was not God's will might be authentic.

[141] Ibid, 43.

In light of this, Pugh introduces an important modification to Ekstrom's coherence theory, which is apposite here. According to Ekstrom's theory, the agent's preferences need only be rationally warranted in an objectivist sense – that is, that the agent must believe they have reasons to have those preferences, based on their subjective beliefs about what is good. What Ekstrom does not require is that those beliefs are otherwise rationally warranted. Pugh is critical of this for failing to account for the importance of one's evaluative beliefs being theoretically rational. He gives the example of someone suffering from clinical depression to illustrate this point. Although the person may personally authorise a suicidal desire, this authorisation may stem from a belief about the disvalue of their life that they hold irrationally, in the sense that they are not able to offer any cogent reasons as to *why* they hold those evaluative beliefs or to respond to any epistemic reasons with which they are presented against holding such beliefs. In this case, he argues that it is plausible to claim this person lacks autonomy, as their 'endorsement of their motivating desire is based upon an irrational belief about the good'.[142]

On Pugh's account, then, autonomy demands not just practical rationality but also theoretical rationality. The latter 'relates to the set of norms that govern how we come to form and sustain our beliefs', including 'being responsive to evidence in sustaining one's beliefs, drawing logical implications from matters of fact and probability, and holding broadly consistent and coherent sets of beliefs'. This therefore amounts to a significant qualification: if the beliefs that underpin the 'authorising' or 'endorsing' preference are held in a theoretically irrational manner, then they will not be able to 'authorise' the desire in an authoritative sense (i.e., the desire cannot be said to be authentic). The effect will be to discount the authenticity of most desires that are premised on delusional beliefs – since such beliefs will generally be formed in a theoretically irrational manner, being unresponsive to evidence – as well as many of those stemming from depressive values or anorexia nervosa. This is not to say that *all* disordered values are necessarily theoretically irrational. As Pugh himself explains, while many sufferers of anorexia nervosa hold theoretically irrational beliefs that they are overweight (despite being severely underweight), this is not always the case: 'some sufferers understand that they are dangerously underweight, yet harbour a desire to maintain a low weight, a desire that

[142] Ibid, 52.

trumps all others'.[143] Their desires will not necessarily be inauthentic according to his account. Nor is it to say that those who hold theoretically irrational beliefs will always be non-autonomous: one might hold a range of rationally held beliefs alongside these which motivate a given decision. For example, one might have (irrational) anorexic beliefs about their weight, while also (rationally) believing that given the low quality of life they experience with that disorder, dogged as it is by hospital admissions and forced feeding, they would prefer to end their life. But there will be instances in which the beliefs that underpin an agent's preference are held in theoretically irrational ways, which, on Pugh's account at least, undermines the autonomy of the decision.

Pugh therefore accounts for concerns about the origins of one's beliefs, not through examining the person's subjective attitude towards those beliefs in light of their causal origins, but through examining those beliefs themselves and whether they are held in theoretically rational ways, and are otherwise coherent with the person's character system. In doing so, he demands more for a decision to be authentic than Christman: it is not enough simply that a person sanctions a desire as part of a '*coherent* and acceptable self-narrative'.[144] Rather, the agent must have sufficient reasons to hold a preference for a desire to be effective, based on beliefs which are held in a theoretically rational way.

What are the implications of this divergent approach for mental disorder? For the most part, very little in practice, since these accounts are likely to reach the same answer to the question of whether disordered values and beliefs are authentic, albeit through different mechanisms. The agent is, after all, very likely to feel alienated from beliefs that are held in theoretically irrational ways and which are incoherent with their character system: most of us do not seek to act on the basis of beliefs we know to be held irrationally. But this will not invariably be the case, and cases such as that of Mr B in *Wye Valley*[145] put strain on these different accounts of authenticity. On Christman's account, it is possible that Mr B would be deemed authentic, since it is plausible that even knowing that his religious beliefs stem from auditory hallucinations, he would not feel deeply alienated from them. But he will likely be inauthentic on Pugh's account because his beliefs are held in theoretically irrational ways, being maintained despite clear evidence that they derive from

143 Ibid, 28.

144 Christman, *The Politics of Persons*, 144.

145 [2015] EWCOP 60.

hallucinations brought about from psychiatric disorder. The theories would thus seem to diverge on the question of whether someone can act authentically if they decide in accordance with theoretically irrational beliefs. In the view of Pugh, they cannot: an agent simply cannot incorporate attitudes into one's authentic self which they regard as irrational. It is the agent 'herself who decides how to shape her authentic self on the basis of her own values and conception of the good',[146] and her beliefs about the good must be held in a theoretically rational manner. By contrast, Christman's account does not explicitly preclude a person from acting authentically on the basis of theoretically irrational beliefs, provided the person has critically reflected on them 'adequately without constriction, pathology, or manipulation'.[147] This reflection, he stresses, involves an affective element, not just a cognitive one, and so it is possible that one may not feel alienated in the sense that they do not experience a negative affect, even if they may judge something to be unacceptable on normative grounds. He gives the example of someone who, coming from a socially conservative background, judges holding certain sexual desires as immoral, 'but the feelings not only remain in force, they are not unpleasant and not the cause of conflicting desire'.[148]

It is not necessary for the purposes of this discussion to formulate a precise view on whether Pugh is right to exclude the possibility that decisions based on theoretically irrational beliefs can be autonomous. The effect, however, is to severely restrict the instances in which decisions taken on the basis of disordered beliefs or value systems will be regarded as authentic, given that very many of them will rest on theoretically irrational beliefs. Certainly, there is some intuitive appeal to the idea that someone could still act authentically if they sanctioned a belief knowing it to be irrational, given human propensity to deeply value things even when to do so is irrational. Mental illness is one such instance,[149] but there are plenty of more prosaic examples, including holding certain religious beliefs in irrational ways,[150] or falling in love with someone

146 Pugh, *Autonomy, Rationality, and Contemporary Bioethics*, 55.

147 Christman, *The Politics of Persons*, 147.

148 Ibid, 145.

149 Although denying that such a decision could be authentic, Pugh gives the example of an anorexic patient who regarded 'her desire to refrain from eating as irrational, and yet also regarded it as providing her with sufficient justificatory reason to refrain from eating': Pugh, *Autonomy, Rationality, and Contemporary Bioethics*, 54.

150 Pugh regards religious beliefs as autonomous in certain cases, 'as long as the operative cognitive states here are not strictly beliefs (held in a manner that fails to meet standards

with whom a person knows they ought not to. Suzy Killmister gives many such examples, in which an agent appears to hold a motivational attitude that they know to be unreasonable (or irrational), yet still regard this as an integral part of themselves, and so be motivated to act on the basis of it.[151] Where this is the case, and the person knowingly accepts it as part of their coherent self-narrative, it seems plausible that it becomes part of their authentic self, understood as embodying one's values, commitments, and beliefs about the good, in an affective and not purely cognitive sense.

However, regardless of one's stance on this particular issue, one thing is clear: that whether a desire is authentic must rest on more than simply its causal origins and whether its development can be attributed to a mental illness. The mere fact that a value or belief is thought to derive from a mental illness is not therefore sufficient in itself to impugn it: rather it must be shown that that value or belief is inauthentic and so the decision based on it is non-autonomous. This must, *at a minimum*, hinge on the agent's attitude towards that desire: whether knowing how they came to hold it, the agent nonetheless accepts it as being a part of their self-narrative or character system. Some, such as Pugh, suggest that it will further depend on whether the endorsing preference is coherent with the person's character system. It follows that while most people suffering from mental disorders would not endorse or sanction desires known to be motivated by that disorder (and so doctors are right to deem them non-autonomous), this will not always be the case. There will be some people, particularly those suffering from chronic mental illness, who do (or could) sanction those desires as consistent with their character

of theoretical rationality), but rather items of faith': see Pugh, *Autonomy, Rationality, and Contemporary Bioethics*, 220.

151 S. Killmister, 'The Woody Allen Puzzle: How "Authentic Alienation" Complicates Autonomy' (2015) 49(4) *Noûs*729–747. She termed this problem 'authentic alienation'. In order to account for this problem, Killmister argues that we must recognise different dimensions of autonomy: self-definition (which is concerned with the reasonableness of an agent's attitudes) and self-realisation (both internal, which is concerned with 'whether the agent's intention tracks what she takes herself to have most reason to do, given her motivational attitudes and beliefs' (p. 735) and external, which is concerned with 'the extent to which the actions performed accord with, and are brought about by, our intentions' (p. 735)). In her view, one may lack this self-definition dimension of autonomy and so not be fully self-governing, while retaining the self-realisation dimension. This, she stated, means 'that they are less autonomous than they otherwise could be, if they were acting on the basis of attitudes that they deemed both reasonable and reasons for actions' (p. 741).

system. Where this is the case, providing the process of critical reflection is not itself undermined by the disorder, and the agent's other capacities are intact, there is little justification for them to be found to lack capacity when acting on those desires.

3.3 Conclusion

In Chapter 2, it was established that notwithstanding the apparent value neutrality of the test for capacity, in fact doctors and judges *are* taking account of the substance of the values or beliefs underpinning a decision when determining a person's capacity to take it. Often this will be because of concerns over the disordered nature of the values or beliefs motivating a decision, which lead the person to make evaluative judgements that they might not make, were it not for the effects of that disorder. Not only does this involve a straining of the statutory language of 'using' or 'weighing' information about a decision, but addressing concerns about the substance of the person's values in this way also obscures the normative assumptions that underpin such claims.

These claims were examined in this chapter, which concludes – albeit tentatively – that while the line between order and disorder are not always clear cut, there are nonetheless characteristics of disorder which ought to distinguish it from non-disordered abnormal behaviour. Moreover, in many cases, the fact that the value or belief motivating a decision is disordered will be a good reason to consider it inauthentic and thus non-autonomous, because very often the fact that a value stems from a disorder also means that the person would not accept it as part of their character or life narrative if they did not have that disorder. Or to put it another way, absent the disorder, they would decide differently, in a way which better reflected those things that truly matter to them. There will, however, be some rare instances in which a person *would* sanction beliefs or values originating in their mental illness, even knowing of their origins. To find them to lack capacity in such cases is thus hard to justify, even if our limited ability to accurately test for this in practice may mean that this is not a distinction on which the law can rely – as Chapter 4 will explore.

Yet while the conclusions reached here indicate that assessors are not necessarily acting illegitimately when they deem an agent to lack capacity on the basis of their disordered values, the way in which the law currently deals with this issue is deeply unsatisfactory. Rather than being addressed explicitly, considerations are shoehorned within the assessment of whether the agent can use or weigh information, with the agent often being found to be unable to use or weigh the information, because their disorder 'compels' them to weigh up the information in a certain way. The effect is to blur the distinction between an agent's capacity to weigh and how they in fact choose to attribute weight to information, in a way which is difficult to reconcile with the liberal ideals on which the MCA is based. But more importantly, given the unclear boundaries of mental disorder, both at a conceptual level (given it must be defined partly by reference to changing social values) and at a practical one (relying as it does on substantial clinical judgement), coupled with the uncertainties inherent in identifying when an agent's values or beliefs are 'authentic', it is essential that where assessments of this nature are being made, they are done so openly so that they can be subject to scrutiny, both by the individual and by society more generally.

This transparency may also be important legally, since the boundary between disorder and genuine religious belief may define the scope of human rights protections. Article 9 ECHR protects the right to manifest one's religion and beliefs freely,[152] including in respect of treatment decisions.[153] Although Strasbourg has not considered protections afforded to delusional beliefs directly, the Council of Europe has been clear that to benefit from article 9 protections, a belief 'must attain a certain level of cogency, seriousness, cohesion and importance'.[154] The threshold for this should not be set too high: as Lord Nicholls noted in *R (Williamson and Others) v. Secretary of State for Education and Employment*,[155] religious beliefs are not always 'susceptible to lucid exposition' or 'rational justification', and 'depending on the subject matter, individuals cannot always be expected to express themselves with cogency or precision'.[156] This implies, however, that whether or not a disordered belief warrants prima facie protection will depend on the nature of the belief itself and its coherence and cogency: some will, such

[152] Convention for the Protection of Human Rights and Fundamental Freedoms (European Convention on Human Rights, as amended) (ECHR), article 9.

[153] See, for example, *Jehovah's Witnesses of Moscow and Others v. Russia*, ECHR, Application no. 302/02, concerning the rights of Jehovah's Witnesses to refuse blood transfusions.

[154] Council of Europe, 'Guide on Article 9 of the Convention – Freedom of thought, conscience and religion' (31 August 2022), [16].

[155] [2005] UKHL 15.

[156] Ibid, [23].

as Mr B's beliefs in *Wye Valley*[157] (which, Mr Peter Jackson accepted, were protected by article 9), others will not. Transparency about when and why certain beliefs warrant protection and others do not is therefore important.

Of course, even if a disordered belief does constitute a protected belief under article 9, it does not follow that interference with that will necessarily be illegitimate. In *Jehovah's Witnesses of Moscow and Others v. Russia*,[158] the court acknowledged that 'given that health and possibly life itself are at stake in such situations, the authenticity of the patient's refusal of medical treatment is a legitimate concern'.[159] Although they did not address the issue directly, implicit in their judgment seems to be an acceptance that interference with article 9 could be acceptable if the person is not making an autonomous choice to manifest such beliefs, either because they lack capacity or because the person's will has been 'overborne' by another.[160] Given this, ascertaining (and justifying) the impact of the disordered belief on the person's capacity for autonomous decision-making is important. The conclusion reached by Mr Peter Jackson in *Wye Valley*[161] that Mr B's beliefs were protected by article 9 was easier to reach given that he ultimately found it to be in Mr B's best interests to not receive treatment, in line with those (disordered but religious) beliefs. Had he concluded the opposite, however, namely that it would be in Mr B's best interests for his religious beliefs to be frustrated, a tension might well have arisen between Mr B's right to freedom of religion under article 9 and the court's role in determining and giving effect to his best interests under the MCA. The court would then be required to justify any interference with his human rights, necessitating greater engagement with the relationship between his disordered values and capacity for autonomy. The aim of Chapter 4 will therefore be to propose a new framework for dealing with such cases under the MCA, which mitigates some of the problems that have been identified with the current approach.

It should, of course, be noted that although the focus has been on the implications for the MCA, this discussion of the nature of mental disorder and its impact on autonomous decision-making may also cast

157 [2015] EWCOP 60, [14].
158 ECHR, Application no. 302/02.
159 Ibid, [138].
160 Ibid.
161 [2015] EWCOP 60.

doubts on the legitimacy of the Mental Health Act 1983. It implies that at least some people with mental disorders *can* decide autonomously and thus lends further support to those who argue that forcibly detaining and treating such people may be hard to justify. While it is not my intention to rehearse arguments for reforming the MHA here, it may therefore lend credence to those seeking to move mental health legislation away from a risk-based framework towards one that accords greater respect to individual autonomy, through the fusion of mental health and mental capacity legislation.[162] Crucially, however, this chapter makes clear that before any such changes are introduced, it is essential that changes are made to the test for capacity to ensure that the capacity framework better accounts for the impact of disorder on autonomous decision-making. These changes will be outlined in Chapter 4.

[162] For a discussion of this, see Dawson and Schmukler, 'Fusion of Mental Health and Incapacity Legislation', 504–509; N. Rees, 'The Fusion Proposal'; Richardson, 'Mental Disabilities and the Law', 333–354. This is discussed in detail in 'Special Issue: A Model Law Fusing Incapacity and Mental Health Legislation – Is It Viable; Is It Advisable?' (2010) 20 *Journal of Mental Health Law*. In the Final Report of the Independent Review of the Mental Health Act 1983 ('Modernising the Mental Health Act: Increasing Choice, Reducing Coercion'. Available at https://assets.publishing.service.gov.uk/government/uploads/system/uploads/attachment_data/file/778897/Modernising_the_Mental_Health_Act_-_increasing_choice__reducing_compulsion.pdf), published in December 2018, the authors recognised the many benefits of fused legislation, but ultimately decided not to recommend it because of the time it would take in order to do so.

4

Accommodating Values in the Test of Capacity

Chapter 3 concluded that some degree of paternalistic intervention may be justified where a mental disorder or impairment distorts the value or belief system of the agent, and this undermines their ability to make an authentic decision. The key question for this chapter is therefore how to best reflect such impairments in autonomy in a test for capacity. In other words, where a disorder or impairment results in a person holding values or beliefs that they would not otherwise hold, which they do not sanction, and which distort the way that they evaluate relevant information, how do we best ensure that they are found to lack capacity?

Establishing a role for values in capacity assessments requires charting a difficult course between unwarranted paternalism on the one hand and a failure to protect those whose autonomy is in doubt on the other. As Jillian Craigie has explained:

> Understand the concept [of mental capacity] too broadly, or apply it too stringently, and this will result in inappropriate infringements on personal liberty. However, an overly narrow conception, or undemanding application of the concept in practice, will result in failures to care appropriately for some who need the state to intervene in their private affairs.[1]

The challenge for the law is to navigate these competing harms. And this must be done with a keen eye on the practical realities and limitations faced by assessors in the kinds of complex cases they encounter on the ground.

This chapter will consider different ways in which concerns about the substance or origins of the values underpinning an agent's decision might better be captured. Given its inclusion in the legislation of other jurisdictions – most significantly in Northern Ireland's Mental Capacity Act

[1] J. Craigie, 'Introduction: Mental Capacity and Value Neutrality' (2013) 9(1) *International Journal of Law in Context* 1–3, 1.

2016 – the chapter will begin by exploring the merits of including an 'appreciation' criterion into the test for capacity. While this would certainly help to capture some autonomy-subverting influences which are not properly accommodated at present (such as delusions resulting in mistaken beliefs), it will be suggested that this would not capture *all* the problems identified in Chapters 1–3 (such as how disorder affects evaluative judgement) or, at the very least, can do so only through including *implicit* substantive conditions on the kinds of value systems a person can reasonably hold. Moreover, since assessors would still have to discern whether the failure to 'appreciate' information is due to an impairment or merely an alternative belief system, they would still have to examine the nature and origins of the agent's beliefs. But since this will not be an explicit part of the assessment process, an appreciation limb will do little to enhance the conceptual clarity or transparency of assessments, merely replicating many of the issues that currently afflict the 'use or weigh' limb.

If the MCA 2005 is to address the concerns raised in Chapters 1–3 and capture the full extent of ways in which an agent's capacity for autonomous decision-making may be undermined, it must instead abandon its pretence of value neutrality and acknowledge some role for substantive (and value-laden) conditions in the assessment of capacity. This chapter will therefore explore different forms of substantivism (weaker and stronger accounts), as well as different types of conditions which might be imposed (reflecting the different notions of authenticity discussed previously). It will conclude that a separate limb ought to be introduced into the test for capacity which would apply if the agent was unable to make a decision because the values or beliefs by which the agent is evaluating the relevant information have been caused by or altered as a consequence of the agent suffering from a disorder, illness, or impairment. While the nature of mental disorder diagnosis means this necessarily involves the imposition of some substantive conditions and, as such, conflicts to some extent with liberal conceptions of autonomy and capacity, it will be argued that in practice, the enhanced scrutiny that such an addition to the test allows for minimises the scope assessors have available for paternalistic judgments, and so should be preferred to a limb based on the agent's 'ability to value authentically'.

Before considering the various options that the law could adopt, it should be noted that the concern here is only with the effect of a disorder or impairment on a person's ability to decide authentically: it is not concerned with the many other social or relational influences which could undermine the authenticity, and thus autonomy, of a decision. As noted earlier, section 2(1) of the MCA currently imposes a requirement that the person's inability to make a decision must be caused by an 'impairment of, or a disturbance in the functioning of, the mind or brain',[2] which, as the Code of Practice explains, includes situations where a person suffers from 'a disability, condition or trauma' which affects the way their mind or brain works.[3] While this provision has been subject to criticism for being under-inclusive, it is not my intention to challenge it here. Chapter 3 highlighted the complex relationship between mental disorders, the beliefs and evaluative stances they can cause a person to hold, and decision-making autonomy. But this pales in comparison to the complex role that social and familial interactions, and cultural norms play in the generation and maintenance of our value and belief systems. While concerns about authenticity doubtless arise outside of the context of disorder and impairment, the difficulty for those seeking to accommodate the multitude of ways in which an agent's autonomy can be undermined within a test for capacity is thus being able to distinguish those relationships and social interactions which are constitutive of a person's identity and sense of self, from those which serve to undermine it.[4] Since this cannot be done reliably or accurately, abandoning section 2 (1) at this time would, as the Conclusion will explore further, serve merely to expand the scope for paternalistic interference under the MCA. And given the existence of the inherent jurisdiction which plugs the gap in the law's protection for vulnerable adults suffering from undue influence or coercion, there is no reason to believe that doing so would necessarily result in better protection than is already provided under that jurisdiction. These broader authenticity-based concerns will therefore not be considered in detail here.

4.1 'Appreciation' in the Test for Capacity

One possible solution to the problems identified in Chapters 1–3, which has been adopted by other jurisdictions, is the inclusion of an 'appreciation' limb in the test for capacity. In the Mental Capacity Act (Northern Ireland) 2016, for example, although the test for capacity broadly mirrors

[2] Mental Capacity Act, s2(1).

[3] Department for Constitutional Affairs, 4.3.

[4] For a discussion of this in the context of adolescents, see Auckland, 'Authenticity and Identity in Adolescent Decision-Making'.

that in the English legislation, a person will be deemed unable to make a decision if he or she 'is not able to appreciate the relevance of that information and to use and weigh that information as part of the process of making the decision'.[5] Appreciation here was expressly included to allow 'for things, such as lack of insight, delusional or distorted thinking, to be taken into account when assessing someone's ability to make a decision'.[6] As the Department of Health's consultation paper explained:

> This goes further than the equivalent statutory provision in England and Wales because of the inclusion of the appreciation element. Its inclusion means that, under the draft Bill, it will not be sufficient for a person to have a cognitive understanding of the information relevant to the decision if he/she is to be deemed to have capacity. A person whose insight is distorted by their illness or a person suffering from delusional thinking as a result of their illness, may not, therefore, meet this element of the test.[7]

Responses to the inclusion of appreciation were, at the time, mixed. The Royal College of Psychiatrists supported its inclusion, arguing that an appreciation limb would help the Act to respond to criticisms that the MCA 2005 'does not lend itself well to psychiatric disorders where cognitive processes may be intact, but the person lacks insight or is affected by delusional thinking'.[8] In their view, the 2005 Act is 'less practically applicable to people with psychiatric disorders', and an appreciation criterion would help to address that.[9] However, such support was not shared by the wider medical establishment, with the British Medical Association opposing its inclusion, concerned that it might make the capacity criteria 'more stringent and raise the bar in relation to the threshold for capacity'.[10] In particular, they raised concerns about the potential scope for differing interpretations of 'appreciation', noting that

[5] Mental Capacity Act (Northern Ireland) 2016, s4(1)(c).

[6] Mental Capacity Act (Northern Ireland) 2016 Explanatory Notes: Part 1 Section 4: 'Meaning of "unable to make a decision"'.

[7] Department of Health and Social Services and Public Safety, Northern Ireland, Department of Justice. *Draft Mental Capacity Bill (NI): Consultation Document*. DHSSNI 'DOJ, 2014. Available at: www.health-ni.gov.uk/sites/default/files/consultations/dhssps/mental-capacity-consultation-document.pdf, 2.22.

[8] Ibid, [45] and Appendix A.

[9] Ibid.

[10] Northern Ireland Assembly Ad Hoc Joint Committee on the Mental Capacity Bill, 'Report on the Mental Capacity Bill' (Report: NIA 252/11-16) (25 January 2016), Appendix A: www.niassembly.gov.uk/globalassets/documents/ad-hoc-mental-capacity-bill/report-on-the-mental-capacity-bill2.pdf.

> there are no legal precedents for the judicial interpretation of what "appreciate" means. The term is subjective and open to interpretation. Great care needs to be taken to ensure that this clause does not result in many more people being found to lack capacity.[11]

This concern is a valid one, particularly given the potential breadth of interpretations that the Explanatory Notes to the Act would allow. While the notes explicitly refer to a lack of insight or delusional thinking, they also regard the provision as capturing situations where there is 'distorted thinking', which could encompass any number of impairments.

In the medico-legal literature, 'appreciation' is also understood in different ways. The notion derives from the work of Thomas Grisso and Paul Appelbaum,[12] who proposed four criteria for decision-making capacity: (1) the ability to understand relevant information, (2) to appreciate the significance of the given information about the illness and possible treatment for one's own situation, (3) to reason about that information, and (4) to express a choice. These now form the criteria for assessing capacity using the MacArthur Competence Assessment Tool for Treatment (MacCAT-T) – the 'gold standard' instrument for testing capacity in clinical psychiatry – as well as the legal test in a number of jurisdictions of the United States. The MacCAT-T instrument assesses both the person's appreciation of their disorder and their appreciation of the treatment benefits. Most subsequent uses in the literature have sought to emulate this, with appreciation generally being thought to filter out situations in which the person understands the information, but does not truly believe it, or they do not believe that it applies to *them* (even if they could accept it may be true of others). An example might be where someone's delusion leads them to not believe that what their doctor says is true, making them unresponsive to evidence (what Pugh termed 'theoretical irrationality'[13]). In this sense, appreciation is similar to the clinical concept of 'insight': the question is whether the person fully appreciates their condition and circumstances?

However, others have gone beyond this, incorporating more elements in their definition of the capacity to appreciate information. Buchanan and Brock, for example, have argued that appreciation involves the capacity to

[11] Ibid.

[12] *The Assessment of Decision-Making Capacity: A Guide for Physicians and Other Health Professionals* (Oxford: Oxford University Press, 1998), 42–52.

[13] C.f. the discussion on this in Chapter 3.

> appreciate the nature and meaning of potential alternatives – what it would be like and "feel" like to be in possible future states and to undergo various experiences – and to integrate this appreciation into one's decision-making.[14]

Clearly, the latter would be very hard to test for in any meaningful sense, given the impossibility of knowing how another person truly feels. But it would also place the threshold for establishing capacity very high; after all, people are frequently unable to truly appreciate what certain medical outcomes (death, extreme pain, or disability) would 'feel' like. In fact, one criticism frequently made of advance directives is that people are bad at anticipating how certain events will make them feel, and there is ample literature from psychology examining people's 'affective forecasting', which suggests that humans typically discount the future, overestimate the effects of events and changes in circumstances on their level of well-being, and underappreciate their ability to adapt to new circumstances.[15] Humans are often unreliable at predicting how future events will make them feel, just as they tend to forget exactly how past events felt at the time.[16] Crucially, as Jodi Halpern and Robert Arnold note, they also have a tendency to 'overestimate the impact and duration of negative emotions in response to loss'.[17] This, they explain, is due to three common 'affective forecasting errors':

> focalism, in which people focus more on what will change than on what will stay the same; immune neglect, in which they fail to envision how their own coping skills will lessen their unhappiness; and failure to predict adaptation, in which people fail to envision shifts in what they value.[18]

This suggests people are frequently very bad at anticipating how they will 'feel' in different eventualities and so they often lack 'appreciation' (in the Buchanan and Brock sense) of the implications of their decision.

14 Buchanan and Brock, *Deciding for Others*, 26.

15 See, for example, P. A. Ubel, G. Loewenstein, N. Schwarz, and D. Smith, 'Misimagining the Unimaginable: The Disability Paradox and Health Care Decision Making' (2005) 24 (4S) *Health Psychology* S57–S62; G. Loewenstein, 'Hot-Cold Empathy Gaps and Medical Decision Making' (2005) 24(4S) *Health Psychology* S49–S56; G. Loewenstein, 'Projection Bias in Medical Decision-Making' (2005) 25(1) *Medical Decision Making* 96–105.

16 See, for example, N. Levy, 'Forced to Be Free? Increasing Patient Autonomy by Constraining It' (2014) 40 *Journal of Medical Ethics* 293.

17 J. Halpern and R. Arnold, 'Affective Forecasting: An Unrecognized Challenge in Making Serious Health Decisions' (2008) 23(10) *Journal of General Internal Medicine* 1708–1712.

18 Ibid, 1708.

There is also evidence that people without disabilities or illnesses estimate the quality of life of people with them to be far lower than that reported by those who have them.[19] This has been found in respect of a range of conditions, from chronic dialysis,[20] breast cancer,[21] and living with a colostomy,[22] to arthritis and acne.[23] People may therefore believe that the outcome of a treatment decision will leave them very badly off, when in fact they may not find their quality of life to be as reduced as they anticipate.

This wealth of evidence that humans are poor at 'affective forecasting' calls into question whether the ability to appreciate how different outcomes will make one 'feel' is a reasonable requirement for a capacity threshold. There is a clear risk that placing the threshold for capacity too high may result in many agents being deemed to lack capacity to take a decision because of the inevitable limitations humans face in anticipating their future emotions. However, even embracing appreciation in the former, less-demanding sense (as a legal equivalent of the clinical notion of 'insight'), there are still reasons to question whether this will adequately address the difficulties identified in Chapters 1–3. One such reason is that it is not clear that this would capture all of the challenging situations discussed previously. A person's misperception of reality due to a delusion or hallucination, which renders them unable to believe objectively true information, would doubtless fall within the capacity to

[19] See, for example, P. A. Ubel, G. Loewenstein, J. Hershey, J. Baron, T. Mohr T., D. A. Asch, and C. Jepson, 'Do Nonpatients Underestimate the Quality of Life Associated with Chronic Health Conditions Because of a Focusing Illusion?' (2001) 21(3) *Medical Decision Making* 190–199. There is also evidence suggesting that people adapt well to disability. For example, those rendered paraplegic by an accident were found to be almost as happy as other people a few years after an accident (and comparable to those who had won the lottery): P. Brickman, D. Coates, and R. Janoff-Bulman, 'Lottery Winners and Accident Victims: Is Happiness Relative?' (1978) 36 *Journal of Personality and Social Psychology* 917–927; L. C. Vogel *et al.*, 'Long-term Outcomes and Life Satisfaction of Adults Who Had Pediatric Spinal Cord Injuries' (1998) 79 *Archives of Physical Medicine and Rehabilitation* 1496.

[20] D. L. Sackett and G. W. Torrance, 'The Utility of Different Health States as Perceived by the General Public' (1978) 31 *Journal of Chronic Diseases* 697–704.

[21] D. L. Buick and K. J. Petrie, '"I Know Just How You Feel": The Validity of Healthy Women's Perceptions of Breast Cancer Patients Receiving Treatment' (2002) 32 *Journal of Applied Social Psychology* 110–123.

[22] N. F. Boyd, H. J. Sutherland, K. Z. Heasman, D. L. Tritchler, and B. J. Cummings, 'Whose Utilities for Decision Analysis?' (1990) 10 *Medical Decision Making* 58–67.

[23] J. Baron, D. A. Asch, A. Fagerlin, C. Jepson, G. Loewenstein, J. Riis *et al.*, 'Effect of Assessment Method on the Discrepancy between Judgments of Health Disorders People Have and Do Not Have: A Web Study' (2003) 23 *Medical Decision Making* 422–434.

appreciate information. But more contentious is whether a failure to 'appreciate' also filters out cases of 'pathological' or disordered valuing, as occurs to some people with depressive illnesses or anorexia nervosa, which affects their evaluative judgements. This will be explored in Section 4.1.1.

4.1.1 Does an Appreciation Limb Capture Instances of Disordered Valuing?

In the view of Jacinta Tan and others,[24] an appreciation limb would not filter out cases in which disorder has affected a person's evaluative judgements. Conducting a study into patients with anorexia nervosa, they found that patients typically scored highly for appreciation on the MacCAT-T test, because they very often have good insight into their illness and *can* appreciate (at least at a cognitive level) that they suffer from anorexia nervosa and will die without the treatment. Aside from two of the participants, they described the young women who took part in the study as being 'able to describe their own difficulties with great insight, clarity, and articulateness',[25] indicating good appreciation of their illness and circumstances. This would suggest that an appreciation criterion would not help to capture the nature of the impairment in such cases, as if it were strictly applied; the person would still be found to have capacity to refuse treatment.

Such a conclusion has, however, been refuted by Grisso and Appelbaum, who contend that an appreciation limb can capture impairments in evaluative judgements too. They argue that if a value (defined as 'a person's belief about the importance or merit of something'[26]) is applied in a way that involves a distortion of reality, this amounts to a lack of appreciation.[27] To illustrate their point, they give the following example. If a person refuses treatment for a hip fracture because he says that he values freedom from pain so much that he would rather lie immobile in bed than endure the pain of being moved, then in their view he lacks appreciation of the consequences of his decision because 'the strength of the value represents a distortion of reality in that it

[24] Tan *et al.*, 'Competence to Make Treatment Decisions in Anorexia Nervosa', 267–282.

[25] Ibid, 277.

[26] T. Grisso and P. Appelbaum, 'Appreciating Anorexia: Decisional Capacity and the Role of Values' (2006) 13(4) *Philosophy, Psychiatry and Psychology* 293–297, 294.

[27] Ibid, 295.

ignores the fact he cannot literally lie there forever'.[28] In fact, they suggest that most cases in which a lack of appreciation is identified involve values being applied in a manner that entails a distortion of reality, with appreciation resting 'substantially on an assessment of the person's beliefs about his or her illness and about the likelihood of benefit from the proposed treatment'.[29] In the context of anorexia nervosa, for example, many patients would not believe that they benefited from treatment. Their reasons for this would be based on a number of distortions of reality – that the only thing that matters is thinness, above all else, and that they would not be liked if they gained weight – and so, in Grisso and Appelbaum's view, they lack appreciation.

Helena Hermann *et al.* are rightly critical of this approach for merging notions of values and beliefs.[30] As they explain, there is an important conceptual difference between making a decision 'based on untrue beliefs about reality and being responsive to evidence but basing a decision on evaluative judgments relating to those facts'.[31] This distinction is evident when one interrogates the first example given by Grisso and Appelbaum, of the person refusing treatment for a hip fracture. They suggest that the flaw in that person's decision-making is that it 'ignores the fact that he cannot literally lie there forever'.[32] But if this is the case, then arguably the patient does not fully understand the consequences of his decision, since it is a matter of fact that either way he will, at some stage, have to be moved and thus be subjected to pain; it is simply a question of when that will be.[33] This is, however, a very different scenario from that where the facts are not disputed, but a person makes an evaluative judgement about those facts based on their values. An example of the latter situation would be where the person knows he will have to be moved at some stage, but says he simply cannot face the pain now, so would rather delay it until he *has* to be moved, even if he knows that this will cause long-term immobility.

It is the latter kind of concern that underpins the most conceptually challenging of the anorexia and depression cases discussed previously,

28 Ibid.

29 Ibid.

30 Hermann *et al.*, 'Emotion and Value in the Evaluation of Medical Decision-Making Capacity', 765, 8.

31 Ibid, 2.

32 Grisso and Appelbaum, 'Appreciating Anorexia', 293–297, 295.

33 If this is the case, there may in fact be no need for recourse to an appreciation standard, given that under the MCA, he could be found to lack the requisite understanding.

where the decision-maker may accept information to be true, yet still not place weight on certain information or outcomes because of their disordered or pathological values. Grisso and Appelbaum evade this by characterising the beliefs underpinning a person's evaluative judgements in such cases as being objectively untrue, and thus reasoning that the decisions rest on distortions of reality (a term that they leave undefined).[34] However, such an approach is difficult to sustain.

There may well be some cases where a person believes they are fat when they are not, or that people will not love them if they put on weight, which the doctor knows from those around them to be untrue. In *NHS Foundation Trust v. X*, for example,[35] the doctors stressed that X's 'false beliefs about her weight shape and nutritional state and absolute fear of weight gain' meant she was 'unable to apply the information to herself or believe in the need for it'.[36] Consequently, 'the reality and importance of the associated risks including death in her malnourished state are therefore not truly appraised',[37] meaning she lacked capacity. While this was decided under the 'use or weigh' limb, this may be more accurately analysed as a failure to appreciate how the information applies to her (despite her ability to weigh it up abstractly). However, not all the claims which Grisso and Appelbaum rely on as being 'distortions of reality' are themselves objectively verifiable, and so in deeming them such, the authors are in fact making certain value judgements (for example, that thinness should not be the paramount consideration), which, while understandable, nonetheless import substantive content into the capacity assessment through the backdoor.

Moreover, even if some anorexia nervosa cases do involve distortions of reality, this will not be the case in *all* cases involving an anorexic patient who refuses treatment. In *A Local Authority v. E*,[38] for example, a woman had been controlling her eating since the age of eleven and had spent over half her time between the ages of twenty-six and thirty in specialist units. Despite numerous treatments, nothing had cured her anorexia. Given her years of suffering, and very low chance of ever

[34] In the context of anorexia, for example, they state that the person's reasons for not believing treatment can be of benefit to them 'can only be called distortions of reality' (p. 296) that people will only like them if they are thin, or that nothing else matters in the world except their thinness.

[35] [2014] EWCOP 35.

[36] Ibid, [27].

[37] Ibid.

[38] [2012] EWCOP 1639.

recovering, she expressed a consistent and unequivocal wish to be entitled to refuse treatment, even if that ended her life:

> She describes her life as "a pure torment". All the things she had wanted to do have proved impossible because of her illness. She cannot achieve any of her goals and she feels crushed. She feels she is in a situation where she is able to give nothing to the world and the world is able to give nothing to her.[39]

She did not believe the treatment would benefit her, but not because of a distortion of reality. The treatment had only a 10–20 per cent chance of being successful and would necessitate 'forcible feeding under physical or chemical restraint for not less than a year'.[40] This, as Mr Justice Peter Jackson acknowledged, would 'not merely entail bodily intrusion of the most intimate kind, but the overbearing of E's will in a way that she experiences as abusive',[41] as it replayed the serious sexual abuse she had suffered as a child.[42] Even if it succeeded, much that E had valued in life had become impossible as a result of her illness: she had had to abandon hopes of becoming a doctor, was now unable to have children, and had not been able to form any meaningful relationship with her sister's children. For this reason, she advocated for her right to die. Of course, this decision was affected by the importance she attached to calorie avoidance and by the inevitable trauma that force-feeding would entail (which could be avoided if she accepted treatment voluntarily). However, to attach disproportionate weight to a particular objective is not to make any claim about objective fact. It does not, therefore, 'distort reality' in the sense claimed by Grisso and Appelbaum.

In *Northamptonshire Healthcare NHS Foundation Trust v. AB* too,[43] the treating team found that while AB, a patient with anorexia, accepted that her refusal to eat was putting her life at immediate risk, she 'finds the treatments so aversive that this risk is accepted by her'.[44] As she herself explained:

> I do understand that my weight is dangerously low, and that the consequence of not eating enough to gain weight is death. I do not want to die, and I do understand what the illness is doing to me, and the consequences

[39] Ibid, [76].
[40] Ibid, [88].
[41] Ibid, [131].
[42] Ibid, [89].
[43] [2020] EWCOP 40.
[44] Ibid, [42].

> of continuing down the path that I am on. Similarly, though, I also understand what the physical risks, as set out by [Dr B] of forcibly feeding me now are, and I wonder in addition whether in fact the mental stress of being treated against my will would kill me.[45]

She described in detail the trauma she had suffered at past treatment[46] and, on this basis, concluded that 'it is just cruel to keep putting me through this'.[47] In her own words, she explained:

> The illness is a part of me, yes. It is a voice, yes. It is a bullying and powerful voice, yes. But the voice making this particular decision is mine. It is a voice made hoarse by screaming, and tearful by the prospect of being forcibly treated against my will – knowing all the while both that any such treatment may cause my death in any event, and that, even were it not to, the likelihood of it 'working' is minute. I do not believe that anyone would agree to undergo further inpatient treatment knowing what it entails, and if told, as I have been, that the chances of 'success' – whatever that actually means – are so low.[48]

It is hard to accept that in these cases, the decision by the patient rests simply on a 'distortion of reality' in the way Grisso and Appelbaum argued. Indeed, even for patients like X (discussed previously) who *do* suffer from some distortion of reality, this may not be the only reason for believing the treatment does not benefit them. Rather, they may have a number of reasons or beliefs – some true, others untrue – which collectively influence their decision to refuse treatment. While there may be some instances in which an 'appreciation' limb of the capacity test would better capture the nature of the impairment in anorexia nervosa cases, therefore, it will not capture *all* instances in which the agent appears to attribute weight on the basis of their disordered value system.

The same is true in instances of depression. Refusing treatment because you do not care if you live or die, or you do not believe there is any value or worth to your life, may be a tragic misrepresentation of your life and opportunities, but it would seem odd to suggest that it demonstrates a failure to 'appreciate' information. To do so would once again risk conflating the question of an agent's ability to weigh with the question of the weight that they do in fact give to information, since it would necessarily involve the implicit assumption that a person *ought* to

45 Ibid, [48].
46 Ibid, [48].
47 Ibid, [47].
48 Ibid, [48].

believe their life to be valuable, worthwhile, and worth prolonging, and so the failure to think in this way indicates a lack of capacity. As the British Medical Association feared, this may serve only to increase the scope for paternalistic judgements by capacity assessors.

An appreciation limb may therefore capture *some* impairments which are not currently accounted for properly in the test for capacity (such as delusional thinking leading to mistaken beliefs) and thus represent a step forward from the current law. But it will not capture all those challenging cases where concerns have been raised about the way in which disorder affects the individual's evaluative judgement, except through misleadingly characterising those evaluations as objectively 'wrong'. Moreover, there is a risk that an appreciation limb would serve to duplicate concerns raised previously about the application of the 'use or weigh' criterion. As Chapter 2 explained, agents disbelieve information about their condition or the treatment for all sorts of reasons, and making a mistake is not the same as lacking capacity. Distinguishing between a failure to believe that information applies to one's case because an impairment prevents the agent from doing so and failing to believe it because one has chosen not to – whether that is on account of holding a contrary belief or simply making a mistake – will thus be difficult. It will require the assessor to first examine why it is that the agent does not believe the information that is being told to them (let us say, because it is incompatible with other beliefs that the agent holds to be true) and then to consider whether that amounts to an impairment (for instance, is the alternative belief system the product of a disorder or not). To use the example of a person dismissing the doctor's evidence that they will die without medical intervention, out of a conviction that prayer will heal them, is this the belief of a Christian Scientist or a delusional paranoid schizophrenic? In assessing this, many of the obscured value judgements that were identified in Chapter 2 in the context of the 'use or weigh' limb will be reintroduced under an appreciation limb, together with new value judgements about whether a belief amounts to a 'distortion of reality' in the sense that it can be said to be factually untrue. This will do little to enhance transparency and may in fact reduce it by introducing a new broadly framed limb within which to conceal such judgements.

A better way of tackling the issue of inauthentic values must therefore be found which not only captures how they affect evaluative judgement but also examines more clearly why the origins or content of the person's values or beliefs is thought to be negatively interfering with their decision-making capacity. In order to do this, however, a fundamental tension must be addressed, between attempts to capture concerns about the disordered nature of values and the value neutrality at the heart of the Act. As Fabian Freyenhagen and Tom O'Shea explain:

> Defenders of normative neutrality aim to avoid making a person's autonomy conditional upon adherence to values or norms which they do not accept, and thus face a challenge: can they account for the capacity-subverting influences of those mental disorders which affect evaluative orientation and judgement without lapsing into a form of substantivism?[49]

The simple answer to this is that they cannot. Any attempt to require the values or beliefs driving a decision to be 'authentic' in the sense that they are not caused or altered by mental illness or impairment necessarily involves placing some substantive conditions on the kinds of values or beliefs a person can act in accordance with practice, which threatens neutrality. As Section 4.2 will explain, however, acknowledging this does not necessitate a descent into unbridled paternalism, and may in fact limit the scope for paternalistic judgements in practice.

4.2 Abandoning Value Neutrality

While there is much opposition to introducing any substantive conditions on autonomy, it is important to note that substantive accounts take many different forms. At one end of the spectrum are 'strong' substantive accounts which, as Paul Benson explains, 'directly [impose] normative restrictions on the contents of the preferences or values that agents can form or act upon autonomously'.[50] At a minimum, this requires that

> there must be some things that autonomous agents cannot prefer or value without sacrificing some autonomy, where this restriction depends immediately on the substance of such preferences or values.[51]

These are the kinds of 'ideal desire' accounts of autonomy referred to previously. Beyond this, however, exists a 'largely unmapped expanse of theoretical terrain that stretches between strong substantive theories and

[49] F. Freyenhagen and T. O'Shea, 'Hidden Substance: Mental Disorder as a Challenge to Normatively Neutral Accounts of Autonomy' (2013) 9(1) *International Journal of Law in Context* 53–70, 56.

[50] Benson, 'Feminist Intuitions and the Normative Substance of Autonomy', 124–142, 125.

[51] Ibid, 133.

strictly neutral ones',[52] within which lies a series of weak or indirect forms of substantivism which do not directly constrain the types of preferences or values a person can have, but still incorporate substantive standards into the assessment of autonomy (and thus implicitly of a person's capacity to take autonomous decisions).

Although considering autonomy in the context of social and relational influences as opposed to the effect of disorder, Benson advocates one such indirect form of substantivism – a normative competence theory – which demands 'that the agents' capabilities of perception, reasoning, and motivation be connected in the right sorts of ways to what is really valuable or reasonable for them'.[53] This account is substantive in the sense that what is 'really valuable' to a person may not necessarily be what they think is valuable to them at any given time, yet by focusing on the individual's *capabilities* rather than the content of their values or preferences, such theories maintain space for different value systems, provided the agent is not subject to an impairment which prevents them from acting in accordance with what really matters to them. And as weak or indirect substantive theories do not directly constrain the content of the values, beliefs, or preferences that a person may have, they also do not run into the same attacks of paternalism as strongly substantive theories. As Freyenhagen and O'Shea argue,

> indirect substantivism would not fall prey to the same false positives as normatively neutral accounts of autonomy, yet promises to be less prescriptive than direct substantivism. In emphasising abilities and skills, there is also a focus on functions instead of status, thereby minimising the discrimination that status-based approaches to capacity are often thought to imply.[54]

The theory of weak substantivism adopted by Benson[55] is too imprecise to form a legal basis for intervening in a decision. There is too much ambiguity surrounding the capacities listed (perception, reasoning, and motivation) as well as what 'the right sort of ways' for connecting with values are; meanwhile, the notion of what is 'really valuable' to a person presupposes that someone might have values which are not 'really valuable' to them, yet Benson does not elaborate on when this will be the case. However, similar concerns have led to the development of other

52 Ibid, 124–142, 136.
53 Ibid, 134.
54 Freyenhagen and T. O'Shea, 'Hidden Substance', 53–70, 66.
55 Benson, 'Feminist Intuitions and the Normative Substance of Autonomy', 124–142, 134.

weak substantivist theories, more closely connected to the accounts of authenticity advocated earlier, which could form the basis for a legal test of capacity. Scott Kim, for example, has suggested that rather than focusing on 'pathological values' themselves, which inevitably involves 'passing judgment on the worthiness of values that a person holds',[56] we should instead be concerned with the agent's 'ability to value'. This may be impaired if two conditions are present. First, the decision-maker must suffer from 'some type of pathology, psychiatric or cognitive, or malfunctioning of brain processes that can reasonably be determined to be the source of the impaired ability to value'.[57] Second, the desire expressed must be 'patently inconsistent with the set of values and history that roughly constitute the person's identity'[58] (though he is clear that the notion of authenticity espoused here must not be too strong[59]). As he explains:

> If the value is out of line with the person's prior set of values *and* arises out of a psychopathologic or cognitive dysfunction, then it seems reasonable to say that the person's ability to value is impaired. Thus, the judgment here is not that the person fails to confirm of the values dictated by society but rather that, due to a pathology, she is being prevented from being herself, as it were.[60]

While the gist of his argument is not dissimilar from the justification offered in Chapter 3 for intervening in such cases, it is questionable whether an impaired 'ability to value' is the best way of expressing what is problematic in such cases. As Jennifer Hawkins argues, this

> suggests a contrast between those who have some evaluative outlook or other, and those who entirely lack one. But for the most part, the cases that interest us are not cases in which a person lacks any sense that things matter. Rather the problem is that her sense of what matters is off-base, flawed, mistaken, or bad.[61]

In the case of someone suffering from anorexia nervosa, for example, it is not that they cannot value anything, but that they value

56 Kim, 'The Place of Ability to Valuc in the Evaluation of Decision-Making Capacity', 189–203 at subsection 3 (eBook).

57 Ibid.

58 Ibid.

59 As he explains, 'it would be a mistake to tie DMC to a high standard of authenticity in the sense that a person's decision must be part of some tight set of identity-conferring "projects, relationships, and life plans"'(at subsection 3, eBook).

60 Ibid.

61 Hawkins, 'Decision-Making Capacity and Value', 204–213 at subsection 6 (eBook).

something – thinness – more than we think they ought to. Likewise, a person with depression is unlikely to be unable to place value on anything; they simply place less value on certain things – their life – than they might otherwise do. People with schizophrenia or other psychotic illnesses similarly retain *a* belief system and evaluative outlook; it is just one heavily altered by their disordered beliefs about the world, including the generation of new beliefs that they would not have if they did not suffer from the psychopathology.

If this is the case, and the issue lies not with the person's ability to formulate values, but with the way in which the person's values have been altered or distorted by an illness, then the terminology of 'ability to value' does not fully capture what is impaired in the context of such conditions. More apt would be to describe it as the 'ability to value authentically' – or, more specifically, the ability to formulate values that are unaffected by any type of 'pathology, psychiatric or cognitive, or malfunctioning of brain processes'. Indeed, Kim himself gives an example of a person who understands the consequences of not accepting medical treatment but believes he will be saved by the 'Universal Force of All Reality'. Of him, he explains:

> The underlying spiritual value that trumps the value of medical benefits for the patient refusing a recommended therapy is *inauthentic* in the sense that, were the person not suffering the psychopathology, he would not have such a value or desire.[62] [Emphasis added]

One problem with this approach is that it still fails to elucidate the relationship between the disordered values and the agent's decision-making. If the agent is deemed unable to make a decision because they cannot 'value authentically', this still raises the question of how exactly the purported values impair their decision-making. Of course, what matters is not what values an agent holds, or even whether those values are disordered, but whether those particular values are instrumental in leading the agent to make the decision that they have made, such that without them, they would have made a different decision. A failure to be clear about the effect of the agent's valuing on the decision thus risks being over-inclusive, capturing inauthentic values which are not causally connected to the decision outcome, and so do not directly affect the agent's ability to make decisions.

[62] Kim, 'The Place of Ability to Value in the Evaluation of Decision-Making Capacity', 189–203 at subsection 3 (eBook).

As Kim himself recognises, determining if and when a person can 'value' is also hugely complex. He explains that 'valuing as endorsing or identifying with can be conceptualized as involving several factors'.[63] These include 'the motive or impulse or a desire', the process of 'endorsing or identifying with a motive' and the 'comparing, contrasting, weighing or choosing between different motives or values'.[64] Evaluating this competency is therefore far from straightforward and provides ample room for capacity assessors to invalidate a decision. Furthermore, if the ability to value encompasses the agent's ability to contrast different values that they hold and attribute weight to them, then this would seem to encroach heavily on the agent's evaluative judgement, providing scope for the assessor to deem someone unable to properly choose as between motives, where they choose to prioritise some less-palatable motives over others.

More importantly, however, it is questionable whether this approach really represents a less direct challenge to liberal principles than a more directly substantive theory would do. While in principle, focusing on the agent's capabilities rather than on the content or substance of the values themselves is easier to accommodate within the liberal framework, in reality it involves making exactly the same assessments, but without the transparency that a criterion which looked explicitly at the nature of the values or beliefs and their effects on the agent's evaluative judgements would bring. For example, Kim is clear that in cases of delusional beliefs, despite ostensibly looking at the agent's 'ability to value' and not the values themselves, the agent holds a value that they would not hold if they did not suffer from the psychopathology.[65] In the context of a depressive illness, meanwhile, which he describes as the 'paradigmatic case of an impaired ability to value', he explains that the depressive disorder '*directly distorts, creates, or eliminates a drive, desire, or inclination* the agent would otherwise have, as in a severely depressed person with no desire to live, or with a desire to die'.[66] In both cases, the premise on which the agent has been assessed to be unable to value would seem to be that the value or belief they are expressing is 'inauthentic', in the sense that it has been caused by a disorder and is otherwise inconsistent with the values that constitute the agent's identity or character. Therefore, if

63 Ibid, at subsection 5 (eBook).
64 Ibid.
65 Ibid.
66 Ibid.

framing the question as to whether the values are authentic to the agent or whether the person is able to value authentically, the assessment still involves establishing that certain values or beliefs can be attributed to a recognised mental disorder, and are not consistent with the agent's character, and so to act on the basis of them would undermine the autonomous quality of the decision. But rather than confront the basis on which the particular value is being impugned head-on, this assessment is once again concealed within the language of the agent's capabilities.

Indeed, if this is the case, and a criterion based on the ability to value still involves an evaluation of the disordered nature of a particular value or belief, then it may be questioned whether such an approach is really an 'indirect' form of substantivism at all. At one level, an approach which judges an agent's values and beliefs based on their causal origins might be said to focus not on the content or substance of the values but on what causes the agent to commit to these values. For example, it is not that an agent cannot authentically believe that God will cure them through prayer; it is simply that where that belief derives from a disorder, and the agent would not have it but for that disorder, it may be deemed inauthentic and, thus, to impair an agent's ability to value.

In practice, however, the diagnosis of mental disorder depends not on some objective piece of evidence (like a blood test) but on evaluating the agent's belief systems and behaviour relative to symptoms of known disorders. Determining if a belief has been caused by an illness will thus often entail scrutinising the content or substance of that agent's belief, in order to then consider how that maps onto the common symptoms of different disorders. Consider, for example, the DSM-5 diagnostic criteria of narcissistic personality disorder, according to which the agent must present a 'pervasive pattern of grandiosity (in fantasy or behavior), need for admiration, and lack of empathy, beginning by early adulthood and present in a variety of contexts'.[67] This may be indicated by five or more of the following characteristics:

(1) Has a grandiose sense of self-importance (e.g., exaggerates achievements and talents, expects to be recognized as superior without commensurate achievements).
(2) Is preoccupied with fantasies of unlimited success, power, brilliance, beauty, or ideal love.

[67] American Psychiatric Association, 669–670.

(3) Believes that he or she is 'special' and unique and can only be understood by, or should associate with, other special or high-status people (or institutions).
(4) Requires excessive admiration.
(5) Has a sense of entitlement (i.e., unreasonable expectation of especially favorable treatment or automatic compliance with his or her expectations).
(6) Is interpersonally exploitative (i.e., takes advantage of others to achieve his or her own ends).
(7) Lacks empathy: is unwilling to recognize or identify with the feelings and needs of others.
(8) Is often envious of others or believes that others are envious of him or her.
(9) Shows arrogant, haughty behaviors and attitudes.[68]

Deciding whether a belief derives from such an illness will thus involve scrutinising the content of the agent's beliefs and behaviour to determine whether they reflect these indicators. This is just one example, but the same may be true for many other disorders. In determining whether someone has an eating disorder, for example, the paramountcy given to thinness is clearly highly indicative of a disorder, in a way that, for example, simply valuing physical fitness is not. Feelings of worthlessness, hopelessness, or emptiness, meanwhile, are instrumental to the diagnosis of major depressive disorder. And the content of the delusions from which a person suffers might be highly indicative of the disorder they are afflicted by. Grandiose delusions, for example, where a person has an exaggerated sense of their own importance or authority, are a common symptom of paranoid schizophrenia. Clearly one cannot establish if the delusion is one of grandeur without examining the content of it. Consequently, there will be many cases in which the content or substance of beliefs or values will be highly relevant to the determination of whether that belief or value is authentic. This introduces a clear risk of circularity: one is diagnosed as having a disorder *because* they hold certain beliefs, or value things in certain ways; and then precisely because those beliefs or values form part of the diagnostic criteria for a disorder, they are then attributed to that disorder, making any putative decisions based on them inauthentic.

[68] Ibid.

Of course, the fact that the substance of certain beliefs may be relevant to establishing whether they are thought to be caused by a disorder does not mean that it is *determinative* of that assessment. This is aptly illustrated by the decision in *King's College Hospital NHS Foundation Trust v. C & V*,[69] where the evidence was 'equivocal' as to whether C's highly egocentric and impulsive decision-making was the product of a histrionic or narcissistic personality or simply her strong-willed and difficult personality.[70] The question is thus whether there are certain beliefs or values that will *always* be deemed disordered, inauthentic, and indicative of a lack of capacity. If this is the case, then arguably this approach would place limits on the kinds of beliefs and values the person can autonomously act on in some cases – in practice, even if not in theory.

It is certainly very difficult to envisage any set of circumstances in which the belief of Mrs T in the *NHS Trust v. Mrs T*[71] that blood is evil and can cause a person to do evil acts would be regarded as authentic. Similarly, while many people value being thin, valuing thinness to such an extent that it takes precedence over all other considerations (the person's health, relationships, academic or professional success), would seem demonstrably disordered. This is not to suggest that someone with anorexia nervosa could never capacitously refuse food: they may, as in *Northamptonshire Healthcare NHS Foundation Trust v. AB*,[72] have other reasons for deciding as they do, which are not directly connected to how they value thinness. But where someone does hold that value, or prioritises that value to such a destructive extent, that value will invariably be described as disordered. But if this is the case, and in practice there *are* certain beliefs or evaluative stances that will always be considered disordered (and thus any decision based on them, incapacitated), then such an approach would in reality place some substantive limits on the agent's autonomy and capacity: there would, in effect, be certain beliefs or evaluative stances which an agent simply could not act on, while being deemed capacitous.

It seems, then, that while in theory there may be ways of imposing substantive conditions without placing any direct constraints on the kinds of values or beliefs that the person can act upon, in practice, given

69 [2015] EWCOP 80.
70 Ibid, [44] and [94].
71 [2004] EWHC 1279 (Fam).
72 [2020] EWCOP 40.

the nature of diagnosis of disorder (which involves assessing the person's behaviour or beliefs against common symptoms), one must accept that any attempt to intervene on the basis of an agent acting on 'disordered' values or beliefs will involve some substantive conditions being applied. But if this is the case, then paradoxically, while focusing on the values or beliefs that themselves (rather than the agent's capacities) might represent a greater challenge to liberal ideals in principle, it may in fact reduce the scope for paternalistic judgments in practice through allowing for greater scrutiny of decisions. Rather than merely stating that a certain set of beliefs undermined the agent's ability to 'value authentically', assessors would be required to justify why they consider a specific belief or evaluative outlook to be the product of disorder or impairment, as well as how it is affecting capacity for autonomous decision-making. And if disputed, the agent would have the opportunity to adduce evidence of the authenticity of the belief or value, as indeed the agent did in *C & V*.[73] This would thus introduce far greater transparency into assessments, allowing for proper interrogation of the contested boundaries of disorder in given cases, and enhanced scrutiny of the conclusions reached by capacity assessors. As Ruck Keene and others note, such transparency is 'critical for two reasons':

> The first is that it enables individual accountability, by allowing either the person or anyone else more easily to challenge the outcome of the determination reached. The second is that – at a systems level – transparency is the best way to enable patterns of practice (good or bad) to be identified.[74]

The question, then, is how the law can best attempt to capture this.

4.3 An Authenticity Limb

One way of tackling this issue would be to introduce a new limb to the capacity test that looked explicitly at whether or not the person was unable to make an authentic decision because of the effect of inauthentic values or beliefs on the decision-making process. The discussion in Chapter 3 explored a series of influential accounts of authenticity in the philosophical literature, concluding that authenticity should not depend merely on the causal origins of a given desire or value, but must include some consideration of the agent's attitude towards it. It might seem from

[73] *King's College NHS Foundation Trust v. C and V* [2015] EWCOP 80.
[74] Ruck Keene *et al.*, 'Mental Capacity', 16.

this that any new limb of the test for capacity ought to be directed towards ascertaining the agent's attitude towards a given desire (i.e., whether they sanction it as part of their autobiographical narrative or not). However, as the following discussion will explain, the inability to translate this into a workable legal test gives rise to a problem. While finding a person to lack capacity (where their decision-making has been affected by disordered, but nonetheless endorsed or sanctioned, beliefs or values) is hard to justify philosophically, if the law cannot accurately determine an agent's attitudes towards their beliefs, a choice may have to be made between the law being *over*-inclusive (in finding people to lack capacity even if they would endorse those disordered preferences) or *under*-inclusive (by finding people to *have* capacity even if they would not endorse them). In these circumstances, there may be a range of policy reasons which lean in favour of the capacity test being over-inclusive (since the risk of overreach by the state may be mitigated through a conservative application of the best interests test), rather than under-inclusive (where there is no way to mitigate the total lack of protection offered).

Despite widespread support for the idea that authenticity depends, in some form, on the agent's attitude towards their desire, there is much disagreement in the literature about what exactly that attitude should entail (does it require endorsement, sanctioning, or merely non-alienation?) and about whether it ought to require actual sanctioning or endorsement (as Pugh and Ekstrom suggest[75]), or whether hypothetical endorsement is sufficient (as Christman suggests[76]). Irrespective of what stance one takes on these issues, all result in substantial difficulties when attempts are made to apply them as a legal test, assessed by an outside observer. Posed as an empirical question (i.e., does the person endorse that desire?), the answer is very difficult to establish with any degree of certainty. This is particularly so in the context of mental illness, where it can be hard to pinpoint exactly how much insight the agent really has into their disorder and how the illness might be affecting the reflective process itself. In *A Local Authority v. E*, for example,[77] although E undoubtedly understood that her reasons for acting were caused by an illness (anorexia nervosa), and so did possess good insight, it would still be very difficult for her to prove that she nonetheless endorsed or sanctioned the decision to refuse food, since she would have to

[75] Albeit they allow for this taking place subconsciously.
[76] Christman, *The Politics of Persons*, 145.
[77] [2012] EWCOP 1639.

demonstrate that that endorsement of it was not itself affected by the disorder. But how could an assessor be sure that an agent's sanctioning of a desire – especially one so self-destructive and dangerous – is untainted by their mental disorder, such that they can be confident that it is autonomous?

Pugh and Ekstrom's coherence theory might be of assistance here, since the question is not whether they endorse a desire per se but whether the desire has been endorsed by a preference which is coherent with the agent's character system, in the sense that the agent has sufficient reason to want that desire to be effective in light of their preferences and acceptances. It thus evades the problem of regress, and the risk that the endorsement or authorisation process might itself be affected by the autonomy-subverting disorder. Yet such a test is no easier to apply in practice, requiring the assessor to possess a comprehensive account of the agent's beliefs about what is true and good (i.e., the preferences and acceptances that make up their character system), with a view to then assessing whether in light of these, the agent has 'sufficient reason' to want a given desire to be effective.

Of course, no person has an entirely coherent narrative, and many people's beliefs when taken together might seem contradictory, even incoherent. To try to formulate some sense of an agent's coherent character with sufficient clarity as to be able to discern whether they have sufficient reason to act in a given way will therefore be extremely difficult, particularly in the context of chronic mental disorder, given that many mental illnesses are characterised by unstable preferences, changeable behaviour, and shifting value systems. How does one formulate a narrative for someone suffering from chronic bipolar disorder, for example, for whom erratic, impulsive, and changeable behaviour is 'normal'? And even if, through prolonged engagement with the agent and those close to them, one can form a sense of their preferences and acceptances, it is clearly the case that within the treatment and care context, a change in the agent's circumstances – being ill or disabled, or vulnerable and dependent on others – might well trigger a change in perspective, causing the agent to reassess those things they value most highly. Neither Pugh nor Ekstrom commit to the idea of the 'self' as a static, extant, and immutable essence – on both accounts, one's character may change over time as one's preferences and acceptances evolve, even if many aspects of one's 'core character' will remain relatively stable. Accordingly, the character against which an assessor attempts to assess an agent's desires may well be shifting as such decisions are being taken.

Given this, there is a risk that any attempt to assess whether the endorsing preference is coherent with an agent's character system becomes contingent on the assessor, and what importance they attach to different behaviours or expressions of value. Are these incoherent with the agent's character system or demonstrative of changes in one's preferences and acceptances? To use a crude example, if an adherent Roman Catholic who has always professed to be heterosexual and expressed religious-based objection to the practice of homosexuality suddenly announced himself to be gay, an outside observer might be disinclined to regard this as him acting 'inauthentically'. This is based, however, on a judgement that this 'new' expression of the agent's preferences or acceptances is in some way more significant than their previous ones. Their perception of the agent's character system is thus reconfigured to include this development, rather than regarding it as outlying and inauthentic. In this way, the assessment of authenticity becomes dependent on the assessor's own judgements about what coheres with the agent's character and what does not.

This problem might be lessened if the bar for coherence were set lower. In Kim's formulation, for example, the decision must be 'patently inconsistent with the set of values and history that roughly constitute the person's identity' to be inauthentic, which would seem easier to establish than the extent to which a person's set of values or history provide them with sufficient reason for action. However, the effect is to shift the focus from the agent's attitude towards that desire, to an objective assessment of the extent to which it appears to be consistent with their character. What matters is not whether *they* think they have good reason to act in a certain way, because, for example, they value something more highly than other things; instead, what matters is whether a desire is, as a matter of fact, consistent with previously expressed values or character. While coherence with pre-existing values might be good evidence of whether or not a value originates in a disorder, and of the agent's likely attitude towards it, the fact that an agent's value is inconsistent with what has gone before would not seem sufficient in itself to regard it as inauthentic. It would seem perverse, for example, to deny the autonomy of a young man who, despite always maintaining that physical independence and agility was essential to his sense of self, without which he would rather die, later wishes for life-saving treatment despite being rendered quadriplegic. As noted previously, the medical context often precipitates changes of attitudes, as people come to adjust to new, often previously undesirable circumstances. And, of course, these problems of applying the test in practice are compounded in cases of chronic mental illness, where precisely the opposite may be true. The desire may well be reasonably consistent with the person's history and previously expressed values, yet they may not consider those values to constitute their identity, precisely because they do not endorse or sanction them, and perhaps even resent having them. Refusal of food because one values thinness above all else may be perfectly consistent for someone with chronic anorexia, for example, yet as studies into their experiences discussed previously showed,[78] they may deem that anorexic self as separate from and harmful to their authentic self, and those values something which they must push against and try and resist. It would seem equally perverse to deem such a person to be acting authentically if they refused food despite their wish to overcome their illness. The test therefore cannot assist in identifying when intervention is acceptable in the very circumstances in which questions of authenticity are most pertinent. Rather it merely generates new questions about what values will 'roughly constitute' a person's identity, which reintroduces the challenges identified previously, concerning assessors attempting to formulate coherent narratives for people from the outside.

Given these problems with answering the question of whether the agent *in fact* endorses a value, one might instead follow Christman's lead and frame the test instead as a hypothetical question: *if* the agent knew of all their reasons for holding that belief, *would* they accept it as part of their self-narrative? However, if this were the test, there is a real risk that the answer to this would depend on scarcely more than whether the assessor regarded that belief as valuable or worthwhile. If there seems to be some value in holding it, then the assessor is likely to be more inclined to say the agent would be likely to sanction or accept it, while a belief that is self-destructive and irrational is unlikely to be thought to be one which an agent would knowingly sanction. For example, since most would agree that prioritising thinness over one's life is neither rational nor beneficial to a person, it is difficult to think of any circumstances in which an assessor would conclude that the agent would hypothetically rationally sanction their desire to be thin at the expense of life, even if they understood it was caused by an eating disorder. The same might be true of Mrs T's belief that blood is evil.[79] Other beliefs or values, however, *might* be regarded as beneficial or valuable to the agent, even if stemming

[78] Tan *et al.*, 'Competence to Make Treatment Decisions in Anorexia Nervosa, 267–282.

[79] *The NHS Trust v. Mrs T* [2004] EWHC 1279 (Fam).

from a disorder. In *Wye Valley*, for example, an assessor might be more inclined to answer the question of whether Mr B would hypothetically sanction his beliefs in the affirmative, given that they provided Mr B with a source of comfort and a positive ethical framework by which to live his life. Or, to use an even clearer example, a widow who 'hears' or 'sees' their dead spouse talking to them and who takes instructions of what to do in certain situations from them. (This is relatively common: a study in 2015 found that between 30 per cent and 60 per cent of widowed people had suffered from a hallucination of this sort.[80]) In this situation, an assessor might be more inclined to say that the widow would sanction this belief, even knowing it was a hallucination, because of the comfort it brings at a difficult time. Posed as a hypothetical question, then, the answer is likely to depend largely on whether the assessor considers the belief to be the kind of belief that someone might reasonably hold, or which might bring about some benefit to them. Not only is this entirely subjective, depending on the particular assessor and their own values or beliefs, but it would also result in the reasoning behind assessments becoming very opaque, which would not enhance the transparency with which the test is currently being applied and might in turn encourage outcome-orientated decisions.

Whether framed as an empirical question or a hypothetical question, it does not seem that sanctionist or coherentist theories (even in their modified forms) can provide a reliable and workable *legal* test for when a motivating value or belief will be authentic, even if they may provide the most convincing theory of authenticity philosophically. Given the problems identified in this discussion, one must attach a very low degree of certainty to any assessment that an agent would have (or has) sanctioned their disordered beliefs. But if this is the case, we should be wary of placing substantial weight on this determination,[81] as would clearly occur if the capacity assessment, and thus the power to intervene and offer any protection to an (ill and vulnerable) individual, rested on it.

Of course, for the most part, originist (or historical) accounts provide a crude proxy for a sanctionist approach, given that most people will not

[80] A. Castelnovo *et al.*, 'Post-Bereavement Hallucinatory Experiences: A Critical Overview of Population and Clinical Studies' (2015) 186 *Journal of Affective Disorders* 266–274.

[81] While determining the origins of beliefs or values also inevitably entails clinical judgement, the parameters of that judgment are set by the diagnostic criteria for disorder contained in the DSM and ICD manuals. It is therefore considerably more bounded than the very open-ended question of what the person's hypothetical attitude towards a belief would be if they were not suffering from a disorder.

sanction beliefs or values that they hold only on account of illness, especially where those beliefs or values cause them distress or an inability to function fully in ordinary life. Those who have insight into their illnesses often state they would rather not suffer from that mental illness; indeed, they seek medical assistance precisely with a view to overcoming it or to lessen its symptoms (which may be those value or belief systems it generates). Meanwhile, there is much evidence from those who have recovered from serious mental disorders that they later come to regret the values that previously informed their decisions. Craigie draws on this in the context of anorexia, explaining where the person placed paramount importance on thinness, this regret does not appear to be based on a failure to do what they wanted ('they pursued the goal of thinness very effectively'). Rather, this regret

> has its source primarily in *what they valued*. Among the themes evident in discussions of regret by people who have suffered from anorexia is the belief that they placed too much importance on particular considerations (e.g., restricting food intake) or failed to recognize the relative importance of other considerations (e.g., relationships, health, education, career).[82]

While Pugh is right to caution against placing too much emphasis on anticipated future regret as a basis on which to find someone to lack capacity,[83] this is nonetheless evidence in support of the idea that absent the influence of disorder, many people suffering from anorexia nervosa would neither sanction nor endorse their valuing of thinness. And of course where a disorder has led a person to hold false beliefs – that they are overweight when they are in fact severely underweight; that they are a world-famous surgeon, when they are not; or that the doctor has sinister intentions, when they do not – and these false beliefs cause them to wish to make harmful choices, this is likely to be even more clearly the case. Few people would endorse or sanction beliefs they knew to be objectively untrue or wish to make decisions on the basis of them.

Given the challenges in translating sanctionist accounts into a viable legal test, coupled with the fact that they will generally overlap with originist accounts, at least in the context of disorder or impairment (it may be different in the context of social or cultural influences), one response might be to opt for the less nuanced originist test, with the

[82] J. Craigie, 'Competence, Practical Rationality and What a Patient Values' (2011) 25(6) *Bioethics* 326–333, 331.

[83] Pugh, *Autonomy, Rationality, and Contemporary Bioethics*, 230–231.

complexities of the agent's attitude towards their disordered beliefs dealt with instead within the best interests assessment. The merits and challenges of such an approach will be considered in Section 4.3.1.

4.3.1 Embracing Originist Accounts of Authenticity in the Law

At first sight, focusing on the cause or origins of a value belief would seem markedly more straightforward than considering the agent's attitude towards that belief or its consistency with their character system. Certainly, many of the examples considered previously could easily be regarded as inauthentic on this basis: in *Mrs T*[84] or *Wye Valley*,[85] psychiatrists were clear that the decision was based on beliefs that stemmed from the agent's hallucinations or delusions, while the values of an agent with anorexia nervosa who refuses food might be easily attributable to their disorder in at least some cases.[86] As Charland explains,

> in anorexia, thinness is usually pathologically overvalued. It is crucial that this pathology in valuation is not simply an idiosyncratic matter of personal choice and 'lifestyle,' a mere social abnormality. In full-fledged chronic anorexia, the value of thinness acquires a different character. It also becomes a medical abnormality that is both caused and reinforced by the disease. Significantly, this medical abnormality in valuation varies with the incidence and severity of disease. When the disease is active, pathological overvaluation of thinness persists or increases. As the disease abates, the pathological overvaluation wanes and may even disappear. This variation between pathological overvaluation of thinness and the incidence and severity of anorexia strongly suggests that the overvaluation of thinness in anorexia is largely a medical abnormality, a causal consequence of disease. This can be contrasted with cases where overvaluing thinness is simply a matter of personal choice based on abnormal social preferences, which an individual can adopt or relinquish at will.[87]

Charland also draws analogies with substance addictions, where 'the drug has become the dominant gravitational center of attraction in that person's value system'.[88] In such cases, it might be thought that we can

[84] *The NHS Trust v. Mrs T* [2004] EWHC 1279 (Fam).
[85] *Wye Valley NHS Trust v. Mr B* [2015] EWCOP 60.
[86] *A Local Authority v. E* [2012] EWCOP 1639.
[87] L. Charland, 'Anorexia and the MacCAT-T Test for Mental Competence: Validity, Value, and Emotion' (2006) 13(4) *Philosophy, Psychiatry, & Psychology* 283–287, 284.
[88] Ibid, 284–5.

confidently attribute certain values to disorders and assess how they might be influencing the agent's evaluation of information.

Sceptical that an originist approach could work in practice, Ahlin has suggested that determining the origins of a person's desires would require 'deep psychological analysis' and 'socio-historical biographical investigation', which would likely 'have to include interviews with people who were close to the desire-holder'.[89] While this may be true (in some cases at least), these are not insurmountable obstacles, particularly given that authenticity concerns will usually arise in the context of psychiatry, where a standard psychiatric assessment would involve taking a detailed history of the agent's life from birth and, if possible, obtaining a collateral history from someone close to the agent. Indeed, many of the most difficult cases are characterised by chronic mental illness, as in *A Local Authority v. E*,[90] *Wye Valley*,[91] and *Re C*,[92]and so the psychiatrist (or social worker) may have had a lasting relationship with the agent reaching back over many years or, at the very least, have access to very extensive notes. While this is not to say that there will not be emergency situations, as in cases such as *St George*,[93] it does suggest that the contexts in which authenticity might have the most traction are those in which comprehensive and detailed assessments can be, and to a large extent already are, made about whether and how the agent's thought processes and belief structure are being affected by illness. This is supported by Kane *et al.*'s study into the capacity assessments conducted by liaison psychiatrists (described in Chapter 2), which found that a key challenge for psychiatrists lay in determining whether a person's beliefs were caused by mental illness, or 'were congruent with the person's own personal or cultural belief systems'.[94] In order to establish this, psychiatrists often had to consider 'the patients' personal history and culture (often through involving others from the same culture)'.[95]

Of course, examining peoples' values and beliefs in this way is in any event required if the agent is found to lack capacity, as the assessor must then decide what is in that agent's best interests, which requires them to

89 Ahlin, 'The Impossibility of Reliably Determining the Authenticity of Desires', 43–50, 48.
90 [2012] EWCOP 1639.
91 *Wye Valley NHS Trust v. B* [2015] EWCOP 60.
92 *Re C* (Adult: Refusal of Treatment) [1994] 1 WLR 290 (Fam).
93 *St George's NHS Trust v. S* [1998] 3 All ER 673.
94 Kane *et al.*, 'Difficult Capacity Cases, 946234..
95 Ibid.

consider the agent's past and present wishes and feelings[96] and the beliefs and values that would be likely to influence their decision if they had capacity.[97] The assessor is also obliged to consult with those involved in the agent's care or interested in their welfare,[98] with a view to helping them elicit information about the agent and what they valued.[99]

Many cases are not borderline, and there is therefore reason to think that assessors will be able to judge fairly reliably whether an agent holds a set of beliefs or values only on account of illness, particularly where that illness manifests in specific ways, such as in eating disorders or, to a lesser extent, depression. It is worth noting here that evidence suggests fairly high levels of inter-rater reliability when it comes to assessments of capacity in the psychiatry context.[100] While the fact that psychiatrists agree is not necessarily evidence that they are 'right', it does give us reason to hope that for the most part, psychiatrists are able to reliably and consistently determine when an agent's behaviour or expression of values is indicative of disorder.

But this will not always be the case and there will be cases which are far from straightforward. Even if a person is known to have a mental illness, it can prove difficult to unpick how, if at all, this is affecting their values and beliefs. This is especially so where the disorder is connected with attitudes, behaviours, or psychosis, the exact nature of which may manifest differently between people. While schizophrenia often gives rise to hallucinations or delusions, for example, the nature of these hallucinations may differ substantially, making it difficult to know which of a person's beliefs (if any) ought to be attributed to that illness, and which to their pre-illness authentic self. This was evident in Kane *et al.*'s study, in which psychiatrists explicitly noted the 'difficulty distinguishing whether [certain beliefs] were due to a delusion or whether they were religious, cultural, or political beliefs'.[101] But it is also apparent from the responses

96 Mental Capacity Act, s4(6)(a).

97 Mental Capacity Act, s4(6)(b).

98 Mental Capacity Act, s4(7).

99 This engagement with the patient's values and priorities is also demanded in other areas of law, such as in determining what risks to disclose to the patients in light of *Montgomery*: *Montgomery v. Lanarkshire Health Board* [2015] UKSC 11.

100 See, for example, V. Raymont, A. Buchanan, A. David *et al.*, 'The Inter-Rater Reliability of Mental Capacity Assessments' (2007) 30(2) *International Journal of Law and Psychiatry* 112–117; D. Okai, G. Owen, and H. McGuire, 'Mental Capacity in Psychiatric Patients' (2018) 191(4) *The British Journal of Psychiatry* 291–297.

101 Kane *et al.*, 'Difficult Capacity Cases', 946234.

of interviewed doctors to the vignette of Max – a schizophrenic Christian refusing treatment for a kidney stone as he believed his pain was God's punishment for his sins[102] – with nearly all interviewees expressing (in different ways) the need to (and challenge involved in) determining whether 'this view about God was a part of his psychotic illness at the moment, or whether that is consistent with his previous belief system' (David, p. 18). The courts faced a similar issue in *Sherwood Forest Hospitals NHS Foundation Trust v. C*[103] and in *Wye Valley.*[104] In the latter case, although it was clear that Mr B's religious beliefs *were* the result of persistent auditory hallucinations in which he heard the voices of angels and of the Virgin Mary, Mr Justice Peter Jackson noted that the line between faith and delusion is not always clear cut: '[R]eligious beliefs are based on faith, not reason, and some can strongly influence the believer's attitude to health and medical treatment without in any way suggesting a lack of mental capacity.'[105] There may also be a cultural dimension to some beliefs which exacerbate these difficulties. Demonic possession is a feature of many shamanic cultures, for example. The boundary between disordered values and unusual or eccentric ones can thus be a very fine one.

Another context in which distinguishing the disordered from the authentic can prove difficult is in cases of chronic mental illness, where, over many years, pre-existing 'authentic' and 'inauthentic' belief and value systems may become inextricably intertwined. In these circumstances, identifying whether a particular value or belief is attributable to illness or disorder may be almost impossible. This was the case in *Wye Valley,*[106] but it is even more clearly the case for someone like Ian Brady, whose personality disorder manifested itself in 'narcissism; egocentricity; histrionicity; obsessionality; need for control; paranoia; litigiousness; lack of remorse; and lack of empathy'.[107] It is difficult to conceive of any of his

[102] Max suffers from schizophrenia and experiences persecutory delusions. He has a kidney stone, which is causing him some abdominal pain, and he requires an operation to remove it. He understands the medical evidence in favour of having the operation, and the consequences of not having it, because he believes the pain is God's punishment for the sins he has committed during his life. He thinks doctors should not interfere with the actions of God, and that it is only God who will decide his fate. As a devout Christian throughout his life, he believes God will not let him die.

[103] [2020] EWCOP 10.

[104] *Wye Valley NHS Trust v. Mr B* [2015] EWCOP 60.

[105] Ibid, [15].

[106] Ibid, [43].

[107] *R v. Collins and Ashworth Hospital Authority ex parte Brady* [2001] 58 BMLR 173, [36].

beliefs or values being totally unaffected by his disorder, making establishing authenticity very challenging. Similarly in *Leicester City Council v. MPX*,[108] Her Honour Judge George concluded that the agent's personality disorder so distorted her 'perception of the world' that she lacked capacity in respect of all the issues before the court,[109] indicating that she considered it to cloud very many aspects of her decision-making in a way which made identifying an otherwise 'authentic' self difficult.

And if cases of mental illness can cause problems in establishing authenticity, even more difficult are those cases in which it is simply not clear whether an agent's values or beliefs evidence a disorder at all. As the previous discussion illustrates,[110] mental illnesses are not objectively either present or absent; rather the assessor must often seek to establish whether, on the basis of the available evidence, the agent's symptoms are sufficiently pronounced to deem them to have a mental disorder. The challenge involved in this is evident in cases such as *King's College Hospital NHS Foundation Trust v. C & V*[111] (where a woman refused dialysis because her life had lost its sparkle) and *Avon and Wiltshire Mental Health Partnership v. WA & Anor* (in which a man refused food in protest at his official date of birth being changed).[112] There will therefore always be hard cases in which it is difficult, perhaps even impossible, to unpick how far an agent's values are being affected by their illness. But that some cases will pose difficulties is not a good reason to abandon any inquiry into it. After all, judgements of this nature form the bedrock of a psychiatrist's work, being an inherent part of diagnosis. This is not to say that such determinations will always be easy. They are a challenging but not uncommon feature of clinical practice, which psychiatrists must grapple with all the time. There is therefore good reason to believe that a provision that looked at the origins of certain values or beliefs could provide a workable means of distinguishing authentic from inauthentic values in practice.

One way of incorporating this into the MCA may be to introduce a part (e) into the list of capacities contained in section 3(1)(a)–(d),[113]

[108] [2019] EWCOP 64.
[109] Ibid, [36].
[110] See Chapter 3.
[111] *NHS Foundation Trust v. C & V* [2015] EWCOP 80.
[112] [2020] EWCOP 37.
[113] Section 3 MCA states that: (1) For the purposes of section 2, a person is unable to make a decision for himself if he is unable to (a) understand the information relevant to the decision, (b) retain that information, (c) use or weigh that information as part of the

which would apply if the agent was unable to make a decision because the values or beliefs by which the agent is evaluating the relevant information have been caused by or altered as a consequence of the agent suffering from a disorder, illness, or impairment. In justifying the use of such a provision, assessors would then have to explain clearly both how and why the agent's values or beliefs were thought to have been caused or altered by the disorder or impairment, and how those values or beliefs were affecting the agent's evaluative judgement in respect of the relevant information. For example, in the context of anorexia nervosa or depression, the psychiatrist must seek to show how the disorder has affected the values or beliefs that the agent holds (which would require them to explain why the values governing the agent's decision-making could reasonably be attributed to anorexia nervosa), as well as the impact of those 'new' or 'distorted' values on their evaluation of the relevant information. Similarly in the context of delusional beliefs, it must be shown both that the beliefs being expressed by the agent are the product of a disorder or impairment (as opposed to merely an eccentric belief system), and how those beliefs affect the judgements they make about the information (e.g., that it is causing them to misunderstand how factually true and relevant information applies to them).

One concern that may arise is how such a provision ought to deal with situations in which an agent has multiple reasons for deciding as they have, only some of which have been affected by illness or impairment. After all, an agent may have multiple values or beliefs which they apply to the relevant information, some of which may be disordered, and others not. This shall be considered in Section 4.3.2.

4.3.2 *Multiple Reasons for Acting*

It is clearly the case that people may apply different values or beliefs to any piece of information, and that not all these values will necessarily be affected by a disorder or impairment, even if a person happens to suffer from one. In *A Local Authority v. E*, for example,[114] while E undoubtedly had disordered values due to her anorexia which affected her evaluative judgement, she also expressed other, perfectly rational reasons for acting, such as to end her perpetual suffering. In *Northamptonshire Healthcare*

process of making the decision, or (d) communicate his decision (whether by talking, using sign language, or any other means).

114 [2012] EWCOP 1639.

NHS Foundation Trust v. AB too,[115] although AB's anorexia clearly affected her decision-making in some ways, she also expressed an understandable desire not to be subjected to a traumatic period of forced feeding for yet another time. Even in cases involving delusional beliefs, it is not uncommon for people to express multiple reasons for their decision, some of which may be driven by delusions, but others not. In *Mrs T*, for example, although one of her reasons for refusing a blood transfusion was that she believed blood was evil; she also felt herself to be in a vicious cycle of cutting herself and then requiring a transfusion, which she no longer wished to endure.[116] Perhaps the clearest and most challenging example of this is in *Re SB (A patient: Capacity to consent to termination)*,[117] which concerned whether a woman suffering from bipolar disorder had the capacity to consent to terminate her pregnancy at twenty-three weeks. During the early weeks of her pregnancy, all the evidence suggested she wanted the baby, and she conscientiously attended scans and other antenatal appointments. But after four months, she stopped taking the medication prescribed for her bipolar disorder, after which she started to exhibit symptoms of being unwell. She now made appointments for a termination, not once but twice, but on neither occasion went ahead with it. The first time she claimed to have insufficient funds to travel to the clinic,[118] while the second time she professed a dislike of the type of procedure proposed.[119] At this time SB was compulsorily detained under the Mental Health Act. Despite her requests for a termination, the hospital did not consider her to have the capacity to make this decision. Although she understood the relevant information,[120] her consultant psychiatrist was '100% clear that she does not have capacity to take the decision',[121] a view supported by the independently instructed psychiatrist.[122] Her reasons were based 'upon flawed evidence and paranoid beliefs',[123] namely that her husband and mother would not support her if she had a baby (a view strongly disputed by them, and contrary to the opinion of the treating psychiatrist who

115 [2020] EWCOP 40.
116 [2004] EWHC 1279 (Fam), [8].
117 *Re SB (A patient: Capacity to consent to termination)* [2013] EWHC 1417 (COP).
118 Ibid, [21].
119 Ibid, [22].
120 Ibid, [23]; [34].
121 Ibid, [32].
122 Ibid, [33].
123 Ibid, [34].

observed her husband to be attentive and caring). Both psychiatrists considered these to be paranoid beliefs, a view corroborated by the strong correlation between the time when she stopped taking her medication and the commencement of these beliefs.[124] Notwithstanding this, Mr Justice Holman found her to have capacity. Even though she had 'some skewed thoughts and paranoid or delusional views with regard to her husband',[125] she also gave many other reasons for requesting a termination.[126] These included the fact that she 'perfectly understand [ably]'[127] did not want to have a child while compulsorily detained under the MHA;[128] her 'entirely rational'[129] worry about her ability to bring up a child;[130] and that she felt suicidal at the prospect of having to carry the child to term, and might well attempt to kill herself if denied a termination.

As these examples from the case law demonstrate, the problem of an individual having multiple reasons for acting is thus not one specific to incorporating a new authenticity limb into the capacity test: it is a problem that judges must often grapple with under the current law too. Section 3 of the MCA provides that a person will be unable to make a decision *if* he is unable to understand, retain, and use or weigh the relevant information when making a decision, but it does not provide specific guidance on how to apply this where the lack of understanding or weighing ability only afflicts *certain* reasons a person gives and not others. Given the lack of explicit judicial engagement with the question to date, coupled with its increased importance under the proposed new capacity criteria, it is nonetheless important to consider how such cases ought to be approached under the alternative legal framework suggested.

The starting point for this is to analyse how judges are currently approaching this issue. Although the approach differs across preceding cases, broadly, the touchstone for whether the person is found to have capacity in these circumstances would seem to be whether or not the person would have reached the same decision regardless of (or 'but for') the disorder or impairment. Sometimes the focus of the assessment will be on the relationship between the disorder and the decision reached,

124 Ibid.
125 Ibid, [41].
126 Ibid.
127 Ibid, [42].
128 Ibid.
129 Ibid, [42] and [43].
130 Ibid.

underpinning which is the idea that if the disordered belief is not directly connected with the nature of the decision to be taken, then there must be something else causing the agent to decide as they are, which is unaffected by their impairment. In *Re C (Adult: Refusal of Treatment)*,[131] for example, the court was called upon to decide whether a sixty-eight-year-old man with paranoid schizophrenia had the capacity to refuse the amputation of his gangrenous foot, without which there was an 85 per cent chance he would die. C, who suffered from persecutory delusions that any treatment was intended to destroy his body, along with delusions of grandeur that he had enjoyed a distinguished career as a doctor and had never lost a patient, opposed the treatment. Despite understanding his prognosis, he expressed complete confidence that he would survive his current condition, aided by God, the doctors, and the nurses. While aspects of his reasoning were thus clearly irrational, others were perfectly rational. He was clear, for example, that he 'would rather die with two feet than live with one' – an understandable decision for an elderly man detained in a secure hospital, who did not want to have to adapt to using a prosthetic limb. Below-the-knee amputation also carried a 15 per cent risk of death, and while he rejected the surgery proposed, he agreed to more conservative surgery (subject to not having a more localised spinal injection because of the risk of paralysis).

The medical professionals in the case could not reach agreement over the extent to which his delusions were affecting his ability to make such a decision. In the view of one psychiatrist, Dr Eastman, although C's capacity was 'plainly' reduced by his mental illness, 'whether it is sufficiently reduced remains marginal in the absence of any direct link between the persecutory delusions and his present condition'.[132] Dr Gall reached a similar conclusion, with both doctors attaching considerable weight to the 'rational' reasons he gave for his refusal. Dr Ghosh, meanwhile, described this as a case that, 'far from being on the borderline', was 'very clear cut'. While she acknowledged that his capacity was 'not absent', she found it to be 'very seriously reduced' by his persecutory and grandiose delusions.

[131] *Re C* (Adult: Refusal of Treatment) [1994] 1 WLR 290 (Fam). Although this case was heard prior to the introduction of the MCA, given the very similar test for capacity applied (which drew on the Law Commission's suggestions for reforming the law in this area), its discussion on this issue is apposite.

[132] Ibid, 292 G.

It was Dr Eastman and Dr Gall's evidence that ultimately found favour with Mr Justice Thorpe, who did not find sufficient evidence of the link between C's refusal and his persecutory delusions.[133] This was in part because Dr Ghosh was found not to have known the full consequences of C refusing treatment at the time, information which Mr Justice Thorpe considered would have 'influenced her appraisal of the critical equation and of C's approach to it'.[134] Importantly, however, he also held that while C's schizophrenia impaired his 'general capacity', it could not be shown that he lacked sufficient understanding of the 'nature, purpose and effects of the treatment he refuses'.[135] Accordingly he found C to have capacity regarding his decision to 'result from sincerely held conviction'.[136]

The focus of the judge's assessment in this case was on the relationship between the disordered beliefs and the content of the decision. Since there was no direct link between C's disordered beliefs and his decision to refuse the amputation, his disorder could not be said to be the cause of the decision. Very similar issues and reasoning arose in *Heart of England NHS Foundation Trust v. JB*,[137] also concerning a patient with paranoid schizophrenia who refused an amputation notwithstanding her gangrenous foot having come off 'naturally', leaving an unresolved wound prone to infection. This again led to a disagreement between JB's community psychiatrist (who felt her ability to weigh the information was 'compromised by her tendency to minimise and disbelieve what the doctors are telling her'),[138] and an independent psychiatrist who found her to be 'consistent in her views and reasoning process', namely that she wished to keep her leg as long as possible.[139] The latter view was supported by the surgeon and later the judge, who was similarly unsatisfied that a link between JB's mental illness and alleged incapacity in taking that specific decision had been established.[140]

133 Ibid, 295 E.
134 Ibid, 294 B.
135 Ibid, 295 E.
136 Ibid, 294 C.
137 *Heart of England NHS Foundation Trust v. JB* [2014] EWHC 342 (COP), per Peter Jackson J. at [28].
138 Ibid, [30].
139 Ibid, [33].
140 Ibid, [40].

The opposite conclusion was reached in *A Local Authority v. E*[141] and *Northamptonshire Healthcare NHS Foundation Trust v. AB*,[142] both concerning refusals of treatment by women with chronic anorexia nervosa. This is clearest in respect of *AB*, in which counsel for AB, Katie Gollop QC, sought to argue precisely that there was a lack of direct link between her disorder and the decision to refuse force-feeding, because her decision was based not on a compulsive desire to avoid calories entering her body (that was undoubtedly characteristic of anorexia), but on a number of other perfectly 'reasonable' reasons. These included:

(1) the effect of her past experience and the violence it has done to her sense of self and her personal dignity,
(2) the risks and futility of further tube feeding,
(3) the desire to be at home, and
(4) the desire to focus on quality, not quantity, of life.[143]

Ms Gollop QC drew a distinction between AB's 'wish not to endure further trauma and her avoidance of the option of tube feeding in order to avoid ingesting calories and putting on weight'.[144] While she accepted that her motives for refusing force-feeding may be plural, at least one of these was to avoid the 'threat, fear and risk of another episode of forcible feeding'. To characterise that as 'illness impaired reasoning' would be to 'negate the reality of what AB has been through and its true effect on her'.[145] And so even if one reason was to avoid putting on weight, the impact of her disorder on her decision-making was 'tangential at best'.[146] Mrs Justice Roberts roundly rejected this argument, holding that

> given the chronic nature of AB's illness and its current clinical presentation, her decisions in connection with food, calorific intake and consequent weight gain are so infected and influenced by her fixated need to avoid weight gain at all costs that true logical reasoning in relation to these specific matters is beyond her capacity or ability.[147]

Her decision was thus inextricably linked to – and influenced by – her disordered evaluation of the importance of avoiding calories. And so

141 *A Local Authority v. E* [2012] EWCOP 1639.
142 [2020] EWCOP 40.
143 Ibid, [59].
144 Ibid, [58].
145 Ibid.
146 Ibid, [60].
147 Ibid, [64].

while she did hold 'very sound and straightforward reasons for not wishing to experience the trauma and pain of further admissions to hospital', her judgement in relation to the need to gain weight was 'critically impaired by an intense and irrational fear of weight gain',[148] which left her 'powerless to reach any other decision'.[149] Her disorder was thus taken to have distorted her evaluative judgement to such an extent that she could not be said to have separate reasons unconnected to it, which would otherwise have led to the decision outcome.

Other judgments have not been concerned expressly with the causal relationship between the disorder and the decision, but with the *other* reasons that the agent has given in support of their decision. As noted previously, in *Re SB* for example, Mr Justice Holman appeared to take the view that if the agent had *some* rational reasons for wanting to have an abortion, this was sufficient to find them to be able to take a decision. In this case,

> even if aspects of the decision-making are influenced by paranoid thoughts in relation to her husband and her mother, she is nevertheless able to describe, and genuinely holds, a range of rational reasons for her decision.[150]

Although the rationale for this was not explained, the assumption underpinning this may have been that these 'rational reasons' would have led SB to make the same decision anyway, and so her 'paranoid thoughts' were inconsequential and did not disbar her from being able to 'make a decision' within the terms of the Act. Nonetheless, the mere fact that an agent holds 'rational' reasons should not be sufficient to deem them to have capacity if those reasons would not alone have led the agent to take the decision in question. The key question ought to be whether *that* agent would have reached the decision they have were it not for the effect of the disorder on their evaluative judgement; it is not about whether someone else could capacitously make that decision based on the reasons given. In this case, for example, the crux of the issue ought to have been whether her 'rational' reasons would have led her to desire an abortion even if she was not suffering from paranoid delusions. If the answer is no, then the decision reached was still an inauthentic one *for her*, even if it might well have been an authentic one for someone else. One concern with Mr Justice Holman's formulation is thus that a failure to examine the

[148] Ibid.
[149] Ibid.
[150] Ibid, [44].

relationship between the disordered beliefs and the decision outcome might result in an assessor applying the MCA to find agents to have capacity, notwithstanding the fact that they are seeking to make inauthentic decisions. In this case, it also led to a failure to explore how the SB's paranoid beliefs might have affected both the existence of and the weight given to her apparently 'rational' reasons. For example, her fear of not being able to bring up the child, and the consequent risk that the child might be taken into care, may well have been influenced by her conviction that her husband and mother would not support her in caring for the child. Given the clear correlation between the abandonment of her medication and her relapse, it also might be argued that once she resumed her medication, SB might have conquered her suicidal thoughts and felt better placed to cope as a parent. Her decision may therefore have been an inauthentic one, notwithstanding her seemingly being able to offer 'rational' reasons in support of it.

Despite the criticisms which may be made of *Re SB*, the overarching approach of the courts in cases of this kind is nonetheless a good one. Underpinning the judgements seems to be an attempt to answer the question of when an agent will be 'unable to make a decision' by looking at the causal relationship between their impairment and the decision outcome. Have the 'impaired' reasons led to the decision being made, or would the agent have made the same decision even if aspects of their reasoning had *not* been affected by the impairment, because, for example, they had other reasons for deciding as they have? This approach ought to be continued if the amendments proposed are adopted. After all, if someone holds non-disordered beliefs or reasons which would have led them to the same conclusion, then the outcome of the decision has not been affected by the disorder. And so, it would seem unduly harsh to find them to be 'unable to make a decision' merely because they also happen to hold a disordered belief, which in their eyes would lend further support for a decision they otherwise seek to make. To do so risks descending into a status-based approach to capacity whereby the mere fact of holding disordered beliefs or values renders someone incapacitated, even if those beliefs or values do not influence decision-making in a meaningful way.

Introducing the proposed new limb will not therefore necessitate a new approach, but it might enhance the transparency with which such assessments are made. Currently one of the difficulties with these judgments is that judges are attempting to grapple with what the impact of disordered beliefs or values are on the agent's decision-making process, without having the 'language' or 'framework' to do so. In cases involving chronic anorexia, for example, underpinning the judgments seems to be an assertion by the judges that even though the agent may be able to understand, use and weigh information, and thus provide some rational reasons for their decision, the entire evaluative outlook that they apply to the information and decision-making process is shaped by their anorexia nervosa, such that none of the reasons they give are wholly unconnected with their disorder. Similarly in *Re SB*, the real crux of the issue is around how SB's paranoid beliefs and lack of insight into her condition are affecting her evaluation of other issues, namely her capacity to cope with the demands of parenting. Yet it is hard to capture these assessments within the question of whether the agent can use or weigh information. The new criteria would thus allow for greater precision in the language used to describe the impact of disorder or impairment in such cases. In *Re C*, for example, it would have been open to the judge to conclude that either C's disordered beliefs that he would survive without the amputation were not affecting the way he was evaluating the 'relevant' information, because there was no direct link between the content and nature of his beliefs and his decision to refuse, or the judge could have decided that they were affecting the way he is evaluating some, but not all, of the information, and applying the previous logic, not in a way sufficient to render him unable to make the decision on the balance of probabilities. In *AB*, meanwhile, the judge might have reached the opposite conclusion: that AB's values had become distorted by her anorexia nervosa in a range of ways, which were affecting how she evaluated all information relevant to the question of whether to refuse force-feeding. These assessments must, of course, be made against the background position that where it is not possible to say the extent to which the disordered or impaired values or beliefs are affecting the agent's evaluation of the relevant information, the presumption of capacity ought to apply.

In fact, this discussion highlights once again the potential harshness of the capacity cliff edge. In both *Re C*[151] and *Re SB*,[152] despite holding both rational and delusional beliefs, the agent was found to have capacity, and their expressed wishes were respected. In *E*, by contrast, the consequences could not have been more different: E was found to lack capacity and was subjected to the most invasive of treatments against her clearly expressed wishes. While a separate limb of the capacity test will not

[151] *Re C (Adult: Refusal of Medical Treatment)* [1992] 4 All ER 649.
[152] *Re SB (A patient: Capacity to consent to termination)* [2013] EWHC 1417 (COP).

overcome the difficulties inherent in people having multiple reasons for acting, by placing a greater onus on the assessor to show how the agent's disordered values are rendering them 'unable to make a decision', this brings some of the assessor's reasoning out into the open, which may facilitate a more nuanced response to people found to lack capacity.

4.4 Conclusion

This chapter has considered how the law could seek to accommodate concerns about the disordered nature of an agent's values or beliefs in a way that enhances the transparency and analytical rigour with which the Act is applied, without undermining its conceptual coherence. One means of doing so is to introduce a separate limb of the test for capacity that would apply where the agent is unable to make a decision because the values or beliefs by which they evaluate the relevant information have been caused by or altered as a consequence of the agent suffering from a disorder, illness, or impairment. It is hoped that this would give assessors and judges a more legitimate basis on which to intervene in decisions where they have reason to believe that the agent's decision is being driven by evaluative outlooks or epistemic beliefs that have been distorted by disorder or impairment. And that this, in turn, will improve the transparency of assessments, meeting Ruck Keene and others' call for greater openness about the normative dimension of capacity assessments and 'the application of those norms by those charged with carrying out assessment'.[153]

While there is every reason to believe that such a provision could be workable in practice, the problem with such an approach lies in its potential to be over-inclusive. In Chapter 3, it was explained that disordered values do not necessarily undermine a person's capacity for autonomous decision-making if the person would otherwise sanction or endorse those values or beliefs as part of their self-narrative. As currently drafted, however, values or beliefs caused by a disorder which affected evaluative judgement would be included irrespective of the agent's real or hypothetical attitude towards them, indeed even if they were otherwise coherent with the agent's character system, and thus which are ostensibly authentically held. This limb could therefore result

[153] Ruck Keene *et al.*, 'Mental Capacity', 13.

in certain people being deemed to be unable to make an autonomous decision when this is not, in fact, the case.

Two things should, however, be borne in mind. The first is that a finding of incapacity does not give assessors or judges carte blanche to impose paternalistic judgments on individuals. Rather – as Chapters 5 and 6 will explore – they ought to take account of the agent's deeply held wishes, feelings, beliefs, and values, and attempt to give effect to these when determining their best interests. Finding the agent to lack capacity because their motivating belief is disordered does not therefore mean that it will necessarily be right to interfere with it, and the court may, as in *Wye Valley* and *Avon and Wiltshire Mental Health Partnership v. WA & Anor*,[154] choose to respect that wish through determining that it is in their best interests to do so, notwithstanding the potential harm it causes. The assessor or judge can therefore mitigate the potential over-inclusivity of the capacity test via their application of the best interests standard, taking account of the agent's attitude (or hypothetical attitude) towards their disordered belief when determining the weight to be given to it. By contrast, if they were to go down the alternative path of finding the agent to *have* capacity on the basis of a highly speculative assumption that they might hypothetically sanction their disordered belief, then the assessor will be left with no further powers to intervene: impotent, irrespective of how harmful the decision is. This should lead us to conclude that when faced with a choice between over-inclusivity (capturing people who may sanction their disordered beliefs) and under-inclusivity (erroneously deeming them capacitous based on speculative assumptions about their attitudes), the former is the better bet, since the harmful consequences of that path can be mitigated in a way that the latter cannot.

The second is that even if there is a risk of unjustified paternalism in rare instances, the problems being considered here are not new or unique to an authenticity limb. As the discussion in Chapter 2 has highlighted, assessors and judges *are* taking account of the disordered nature of the agent's values when determining whether they have capacity, with the agents at the heart of the cases discussed previously (Mr B, E, Mrs T etc.) all found to lack capacity, irrespective of whether they might have endorsed those values (which was at least possible in the case of Mr B). While an authenticity limb demands more direct engagement with these

[154] [2020] EWCOP 37.

issues, it does not create them: there is an equal risk under the current law that people may be found to lack capacity where their decisions are thought to be motivated by disordered value or belief systems, even if they would in fact have sanctioned those desires. What these changes do is require assessors to be more precise in their description of how illness affects the agent's autonomous decision-making. This will not only allow for greater scrutiny of the normative and empirical claims underlying capacity assessments, but will also help to expose more clearly those cases on the cusp of capacity, where determining the effect of an illness on the agent is not clear cut.

This is important at a practical level, because understanding where the complexities or ambiguities lie in an agent's capacity assessment is crucial to determining how one should then assess their best interests. Whether the issue relates to an impairment in their cognitive capacities or a disruption of their authentic values is clearly essential to how one can best maximise their welfare in decisions being taken for and about them. But highlighting the fragility of capacity assessments and the resulting grey area that exists on the cusp of capacity is also conceptually important, because it calls into question the 'cliff-edge' approach we currently adopt whereby a person either has capacity, in which case they may decide as they wish, no matter how harmful that decision may be, or they lack it, in which case a decision will be taken for them, which 'takes account' of their wishes but does not necessarily follow them. Greater recognition of the challenges involved in accurately assessing the impact of disorder or impairment on autonomous decision-making is thus important when it comes to evaluating the capacity framework as a whole, particularly whether it gives sufficient weight to the wishes of those found to lack capacity. In Chapters 5 and 6, the implications of this discussion for best interests decision-making will therefore be explored, in order to evaluate the extent to which the current framework adequately accommodates these inherent shortcomings in testing for capacity.

5

Reflecting Ambiguity on the Cusp of Capacity

Chapters 1–4 have highlighted the fundamental fragility of assessments of capacity, which hinge on a series of complex yet unavoidable clinical judgements about the agent's cognitive capacities and the origins of the beliefs or values that motivate their decision. This is particularly apparent in cases in which the agent is thought to suffer from a mental disorder, the diagnosis of which requires evaluation of the agent's behaviour against the backdrop of evolving social and cultural norms. While it is hoped that the reform suggested in Chapter 4 will enhance the conceptual clarity and transparency of such judgements, it will not remove the need for them to be made, nor for the complex assessments lying at the heart of them. The next step must therefore be to consider whether the capacity framework as a whole adequately accommodates these inevitable limitations inherent in testing for capacity. After all, if the line between those with, and those without, capacity is blurred and at times porous, then one must question the legitimacy of the law adopting a cliff-edge approach to capacity, which accords little weight to the views of the agent once they are found to lack it.

This chapter will focus on three implications of the foregoing analysis for best interests decision-making. The first of these is the recognition that agents may be subject to different impairments, which vary both in kind and in degree. As Chapter 1 explained, the MCA as it currently stands focuses only on cognitive impairments – that is, those that relate to the agent's capacities to understand, retain, and reason about information – and does not seek to capture impairments in the agent's values or beliefs. However, once it is accepted that impairment of cognitive capacities and the disruption of values may not always go hand in hand, it follows that just as an agent's values and beliefs may have been affected by disorder without any impairment of the agent's cognitive processes, so too an agent's cognitive capacities may be impaired without undermining or distorting the values, beliefs, and priorities which the agent holds. As Mary Donnelly explains:

> [C]apacity impairment is not necessarily a barrier to people having views and preferences (acting autonomously in a thin sense) or having values, life narratives and a sense of selfhood, and seeking to formulate ways in which to give effect to these (acting autonomously in a thicker sense).[1]

The agent may therefore retain authentically held values, even if they have lost the ability to act on them or cannot fully comprehend the implications of pursuing them. District Judge Eldergill captured this eloquently in *Westminster City Council v. Sykes*, when he suggested that Ms Sykes (who was suffering from dementia) was

> still able to appreciate and express the value of being at liberty and being allowed autonomy. The importance of individual liberty is of the same fundamental importance to incapacitated people who still have clear wishes and preferences about where and how they live as it is for those who remain able to make capacitous decisions. This desire to determine one's own interests is common to almost all human beings. Society is made up of individuals, and each individual wills certain ends for themselves and their loved ones, and not others, and has distinctive feelings, personal goals, traits, habits and experiences. Because this is so, most individuals wish to determine and develop their own interests and course in life, and their happiness often depends on this. The existence of a private sphere of action, free from public coercion or restraint, is indispensable to that independence which everyone needs to develop their individuality, even where their individuality is diminished, but not extinguished, by illness. It is for this reason that people place such weight on their liberty and right to choose.[2]

This may be particularly true when the agent suffers from a condition such as dementia, where their impairment often relates to their attention and recall, rather than distorting their fundamental values and beliefs. If the justification for paternalistic intervention is to maximise individual welfare, this must be achieved through attempting to give effect to the agent's authentic values or desires via the best interests determination so that the agent can continue to pursue those things that matter to them.[3]

[1] M. Donnelly, 'Best Interests in the Mental Capacity Act: Time to Say Goodbye' (2016) 24 (3) *Medical Law Review* 318–332, 322.

[2] *Westminster City Council v. Sykes* [2014] EWHC B9 (COP), [2014] MHLO 11.

[3] It is accepted here that the question of what is good for a person inevitably engages questions of prudential value theory (see, for example, D. DeGrazia, 'Value Theory and the

Secondly, through examining what it means for a decision to be autonomous, the aforementioned analysis unearthed a problem. While it is theoretically possible for an agent to endorse a belief even knowing it originated in a mental illness – and thus, at least on most sanctionist theories, for that belief to be authentic to them – given the difficulties in establishing an agent's attitude towards their belief, there is no way for the law to reliably accommodate this within the test for capacity. It is therefore possible that people may on occasion be found to lack capacity to take a decision, even though that decision is both autonomous and welfare maximising. This ought to be reflected in the weight accorded to those values or beliefs in the best interests determination.

Finally, the foregoing analysis has highlighted the inherent fragility of capacity assessments (empirically, though also normatively). Establishing whether a disorder or impairment is affecting the values or beliefs that an agent has, and how this undermines their capacity for autonomy, is not an exact science but relies heavily on the exercise of clinical judgement. Given this, there is reason to doubt whether the capacity test always delineates the autonomous from the non-autonomous with perfect accuracy, and a substantial grey area remains on the cusp of capacity, where the 'right' answer is far from clear. While this ambiguity is unavoidable, it ought to be reflected in the way the law responds to a finding of incapacity, and the weight ascribed to the agent's wishes and feelings in any best interests assessments being made about them. As Jonathan Herring observes, the wishes of the incompetent person should not be treated as though they are 'no more than the grunts of an animal'.[4] There are many people with clearly and strongly held wishes, feelings, beliefs, and values, who are perfectly able to appreciate the effects of a decision on them or to feel distress at having their wishes frustrated. The determination of incapacity should not represent an 'off switch' for respecting those wishes.

Collectively, these findings suggest the need for the agent's values and beliefs – at least where authentically held — to be given proper weight in any assessment of their best interests. Section 5.1 will therefore explore the extent to which the current law achieves this, both on the face of the statute and in how it is being applied in the courts and in practice.

Best Interests Standard' (1995) 9(1) *Bioethics* 50–60). Full discussion of this is beyond the scope of this discussion; however, this issue is engaged in more detail at footnote 847.

4 J. Herring, 'Losing It? Losing What? The Law and Dementia' (2009) *Child and Family Law* Quarterly 3, 14.

5.1 Best Interests Assessments under the MCA

As Chapter 1 explained, while the MCA does not define what an agent's best interests are, it does set out a number of factors which the assessor must take into account when determining them. Certain of these factors are designed to ensure that the wishes of the incompetent person are properly heard in decisions being taken about them, including the fact that the assessor must 'permit and encourage the person to participate' in the decision,[5] and that they must take into account 'if it is practicable and appropriate to consult them', and the views of others engaged in the care of the agent and those interested in their welfare.[6] Importantly, the assessor must also, 'so far as is reasonably ascertainable', consider:

(d) the agent's past and present wishes and feelings (and, in particular, any relevant written statement made by [them] when [they] had capacity),
(e) the beliefs and values that would be likely to influence [their] decision if [they] had capacity, and
(f) the other factors that [they] would be likely to consider if [they] were able to do so.[7]

These provisions introduce an important element of substituted judgement[8] despite the Act's focus on the agent's objective best interests.[9] As Mary Donnelly observes, they aim to represent 'a more appropriate and workable response to the goal of preserving patient autonomy notwithstanding the patient's loss of capacity'.[10] Whether they achieve this aim, however, depends on how the best interests assessor weighs these factors within the overall assessment.

None of the factors in section 4 is, on the face of the statute, accorded priority in the best interests assessment. This was deliberate. Both the report of the Joint Committee on the Draft Mental Incapacity Bill[11] and

[5] Mental Capacity Act, s4(4).
[6] Ibid, s4(7).
[7] Ibid, s4(6).
[8] According to which the surrogate decision-maker ought to choose as the incompetent person would do were they competent to do so: Buchanan and Brock, *Deciding for Others*, 112.
[9] *Mental Incapacity*, Law Com. No. 231 (HMSO, 1995), 3.25.
[10] M. Donnelly, 'Best Interests, Patient Participation and the Mental Capacity Act 2005' (2009) 17 *Medical Law Review* 1, 16.
[11] HL 189-1, HC 1083-1 (TSO, 2003).

the government's response to this report[12] commented at the time of drafting that the need for flexibility when it came to making such assessments was best served by leaving it to the assessor to 'take account of a variety of circumstances, views and attitudes which may have a bearing on the decision in question'.[13] To prioritise one factor, it was felt, would 'unnecessarily fetter their operation in the many and varied circumstances in which they might fall to be applied'.[14] As a result, the Code of Practice accompanying the MCA is clear: while the individual's wishes and feelings, beliefs, and values 'should be taken fully into account', they will 'not necessarily be the deciding factor'.[15]

The effect of this is to leave the best interests assessor – be that clinician, carer, or court – a large degree of discretion to decide how to balance the various factors set out in section 4, so as to come to a conclusion about what constitutes the agent's best interests. In order to evaluate whether the empowering provisions in section 4 are sufficient to 'soften' the harsher edges of the capacity cliff edge, it is thus necessary to understand how assessors exercise this discretion and whether they *are* giving substantial weight to the empowering provisions of ss4(4) and 4(6) when assessing what is in a person's best interests – both in decisions being made in the courtroom and those made by doctors or carers 'on the ground'. This will be considered in Section 5.2.

Before doing so, it is important to note the distinction drawn in section 4 between the agent's 'wishes and feelings' (section 4(6)(a)) and their 'values and beliefs' (section 4(6)(b)). While the Act provides that the best interests assessor must consider both the past and *present* 'wishes and feelings' of the individual, it is only those 'beliefs or values' which are 'likely to influence [their] decision if [they] had capacity' which must be considered. Arguably, implicit in this is the suggestion that the *current* values or beliefs of the agent – that is, those they hold while lacking in capacity – are relevant only insofar as they are thought to be values which would also have a bearing on the individual's capacitous decision-making. The effect is to tacitly exclude values or beliefs that are thought to have been developed as a result of the incapacitating impairment.

[12] Government Response to the Scrutiny Committee's Report on the Draft Mental Incapacity Bill (February 2004) Cm 6121.

[13] Report of Joint Committee on the Draft Mental Incapacity Bill, HL 189-1, HC 1083-1 (TSO, 2003), [89].

[14] Government Response to the Scrutiny Committee's Report on the Draft Mental Incapacity Bill, 15.

[15] Department for Constitutional Affairs, 5.38.

As cases such as *Wye Valley* show, there has been a tendency by judges to read down this provision, with judges attributing weight to the agent's values even where they might not have held them absent the incapacitating impairment. Nonetheless, this distinction is worth noting, since it reflects the tension explored in the preceding chapters between authentic and inauthentic values or beliefs, with the question of whether the agent's decision-making would, notwithstanding their impairment, still be influenced by those values being a very similar one to that of whether they would hypothetically sanction or endorse them in the absence of the disorder or impairment. The significance of the authenticity of the agent's values or beliefs for the weight attributable to the agent's wishes will be considered in detail in Chapter 6.

5.2 How Are Best Interests Decisions Being Made by the Courts?

The approach of the courts to applying section 4 has evolved over the last two decades, with the importance ascribed to the agent's values and wishes increasing with time. Given the lack of guidance in the Act on how the factors in section 4 ought to be balanced, it is no surprise that in the early years of the MCA, competing views emerged on how section 4 ought to be interpreted.[16] In *Re S and S* (Protected Persons), for example,[17] Judge Marshall QC regarded there as being a rebuttable presumption in favour of following the agent's wishes and feelings, where these were not irrational, impracticable, or irresponsible given the agent's resources.[18] As she explained:

> What, after all, is the point of taking great trouble to ascertain or deduce P's views, and to encourage P to be involved in the decision making process, unless the objective is to try to achieve the outcome which P wants or prefers, even if he does not have the capacity to achieve it for himself?[19]

However, just months later in *Re P*, Mr Justice Lewison accused Judge Marshall of 'slightly overstat[ing] the importance to be given to P's

[16] For a more detailed discussion, see A. Ruck Keene and C. Auckland, 'More Presumptions Please? Wishes, Feelings and Best Interests Decision-Making' (2015) 3 *Elder Law Journal* 293–301.

[17] *Re S and S* (Protected Persons), *C v. V* ([2009] WTLR 315.

[18] Ibid, [57].

[19] Ibid, [55].

wishes',[20] a view which then gained the support of Mr Justice Munby in *Re M*,[21] who thought that although 'wishes and feelings will always be a significant factor to which [the assessor] must pay close regard',[22] the weight to be attached to them 'will always be case-specific and fact-specific'.[23] In some cases, they may be 'preponderant'; in others, they would carry 'little weight'.[24] Far from there being a rebuttable presumption, therefore, the agent's wishes and feelings were just one among many factors which must be weighed in the balance sheet. He set out some of the factors which would influence the weight to be accorded to these wishes:

(a) With regard to the degree of P's incapacity, for the nearer to the borderline the more weight must in principle be attached to P's wishes and feelings.
(b) The strength and consistency of the views being expressed by P.
(c) The possible impact on P of knowledge that her wishes and feelings are not being given effect to.
(d) The extent to which P's wishes and feelings are, or are not, rational, sensible, responsible, and pragmatically capable of sensible implementation in the particular circumstances.
(e) Crucially, the extent to which P's wishes and feelings, if given effect to, can properly be accommodated within the court's overall assessment of what is in her best interests.[25]

While Mr Justice Munby's view has been reiterated in many of the cases that followed,[26] disagreement nonetheless remained,[27] prompting the Supreme Court to clarify the application of section 4 in *Aintree*

20 *Re P* [2009] EWHC 163 (Ch) at [41].
21 [2009] EWHC 2525 (Fam).
22 Ibid, [35].
23 Ibid.
24 Ibid.
25 Ibid.
26 See, for example, *VAC v. JAD and Others* [2010] EWHC 2159 (Ch), and *NT v. FS and Others* [2013] EWHC 684.
27 In *Re G* (TJ) [2010] EWHC 3005, for example, Morgan J seemed to go further than Munby J had when he remarked that best interests could include an 'element' of substituted judgement, and in the absence of any countervailing factors, respect for the agent's wishes could define what would be in their best interests. The court was not obliged to give effect to what the agent wanted, but what they wanted would often be what was best for them.

v. James.[28] In determining what is in a person's 'best interests', Lady Hale suggested that the assessor

> must look at his welfare in the widest sense, not just medical but social and psychological; they must consider the nature of the medical treatment in question, what it involves and its prospects of success; they must consider what the outcome of that treatment for the patient is likely to be; they must try and put themselves in the place of the individual patient and ask what his attitude to the treatment is or would be likely to be; and they must consult others who are looking after him or interested in his welfare, in particular for their view of what his attitude would be.[29]

She rightly rejected the Court of Appeal's suggestion that the patient's wishes and feelings ought to be considered objectively (what a 'reasonable patient' would have thought), noting that 'the purpose of the best interests test is to consider matters from the patient's point of view'.[30] That did not mean that the agent's wishes would always prevail, but

> insofar as it is possible to ascertain the patient's wishes and feelings, his beliefs and values or the things which were important to him, it is those which should be taken into account because they are a component in making the choice which is right for him as an individual human being.[31]

While this judgment emphasises the individual at the heart of the decision and the need to approach the question of what is best for them through the lens of what *they* value and prioritise (and not what they ought to value), Lady Hale certainly could have been more firm about how later courts should approach the weighting of factors in section 4. Noting that the agent's wishes and feelings should be 'taken into account' because they are a 'component' in making the choice that is best for them implies that there are other components that might also be important in determining what is best for that agent, while giving no guidance as to how these different 'components' ought to be weighted. It does not, then, go as far as Mr Justice Morgan in *Re G* (TJ),[32] when he suggested that respecting an agent's wishes, beliefs, and values will *often* be what is best for the agent, indicating that it should be the starting point of any assessment. Perhaps as a result, there has been some inconsistency in later judgments over how this statement ought to be interpreted. While

[28] *Aintree University Hospitals NHS Foundation Trust v. James* [2013] UKSC 67.
[29] Ibid, [39].
[30] Ibid, [45].
[31] Ibid, [45].
[32] [2010] EWHC 3005.

most of the judges in the cases that have followed have read Lady Hale's judgment as requiring great weight to be placed on the agent's wishes and values (some, far more so than her judgment in fact supports), discrepancies remain between judges, with some judges attaching relatively little weight to the views of the individual involved.

5.2.1 *Post-*Aintree *Patient Empowerment*

Lady Hale's judgment has pervaded the cases that have followed *Aintree* in *Re M* (Best Interests: Deprivation of Liberty),[33] Mr Justice Peter Jackson was clear that 'the court must surely have regard to the person's *own assessment* of her quality of life',[34] rather than striving merely to prolong the person's life at all costs. Likewise, in *Westminster City Council v. Sykes*,[35] District Judge Eldergill said of a woman with dementia who wished to remain living at home:

> It is her welfare in the context of her wishes, feelings, beliefs and values that is important ... In this important sense, the judge no less than the local authority *is her servant, not her master.* [Emphasis added.][36]

In *Newcastle upon Tyne Foundation Trust v. LM*,[37] Mr Justice Peter Jackson went even further. Although he found P (a Jehovah's Witness) to have the capacity to refuse a blood transfusion, he continued that even had she lacked capacity, he would still have maintained that a transfusion was not in her best interests despite its life-saving potential: 'applying s.4(6) in relation to the specific issue of blood transfusion, her wishes and feelings and her long-standing beliefs and values carried *determinative weight*'.[38]

Nowhere is this point made more clearly than in *Wye Valley*.[39] Responding to the Trust's submission that 'views expressed by a person lacking capacity were in principle entitled to less weight than those of a person with capacity',[40] Mr Justice Peter Jackson stated:

> This is in my view true only to the limited extent that the views of a capacitous person are by definition decisive in relation to any treatment

33 [2013] EWHC 3456 (COP).
34 Ibid, [38].
35 *Westminster City Council v. Sykes* [2014] EWHC B9.
36 Ibid.
37 [2014] EWCOP 454.
38 Ibid, [23].
39 *Wye Valley* [2015] EWCOP 60.
40 Ibid, [10].

> that is being offered to him so that the question of best interests does not arise. However, once incapacity is established so that a best interests decision must be made, there is no theoretical limit to the weight or lack of weight that should be given to the person's wishes and feelings, beliefs and values. In some cases, the conclusion will be that little weight or no weight can be given; in others, very significant weight will be due.[41]

He went on to explain:

> This is not an academic issue, but a necessary protection for the rights of people with disabilities. As the Act and the European Convention make clear, a conclusion that a person lacks decision-making capacity is not an *"off-switch"* for his rights and freedoms. To state the obvious, the wishes and feelings, beliefs and values of people with a mental disability are as important to them as they are to anyone else, and may even be more important. It would therefore be wrong in principle to apply any automatic discount to their point of view.[42]

It was important that people were not, by virtue of their disability, 'deprived of the range of reasonable outcomes that are available to others'.[43] Indeed denying people with a disability control over their own lives 'may be experienced as an even greater affront that it would be to others who are more fortunate'.[44] Accordingly, he acceded to Mr B's wish to refuse a leg amputation, even if it would result in his death. He could see no benefit in

> tak[ing] away his little remaining independence and dignity in order to replace it with a future for which he understandably has no appetite and which could only be achieved after a traumatic and uncertain struggle that he and no one else would have to endure.[45]

Similarly, in *Avon and Wiltshire Mental Health Partnership v. WA & Anor*,[46] despite finding that WA – a refugee from Palestine who was refusing food and drink in protest at the Home Office's determination of his date of birth – lacked capacity, Mr Justice Hayden nonetheless found it not to be in his best interests to subject him to forced feeding. As he explained:

> WA has expressed himself in language which not only conveys the depth of his wishes and feelings but also communicates them in terms which

41 Ibid, [10].
42 ibid, [11].
43 Ibid, [12].
44 Ibid.
45 Ibid, [45].
46 [2020] EWCOP 37.

> permit of absolutely no ambiguity. He has consistently maintained that he has "*had enough*" and does not wish to live with his identity compromised by his bureaucratically assigned date of birth. I have concluded that the rigidity of his thinking in this regard has occluded his capacity, in the sense that its overwhelming importance to him inhibits his ability to weigh the advantages and disadvantages of his decision to reject CANH. This does not mean that I regard WA's reasoning as delusional or even as flawed. On the contrary, I have little difficulty in understanding how important a date of birth is to a young man deracinated from his family and homeland and whose autonomy was, during the course of his childhood and adolescence, crushed by sadistic torture and subsequent sexual abuse. The fact that this aspect of WA's thinking overwhelms all else does not mean that it does not weigh heavily in the balance when determining where his best interests lie. I consider a decision such as this that is, of itself, entirely coherent, clearly articulated and consistently expressed, requires to be given very great weight. In many circumstances such a decision, even where P is incapacitous, would nonetheless be determinative. It is also important to emphasise that all the evidence indicates that the question of capacity is finely balanced. This serves to reinforce the weight to be given to WA's consistently expressed views.[47]

This was notwithstanding the fact that WA was an otherwise healthy young man, with 'a great deal to offer the world as well as much to receive from it'.[48]

The clear trend discernible since *Aintree* in favour of giving priority to the agent's wishes has in part been facilitated by increased participation by the agent in legal proceedings, aided by amendments in 2015 to the Court of Protection Rules which require the Court to consider how the agent ought to participate in proceedings, including whether they 'should have the opportunity to address (directly or indirectly) the judge determining the application'.[49] In *Wye Valley*, for example, 'given the momentous consequences of the decision either way', Mr Justice Peter Jackson did not feel able to reach a conclusion without meeting Mr B himself.[50] He found that the advantages of face-to-face meetings 'can be considerable, and proved so in this case',[51] giving him a 'deeper understanding of Mr B's personality and view of the world',[52] which manifested in the

47 Ibid, [93].
48 Ibid, [102].
49 The Court of Protection (Amendment) Rules 2015. Available at: www.legislation.gov.uk/uksi/2015/548/pdfs/uksi_20150548_en.pdf, 3A(2)(d).
50 *Wye Valley NHS Trust v. Mr B* [2015] EWCOP 60, [18].
51 Ibid.
52 Ibid.

scrupulous description he later gave of him.[53] This 'eloquent, moving and lucid judgment'[54] inspired Mr Justice Mostyn to meet the patient for himself in the later case of *A Hospital NHS Trust v. CD*,[55] something he described as an 'enlightening experience' which he would 'recommend to any judge hearing a similar case',[56] albeit that following *Re AH* (Serious Medical Treatment),[57] judges must be alive to the procedural implications of attaching very great weight to conclusions drawn from their visit, which they may lack the clinical expertise to properly interpret.

The emphasis now placed on the agent's wishes has even extended beyond those on the cusp of capacity, to cases in which the agent, though not currently able to contribute to the decision (being in a coma or minimally conscious state (MCS)), has previously expressed views which indicate what they would now want. This is exemplified by comparing three cases on withholding artificial nutrition and hydration (ANH) from someone in MCS.[58] In the pre-*Aintree* case of *W v. M*,[59] Mr Justice Baker

[53] Mr Justice Peter Jackson said of him: 'Mr B has had a hard life. Through no fault of his own, he has suffered in his mental health for half a century. He is a sociable man who has experienced repeated losses so that he has become isolated. He has no next of kin. No one has ever visited him in hospital and no one ever will. Yet he is a proud man who sees no reason to prefer the views of others to his own. His religious beliefs are deeply meaningful to him and do not deserve to be described as delusions: they are his faith and they are an intrinsic part of who he is. I would not define Mr B by reference to his mental illness or his religious beliefs. Rather, his core quality is his "*fierce independence*", and it is this that is now, as he sees it, under attack': ibid, [43].

[54] [2015] EWCOP 74, [18].

[55] Ibid.

[56] He further explained: 'The reason it was enlightening for me was that the person I met was different in many respects to the person described in the papers. CD was engaging and polite. She was articulate. She was amusing. She listened carefully to questions and answered them equally carefully. True, there were comments that suggested powerful delusional forces; and Dr FH explained that she was heavily medicated. But even so, the person I met was a world away from the violent sociopath described in the papers': ibid, [31]. This could be taken further. Emily Jackson, for example, suggests that there ought to be a presumption that the judge should, where reasonably practicable, meet [the patient] in order to hear from her directly which would certainly help the judge gain a clearer sense of the person's character, priorities, and values which would assist in assessing capacity as well as best interests: E. Jackson, 'From "Doctor Knows Best" to Dignity: Placing Adults Who Lack Capacity at the Centre of Decisions about Their Medical Treatment' (2018) 81(2) *Modern Law Review* 247–281.

[57] [2021] EWCA Civ 1768.

[58] For a detailed assessment of all the recent case law on those in a minimally conscious state, see R. Huxtable and G. Birchley, 'Seeking Certainty? Judicial Approaches to the (Non-)Treatment of Minimally Conscious Patients' (2017) 25(3) *Medical Law Review* 428–455.

[59] [2011] EWHC 2443 (Fam).

stuck rigidly to the 'conventional' balance sheet approach, finding it to be in the patient's best interests to continue life-sustaining treatment, despite the evidence of her family that she would not have wanted to live in her current condition. Mr Justice Baker found earlier statements by her that Tony Bland ought to be 'allowed to die' to be 'informal' and so did not attach substantial weight to them.[60] This was a wholly different approach to that taken three years later in *United Lincolnshire NHS Trust v. N.*[61] Despite the evidence being no more convincing than that in *W v. M*[62] (arguably even less so), Mrs Justice Pauffley attached far greater weight to it, suggesting that 'what the views of the patient might be, and what the views of the family are, are *highly material factors* when considering best interests, although not determinative'.[63] Drawing on Lady Hale's judgment in *Aintree*, she was left 'utterly convinced' that continued treatment was not in the patient's best interests.[64] Similarly, in *M v. Mrs N*,[65] Mr Justice Hayden engaged in the most detailed and intimate examination of Mrs N's values and personality, drawing on the accounts of her family and calling on evidence going back to when she was eighteen years old.[66] This left him with 'little doubt' that she would not wish to continue as she is.[67]

But nowhere is this trend clearer than in *Barnsley Hospitals NHS Foundation Trust v. MSP*,[68] concerning whether to withdraw life-sustaining treatment from a thirty-four-year-old with complex abdominal problems but no life-threatening injury. The patient, MSP, had suffered from serious gastrointestinal problems for ten years which had resulted, amongst other interventions, in a stoma being formed in October 2019. MSP strongly objected to having a stoma and so it was removed some months later at his instigation. During this time, he also signed an advance directive, in which he sought to refuse the formation of any future stoma 'that is expected to be permanent or with likelihood of reversal of 50% or under',[69] even where it was necessary to sustain or

60 Ibid, [6]–[7].
61 [2014] EWCOP 16.
62 *W v. M* [2011] EWHC 2443 (Fam).
63 Ibid, [58].
64 Ibid, [66].
65 [2015] EWCOP 76 (Fam).
66 Ibid, [50]–[61].
67 Ibid, [60].
68 [2020] EWCOP 26.
69 Ibid, [9].

prolong life. However, this failed to comply with the requirement set out in section 25(6) of the MCA that the directive be signed by a witness[70] and, consequently, was not valid. Not long after this, he became ill once again, necessitating the urgent formation of a new stoma. Surprisingly, given his clearly expressed objections to having a stoma in the past, MSP consented to it. His consent was, the judge accepted, capacitous at the time MSP gave it, albeit that it may well have been influenced by Mr M's clear 'optimism' that the stoma would be capable of being reversed in the future. Although the judge did not engage in detail with what the prospect of the stoma being reversed now was, underpinning the application was a seeming acceptance that it was now remote.

In determining his best interests, Mr Justice Hayden attached great significance to the previously expressed wishes of MSP. The evidence – from his family, two of MSP's previous doctors, and his recent 'carefully crafted' advance directive – was striking in its strength and consistency. Although his advance directive was not binding on the court, it provided strong evidence of his previously held wishes which was of 'significant relevance when evaluating MSP's best interests'.[71] Against this should be weighed the most recent expression of his wishes, evidenced in his recent capacitous consent to the stoma. However, the judge appeared to accept that such consent was 'predicated on Mr M's optimism that the stoma could, potentially, be reversed',[72] and that had Mr M 'been pessimistic, as to the prospects of a reversal', MSP would have rejected it.[73] Consequently, he concluded that MSP would not wish to continue to live with a stoma and so would wish that artificial nutrition and hydration were withdrawn from him, leading to his death. This was notwithstanding the fact that MSP was a young man who was not suffering from any terminal or fatal illness, who would likely regain consciousness in the near future without any substantial long-term impairment to his cognitive capacities.[74]

Yet while the general tenor of judgments since *Aintree* has emphasised the importance of the agent's wishes and values, none of the cases set out

[70] Ibid, [19].
[71] Ibid.
[72] Ibid, [42].
[73] Ibid, [46].
[74] For a more detailed discussion (and critique) of this case, see C. Auckland, '*Barnsley Hospitals NHS Foundation Trust* v *MSP* [2020] EWCOP 26: The Need for Caution When Establishing the Wishes of Incapacitated Patients' (2021) 29(2) *Medical Law Review* 347–358.

any strong statement of principle about the weight that ought to be accorded to the agent's wishes and values. Instead, judges have reiterated that this is case-specific and fact-specific. In *Wye Valley*, for example, notwithstanding the careful and empathetic judgment of Mr Justice Peter Jackson, he remained clear that 'in some cases, the conclusion will be that little weight or no weight can be given; in others, very significant weight will be due'.[75] In *M v. N*, meanwhile, Hayden J stressed that:

> Respecting individual autonomy does not always require P's wishes to be afforded predominant weight. Sometimes it will be right to do so, sometimes it will not. The factors that fall to be considered in this intensely complex process are infinitely variable e.g. the nature of the contemplated treatment, how intrusive such treatment might be and crucially what the outcome of that treatment may be for the individual patient. Into that complex matrix the appropriate weight to be given to P's wishes will vary.[76]

While the weight to be accorded to the agent's wishes is fact- and case-specific, it is nonetheless possible to discern some factors which appear to be influencing the weight being accorded to the agent's wishes in cases coming before the Court of Protection. These include the authenticity, strength, and consistency of the views being expressed; the impact on the agent of knowing their wishes have been frustrated; the degree of incapacity; and whether respecting the agent's wishes will preclude future enjoyment of life. Each of these shall be considered in turn.

5.2.1.1 The Authenticity of the Agent's Wishes

In *M v. N*, Mr Justice Hayden noted that where the wishes and feelings of an incapacitated adult had 'similar cogency and authenticity', they 'are to be afforded no less significance than those of the capacitous',[77] indicating that the authenticity of the wish was an important factor in determining the weight to be ascribed to it, and that where the wish expressed *was* authentic, it ought to be respected. This attempt to grapple with the authenticity of the wishes being expressed also underpins other judgments. In *An NHS Foundation Trust v. An Expectant Mother*,[78] for example, Mr Justice Holman was called upon to decide whether an agoraphobic pregnant woman who wished for a home birth ought to

[75] *Wye Valley* [2015] EWCOP 60, [10].
[76] *M v. N* [2015] EWCOP 76 (Fam), [28].
[77] Ibid, [32].
[78] [2021] EWCOP 33.

be forcibly removed to hospital if something went wrong. In finding that it was in her best interests to do so, the judge held that:

> The mother herself says that she would prefer to give birth at home, but she clearly expresses that that is due to her agoraphobia and fear of going out. I am satisfied that, but for her agoraphobia, the mother herself would opt for a hospital birth, as encouraged by her mother and partner.[79]

As the expectant mother's wishes were deemed inauthentic, being attributable to a disorder (agoraphobia) and not authentically held beliefs or values, they did not demand that the same weight be attached to them. Similarly, in *University Hospital Birmingham NHS Foundation Trust v. AI & K*,[80] concerning a forty-eight-year-old man with schizophrenia and end-stage kidney disease refusing dialysis, the judge found that while 'his belief system may be delusional, his exhaustion is real': it was clear he had 'had enough'.[81] Again, the judge here appears to be attempting to unpick authentic feelings (of having become 'tired by the effort of the dialysis'[82]) from his inauthentic schizophrenic beliefs, attributing significant weight only to the former in the best interests assessment.

This proved particularly challenging in *SS v. LB Richmond on Thames and SWL CCG*,[83] where the court was called upon to determine whether or not to vaccinate an eighty-six-year-old with dementia for Covid-19 against her wishes. In recent times, she had become increasingly resistant to medical interventions of any kind, though it was not clear whether this was a consequence of her dementia or longer-term (and authentically held) beliefs about the role of medical science. Mr Justice Hayden thus engaged in a detailed examination of her belief structure. While more recent opposition to medical interventions appeared to stem from a newspaper article which she had read as indicating that medicine did 'more harm than good',[84] SS's medical records dating from 1997 revealed no evidence of her ever having received a vaccination. 'Unambiguous notes' suggested that SS had declined both seasonal influenza and pneumococcal vaccines in 2002, 2010, 2012, and 2014,[85] indicating 'a clear and consistent pattern of behaviour which predates SS's diagnosis of

79 Ibid, [22].
80 [2021] EWCOP 37.
81 Ibid, [16].
82 Ibid.
83 [2021] EWCOP 31.
84 Ibid, [18].
85 Ibid, [20].

dementia by a significant period'.[86] This led Mr Justice Hayden to conclude that if SS was capacitous, she would most likely have declined the vaccination. The fact that she 'plainly resisted vaccinations'[87] throughout her life was good evidence that this was an authentically held preference, and not one attributable to her disorder. These cases therefore suggest that judges are, in some cases at least, grappling with the authenticity of a value or belief (or wishes based on them) when determining the weight to accord it in the best interests assessment.

5.2.1.2 The Strength of the Wish Being Expressed

In other cases, it is the perceived strength with which the agent held a wish (or a belief motivating a wish) which has dictated how much weight is attached to it. In *East Lancashire Hospitals NHS Trust v. PW*, for example,[88] concerning whether to authorise an amputation for a sixty-year-old man with sepsis, who suffered from paranoid schizophrenia. Despite his clear and unwavering opposition to the surgery, Mrs Justice Lieven nonetheless authorised it as being in his best interests. In doing so, she distinguished this case from *Wye Valley* (discussed previously) on the basis that she did not think (although she could not be 'totally confident') that 'PW's opposition to the operation is as deep seated, or as fundamental to his dignity, as was Mr B's'.[89] Consequently, it was hoped that overriding his wishes would not 'fundamentally undermine his dignity and his independence' in the way that it would have for Mr B.[90]

Similarly, in *Manchester University NHS Foundation Trust v. DE*,[91] the judge had to decide whether to authorise the use of blood products should they become necessary during an operation on a Jehovah's Witness's leg. The crux of the judgment concerned how important her religious beliefs and commitments were to her, and thus 'the degree to which DE's wishes and feelings would be overborne by a decision to allow a blood transfusion'.[92] The evidence from the hearing indicated that

> DE's beliefs and her commitment to the Jehovah's Witness religion was fairly scant. She attends services, but her mother described her as not

[86] Ibid, [20].
[87] Ibid, [25].
[88] [2019] EWCOP 10.
[89] Ibid, [33].
[90] Ibid.
[91] [2019] EWCOP 19.
[92] Ibid, [28].

> being a practising Jehovah's Witness. She can recite the scriptures, but I got no sense of the degree to which she understood them or believed them or the degree to which they played an important part in her life.[93]

On this basis, Mrs Justice Lieven concluded that although DE would describe herself as a Jehovah's Witness, 'she was not someone for whom those beliefs were central to her personality or sense of identity',[94] and overriding her wishes would not cause her to feel 'deeply upset'.[95] Consequently, her position was 'quite different' from that of Mr B in *Wye Valley*, whose religious beliefs were 'fundamental to B's sense of who he was'.[96]

The opposite conclusion was reached in *London Borough of X v. MR & Ors*,[97] in which determining the significance of an eighty-six-year-old's Jewish beliefs to him was an essential part of establishing whether it would be in his best interests to move from a secular to a Jewish care home. Although evidence from his relatives was contradictory, having considered his life in its entirety and sought evidence from his local rabbi, District Judge Eldergill concluded that he was a 'devoted and committed' Jew who would have chosen to live in a Jewish care home if he had had the capacity.[98] He declared it to be in MR's best interests to receive care 'in a manner that more fully accords with his values and the way he chose to live out his life'.[99]

5.2.1.3 The Impact on the Agent of the Knowledge That Their Wishes Had Been Frustrated

Closely related to the strength of the agent's wishes was the likely impact that frustrating them would have on them, and the harm that would be likely to materialise. In *DE*, for example,[100] Mrs Justice Lieven 'did not get any sense that [DE] would feel deeply upset if an order was made in the form sought, or that she would feel a deep conflict with her religious beliefs',[101] indicating that knowledge that her wishes and feelings had not

93 Ibid, [13].
94 Ibid, [28].
95 Ibid, [28].
96 Ibid.
97 [2022] EWCOP 1.
98 Ibid, [100].
99 Ibid, [102].
100 [2019] EWCOP 19.
101 Ibid, [28].

been given effect to would not cause substantial psychological or emotional harm or distress.

In *NHS Foundation Trust v. QZ*,[102] the likely impact of overriding her refusal was unclear, with healthcare professionals giving diverging opinions on how it might affect her mental health. While all agreed that it would lead to deterioration, reinforcing QZ's delusional beliefs that she was at risk of sexual violation by her doctors, there was disagreement over her ability to overcome this in time. Dr O'Donovan was concerned that QZ would suffer from a 'serious and potentially prolonged collapse in QZ's general mental well being' which would reduce her quality of life 'in terms of her stability and emotional security' to such an extent that it had to be 'evaluated with a very critical eye alongside the preservation of her life in the event she had cancer'. Her treating psychiatrist, by contrast,

> was distinctly more positive about QZ's ability to regain trust and learn again in future to work effectively with professionals. That she had been able to do so in the past, he reasoned, was a good prognostic indicator of her capacity to do so in the future. That said, he did not for one moment underestimate the enormity of the impact that this intrusive medical process might have on this particular woman, nor did he shy away from saying that a significant mental health deterioration was, in effect, inevitable.[103]

Mr Justice Hayden ultimately found this evaluation of QZ's resilience to be more compelling. Consequently, 'the prospect that following medical investigation and or treatment and a period of profound mental distress QZ may recover a life which has both happiness and dignity incorporated into it, is one which is very real'. The gynaecological investigation was thus thought to be in her best interests,[104] precisely because it was not thought that knowledge that her wishes had been frustrated would cause lasting harm to her.

The opposite conclusion was reached in *Wye Valley*, in which Mr Justice Peter Jackson was concerned that the process of recovery and rehabilitation would 'occupy a considerable part of Mr B's remaining lifespan', during which time 'the loss of his foot will be a continual reminder that his wishes were not respected'.[105] Moreover, 'his religious sentiments will undoubtedly continue and he will believe that the amputation was carried out against the Lord's wishes',[106] causing him

[102] [2017] EWCOP 11.
[103] Ibid, [20].
[104] Ibid, [32].
[105] *Wye Valley NHS Trust v. Mr B* [2015] EWCOP 60, [37].
[106] Ibid.

continued frustration and distress at the knowledge that the intervention had taken place against his will and that of God. And similar concerns underpinned *Avon and Wiltshire Mental Health Partnership v. WA & Anor*,[107] concerning a refugee from Palestine who was refusing food and drink in protest at the Home Office's determination of his date of birth. Although Mr Justice Hayden found him to lack capacity, he nonetheless found it not in his best interests to subject him to forced feeding. WA was clear that he could no longer live 'without the reinstatement of what he is certain is his true date of birth'.[108] There was a risk that any coercive treatment may reignite past trauma,[109] and thus would be 'antitherapeutic' and 'most likely harmful' to him.[110] Given the risk of re-traumatising him, Mr Justice Hayden concluded that force-feeding was irreconcilable with the 'protection of WA's autonomy'.[111] While efforts should be made to encourage him to accept nutrition and hydration of his own accord, it should not be forced upon him: '[W]hen WA says no to CANH his refusal should be respected. No must mean no!'[112]

It is clear therefore that the impact of the knowledge that the agent's wishes have been frustrated, and the possible harm it may cause them, has proved highly relevant to the weight ascribed to such wishes. It is notable in this regard that in a recent case concerning whether to override the wishes of a Gillick-competent adolescent, Mr Justice Munby drew an analogy with the position of incapacitated adults,[113] when holding that a 'particularly important aspect' of 'any welfare analysis' is 'the possible impact on P of knowledge that her wishes and feelings are *not* being given effect to'.[114]

5.2.1.4 Whether Respecting the Agent's Wishes Would Preclude Future Enjoyment or Fulfilment in Life

Even where the impact of frustrating the agent's wishes would be profound, this has been tolerated in some cases where the effect of respecting such wishes would be to preclude future enjoyment from life. In *QZ*, for example, the judge differentiated the current case from *Wye Valley* on the

[107] [2020] EWCOP 37.
[108] Ibid, [98].
[109] Ibid, [94].
[110] Ibid, [99].
[111] Ibid, [102].
[112] Ibid.
[113] *NHS Trust v. X* [2021] EWHC 65 (Fam).
[114] Ibid, [25].

basis that QZ's circumstances were different, having 'the prospect of many years ahead'.[115] He concluded that after a 'period of profound mental distress', QZ was likely to 'recover a life which has both happiness and dignity incorporated into it'.[116] Permitting investigations into and treatment of her potential cancer was therefore 'fighting on her behalf' to enable her to enjoy such a life, notwithstanding 'her paranoid and delusional beliefs'.[117]

Similarly, in *A Local Authority v. E*,[118] Mr Justice Peter Jackson authorised forced feeding as being in E's best interests notwithstanding her describing her life as 'pure torment',[119] and experiencing the intervention as abusive,[120] replaying the serious sexual abuse she had sustained as a child.[121] This case will be discussed in more detail, but suffice to say for the present that the reason for this was that there was an estimated 20 per cent chance that she might recover, in the sense of returning to a quality of life that she would regard as worthwhile. As the judge explained,

> We only live once – we are born once and we die once – and the difference between life and death is the biggest difference we know. E is a special person, whose life is of value. She does not see it that way now, but she may in future.[122]

Respecting her wishes would have led to her imminent death. By contrast, by frustrating them, the judge pursued the possibility that she might be able to realise a fulfilling life in the future.

These cases can be contrasted with other cases in which, although treatment might preserve a person's physical existence, it cannot alleviate their mental distress, even perhaps their physical disability, and so cannot secure them a quality of life they find acceptable. *Wye Valley* is one such example, where the effect of an amputation would be to put Mr B into a position he would find unacceptable. This led Mr Justice Peter Jackson to conclude that

> it would not be in Mr B's best interests to take away his little remaining independence and dignity in order to replace it with a future for which he

115 QZ [2017] EWCOP 11, [32].
116 Ibid, [32].
117 Ibid.
118 *E* [2012] EWCOP 1639.
119 Ibid, [76].
120 Ibid, [131].
121 Ibid, [89].
122 Ibid, [137]–[138].

> understandably has no appetite and which could only be achieved after a traumatic and uncertain struggle that he and no one else would have to endure.[123]

5.2.1.5 The Degree of Incapacity

Finally, judges have indicated that the agent's wishes ought to be given greater weight where their capacity is closer to reaching the threshold for capacity. This was one of the factors which Mr Justice Munby outlined in *Re M*,[124] as affecting the weight to be accorded to the agent's wishes, noting that 'the nearer to the borderline the more weight must in principle be attached to P's wishes and feelings'.[125] This, he explained, was because for those closer to the cusp of capacity, the greater the 'distress', 'humiliation', and 'anger', the person may feel at others taking intensely private decisions on their behalf.[126] In *Avon and Wiltshire Mental Health Partnership v. WA & Anor* too,[127] Mr Justice Hayden held that:

> I consider a decision such as this that is, of itself, entirely coherent, clearly articulated and consistently expressed, requires to be given very great weight. In many circumstances such a decision, even where P is incapacitous, would nonetheless be determinative. It is also important to emphasise that all the evidence indicates that the question of capacity is finely balanced. This serves to reinforce the weight to be given to WA's consistently expressed views.[128]

The fact that WA sat on the cusp of capacity was thus reason to give his views especial weight in the best interests determination.

While this section has sought to highlight some of the factors that appear to be affecting the weight accorded to the agent's wishes and feelings by the Court of Protection, such factors have typically been drawn upon on a case-by-case basis by first instance judges, and do not have the weight of authority or the value of precedent. There is therefore no requirement for judges to consider such factors in order to perform the best interests evaluation correctly; indeed there is no guidance whatsoever on the weight to be accorded to the agent's wishes, either in the

123 [2015] EWCOP 60, [45].
124 *Re M* [2009] EWHC 2525 (Fam), [35].
125 Ibid, [35].
126 Ibid, [124].
127 [2020] EWCOP 37.
128 Ibid, [93].

Act[129] or from the Supreme Court. In the absence of this, it is unsurprising that, notwithstanding the humane and compassionate way that many of these judges have engaged with the individual, they have still not felt able to enshrine a particular approach as a matter of principle applicable more widely. This may enable judges to retain maximal flexibility in the cases that come before them, but as Section 5.2.2 will explore, the effect has been to introduce a lack of clarity over the level of importance that ought to be attached to the individual's values and wishes. Importantly, it has also created space for 'extra-legal values' to influence judgments, giving rise to 'possible tensions between P's values and those of judges'.[130] Kong *et al.* have identified a range of internal judicial values (that is, social, political, and moral values such as autonomy, sanctity of life, dignity) and external judicial values (which include rule-of-law values such as impartiality or integrity) that influence both the extent to which the agent participates in legal proceedings and the substantive weight given to their values in the best interests determination.[131] As they observe, these findings challenge 'the tendency to either deny the presence and influence of extra-legal values . . . or uphold an ideal of impartiality and disengagement from values'.[132] Given this, it is perhaps unsurprising that the approaches of judges have differed.

5.2.2 Diverging Approaches to Best Interests

The consequence of the lack of framework for grappling with the agent's best interests is that judgments have diverged, both in the *obiter* comments of different judges over the appropriate weight to be accorded to the individual's wishes or values, and in the approach adopted in those cases. The fact that two judgments have recently been appealed to the Court of Appeal on the basis of attaching insufficient weight to the individual's wishes – one successfully – lends further credence to this.[133]

[129] This was explicitly recognised by Lady Justice King in *Re AB* (Termination of Pregnancy) [2019] EWCA Civ 1215 who noted that 'limited guidance as to the proper approach to the "best interests" analysis is found in Section 4 MCA' [28].

[130] C. Kong, J. Coggon, M. Dunn, and P. Cooper, 'Judging Values and Participation in Medical Capacity Law' (2019) 8(3) *Laws* 16.

[131] Ibid. See also Kong *et al.*, 'The "Human Element" in the Social Space of the Courtroom', 715–734.

[132] Kong *et al.*, 'The "Human Element" in the Social Space of the Courtroom', 715–734, 732.

[133] *Re AB* (Termination of Pregnancy) [2019] EWCA Civ 1215.

There are certainly examples which indicate that different judges may attach differing levels of importance to the agent's wishes in the best interests determination. Notwithstanding the outcome in *M v. Mrs N*,[134] for example, Mr Justice Hayden's dictum appears to ascribe less weight to the agent's wishes and feelings than other judges have been prepared to do, with him deducing from *Aintree* only that while wishes and feelings, where ascertainable, are to be afforded 'great respect'; they 'will rarely, if ever, be determinative of P's 'best interests'.[135] This reading would seem to dilute the strength of Lady Hale's judgment even further: to say (as she did) that a person's wishes ought to be taken into account because they are a component of what is best for them suggests that there are other components which may also contribute to the determination of what is best. She does not, however, say anything about how these different components ought to be weighted. To take from this, then, that other components will almost always outweigh the agent's wishes, and so the wishes will rarely, if ever, be determinative, would seem to go a step further than Lady Hale was willing to go. By contrast, Mr Justice Peter Jackson clearly does think that a person's wishes can be determinative of what is in their best interests: in *LM*, for example, the Jehovah's Witness's values *did* carry 'determinative weight'.[136] While a Jehovah's Witness refusing blood transfusions *could* be one of the 'rare' situations that Mr Justice Hayden envisages here, it is certainly not an entirely exceptional situation.

There also remain some cases in which very little weight appears to be given to the agent's clearly ascertainable views, or attention given to explaining why they have not been followed. *RB (By His Litigation Friend the Official Solicitor) v. Brighton and Hove City Council*,[137] for example, concerned whether a former alcoholic, who had sustained a serious head injury (in addition to other injuries, including the effective loss of the use of his left hand), ought to be able to leave his neuroreh-abilitation facility and resume living independently. To start with, he cooperated with his treatment programme, but after arrangements to move him into his own flat collapsed, he resumed his former lifestyle, habitually going out and getting drunk. Accordingly, the council obtained various authorisations, including to restrain him at the care

134 [2015] EWCOP 76 (Fam).
135 *M v. N* [2015] EWCOP 76, [28].
136 *Newcastle upon Tyne Foundation Trust v. LM* [2014] EWCOP 454.
137 [2014] EWCA Civ 561.

home and to permit him to leave only with an escort. These restrictions were strongly resisted by RB: while accepting that he needed some support (with showering, dressing, and cutting up food), he maintained that he could, with assistance, live independently. The court, however, scarcely engaged with RB at all, saying:

> Both the Council and the court are aware of RB's wishes, namely to live independently in the community. The MCA section 4(6)(a) requires both the Council and the court to take those wishes into account. I do so. Unfortunately it is not possible for the time being to comply with those wishes.[138]

Little was provided by way of reason for this clear dismissal of RB's wishes, with Lord Justice Jackson stating only that

> RB's physical and mental disabilities are such that he is not currently capable of independent living outside an institutional setting. Such a setting is necessary (a) to deliver day to day personal care and (b) to prevent RB drinking to excess and suffering dire consequences.[139]

While there may well have been reasons why independent living was not possible for RB, a more detailed discussion of why this was, and whether there were other, less-intrusive means by which he could have been protected, would certainly have been welcome.

Similarly, in *Hull University Teaching Hospitals NHS Trust v. KD*,[140] concerning a fifty-seven-year-old woman with paranoid schizophrenia who required surgery for a collapsed lung, almost no reference was made to the importance of balancing the clinical advice against her clearly expressed wishes. The judge did refer to the fact that KD was resistant to the surgery (fearful that it might change her mental state and that it was ill-advised to undergo the procedure on particular dates of the month),[141] and that concerns about her resistance to post-operative drainage of the lung would require her to wear gloves or mittens 'rather like boxing gloves' to prevent her from removing the drains.[142] However, the judge did not appear to attach substantial weight to these when deciding her best interests, stating merely that it was 'clear' that the treatment was in her best interests.[143] Indeed, the only reference made to the fact that the

[138] Ibid, [81].
[139] Ibid, [80].
[140] [2020] EWCOP 35.
[141] Ibid, [13].
[142] Ibid, [18].
[143] Ibid, [15].

order entailed authorising a surgical intervention against KD's wishes, in circumstances where she would then have to wear intrusive gloves to ensure post-operative care was successful, was right at the end of her judgment, when the judge recognised that 'any judgment of this kind, involving treatment to an incapacitated individual against their expressed wishes, always requires proper public scrutiny'.[144]

In *University Hospitals Bristol NHS Foundation Trust v. ED*,[145] Counsel raised the fact that the judge had failed to address section 4(6) (b), namely what beliefs and values would likely have influenced the agent's decision if they had had the capacity.[146] While Mr Justice Moor accepted that he had failed to do so, his subsequent treatment of the issue was cursory, taking the view that had ED had the capacity, she would have recognised that it was futile (and thus not in her best interests) to have received further treatment in the ICU or CPR, as it would have likely caused her pain and suffering without achieving any advantage.[147] In effect, then, he concluded simply that had she had capacity, she would have taken the same view as he did on the evidence.

In other cases, the dismissal of the agent's views is less overt, but there still appears to be less weight being accorded to the agent's wishes and feelings in the best interests assessment. In *A Local Authority v. E* (described previously),[148] a woman with chronic anorexia expressed a consistent and unequivocal wish to be entitled to refuse treatment, even if that ended her life:

> She describes her life as "a pure torment". All the things she had wanted to do have proved impossible because of her illness. She cannot achieve any of her goals and she feels crushed. She feels she is in a situation where she is able to give nothing to the world and the world is able to give nothing to her.[149]

Even her parents supported her in this wish, believing her to have 'suffered enough'.[150] Given the seriousness of E's case, any therapies for her eating disorder (and other problems) could only be embarked on if her BMI could be raised to 17 (it was currently 11.3), which would

144 Ibid, [22].
145 [2020] EWCOP 18.
146 Ibid, [37].
147 Ibid, [38].
148 [2012] EWCOP 1639.
149 Ibid, [76].
150 Ibid, [80].

necessitate 'forcible feeding under physical or chemical restraint for not less than a year'.[151] This, as Mr Justice Peter Jackson acknowledged, would 'not merely entail bodily intrusion of the most intimate kind, but the overbearing of E's will in a way that she experiences as abusive',[152] as it replayed the serious sexual abuse she had suffered as a child.[153] Nor was this treatment plan without its own risks, with doctors predicting that, given her frailty and the intensity of this medical intervention, 'her chances of surviving or not surviving treatment are no more than equally balanced'.[154] Dr Glover, the court-appointed expert, described it as 'a gargantuan task to take her from where she is now to where we want to go'.[155] Against these 'weighty factors', however,[156] weighed E's life, and it was estimated (albeit with some caution) that there was around a 20 per cent chance of recovery (defined as 'returning to a quality of life that she would regard as being worthwhile'[157]). It was this which ultimately dictated the outcome:

> The competing factors are, in my judgment, almost exactly in equilibrium, but having considered them as carefully as I am able, I find that the balance tips slowly but unmistakably in the direction of life-preserving treatment. In the end, the presumption in favour of the preservation of life is not displaced.[158]

One does not envy the position of Mr Justice Peter Jackson in this case. Arguably, however, it is precisely in cases such as this – in which the factors on each side of the assessment are so finely balanced – that the agent's own perception of what is best for them ought to take on the greatest significance. That E lacked capacity to make decisions about the ingestion of food did not in any way diminish her ability to experience suffering at her situation. As the judge himself noted, her wishes are 'not the slightest bit less real or felt merely because she does not have decision-making capacity'.[159] Given this, to override her clear and consistent wish – especially in such a physically invasive and psychologically traumatic manner – would seem very difficult to justify.

151 Ibid, [88].
152 Ibid, [131].
153 Ibid, [89].
154 Ibid, [71].
155 Ibid, [98].
156 Ibid, [136].
157 Ibid, [72].
158 Ibid, [140].
159 Ibid, [127].

It is clear, then, that while judges in the Court of Protection have generally been alive to the importance of respecting the agent's authentic values, the failure of either Parliament or the Supreme Court to lay down any firm statement of principle about either how *much* weight should be given to the agent's expressed wishes or what factors to take into account when determining this has allowed for diverging dicta and outlying cases. As the Law Commission aptly summarised:

> [T]he law fails to give sufficient certainty for best interest decision-makers on how much emphasis should be given to the person's wishes and feelings. On the one hand, it can be said that there is no hierarchy between the various factors listed in section 4. This was clearly the policy intention behind the legislation. On the other hand, the Supreme Court has clarified in the *Aintree* case that best interests requires consideration of matters from the person's point of view and that the person's wishes and feelings are an important factor, arguably attaching some level of primacy to this factor. Similarly, in some cases the Court of Protection has gone to great lengths to make the decision the person would have wanted. But equally, in other cases, the outcomes have been expressly inconsistent with what the person wants or would have wanted.[160]

Nowhere is this clearer than in *Re AB* (Termination of Pregnancy),[161] which concerned a twenty-four-year-old with moderate learning difficulties who had fallen pregnant in unknown circumstances while visiting family in Nigeria. The question was whether or not it would be in her best interests to undergo an abortion, a course of action which was strongly opposed by her adoptive mother, CD, who was a devout Roman Catholic, and professed the view that in Nigeria, it would be simply unheard of to have an abortion. Significantly, by the time the case was heard by the trial judge, AB was at the end of her twenty-second week of pregnancy, and by the Court of Appeal hearing, she was twenty-three weeks pregnant – the statutory limit for an abortion being twenty-four weeks. Having heard the closely balanced evidence, Mrs Justice Lieven authorised the abortion, deciding that it was ultimately in her best interests, despite being against AB's wishes. She explained that:

> AB's wishes and feelings are plainly a relevant consideration. There are cases where wishes and feelings would be determinative, even where the

[160] Law Commission, 'Mental Capacity and Deprivation of Liberty', Consultation Paper No. 222, 12.47. Available at: www.lawcom.gov.uk/wp-content/uploads/2015/07/cp222_mental_capacity.pdf, 12.42.

[161] [2019] EWCA Civ 1215.

> person has no capacity. If AB's wishes and feelings were clearly expressed and I felt she had any understanding (albeit non-capacitous ones) of the consequences of giving birth, I would give them a great deal of weight. However AB's wishes are not clear. She likes being pregnant, she would probably like to have the baby, but she has no sense of what this means. As I have said I think she would like to have a baby in the same way she would like to have a nice doll. I just do not feel I can give very much weight to those expressions of wishes and feelings.[162]

In the Court of Appeal, Mrs Justice King found that the trial judge had 'failed to take sufficient account of AB's wishes and feelings in the ultimate balancing exercise'.[163] Her conclusion as to AB's best interests was 'substantially anchored in the medical evidence',[164] with 'inadequate weight' given to non-medical factors.[165] In particular, she had failed to give due weight to evidence of 'those who know her best, namely CD and her social worker', who 'believe it to be in AB's best interests to proceed with the pregnancy, as does the Official Solicitor who represents her in these proceedings'.[166] Ultimately, in the view of the Court of Appeal, 'the evidence taken as a whole was simply not sufficient to justify the profound invasion of AB's rights represented by the non-consensual termination of this advanced pregnancy'.[167]

This case starkly demonstrates the concerns raised here. On appeal, notwithstanding the lack of direction in the Act on the weight to be accorded to the agent's wishes, the Court nonetheless concluded that the judge had incorrectly weighed the factors in section 4 and failed to give adequate weight to AB's wishes, or those who knew her best. Yet the consequence of this failure was very nearly grave: AB was due to undergo the first part of her termination of the following day, and there was only a matter of days left in which such an intervention could be lawfully performed. The consequence of 'getting it wrong' in this case was therefore very nearly one of the most profound invasions imaginable: the non-consensual abortion of a woman's child. While the logic of the best interests approach may be that judges ought to be accorded substantial discretion to reflect the fact- and person-specific nature of best interests

[162] [2019] EWCOP 26, [60].
[163] [2019] EWCA Civ 1215, [55].
[164] Ibid, [73].
[165] Ibid, [77].
[166] Ibid, [72].
[167] Ibid, [77].

assessments, judges may nonetheless benefit from a more unified starting point to better ensure that consequences such as this are avoided.

Yet only a very small proportion of cases ever come before the courts. It is therefore essential to examine not only how judges interpret and apply these provisions but also how they are being applied in practice, both by doctors on the wards making treatment decisions and by local authorities when deciding about a person's care arrangements. As Section 5.3 will show, this indicates that the empowering approach of the courts has not percolated through to the decisions being made on the ground.

5.3 Best Interests Assessments on the Ground

In its post-legislative scrutiny of the MCA in 2014, the House of Lords was critical of the way that the provisions in s4(6) had been implemented in practice, observing that 'the empowering ethos of the Act has not been widely implemented'.[168] It found that the wishes, thoughts, and feelings of the person lacking capacity were 'not routinely prioritised',[169] rather 'clinical judgements or resource-led decision-making predominate'.[170] These criticisms were echoed shortly after by the Department of Health in respect of people with learning disabilities, autism, and mental health conditions.[171] Most recently, the Law Commission received evidence that families and carers often felt professionals would 'pick and choose' at random which of the factors in section 4 to prioritise.[172] They quoted from an advocacy provider (Pohwer), who said that:

> Whilst the best interest checklist was well crafted in the Mental Capacity Act, inherent risk aversion within the health, social care and other sectors too frequently results in insufficient weight being given to the wishes and feelings of people subject to the Act.[173]

168 House of Lords Select Committee on the Mental Capacity Act 2005, '*Mental Capacity Act 2005: Post-legislative scrutiny*' (HL Paper 139, 13 March 2014) (also House of Lords Debate on the Select Committee Report), [8].

169 Ibid, [104].

170 Ibid.

171 Department of Health, 'No Voice Unheard, No Right Ignored – A Consultation for People with Learning Disabilities, Autism and Mental Health Conditions' (2015) Cm 9007, 13, 33–34.

172 Law Commission, 'Mental Capacity and Deprivation of Liberty – Consultation Analysis available at: https://s3-eu-west-2.amazonaws.com/lawcom-prod-storage-11jsxou24uy7q/uploads/2017/03/cp222_mental_capacity_responses_analysis.pdf. Accessed 25 September 2018.

173 Ibid.

Similar conclusions were also reached by the Alzheimer's Society who, in gathering evidence for the Department of Health, found that 'almost one in five people with dementia who responded felt that, either all or most of the time, decisions were made for them without them being asked first'.[174] Meanwhile, a recent review by the National Mental Capacity Forum found that '11% of healthcare respondents, 9% of respondents from social care settings and 16% of those from other groups reported that the person's wishes, thoughts and feelings were "rarely" given proper weight when best interests decisions are made'.[175] It seems, then, that the general trend towards greater empowerment seen in the case law has not yet trickled down to the decisions being made on the ground.

Evidence from the interviews conducted as part of this research supports these findings, with best interests often conceptualised not as a question about what clinical course of action is best *in light of* the agent's values and priorities, but rather as though there is an objective right clinical course, which must be qualified in certain instances by the agent's wishes and feelings. Some clinicians interviewed clearly regarded best interests as a clinical decision, with the patient's wishes being only a secondary consideration. One doctor, for example, gave the following example of a woman with dementia in a care home who fell and broke her hip:

> I know that she will be better cared for going into hospital, having her hip fixed, and then coming back out again. I'm not really interested in what she is going to say about going into hospital or not, I know that her suffering will be made worse – much, much longer – and she will be disabled for longer if we do nothing about this. What is in her best interests I will enforce on her, irrespective of what is in the care plan. Just simply because that's an inalienable truth. Certainly, the Capacity Act would say, actually you have to probably work out what everybody else will feel about that [but] ... while somebody is lying on the floor, you cannot have that conversation. (Niamh, p. 13)

By contrast,

> If somebody with cancer was to develop renal failure, would I do anything about it? No. Because, what I'd be doing is perpetuating that individual's

[174] S. Cox, 'Decision-Making and Dementia–How Well Does the Mental Capacity Act Serve People Living with the Condition?' (2015) 2 *Elder Law Journal* 74–83, 79.

[175] National Mental Capacity Forum, *Fourth Report of the National Mental Capacity Forum* (August 2020), 34. Available at: https://assets.publishing.service.gov.uk/government/uploads/system/uploads/attachment_data/file/908360/nmcf-chair_s-fourth-annual-report-2019-20.pdf. Accessed 29 September 2022.

> pain and suffering from their underlying illness. You've got to die of something, and dying of renal failure is not that bad. If somebody developed a chest infection, and they got severe CAPD, or pulmonary breath loss, severe heart failure or severe dementia – well in fact, dying from pneumonia is not that bad either, you just go to sleep. (Niamh, p. 14)

While acknowledging that they could 'get pulled up in court' for some of their decisions, this doctor explained that they would defend themselves on the basis of their 'Hippocratic Oath, or the Good Samaritan approach to things' (Niamh, p. 14). Central to this is that they regard themselves as doing the 'right' thing for the patient, even if this is not what the patient says they want. They went on to appraise the MCA in the following way:

> It does not give me carte blanche to overrule what an individual says. There are times where I find it intensely frustrating, because I think that people may not necessarily make the right decisions, but I think, as an older doctor, I'm now happy to live with that, because not everybody does what you tell them to do. (Niamh, p. 15)

Another doctor spoke of the need to 'coax' patients into making the decision which was best for them (Conor, p. 3), while yet another suggested that patients are not always 'emotionally equipped' to make treatment decisions (Jerry, p. 6). Drawing an analogy with a six-year-old with a fear of needles who required chemical therapy for leukaemia, they said:

> The law does not allow children capacity to make that decision because it recognises they just cannot. They're not emotionally equipped to do so. The thing is many adults are also not emotionally equipped to do so but the law makes no allowance. (Jerry, p. 6)

These views were not, however, representative of all the clinicians interviewed, and certainly within some specialisms (in particular, psychiatry and geriatrics), doctors appeared to place much greater emphasis on the importance of giving effect to the person's wishes even where they lacked capacity. One geriatrician reported 'we generally try and facilitate the patients' wishes, even if we feel that there may be an element of risk or unwiseness' (David, p. 5), while another explained that their aim when treating patients is to be flexible: 'We are not saying to the person, "Look, you do this." What we are saying is, "How can we facilitate? How can we work with you?"'(Sarah, p. 6). Another doctor explained that 'what you are usually doing is trying to listen to what they are saying and see how far you can go along that route without significant harm being caused' (Jonathan, p. 9). So while there are certain areas (and perhaps specialisms) in which medical paternalism may dominate, it should not be assumed that this is the case for all doctors.

This difference of approach appeared to reflect a deeper divergence of opinion over what the 'best interests' test was attempting to ascertain, reminiscent of the dialogue seen in the early case law. Some doctors presented best interests as an objective 'cost–benefit' analysis: 'the potential benefit and the potential harm of doing something versus the potential benefit and potential harm of not doing the thing or doing an alternative' (Oliver, p. 3). This tended to place greater emphasis on the clinical factors – which aligns with the House of Lords finding that 'best interests' is 'all too often' interpreted 'in a medical/paternalistic sense'.[176] Others portrayed best interests as involving two separate constituent elements – the clinical view of what was best for the agent and the agent's wishes. The final determination was often viewed as a 'compromise' between these two elements, with the objectively 'best' clinical course having to be qualified in certain situations by the agent's wishes and feelings.

Some doctors, meanwhile – particularly in geriatrics and psychiatry – regarded best interests as having a much greater subjective element. For one doctor, the best interests assessment was a means of determining 'what would they want for themselves if they can choose for themselves?' (Tatiana, p. 2). Several suggested that they would want to talk to the family to discover what 'the person would have wanted, and what their previous life course was, and what their life decisions had indicated about them' (David, p. 6). They would 'try to get the best idea as to what the patient would have wanted beforehand' (Andrew, p. 7) or 'ask them what they think his wish would have been if he had not been under delusion' (Emily (2), p. 5) or to 'try and understand what the patient's wishes would have been before they lacked capacity, and the type of person they were, and [what] decisions they have made in other similar situations' (David, p. 6). These doctors clearly regarded best interests as bordering on substituted judgement, aimed at ascertaining what the agent would have wanted were they to have capacity. Clearly, then, understandings among clinicians about what constitutes best interests diverge. Given this, it is unsurprising that there is then some inconsistency in the way that they apply the test.

The case law concerning local authorities suggests that their actions in this area are also often dominated by aversion to risk. This is illustrated

[176] House of Lords Select Committee on the Mental Capacity Act 2005, 90.

by numerous instances in which very little weight has been given to the agent's wishes. In *Hillingdon LB v. Neary*,[177] for example, a twenty-one-year-old man with autism and learning disabilities was kept in a residential support unit for a year against his wishes (and those of his father). The judge subsequently found the DOLS authorisation to have been 'flawed' because the best interests assessment had not mentioned his wish to go home at all.[178] Similarly in *G v. E*,[179] Baker J criticised the 'deplorable failure' of the local authority to take into account the close relationship between the young man (who had autism) and his carer, and their 'failure to arrange any contact for several months between this vulnerable young man and the person who had been his carer – his mother-figure – for most of his life'.[180]

While these cases both concerned young men with learning disabilities,[181] *Essex County Council v. RF*[182] concerned a ninety-one-year-old man with dementia who was unlawfully removed from his home and deprived of his liberty for around thirteen months. In a damning indictment of the behaviour of the local authority, District Judge Mort declared himself unable to comprehend why this was 'considered to be a reasonable and proportionate solution to the problem [of his vulnerability to financial abuse] or why his removal and detention was thought to be in his best interests'.[183] In all these cases, local authorities acted in a highly interventionist manner, ignoring the wishes and feelings of the individual at the centre of the decisions.

While these cases may not be representative of the decisions which do not make it to court, the evidence from both the House of Lords inquiry and the Law Commission consultation corroborates the assertion that local authority care decisions are frequently driven by aversion to risk. Dr Ruth Allen, for example, representing the College of Social Work, stated that 'the MCA is not yet fully understood across any profession as

177 [2011] EWHC 1377 (COP).

178 Ibid, [182].

179 [2010] EWHC 621 (Fam).

180 Ibid, [85].

181 While there is no space to consider every case in detail here, other notable examples include *A Local Authority v. WMA & Ors* [2013] EWHC 2580 (COP), and *Northamptonshire Healthcare NHS Foundation Trust v. ML* (Rev 1) [2014] EWCOP 2, both of which concerned young men with learning disabilities being taken out of the care of their families and placed in other living arrangements against their wishes and that of their families.

182 [2015] EWCOP 1.

183 Ibid, [55].

an enabling piece of legislation . . . it is often seen as bolstering the desire to protect and, in some ways, control people's choice making'.[184] Other contributors suggested that social workers veered 'towards overprotection and safeguarding',[185] and that 'most practitioners would feel more comfortable defending a decision to protect rather than being accused of being neglectful'.[186] This was also acknowledged by some local authorities. Lancashire County Council observed that[187]

> enabling someone to take risks is scary, and workers can be under tremendous pressure from families and within their own agencies – what if something goes wrong? Whose name will be headlined? The MCA has not made us any less risk averse.[188]

And here lies the crux of the problem. It is understandable that practitioners should be anxious to avoid any risk, knowing they are ultimately legally responsible for the decision that is being taken, and could face serious liability for any harm that might result. But the way that the current law is framed exacerbates this problem, as it does not provide practitioners with sufficient support for taking reasonable risks with the agent's physical safety, even where doing so respects deeply held values and wishes. The Act instructs practitioners to consider a range of factors, but offers no guidance in situations where these factors pull in different directions, leaving it to each individual decision-maker to perform their own balancing act, based on the aspects that he or she considers most important. As Helen Taylor observes:

> The MCA has drawn attention to the need for decision makers to consider a range of issues wider than the patient's clinical interests, yet provides insufficient guidance on how the statutory principles should be applied in practice.[189]

This is confounded by the fact that unlike judges, who have a rich tapestry of analogous (or semi-analogous) cases on which to draw when seeking to apply the Act, doctors and care workers will rarely be abreast of the specific details of Court of Protection case law, beyond summaries

184 House of Lords Select Committee on the Mental Capacity Act 2005, 86, quoting from response to Q139.
185 Ibid, [87].
186 Ibid.
187 Ibid, [88].
188 Ibid, quoting from Lancashire County Council DoLS Team.
189 H. Taylor, 'What are "Best Interests"? A Critical Evaluation of "Best Interests" Decision-Making in Clinical Practice' (2016) 24 *Medical Law Review* 176.

of the core principles provided by professional bodies. Nor do they have the detailed arguments of Counsel to assist in honing the relevant legal points, whose role it is to draw previous cases (and their analogies or disanalogies) to their attention. They must nonetheless make a decision, and the assessor, struggling to settle on the correct balance between empowering and protecting the individual, finds there is little by way of 'protection' in the Act for them if the agent later suffers harm as a result.[190] It is no defence to say they were acting in accordance with the agent's wishes, since those wishes are only one factor among many which must be 'taken into account' under the Act.

The doctors interviewed for this study were well aware of this difficulty. Even though 'from an intellectual level', stated one, they believed there were circumstances in which it was in a person's best interests to allow them to die, 'from a real-life level, no. Because I think it would be very difficult for me as a hands-on doctor to argue that in court … we would always have to err on the side of life' (Tatiana, p. 9). Another suggested that regardless of their wishes, it is 'rare' for it to be deemed in a person's best interests to not have life-sustaining treatment (Conor, p. 13). Notably, this is not a fear shared by judges, who, unlike doctors, do not risk a negligence claim, disciplinary action, or prosecution if the patient dies, so they feel better able to make empowering decisions.

Conversely, as long as the doctor or care worker can say they 'took into account' the agent's views, it is very difficult to challenge even the most overly paternalistic decisions. As the Law Commission noted:

> Section 4 sets out a procedure, rather than a substantive outcome, and, as one consultee put it, it is difficult to see how almost any best interests decision could be unlawful provided that the decision-maker has consulted the right people and turned their minds to the relevant considerations.[191]

Outside the most extreme cases identified previously in which no mention was made of the agent's wishes in the best interests assessment at all, it is very difficult for a decision to be impugned for not giving 'sufficient' weight to the agent's wishes, with *Re AB* (Termination of

[190] The defence to battery contained in section 5 of the MCA will be considered in more detail in Chapter 6. However, this does not protect doctors who decide *not* to act on the basis of the patient's express wishes.

[191] Law Commission, *Mental Capacity and Deprivation of Liberty* (Law Com. No. 372), 14.11, 13 March 2017. Available at: www.lawcom.gov.uk/app/uploads/2017/03/lc372_mental_capacity.pdf. Accessed 24 August 2018.

Pregnancy)[192] being the only known example of this. By contrast, a claim could (in theory) be brought in negligence if the assessor attached too much importance to the agent's wishes and allowed them to do something harmful as a result. Clearly, then, assessors would be wise to be overly cautious when making these decisions.

The result is that in decisions being taken on the ground, risk aversion may be coming at the cost of enabling individuals to pursue authentically held values. This is a problem from the perspective of the law fulfilling its function, because it implies that best interests determinations may not always be reflecting the agent's own conception of what is good or valuable, as mandated by *Aintree*. But it may also undermine the extent to which the determination reached as to an agent's best interests can really be said to reflect what is 'good' for them at all. The question of what is good for a person and whether this is subjectively or objectively determined is one that has vexed philosophers for centuries, and it is not my intention to examine the vast literature on prudential value theory in depth here.[193] Suffice to say, however, that while there are differing views on the extent to which what is good for a person consists in the satisfaction of their desires (as opposed to the existence of certain 'objective goods' or 'states of affairs', 'regardless of whether one desires them and whether they are satisfying or enjoyable'[194]), in the context of those who *have* capacity, the law clearly determines that what is good for a person is defined by their own subjective preferences or desires, as Chapter 1 explains.[195] In respect of those who *lack* capacity, the position is more complex, since clearly they may face limitations in defining their own well-being, whether by virtue of cognitive impairments or difficulties in accurately identifying their desires because of the impact of mental disorder. For this reason, their well-being cannot be served simply by the satisfaction of their desires, whatever they may be. Indeed, as David DeGrazia points out, 'most desire theorists have adopted conditions for

192 [2019] EWCA Civ 1215.

193 For an interesting (and succinct) discussion of this in the context of making medical decisions, see A. Hall, 'Making Good Choices: Toward a Theory of Well-Being in Medicine' (2016) 37(5) *Theoretical Medicine and Bioethics* 383–400.

194 DeGrazia, 'Value Theory and the Best Interests Standard', 50–60, 55.

195 This is supported in the bioethics literature. See, for example, D. Molyneux, '"And How Is Life Going for You?" – An Account of Subjective Welfare in Medicine' (2007) 33(10) *Journal of Medical Ethics* 568–572; R. Veatch, 'Doctor Does Not Know Best: Why in the New Century Physicians Must Stop Trying to Benefit Patients' (2000) 25(6) *Journal of Medicine and Philosophy* 701–721.

"correcting" actual desires, moving toward informed-desire or rational-desire accounts',[196] precisely to reflect the fact that people's desires may not always be in their interests. Consequently, as Alicia Hall explains, 'determining what is best for the patient under subjective accounts is not always as simple a matter as merely asking the patient what she wants or how she feels',[197] and this will be especially so for those who lack capacity.

Yet the fact that any subjective approach must be tempered by, for example, considerations of the authenticity of the desires expressed, does not mean that we ought to abandon a subjective approach to well-being altogether, and thus disregard the incapacitated agent's preferences entirely in the determination of their best interests. Given that at least some of those who lack capacity may still be able to hold and express deeply and authentically held values and desires, these remain a crucially important dimension to determining what is best for that person, as indeed the MCA acknowledges through its provisions in section 4(6).[198] The account given in Chapter 1 of the importance of being able to live one's life in accordance with one's own priorities and convictions is not simply extinguished because a person lacks the cognitive abilities to decide how different choices might further and reflect those convictions; and to the extent that they remain pertinent to the individual, then it is important to reflect these in decisions taken about them. Rather than disregarding the person's wishes, then, we ought instead to attempt to establish the conditions under which the person's subjective preferences will continue to hold prudential value to them, and give effect to them in those circumstances. This is what Chapter 6 will seek to do.

Such an approach is also instrumentally important, because having regard for the agent's subjective values and beliefs is an important part of treating them as an individual with value. As David Feldman notes, non-consensual treatment may well be experienced as demeaning or undignified, making someone 'subject to demeaning domination by the decision-

[196] DeGrazia, 'Value Theory and the Best Interests Standard', 50–60, 54.

[197] Hall, 'Making Good Choices', 383–400, 392.

[198] Indeed, even some objective list accounts of well-being, which 'identify prudential value with certain kinds of states of affairs, regardless of whether one desires them and whether they are satisfying or enjoyable', might include goods like 'autonomy' among them, thus leaving some space for the person to determine their own interests. Consequently, as DeGrazia notes, many objective list theories also make 'important concessions to subjective theories': see DeGrazia, 'Value Theory and the Best Interests Standard', 50–60, 54–55.

makers, whether medical or judicial'.[199] And so, as Emily Jackson argues, 'preserving a patient's sense that she is a person whose views count is an important way of treating her as a subject, rather than as an object to whom things can be done without asking first'.[200] In fact, this may be especially important in the context of incapacitated individuals, for as Jackson observes, 'one of the most frightening aspects of the loss of capacity through conditions such as dementia is the feeling that one is no longer treated as someone of value'.[201] Engaging with the agent's views is thus also important as a way of demonstrating that they remain someone of value, not diminished in any essential way by the loss of their capacity.

5.4 Conclusion

This analysis has highlighted two key concerns with the current legal framework. The first is that while there is undoubtedly a trend towards the court giving greater weight to the wishes, feelings, beliefs, and values of the incapacitated individual, the lack of direction on how to apply the provisions in section 4 has still resulted in some outlying cases, with different weight being attributed to the agent's wishes, based on a variety of (sometimes implicit) factors, including the authenticity, strength, and consistency of the expressed views. Secondly, this trend towards empowerment is still yet to trickle down to decisions being made by assessors on the ground, which remain characterised by frequent paternalism and risk aversion.

Greater work needs to be done, therefore, to ensure some consistency of approach on the weight being accorded to the agent's wishes, in practice as well as in the courts. This is not intended to suggest that the same weight ought to be accorded in every case: of course, this will depend on the exigencies of any particular case. But there would nonetheless be value to establishing which factors ought to be taken into account when determining the degree of weight to attribute to wishes, and to reframing the law in a way that gives practitioners cause to feel more confident in taking risks, where this accords with the agent's wishes. Mr Justice Munby once observed that:

199 D. Feldman, 'Human Dignity as a Legal Value: Part II' (2000) *Public Law* 61, 69.
200 Jackson, 'From "Doctor Knows Best" to Dignity', 247–281, 264.
201 Ibid.

> The fact is that all life involves risk, and the young, the elderly and the vulnerable, are exposed to additional risks and to risks they are less well equipped than others to cope with. But just as wise parents resist the temptation to keep their children metaphorically wrapped up in cotton wool, so too we must avoid the temptation always to put the physical health and safety of the elderly and the vulnerable before everything else. Often it will be appropriate to do so, but not always. Physical health and safety can sometimes be bought at too high a price in happiness and emotional welfare. The emphasis must be on sensible risk appraisal, not striving to avoid all risk, whatever the price, but instead seeking a proper balance and being willing to tolerate manageable or acceptable risks as the price appropriately to be paid in order to achieve some other good - in particular to achieve the vital good of the elderly or vulnerable person's happiness. What good is it making someone safer if it merely makes them miserable?[202]

The practice of autonomy is not without risks. Under the present law, however, practitioners can only allow an agent to take risks by taking a risk themselves. It is no surprise, then, that they regularly choose instead to shut down all risk, protecting their patient, but also protecting themselves. If people on the cusp of capacity are ever to be empowered to take decisions which are consistent with their authentic values and beliefs, then the legal framework must provide assessors with far greater support for risk-taking at the wish of the agent. It must give practitioners and local authorities the reassurance they need to be able to take decisions which empower the individual – even if doing so exposes the agent to risk, and even, in some cases, if that means allowing the agent to end their own life. How this ought to be done will be considered in Chapter 6.

[202] *Local Authority X v. M* [2007] EWHC 2003 (Fam), [120].

6

Softening the Capacity Cliff Edge

The aim of this chapter is to consider how we can ensure that an individual's wishes – especially those that reflect authentically held values and beliefs – are being prioritised in the best interests decisions being taken about them. The foregoing analysis has made it clear that assessors undertaking best interests assessments could benefit from a more unified starting point and greater clarity on the factors which ought to influence the degree of weight accorded to the agent's wishes. This, it is hoped, would not only achieve greater consistency of approach as between assessors but also give those making decisions on the ground more confidence prioritising the wishes of the agent even in the face of possible harm.

As a starting point, it will be argued that there ought to be a presumption that the agent's wishes and feelings are determinative of what is in their best interests, except where giving effect to them will expose the agent to a risk of significant harm. This would better reflect the fact that frustrating a person's wishes in a way that involves imposing treatment or care interventions on them against their will is likely to cause a level of psychological or emotional harm which can only be outweighed by a serious countervailing harm. However, even where the harms of giving effect to their wishes *are* significant, it might still be legitimate to prioritise the agent's wishes and feelings in some circumstances: where they reflect deeply and authentically held beliefs or values, or where frustrating them will cause the agent a large degree of psychological harm or distress, or force them to endure a life which they find intolerable. Accordingly, this chapter will propose an amendment to section 4 of the MCA, which would outline the factors that ought to be taken into account when determining the degree of weight to be attached to the agent's wishes in the face of such harm. This will be supplemented by changes to the defence to battery in section 5 of the MCA, to bring it in line with the reforms to best interests. The hope is that through these reforms, assessors will not only have a framework to ensure that they are considering the right factors, but also a much-needed flak jacket in those, cases where, having regard to these factors, they consider it right to attach substantial weight to the individual's wishes, even where doing so will expose the agent to a risk of harm.

It should be noted that while this chapter will focus on softening the capacity cliff edge in one direction, through attaching due weight to the wishes of those who have been found to *lack* capacity, judges have, via the development of the Inherent Jurisdiction for Vulnerable Adults, already sought to do this in the other direction. As Chapter 1 observed, the Vulnerable Adults jurisdiction has arisen to plug the 'gap' in the MCA's coverage, protecting those who, despite being deemed capacitous, are nonetheless thought to be especially vulnerable in ways that compromise their autonomy in respect of certain decisions.[1] While it is beyond the scope of this chapter to evaluate the development of this jurisdiction in detail, this does suggest that there has been an acknowledgement at a judicial level of the need to adopt a more nuanced approach to the capacity threshold which recognises the inevitable limitations of the test for capacity as a means of accurately distinguishing those who have the capacity for autonomous decision-making from those who do not have it. It is crucial, therefore, that we acknowledge this in respect of those found to lack capacity in equal measure.

6.1 A Rebuttable Presumption?

Chapter 5 highlighted the difficulties for judges and practitioners called upon to apply section 4 of the MCA, given the variety of ways in which the different factors contained in the provision could be weighed against one another. Consequently, it identified the need to establish a unified starting point for all assessments, which would more clearly define the role that the agent's wishes, feelings, beliefs, and values ought to play in the determination of their best interests, while still retaining some flexibility to reflect the person-, fact-, and circumstance- specific nature of best interests assessments.

This starting point could be established through the creation of a rebuttable presumption in favour of giving effect to the agent's wishes, unless certain circumstances apply. This idea was initially put forward by

[1] *DL v. A Local Authority* [2012] EWCA 253, [65].

the Essex Autonomy Project (EAP), who suggested a 'rebuttable presumption that the reasonably ascertainable will and preferences of [a] person should be given effect to'.[2] This, they considered, would stand in the 'vast majority of cases', but it would not be absolute, and 'in some exceptional circumstances, a proportional and effective strategy for protecting the full range of the person's fundamental rights, freedoms and interests may require action contrary to the person's known will and preferences'.[3] In the consultation that followed, the EAP found there to be 'considerable support' for such a presumption, subject to concerns by some that it was unnecessary, and by others that it did not go far enough in articulating the standard under which the presumption would be rebutted.

Similar problems afflicted the proposals put forward by the Law Commission. In its Consultation Paper, it similarly proposed 'an assumption that the person's wishes and feelings are determinative as to their best interests, although this assumption could be overridden where there are good reasons to do so'.[4] While this gained the support of the majority of people who responded to the consultation (of the 182 consultees who expressed a view on this proposal, 119 agreed, 35 disagreed, and 28 held equivocal positions[5]), criticism remained, echoing concerns raised in the EAP consultation, that section 4 was sufficient without the need to resort to any such presumption. Mr Justice Charles, for example, suggested that the proposal was 'unnecessary and would cause considerable complications when [P's wishes and feelings] have varied over time or cannot be met in practice',[6] a view supported by the Bar Council[7] and Mr Justice Peter Jackson, who in *Wye Valley* stated:

> To elevate one important factor at the expense of others would certainly not have helped the parties, nor the court, in the present case. All that is needed to protect the rights of the individual is to properly apply the [Mental Capacity Act] as it stands.[8]

[2] Martin *et al.*, 'Achieving CRPD Compliance' Essex Autonomy Project, 41.

[3] Ibid.

[4] Law Commission, 'Mental Capacity and Deprivation of Liberty', Consultation Paper No. 222, 12.47. Available at: www.lawcom.gov.uk/wp-content/uploads/2015/07/cp222_mental_capacity.pdf, 12.45.

[5] Law Commission, 'Mental Capacity and Deprivation of Liberty – Consultation Analysis available at https://s3-eu-west-2.amazonaws.com/lawcom-prod-storage-11jsxou24uy7q/uploads/2017/03/cp222_mental_capacity_responses_analysis.pdf, 11.20.

[6] Ibid, 11.34.

[7] Ibid, 11.38.

[8] *Wye Valley* [2015] EWCOP 60, [17].

It is doubtful whether the MCA as it stands *is* sufficient, as Chapter 5 makes clear. The lack of guidance over how section 4 ought to be applied means that it is perfectly possible to 'properly apply' the MCA (at least on the face of the statute), while still giving very little weight to the agent's wishes. This was picked up on by Lucy Series, who suggested that one could be 'diligently following the best interests checklist', yet balance the agent's interests in an entirely different way to Mr Justice Peter Jackson.[9] The Law Commission agreed.[10]

Even if one accepts the need for reform, neither the Law Commission nor the EAP's proposals set out very clearly when the presumption will be displaced. As Mr Justice Peter Jackson noted in *Wye Valley* (supported by other judges of the family division[11]) that 'the Law Commission proposal would not lead to greater certainty, but to a debate about whether there was or was not "*good reason*" for a departure from the assumption'.[12] The Law Commission responded saying that while the proposal would prompt debate, such debate would not be 'wholly undesirable', since a debate over whether there was a good reason to depart from their wishes would at least be a 'step forward from the current focus of the debate on whether *any* weight should be given to wishes and feelings at all'.[13] A similar response had been given by the Essex Autonomy Project, when the same criticism was made of their proposals:

> Any just and reasonable system of law adequate to the practical challenges of this domain of practice will lead to debates. The aim should not be to avoid debate, but to establish a framework for having the debate in terms

[9] Law Commission, 'Mental Capacity and Deprivation of Liberty – Consultation Analysis available at https://s3-eu-west-2.amazonaws.com/lawcom-prod-storage-11jsxou24uy7q/uploads/2017/03/cp222_mental_capacity_responses_analysis.pdf, 11.37.

[10] Law Commission, 'Mental Capacity and Deprivation of Liberty', Consultation Paper No. 222, 12.47. Available at: www.lawcom.gov.uk/wp-content/uploads/2015/07/cp222_mental_capacity.pdf, 14.11.

[11] Law Commission, 'Mental Capacity and Deprivation of Liberty – Consultation Analysis available at https://s3-eu-west-2.amazonaws.com/lawcom-prod-storage-11jsxou24uy7q/uploads/2017/03/cp222_mental_capacity_responses_analysis.pdf, 11.35: this would 'simply lead to debate about whether there is 'good reason' to depart from the assumption and would not produce better outcomes in these difficult cases'.

[12] *Wye Valley* [2015] EWCOP 60.

[13] Law Commission, 'Mental Capacity and Deprivation of Liberty', Consultation Paper No. 222, 12.47. Available at: www.lawcom.gov.uk/wp-content/uploads/2015/07/cp222_mental_capacity.pdf, 14.13.

> that are respectful of the rights, will and preferences of persons with impaired capacity.[14]

A presumption would certainly move the debate on from one focused on what degree of weight, if any, ought to be accorded to the agent's wishes, to one instead centred on why it is not possible to give effect to an agent's wishes. It would also enhance transparency, through requiring the assessor to be explicit about exactly why it is that they are not prioritising the agent's wishes; something that is markedly absent from some of the cases under the current law, such as *RB*[15] and *KD*.[16] Any judge wishing to depart from the agent's wishes would now have to justify their decision to do so.

Although the Law Commission dropped their proposal for a rebuttable presumption that the agent's wishes be given effect to in their final report, the reasons given for this focused on their remit, rather than on principled objections to the idea:

> Whilst we were attracted by the idea of a rebuttable presumption, we do not consider this would fit into the structure of section 4. The requirements of section 4 are largely procedural. Logically, the introduction of a duty to make wishes and feelings generally determinative would require the amendment of section 1 (not section 4), in order to give them a higher status than best interests. However, we did not consult on this and such a reform would be far beyond our remit.[17]

A rebuttable presumption may therefore remain the best way to address concerns over the current application of the best interests test, subject to the concerns raised previously about when such a presumption would be rebutted and whether it fits logically into section 4.

From a practical perspective, neither the framing of the Law Commission's 'assumption' nor the Essex Autonomy Project's 'presumption' would provide the clarity and support that assessors require in order to feel comfortable prioritising the agent's wishes. In both instances, they would be left guessing over how courts might interpret 'good reasons' or 'exceptional circumstances' in any challenge brought against them. After all, there is arguably 'good reason' to intervene wherever an agent's welfare might be adversely affected by their decision, but if this were the case, the assumption would never hold. Moreover, since the 'good

[14] W. Martin *et al.*, 'Achieving CRPD Compliance' Essex Autonomy Project.

[15] *RB v. Brighton and Hove CC* [2014] EWCA Civ 561.

[16] *Hull University Teaching Hospitals NHS Trust v. KD* [2020] EWCOP 35.

[17] Law Commission, *Mental Capacity and Deprivation of Liberty* (Law Com. No. 372), 13 March 2017, 14.4.

reason' or 'exceptional circumstances' that would justify overriding the agent's wishes are left unstated, these presumptions also do not provide a clear rationale for why it is justifiable to override the wishes of the individual in these circumstances (but not others).

Given this, there is a need for a clearer (and more normatively coherent) standard for when such a presumption ought to be rebutted. This is best achieved through a rebuttable presumption that would hold unless following the agent's wishes would expose them to a risk of significant harm. The justification for this is as follows. When determining what is in a person's best interests, it is not only their physical interests which must be taken into account but also their psychological, emotional, and relational interests,[18] all of which may be detrimentally affected by having treatment or care interventions forced upon a person against their wishes. As Lady Justice Hale stated in *R (Wilkinson) v. Broadmoor Special Hospital Authority*,[19] 'most people are able to appreciate that they are being forced to do something against their will even if they are not able to make the decision that it should or should not be done'.[20] Deciding contrary to a person's strongly held wishes may not only result in a decision which is not 'best' for them (in the sense that it does not maximise their well-being, understood to contain a subjective dimension), but it might also have significant psychological and emotional consequences for that person, causing them to feel profoundly disempowered, degraded, and objectified. It is not hard to imagine the distress experienced by someone forced to leave their home in favour of a sterile care home, nor the dehumanising feeling of being a 'thing' which physical interventions are merely 'done to'. And, of course, this is even more clearly the case where the treatment in question is very invasive, as in surgery, where the process of restraining, anaesthetising and then operating on a person constitutes the gravest of infringements to their bodily integrity, which is likely to cause very significant distress for that person.

This is implicitly acknowledged by judges and doctors, who have both suggested that they would be less likely to act contrary to the agent's wishes where the proposed treatment *was* particularly invasive. When listing factors which would influence the weight given to the agent's wishes in *M v. Mrs N*, for example, Hayden J referred to 'the nature of

[18] This was emphasised by Lady Hale in *Aintree University Hospitals NHS Foundation Trust v. James* [2013] UKSC 67.

[19] [2002] 1 W.L.R. 419; [2001] EWCA Civ 1545.

[20] Ibid, [79].

the contemplated treatment' and 'how intrusive such treatment might be',[21] a view he reiterated in *QZ* when he distinguished *Wye Valley* on the grounds of the 'relatively minor level of intrusion involved' in the case at hand.[22] In the interviews, meanwhile, there was near consensus on this issue: where patients were objecting to surgery, it was very rarely regarded as being in their best interests to perform it regardless. This was especially so if the surgery was not being required in an emergency situation or was not necessary to save the person's life. One doctor, for example, described forcing someone to have non-emergency, non-life-saving treatment as 'very hard to justify' (Sarah, p. 10), while another suggested the situation would have to be 'pretty extreme' where 'bodily integrity is compromised' (Oliver, p. 13). Surgery may be particularly intrusive given that the consequences may also be ongoing, with surgery often demanding substantial aftercare and physiotherapy. This will therefore be even more of an affront to a patient who resisted the surgery in the first place.

This is not intended to suggest that all desires, if frustrated, necessarily give rise to harm for the individual. As Joel Feinberg observes, people are commonly left disappointed or dissatisfied without suffering harm.[23] This is because some of our desires are not 'of the appropriate kind to ground ulterior interests', since they are not sufficiently 'stable and durable'[24] or are not linked to our 'longer-range purposes'.[25] When, then, will a desire for something give rise to an interest in some outcome? While being careful not to characterise these as necessary criteria, Feinberg identifies three common hallmarks of when a desire will amount to interest.[26] The first is that it is generally associated with a realistic hope or expectation:[27] one is not harmed by not being able to go to Mars or win the lottery, for example. The second is that the person must want the outcome, at least in part, for the sake of the outcome itself and not purely for the advancement of other, pre-existing interests (such as making money to further other desires that they have).[28] The third common hallmark is that if it is an ultimate interest, it ought to be

21 *M v. N* [2015] EWCOP 76, [28].
22 *NHS Foundation Trust v. QZ* (A Patient) [2017] EWCOP 11.
23 Feinberg, *Harm to Others*, 43.
24 Ibid.
25 Ibid.
26 Ibid, 44.
27 Ibid.
28 Ibid.

capable of promotion by human efforts – there must be ways in which the person can help that goal to be achieved. It is this relationship with personal effort that in Feinberg's view 'converts a mere want into an objective',[29] by creating the necessary investment to give rise to a stake in the outcome.[30] The desire to refuse a treatment or care intervention – whether in pursuit of a good death, religious salvation, or merely being free from excessive interference – clearly exhibits all three of these hallmarks. Forcing treatment or care on an agent in this way is therefore likely to be harmful to them, thwarting their interests in their bodily and psychological integrity, liberty, and freedom from coercion.

Given this, for any such treatment or care decision to be regarded as in the 'best interests' of a patient, the harm to them that will result from giving effect to their wishes must be *sufficient* to outweigh the emotional and psychological harms involved in frustrating them. In other words, to be the decision which *best* promotes the agent's interests, it must be the least harmful of the options available. While there will be situations where the agent may be ambivalent about what happens to them, usually, unless the harm of giving effect to the agent's wishes is significant, this will be outweighed by the psychological harm of overriding their wishes and forcing an intervention on them. To use the example put forward by a doctor in an interview, if a patient refused treatment for a tendon injury, this may well be a poor decision that she will likely regret, but since the harm to her will not be substantial (only slightly diminished function later in life), it cannot justify anaesthetising her and performing surgery against her will (Jerry, p. 2). The injury, then, would have to be markedly graver for non-intervention to be more damaging than the psychological effects of belittling and frustrating the agent in this way. This is also true of care decisions: the risk of an elderly person falling and suffering a physical injury must, for example, be weighed against their loss of independence, routine, home comforts, as well as the (non-negligence) risk of them developing depression as a result of being removed from their home.[31]

Accordingly, it should be presumed that an agent's wishes are determinative of what is in their best interests *unless* giving effect to these

29 Ibid.

30 Ibid.

31 See, for example, C. Sutcliffe, A. Burns, D. Challis *et al.*, 'Depressed Mood, Cognitive Impairment, and Survival in Older People Admitted to Care Homes in England' (2007) 15(8) *American Journal of Geriatric Psychiatry* 708–715.

would result in the agent suffering (or being exposed to a risk of) significant harm. Where giving effect to their wishes would not expose the agent to a risk of significant harm, no further balancing exercise is required by the assessor: the agent's wishes will be respected, since this will be determinative of what is in their best interests. It is only if the presumption is displaced (e.g., the agent is at risk of suffering serious injury or death if their wishes are respected) that the assessor will then have to engage in a balancing of the respective harms, weighing the consequences of giving effect to the agent's wishes against the consequences of frustrating them. (This will be considered further in Section 6.3.)

Given the nature of this presumption, arguably, concerns raised by the Law Commission about the logical structure of section 4 fall away. It is not that the agent's wishes are presumed to have a 'higher status' than their best interests (necessitating a change to section 1), but that the agent's wishes are assumed to *define* the agent's best interests in the absence of them causing significant harm to the agent.

Of course, this presumption must be seen against the background position that there is no legal obligation for doctors to provide any treatment that they do not consider to be clinically indicated, so even if the patient requests treatment which is not harmful to them, the doctor is under no duty to provide it – a position made clear in *NHS v. VT & Anor*.[32] Therefore, in the medical context in practice, this approach only changes the position in respect of treatment refusals.

A similar idea has been put forward by Emily Jackson in the context of refusing medical treatments. She suggests that there ought to be a presumption that 'if [the patient] wishes to refuse a medical intervention, [their] refusal should be respected, unless to do so would result in significant harm to [them]'.[33] This presumption ought, however, to apply to treatment and care decisions across the board, albeit that it is certainly easier to apply to treatment refusals than to care decisions. In the medical context, the harms are often clear and immediate, or at least readily foreseeable. In care decisions, by contrast, the harms are more speculative: the person who insists on living independently despite her frailty *could* fall over and break her hip, or leave the gas ring on, or forget to take her medication – but equally, none of these things might happen. When considering how to apply it in the care context, and in particular when articulating what degree of risk is adequate to rebut the presumption, it

[32] [2013] EWHC B26 (Fam).

[33] Jackson, 'From 'Doctor Knows Best' to Dignity', 247–281, 257.

will therefore be important to draw on the substantial body of jurisprudence that already exists on applying a risk of significant harm standard in the social care context (discussed in Section 6.2).

These changes would not act as a bar to people being placed into a cared-for environment against their wishes, but they would place the onus on any care worker or local authority who sought to do so, to provide strong evidence that the person was at a non-negligible risk in their home, rather than merely asserting that leaving their home would be 'better for them'. This would make it very difficult for behaviour such as that seen in *Essex County Council v. RF*[34] or *Hillingdon LBC v. Neary*[35] to be replicated.

6.2 Understanding 'Significant Harm'

In order that this approach is deemed both applicable in practice and normatively justifiable, there is clearly a need for further elaboration on the meaning of 'significant harm' in this context. The most comprehensive account of 'harm' can be found in the work of Joel Feinberg, who acknowledges the 'vague and ambiguous' nature of the word 'harm',[36] which without further explanation, acts merely as a 'convenient abbreviation for a complicated statement that includes, among other things, moral judgments and value weightings of a variety of kinds'.[37] He distinguishes between different accounts of 'harm'.[38] The first of these conceptualises harm as a 'setback to interests'. According to this understanding, 'it is only when an interest is thwarted through an invasion by self or others, that its possessor is harmed in the legal sense'.[39] The test for whether this invasion has taken place is 'whether that interest is in a worse condition than it would otherwise have been had the invasion not occurred'.[40] His second meaning of the word harm views harm as a wrong to another.[41] Person A wrongs Person B where his 'unjustifiable or [i]nexcusable' conduct violates the rights of

[34] *Essex County Council v. RF* [2015] EWCOP 1.
[35] *Hillingdon LBC v. Neary* [2011] EWHC 1377 (COP).
[36] Feinberg, *Harm to Others*, 31.
[37] Ibid, 32.
[38] The third account, which he describes as harm in a 'derivative or extended sense', he mentions only to dismiss: ibid, 32.
[39] Ibid, 34.
[40] Ibid.
[41] Ibid.

another[42] – which invariably will also involve an invasion of Person B's interests. While almost all harms in the second sense ('wrongs') would amount to harms in the first sense ('setbacks to interests'),[43] not all setbacks to interests will be wrongs: Person A might 'invade [Person B's] interests excusably or justifiably', or thwart interests which Person B 'has no right to have respected'[44] – for example, where Person B has consented to Person A's actions.

When describing a person's self-regarding actions (that is, when a person's decision or actions are causing harm only to themselves), it makes little sense to talk of a person 'wronging' themselves by violating their own rights. This was acknowledged later by Feinberg, who recognised that while the harm principle employed the word harm 'in the sense of wrongful injury', when thinking about the operation of paternalism, harm was rather understood 'in the sense of a simple setback to interest whether "wrongful" or not'.[45] Harm should therefore be understood in the sense of a setback to their interests, with the test being whether or not that interest is in a worse condition than it would otherwise be.

The problem, of course, is that any given person has a variety of interests, which differ in nature. Feinberg, for example, distinguishes between a person's 'ulterior' interests – which encompass their ultimate goals and aspirations[46] – and their 'welfare' interests, which include those interests

> in the continuance for a foreseeable interval of one's life, and the interests in one's own physical health and vigor, the integrity and normal functioning of one's body, the absence of absorbing pain and suffering or grotesque disfigurement, minimal intellectual acuity, emotional stability, the absence of groundless anxieties and resentments, the capacity to engage normally in social intercourse and to enjoy and maintain friendships, at least minimal income and financial security, a tolerable social and physical environment, and a certain amount of freedom from interference and coercion.[47]

In most of the cases being contemplated here – where an agent is thought to require a health or welfare intervention or care plan but is refusing it (or objecting to certain aspects of it) – the agent's actions will invariably be thwarting *some* welfare interest, undermining their physical health or

[42] Ibid.
[43] Ibid, 35.
[44] Ibid.
[45] J. Feinberg, *Harm to Self: The Moral Limits of the Criminal Law* Volume 3 (Oxford Scholarship Online, November 2003), 11.
[46] Ibid, 37.
[47] Ibid.

emotional well-being in a way which could be classed as harmful. Yet they do so out of a conviction that this 'harm' is outweighed by the need to protect *other* interests of theirs, which they, on balance, regard as more important. Where a Jehovah's Witness refuses a life-saving blood transfusion, for example, they will certainly suffer harm to their health, but to act otherwise would be to thwart their ulterior interest in 'achieving spiritual grace'.[48] Meanwhile, an elderly woman who wishes to remain in her own home values her independence and emotional well-being over the increased risk of pain or injury that could result if she were to fall at home, which would undoubtedly represent a setback to her interests. In any decision in this context, then, arguably some interest will be thwarted and some harm will result.

It is for this reason that the 'significance' of the harm becomes important, as without this threshold, the presumption will simply never hold, since a best interests assessor will always be able to point to *some* interest of the agent which is being thwarted by their decision, whether or not the agent in question prioritises that interest. 'Significant harm' is, of course, an inherently relative concept: it must be significant relative to something. However, it is possible to adopt a more objective understanding of significant harm if it is understood as being relative to the agent's previous condition, rather than to the opposing harms (e.g., of not giving effect to a person's wishes). An agent's interest must therefore be in a *substantially* worse condition: the agent's prior physical capabilities must be seriously impaired, the pain or suffering they experience must be substantial, or their life shortened, before the presumption is rebutted.

The *relative* harmfulness of giving effect to versus frustrating the agent's wishes should not, therefore, be considered as part of the determination whether giving effect to their wishes would cause 'significant' harm. It is only *once the presumption has been displaced* (i.e., when the harm is thought to be significant) that the assessor must weigh the harms of giving effect to the agent's wishes against harms of frustrating the agent's wishes, in order to determine which course of action is in the agent's best interests. Otherwise, far from helping to resolve the question of what is best for the agent, applying the presumption would merely descend into a discussion about whether the agent's wishes are rightly regarded as harmful at all, when seen in the context of the consequences of not giving effect to them. Take the example of a Jehovah's Witness

[48] Ibid.

refusing a blood transfusion. If the question of whether giving effect to their wishes amounted to 'significant harm' was answered relative to the harms of not doing so, then a dispute would instantly arise between the assessor (who would undoubtedly regard it as harmful – the person might die) and the agent (who would deem the opposing harm – eternal damnation – to outweigh this). If, by contrast it is only relative to the affect it has on the agent's life, then agreement could be reached over whether it amounts to significant harm.

To facilitate greater consensus over this question, the Code of Practice could provide indicators of what might amount to significant harm, similar to those currently found in the Northern Ireland Mental Capacity Act 2016.[49] In that Act, these arise in the context of the statutory defence to battery rather than best interests. This will be considered in more detail in Section 6.5. However, drawing on these, actions giving rise to significant harm might include those which are likely to cause death or serious injury to or deterioration in the person's physical or mental health; or if it significantly reduces the options they will have available to them in the future. In many cases, there is likely to be a high degree of consensus over these issues: no one would dispute that death, or something seriously and permanently disabling, does not amount to significant harm.

Despite this, there will be some borderline cases where disagreement will arise over whether something constitutes a 'serious' injury or deterioration in the agent's health (as has been the case in other areas of the law where a disability or injury is required to be serious or significant[50]). This might be the case, for example, where something is not life-threatening or grossly debilitating, but it would cause someone substantial pain (e.g., a large kidney stone), or reduce their future mobility (such as refusing a hip replacement). Even within this, while significant pain or suffering invariably amounts to significant harm,[51] there will be a grey area

[49] Mental Capacity Act (Northern Ireland) 2016, s22.

[50] See, for example, *Jepson v. The Chief Constable of West Mercia Police Constabulary* [2003] EWHC 3318, where a judicial review challenge was mounted against the decision of the police not to prosecute a doctor who carried out an abortion under s1(1)(d) of the Abortion Act 1967, which permits an abortion if there 'is a substantial risk that if the child were born it would suffer from such physical or mental abnormalities as to be seriously handicapped'. It was argued by the appellants that a cleft palate and lip could not amount to a 'serious handicap' under the act.

[51] As Joel Feinberg notes, 'when a given condition becomes extremely painful ... it does interfere with the pursuit of various goals and objectives, and that incapacitating effect renders it harmful': Feinberg, *Harm to Self*, 47.

between this and, say, refusing surgery for arthritic joints, which may cause some pain and discomfort, but we might not regard it as *significantly* harmful. While disputes will arise at the margins, this would at least make it incumbent upon the assessor to show why giving effect to the agent's wishes would be seriously harmful to them – a determination which would then be open to challenge if the agent disagreed.[52]

Although writing in the context of decisions about children, Douglas Diekema has further suggested that clinicians understand the concept of 'harm' much better than they understand 'best interests'.[53] While this was not explicitly examined in the interviews, doctors frequently cited what they saw as their fundamental responsibilities – 'avoiding harm', 'relieving suffering', or 'saving life', and there was a high degree of consensus when faced with the vignettes over what constituted a 'negative' or 'harmful' outcome. This suggests it might be easier to gain some consensus over whether something is 'harmful' (a negative value) than over what is 'best' for a person (a positive one). Doctors also appeared to intuitively grapple with the seriousness of the harm to the person, for example, giving greater weight to the agent's wishes where the psychological harms would be greater (such as where the treatment is incredibly invasive, such as surgery), and less where the physical harms would be greater (as in life-saving situations).

Perhaps most importantly, the concept of significant harm is also used successfully in other contexts and is something with which social and care workers are already familiar. Section 31 of the Children Act 1989 prevents a court from making a public law order placing a child in the care of, or under the supervision of, a local authority, unless the court is satisfied that the child is suffering or is likely to suffer significant harm. Social and care workers are thus used to applying this standard, in particular when determining whether a child should remain at home under the care of their family or instead be placed into care. It would not, therefore, seem to be a significant step to apply the same test in relation to whether a person with learning disabilities, brain damage, or dementia should be permitted to remain in their own home or under the care of

52 Where the issue is one of resources (as in *Re LC* [2015] EWCOP 25), this can also be accounted for in a significant harm framework: the question is whether *in light of the resources available to care* for the agent, they would be at risk of significant harm if, for example, left in their own home.

53 D. Diekema, 'Parental Refusals of Medical Treatment: The Harm Principle as Threshold for State Intervention' (2004) 25(4) *Theoretical Medicine* 243–264.

their family, or be moved into a cared-for environment: in both instances, their home environment presents various risks to the individual and the potential for suboptimal (or neglectful) care, and the question is whether these are serious enough to justify moving the person. Given that one of the aims behind the Children Act was to stop the overzealous actions of local authorities in too-readily removing children from their families, it may well be valuable to introduce similar requirements for other vulnerable individuals who require some measure of state supervision and support. It would also mean that there is an existing body of jurisprudence which can be drawn upon by both doctors or social workers and the courts, which would be particularly helpful when applying this standard in the context of care decisions, where the possible harms are less certain.

Differences, of course, remain between the two contexts. In the case of children, there are, in general, two prima facie decision-makers – the parents – who have responsibility for the child, and so the question is in what circumstances the state should be able to displace them as the decision-makers for the child. The bar for this is understandably high, since it dictates when the person who arguably has the most legitimate claim to make the decision about the child, ought to be prevented from doing so. The parents are default decision-makers due to the deeply personal role they have in the child's life and the wide and long-term responsibilities associated with parenthood: there are thus very good reasons why this position should not easily be usurped by other decision-makers. In the current context, however, decisions for an incapacitated adult fall straight to the doctor or carer (subject to there being an LPA) and the question is the basis on which they ought to make the determination of what is best for the agent, rather than when they ought to displace another decision-maker. This might not necessitate such a high threshold.

Far from being problematic, however, this could provide a useful way to reconceptualise the role of the agent in decisions about their treatment and care. Rather than viewing incapacity as a 'switch' which permits the views of others to be substituted for those of the individual agent, this would instead conceive of that agent as holding the strongest claim to know what decision is best for them (even if they lack capacity), which may be displaced *only* in so far as they are doing something which causes significant harm to themselves. A similar approach can be seen in the Irish Assisted Decision-Making (Capacity) Act 2015, under which the co-decision-maker can only refuse to 'acquiesce with the wishes of the appointer' if it is reasonably foreseeable that doing so would result in harm to the appointer (or another).[54] Therefore, their wishes must be given effect to unless harm is likely to result.

Under these proposals for reform, presumptive power is given to the agent's wishes, thus clearly signalling to assessors that it is these which ought to form the starting point in any assessment of what is in their best interests, and which must be respected, unless it can be shown that the harm that will result from doing so is sufficient to outweigh the emotional and psychological harms of frustrating their wishes. This in effect would mean that there is a zone in which people are free to make choices about what is best for them, and to prioritise the values and beliefs that *they* endorse, provided that in doing so, it does not expose them to significant harm. The decision-maker is thus provided with a flak jacket in these circumstances if they wish to uphold an agent's decision to refuse treatment; while if they wish to override it, the onus is on them to justify *why* the decision is so harmful that it outweighs the presumption in favour of respecting their choice. And this debate, of course, results in greater transparency, which will tend to promote more considered and compassionate decisions.

In doing so, the law would arguably strike a better balance under article 8 ECHR, which protects a person's 'right to respect for their private and family life'.[55] This right is qualified and subject to restrictions made 'in accordance with law' where 'necessary in a democratic society' for (amongst other things) 'the protection of health or morals'.[56] However, as the Law Commission explained, this means that departing from a person's wishes and feelings 'should be permitted only where it is necessary and proportionate'.[57] While it might be suggested that *any* intervention which promotes the person's welfare is 'necessary and proportionate', overriding an agent's own assessment of what is 'best' for them merely because it does not accord with what the assessor considers to be 'best', would seem, in the absence of harm, to go beyond what is necessary. In the jurisprudence on article 8, 'necessary' has been

[54] ADMC (Ireland) Act, s19(5).

[55] European Convention for the Protection of Human Rights and Fundamental Freedoms, article 8(1).

[56] Ibid, article 8(2).

[57] Law Commission, *Mental Capacity and Deprivation of Liberty* (Law Com. No. 372), 13 March 2017, 14.18.

taken to imply 'the existence of a "pressing social need" for the interference'.[58] Moreover, the European Court of Human Rights was clear in *Dudgeon v. United Kingdom* that:

> According to the Court's case-law, a restriction on a Convention right cannot be regarded as "necessary in a democratic society" - two hallmarks of which are tolerance and broadmindedness - unless, amongst other things, it is proportionate to the legitimate aim pursued.[59]

If best interests determinations involve a weighting of factors or interests which may legitimately be balanced differently by different people, then it follows that there is room for reasonable disagreement in any given situation, not least between patient and doctor. Given this, frustrating the agent's wishes simply because the assessor would have balanced these factors differently would seem disproportionate to its aim of protecting vulnerable people from harm, especially when considered in the context of the importance attached to 'tolerance and broadmindedness' in a democratic society. A provision which only allowed the agent's wishes to be frustrated where they wished to do something which exposed them to a serious risk of significant harm would thus seem to strike a better balance under article 8, being necessary and proportionate to achieve the aim of protecting the individual from harm.

A presumption would also help to make the law more 'CRPD-compliant'.[60] According to article 12(4), signatories (including the UK), must undertake to 'ensure that measures relating to the exercise of legal capacity respect the rights, will and preferences of the person'.[61] This, as Emily Jackson notes, 'implies more than simply taking [their] views into account',[62] as is all section 4 of the MCA currently requires. According to a General Comment by the UN Committee on the Rights of Persons with Disabilities, the 'best interests' principle is not a

[58] *Dudgeon v. United Kingdom* (1983) 5 EHRR 573, [51].

[59] Ibid, [53].

[60] Although the Supreme Court has dismissed the notion that failure to comply with the CRPD can be invoked as a ground of legal challenge in domestic courts (see Lord Stephens' obiter in *JB* [2021] UKSC 52 at [120] where he refers to it as an 'unincorporated international treaty'; and *R* (SC) *v. Secretary of State for Work and Pensions* [2021] UKSC 26, [77]–[96]), compliance with UN Conventions remains important from the perspective of international law.

[61] UN General Assembly, *Convention on the Rights of Persons with Disabilities: Resolution adopted by the General Assembly*, 24 January 2007, A/RES/61/106, article 12.

[62] Jackson, 'From "Doctor Knows Best" to Dignity', 247–281, 266.

safeguard which complies with article 12 in relation to adults,[63] a view reiterated by a number of other commentators. Mary Donnelly, for example, observes that 'although the expanded best interests standard in the MCA, which requires account to be taken of the person's wishes and feelings, shows more respect for individual subjectivity than prior iterations of the standard, it does not meet the requirements of article 12, as interpreted by GC1'.[64] Others have been explicit about the need for reform. Genevra Richardson maintains that 'the priority afforded to the objective assessment of best interests over the currently expressed wishes of the person might . . . need to be reconsidered'.[65] Peter Bartlett, meanwhile, suggests that including factors other than sections 4(4) and 4(6) in the best interests assessment falls short of the CRPD, and thus 'legislative amendment will be required' if it is to comply.[66]

In appraising compliance between the MCA and the CRPD, the Essex Autonomy Project concluded that a rebuttable presumption in favour of giving effect to a person's wishes *would* strike an appropriate balance between merely 'taking account' of the person's wishes and feelings, which they considered 'falls short of fulfilling a requirement of respect', and total deference to the person's will and preferences as demanded by the CRPD.[67] Similarly in response to the proposals put forward by the Law Commission (which arguably demanded less to rebut the presumption than significant harm), the Equality and Human Rights Commission,[68] Alzheimer's Society,[69] and a number of academics[70] all commented that it would make the law more compatible with article 12 CRPD, even if not entirely compliant.

[63] Committee on the Rights of Persons with Disabilities, *General Comment No 1 (2014) article 12: Equal Recognition Before the Law* (adopted at the Eleventh session of the Committee, 31 March 2014–11 April 2014, Geneva, CRPD/C/GC/1) at [21].

[64] Donnelly, 'Best Interests in the Mental Capacity Act', 318–332, 319.

[65] Richardson, 'Mental Disabilities and the Law', 333–354, 348.

[66] P. Bartlett, 'The United Nations Convention on the Rights of Persons with Disabilities and Mental Health Law' (2012) 75 *Modern Law Review* 752, 766.

[67] W. Martin *et al.*, 'Three Jurisdictions Report: Towards Compliance with CRPD Art. 12 in Capacity/Incapacity Legislation across the UK' (2016) Essex Autonomy Project, 40. Available at: https://autonomy.essex.ac.uk/wp-content/uploads/2017/01/EAP-3J-Final-Report-2016.pdf, 40.

[68] Law Commission, 'Mental Capacity and Deprivation of Liberty – Consultation Analysis available at: https://s3-eu-west-2.amazonaws.com/lawcom-prod-storage-11jsxou24uy7q/uploads/2017/03/cp222_mental_capacity_responses_analysis.pdf, 11.21.

[69] Ibid, 11.22.

[70] Ibid, 11.26.

This proposal would thus strike a better balance from a theoretical perspective, allowing for the discussion of what is in an agent's best interests to take place in a way that is more respectful to the agent as an individual, with their unique values and priorities. But it would also go some way towards providing the guidance and support identified in Chapter 5 as severely lacking from the current law. Being required to base their decisions on such a clear-cut presumption would provide assessors with greater support when making judgements which entail some element of risk. It would offer them more effective protection from legal liability, as anyone challenging the decision would be obliged to adduce evidence that, contrary to what the assessor thought at the time, the agent would have been exposed to significant harm. And this would hopefully have a positive impact on care decisions, where evidence suggests that aversion to risk is often the default position. Instead, the default position would become that an agent's wishes ought to be given effect to, providing the harms that might materialise are not significant.

Of course, that a person's wishes ought to be determinative of their best interests in the absence of a serious risk of significant harm does not tell us how their interests ought to be balanced where there *is* significant harm. Or to put it another way, if the harm is not significant, it will invariably be outweighed by the psychological and emotional harms of overriding their wishes. It does not follow from this, however, that where the harm is significant, it will always outweigh those psychological harms: rather, the harms must be weighed against each other to determine which course of action is the 'least harmful' or 'best' for the person. Section 6.3 will therefore explore when a person's wishes ought to prevail even in the face of 'significant harm'.

6.3 Respecting Values in the Face of Significant Harm

The most taxing decisions are often those where a person resolves to do something deeply harmful to themselves. Yet it is precisely because the consequences are so grave that the person is likely to care about these decisions most strongly. To decide whether to have stitches on a cut to avoid scarring, or a cast versus a splint on a fractured wrist, will scarcely engage the emotions. It is quite another matter to decide where a person is allowed to live or how the final moments of their life should play out. Nowhere is freedom of choice more important than where decisions relate to a person's fundamental sense of self, and it would seem perverse for the law to deny people any say over those decisions that are of profound importance to them, while giving them substantial say over those in which the consequences are relatively unimportant. Thus, significant harm cannot act as a trump card in all such decisions. Rather 'the psychological harm that is done to someone by imposing treatment upon her, where to do so goes against beliefs that are profoundly important to her, should be *put in the balance* with the physical harm that might be caused if she does not receive the treatment [or care] in question'.[71]

When thinking about how to weigh the person's best interests in a case where giving effect to their wishes would put them at a risk of significant harm, it is important to consider both the nature of those wishes (which, as mentioned in Chapter 5, will be relevant to whether satisfaction of them will promote individual well-being) and the likely impact of them on the person's future. People express many wishes: some strongly, others with a degree of ambivalence; some consistently, others transiently; some as part of a broader scheme for one's life, others to enjoy momentary pleasure. While the aforementioned discussion highlights the fact that frustrating a person's wishes and carrying out a treatment or care intervention against their will, will invariably cause *some* emotional or psychological harm to them, it does not follow from this that all frustrations of a person's wishes are equally harmful; rather, the extent and duration of that harm will depend on the nature of the wishes in question, their importance to the individual, and the type of decision being taken.

A useful starting point when determining the weight to attach to a person's wishes is to consider how they relate to the person's more fundamental values or beliefs. In some cases, a person's present wishes may reflect their authentically held values or beliefs. The desire of an incapacitated Jehovah's Witness to refuse a blood transfusion is perhaps the clearest example of this. In others, they may reflect inauthentically held beliefs or values (that is, those held as a consequence of disorder or impairment the person would not otherwise sanction). This might be the case where someone with anorexia nervosa refuses food, or where someone suffering from a delusion refuses treatment on the basis of this delusional belief. And then there will be cases in which a person's wishes do not reflect their broader value or belief system at all, perhaps because the person is unable to reflect upon and give effect to this or where the wishes expressed seem in tension with those values or beliefs that have

[71] Jackson, 'From "Doctor Knows Best" to Dignity', 247–281, 266.

guided their life to date. Each raises different challenges for the best interests assessor, which will be explored in Section 6.3.1.

6.3.1 *Wishes That Reflect Authentic Values and Beliefs*

In the first set of cases, where the person's expressed wishes appear to reflect authentically held values or beliefs, there will generally be very good reason to accord substantial weight to the person's wishes. While the difficulties surrounding notions of authenticity were discussed in Chapters 3 and 4 and will not be rehearsed here, that discussion highlighted two things which are relevant for the present discussion. The first was that since impairments in one's cognitive abilities and in one's values or beliefs do not go hand in hand, a person's authentic beliefs or values may outlive the person's cognitive capacities to consciously act on them. Jaworska explores this in the context of patients with Alzheimer's disease, drawing on medical research to demonstrate how they still often exhibit attitudes which incorporate features of valuing (rather than mere desiring) even after they lose the thread of their life's narrative and are unable to fully direct their lives.[72] It also follows that a person may be able to generate new authentic beliefs or values even after the onset of incapacity. A person who suffers from neurodegenerative decline or a brain injury may come to value new things in life as their cognitive (and perhaps also their physical) capacities deteriorate, for example. The second, and more controversial, consequence of the foregoing discussion was that a person could have authentically held beliefs or values even where those are caused by a disorder or impairment, if the person endorses or sanctions those values notwithstanding knowledge of their origins. Mr B in *Wye Valley* was cited as a possible example of this.

These authentic beliefs or values may affect decision-making in different ways. Sometimes a person will hold beliefs which they deem straightforwardly incompatible with the treatment or care intervention proposed. This might be because it is expressly prohibited within that belief system, as where a Jehovah's Witness refuses a blood transfusion, a Muslim refuses food during the daylight hours of Ramadan, or a Jew refuses porcine-derived medication or foods. Or it might be that although the intervention is not specifically prohibited by their beliefs, they hold certain values on account of those beliefs which lead them to feel that the

[72] Jaworska, 'Respecting the Margins of Agency', 105–138.

intervention would violate them (as where a Catholic woman refuses to terminate a pregnancy even where the foetus carries risks to her, or a Muslim woman wishes to not be examined or intimately cared for by a male nurse). While instances in which refusals are based on specific beliefs often involve a religious element, religious beliefs are by no means the only reason: in *St George's*, for example,[73] the patient's refusal was apparently based on her belief that nature should be allowed to 'take its course', and in *SS v. LB Richmond on Thames and SWL CCG*,[74] the patient wished to minimise medical intervention. And there are other examples of vegetarian patients refusing treatments because they contain animal products (clotting disorders, for example, are often treated with low-molecular-weight heparin, which is prepared from mucosa taken from porcine intestine).

Even where there is no one particular belief which is implicated by a decision, a person's wish may nonetheless reflect values which are deeply important to them, and which they feel would be frustrated or compromised if their wishes were not given effect to. In such cases, there is no objective incompatibility between the value in question and the intervention, but the person may subjectively feel them to be in tension with one another. For example, an intervention may be felt to undermine one's dignity or independence or to impede on their privacy. Such concerns have underpinned a number of recent judgments, where the agent's decision was thought to reflect values and priorities that had been of huge personal importance throughout their life, and which continued to matter deeply to them. In *Re D*, for example, it was D's character as a 'very private man' which led the judge to conclude he would not have wanted his current existence;[75] in *Wye Valley*, Peter Jackson J was motivated by Mr B's 'core quality' of 'fierce independence' which was now under threat,[76] while Manuela Sykes was thought to continue to 'appreciate and express the value of being at liberty and being allowed autonomy'.[77]

In such cases, the fact that a person's expressed wish is consistent with their authentic belief or value system is prima facie a good reason to give

[73] *St George's Healthcare NHS Trust v. S* [1998] 3 All ER 673.
[74] [2021] EWCOP 31.
[75] [2012] EWHC 885 (COP).
[76] *Wye Valley* [2015] EWCOP 60, [43].
[77] A. Ruck Keene *et al.*, *Court of Protection Handbook: A User's Guide* (Legal Action Group, 2014), 3.79.

it very great weight in any best interests assessment. This is because it is very likely to be prudentially valuable or welfare maximising, enabling that person to pursue their own conception of a good life, according to the things that matter to them, even if they are unable to fully guide their lives unaided. Mr Justice Hayden appeared to agree in *M v. Mrs N*,[78] when noting that where the wishes and feelings of an incapacitated adult had 'similar cogency and authenticity', they 'are to be afforded no less significance than those of the capacitous',[79] and as the discussion in Chapter 5 highlighted, the authenticity of a wish has often been a factor in determining the weight to be accorded to it in previous cases. The fact that a person may not have the cognitive abilities to make a decision independently does not simply extinguish these beliefs, or make them irrelevant, and to act in a way that is contrary to them would be to deny respect for the person as an individual and to undermine our commitment to value pluralism and religious freedom. This is especially so given that it is often the very circumstances that render some intervention necessary (say, a blood transfusion) that are causing the person to lack capacity (perhaps due to a severe injury and blood loss). A person would therefore be denied the opportunity to adhere to their beliefs in the very circumstances where that belief has most relevance.

The challenge in such cases is not therefore about whether it is right in principle to accord significant weight to the person's wishes, but in determining *when* a person is acting on the basis of an authentic value or belief. As Chapters 3 and 4 explain, it can be difficult to establish whether a value or belief is itself authentic to a person, or the result of an illness or impairment, and even then it may be difficult to discern what impact different values have on the decision-making process and how they motivate the ultimate wish expressed. While in situations like that of the Jehovah's Witness refusing a blood transfusion, it might be easy to identify the belief in question, assess its relevance to the agent, and apply it to the situation at hand, treatment and care decisions are rarely this clear cut. Most values or beliefs will be far less prescriptive or precise than this. As Johnston *et al.* explain:

> A common value expressed by individuals who witness the decline and mental deterioration of elderly relatives is the desire for dignity towards the end of life, something that many often do not see as compatible with

[78] [2015] EWCOP 76 (Fam).
[79] *M v. N* [2015] EWCOP 76, [32].

> living in a nursing home, being incontinent and requiring assistance with personal care. What this reflects is something about the kind of person one is, what one values, and how one wishes to live one's life. Such values may also provide insight into what would give a person a good death. Such expressions do not provide evidence for particular healthcare/end of life choices in specific (usually unforeseeable) circumstances, but they do provide a rich seam of context in which to make some judgement about what kinds of treatment, or non-treatment, the person would be likely to want in a given situation.. . . They are not individual preferences specific to particular circumstances but general, broad instantiations of the kind of person one is and wants to be, with or without capacity.[80]

Decisions will not therefore always be capable of being explained by reference to a particular value or belief. Rather the agent's previous sentiments or behaviour will assist in formulating a narrative about that agent and their previous values, which may cast light on whether the qualities which previously guided their life are consistent with those wishes currently being expressed but will rarely be definitive. And these concerns about establishing when a decision reflects an authentic value or belief will be even more pronounced where the agent has beliefs that are thought to derive from a disorder, but which are nonetheless deeply meaningful to them, and which have informed their behaviour for some time. Therefore, while there may be good reason in principle to accord great weight to wishes that appear to reflect a person's more fundamental or authentically held values, given the difficulties inherent in establishing this with certainty, these wishes will rarely be *determinative* of their best interests.

It is for this reason that despite the intuitive appeal of Emily Jackson's suggestion to supplement the initial presumption (that the agent's wishes ought to be determinative of their best interests in the absence of significant harm) with a second presumption in favour of respecting decisions grounded in core beliefs and values, this is not the approach advocated here. According to Jackson's proposals, a second presumption would seek to ensure that the agent's refusal of treatment is respected 'if it is grounded in her core values and beliefs, that is, in views that are, or were, of profound importance to [the person]'.[81] This captures a similar idea to that proposed previously, creating a default position that

[80] C. Johnston, N. Banner, and A. Fenwick, 'Patient Narrative: An "On-Switch" for Evaluating Best Interests' (2016) 38 *Journal of Social Welfare and Family Law* 249, 252.

[81] Jackson, 'From "Doctor Knows Best" to Dignity', 247–281, 279.

decisions driven by authentically and deeply held values ought to be respected in best interests determinations.

Concerns may certainly be raised about the practicality of distinguishing 'core' from 'non-core' beliefs, especially in the medical context, in which many beliefs or values which would not have been regarded as 'core' – in the sense that they did not guide the patient's behaviour throughout their lives – may take on new significance. As Jackson herself acknowledges, 'untangling what matters most to the patient, and identifying what might be said to be her core values and beliefs will not always be straightforward'.[82] More significantly, however, creating a rebuttable presumption effectively creates a threshold of significance, above which beliefs are decisive and below which they are just one factor in the best interests determination. In addition to inviting manipulation by assessors, this binary distinction does not reflect the fact that, in reality, an agent's values and beliefs occupy a spectrum of significance for them, which will vary according to the circumstances. It is far from uncommon, for example, for someone to attach renewed significance to their faith in the face of a terrible accident or deteriorating health. Meanwhile, someone who always greatly valued their privacy and dignity may quickly come to tolerate some degree of intrusion into both, as a price worth paying for comfort and independence.

The difficulty is that presumptions work in all-or-nothing terms: it either stands or is displaced. In the context of the first presumption proposed in this chapter, this will (generally) generate a clear 'yes' or 'no' answer: giving effect to the agent's wishes will either expose them to a risk of significant harm or it will not. This then dictates how the assessor should respond. If giving effect to the agent's wishes would *not* cause them significant harm, then the presumption stands and the agent's wishes ought to be given effect to. If it *would*, then the presumption does not apply, and those harms must then be weighed against the harm of frustrating their wishes in the wider determination of their best interests. In the context of this second presumption, however, to produce the same clarity, it would have to treat the categorisation of a belief as 'core' (or to instead use my terminology, 'authentic') as determinative of how we ought to then respond to it. Providing a belief or value is 'authentic', giving effect to it would *always* be in the agent's best interests.

[82] Ibid, 270.

There are two problems with this approach. The first is that noted previously: that determining when a belief or value is authentic (or when a specific wish reflects that authentic belief or value) will not always be clear cut, and so there is a risk in responding to that determination in an all-or-nothing way. Given the ambiguity which inevitably surrounds determinations about the origins of some beliefs or values and their significance to the individual, it is right to be cautious both in the test for capacity and when determining the agent's best interests. This is particularly so where the outcome will bring potentially significant harm to the agent. In fact, the more harmful the outcome, the greater evidence we would wish to see that the agent's wish *was* reflective of authentic and deeply held values, before giving effect to it.

The second is that while the authenticity of a belief means it will generally be welfare-maximising, this will not always be the case. Often in treatment and care decisions, the very fact that the agent is ill or in need of care and support means that certain of their interests or values must be prioritised over others. Or indeed the same value might be implicated, and a decision has to be taken over whether it is better to compromise it in the short term in order to facilitate it in the longer term. Take, for example, an elderly woman who has always been resistant to interference by others and wishes to be left alone to get on with her life on her own terms. This may be facilitated in the long term by undergoing a hip replacement, which could allow her to enjoy greater independence, but this is only possible through substantial interference in the short term. A compromise must therefore be struck, and the authenticity of certain values she holds will not on its own tell the assessor how to strike it. Moreover, independence and freedom from interference might well be authentically held values, and her stated desire to refuse the surgery could reflect those, but giving effect to them may compromise other authentic values in the future, which could prove to be of even greater significance to her. If the pain and impeded mobility prevents her from spending time with family and friends in the future, for example, then respecting her authentic wish now might see her well-being diminished by increasing isolation. The authenticity of a desire is therefore an important dimension to take into account when determining the weight to accord to the agent's wishes, with greater weight generally accorded to wishes which do reflect authentic values or beliefs. But this should not be determinative, since the assessor must also take account of how respecting that value impedes on the agent's ability to pursue the things that matter to them in the future.

6.3.2 *Inauthentic Wishes*

More challenging are those cases in which the agent's wishes appear *inauthentic*. This may be because they are acting on the basis of inauthentic values or beliefs (i.e., those stemming from disorder or impairment). An example of this might be where a person with anorexia nervosa refuses food, or acts on a delusional belief, as happened in *QZ*, in which the patient refused a gynaecological investigation, as she held a delusional belief that she was at risk of being raped by her doctors.[83] Alternatively, we may think a wish is inauthentic because it is difficult to reconcile with their (ostensible) authentically held values. This might be because a person can no longer appreciate their commitment to previous values, such as a Jewish person with dementia eating pork, or they may still hold and appreciate certain values but are unable to decide in a way that furthers these, as in the example given earlier, where a woman who greatly values her ability to live independently refuses hip replacement surgery even though it is necessary for her to continue to live in her own home.

One reason why such cases are complex is that the very fact that the decision is not motivated by authentically held values or beliefs means that respecting those wishes will not necessarily be welfare-maximising. In fact, the opposite may be true: respecting their inauthentic wishes may preclude the agent's ability to experience any kind of future joy or happiness and undermine their welfare in the long term, through preventing them living their life in accordance with those things that they do authentically value. Given this, for it to be in the agent's best interests to accord with such wishes, especially in the face of grave physical harm, the corresponding harms involved in frustrating them would have to be great. Much will therefore depend on the strength or importance of the wishes in question and the likely harm involved in frustrating them. It is possible, for example, that such values or beliefs may be held so strongly and deeply that the agent will not be able to overcome the feelings of invasion, impotency, or anger that result from their wishes being overridden; therefore, even if in theory it may be possible for them to enjoy future happiness if they accept the intervention, in fact the effect of overriding their wishes will make this an impossibility. As noted in Chapter 5, *Wye Valley* may be an example of this,[84] as might *Avon and*

[83] [2017] EWCOP 11.
[84] [2015] EWCOP 60.

Wiltshire Mental Health Partnership v. WA & Anor,[85] where it was feared that force-feeding WA may reignite his past trauma.[86]

In other cases, it is not the psychological harm caused by the frustration of the agent's wishes (or the invasion of their liberty) which might justify respecting their (inauthentic) decisions, but that the effect of treating them against their will would be to condemn them to an existence which they find intolerable. This evidently underpinned the decision in *Wye Valley*, where the judge made clear that to amputate him would be to force him to endure a future for which he had no appetite,[87] and ought to have been more influential in *A Local Authority v. E*,[88] in which forced feeding was authorised, notwithstanding the fact it condemned E to a life she described as 'pure torment',[89] through a treatment course she experienced as abusive. This is not to suggest that the incapacitated agent's assessment of their quality of life will be determinative of what is deemed best for them. After all, for those suffering from mental disorder, particularly those associated with depressive illnesses, an inability to see the future as open and full of possibility may itself be a symptom of their disorder. But the agent's subjective experience of their life must be a relevant factor when determining what the impact of the decision is likely to be on their future well-being.

When it comes to determining the weight to be ascribed to inauthentic wishes, much may therefore depend on the prospect of the agent recovering to attain a quality of life that they would regard as acceptable, or which would enable them to pursue authentic values in the future. In *E*, for example, the departure from her wishes was justified on the basis that there was an estimated 20 per cent chance that with the treatment, she would recover to a quality of life that she would find acceptable. This clearly weighed heavily on the judge; as it did in *NHS Foundation Trust v. QZ*,[90] where the evidence of her treating doctor was that there was every possibility that QZ may 'recover a life which has both happiness and dignity incorporated into it'.[91] The strength, clarity, and consistency of E's wishes, coupled with the 80 per cent chance that such treatment would be in vain, might be reason to question whether the judge struck the right

[85] [2020] EWCOP 37.
[86] Ibid, [94].
[87] [2015] EWCOP 60, [45].
[88] [2012] EWCOP 1639.
[89] Ibid, [76].
[90] [2017] EWCOP 11.
[91] Ibid, [32].

balance in this particular case. But in general, it will only rarely be in a person's best interests to allow them to make life-ending or drastically life-altering decisions on the basis of inauthentic values, where it is thought they have a reasonable prospect of recovery to the point of being able to gain enjoyment from their future life. The application of the law must seek to protect people from the effects of their disorder or impairment, not leave them to bear the consequences of choices driven by harmful psychological dysfunctions alone. And this will sometimes require their wishes to be frustrated in the short term, however distressing that might be, in order to protect their capacity for both autonomy and enjoyment in the future.

Further issues afflict the second category of cases noted previously, in which a person's wish appears to be contrary to their authentically held values, despite them not being subject to the influence of other, inauthentic values. Here, a tension may emerge between the agent's expressed wishes and the assessor's view of their more fundamental 'authentic' values or beliefs. On the one hand, too great a focus on the agent's current wishes risks ignoring the fundamental limitations in their decision-making which led to them being found to lack capacity in the first place. It is precisely because someone is not able to use the information available to make a decision which reflects their values, beliefs, and priorities that causes us to question their capacity for autonomous decision-making. An important part of protecting people whose cognitive capacities are limited is thus in trying to make a choice that best facilitates the things that they find important, even if they, for example, lack the ability to project into the future and see how that decision will affect their future life and choices. On the other hand, there is a clear risk of reifying vague notions of the agent's authentic 'self' or 'values' and bringing them to bear on the decision so as to make a choice that disregards the wishes and feelings – and consequently the humanity – of the individual agent present. This is especially problematic given our inherent limitations when it comes to unearthing a person's values, discussed previously. It may be difficult to distinguish situations where a person's values remain constant, but their cognitive decline prevents them from expressing a wish that reflects those values, from those in which changing experiences and life circumstances result in a natural shift in values and priorities. As the vast literature on advance directives demonstrates,[92] there is a risk in binding someone to their previous

[92] See, for example, Dworkin, *Life's Dominion*, 179–217 and 'Autonomy and the Demented Self', 4–16; R. Dresser, 'Dworkin on Dementia' (1995) 25(6) *Hastings Center Report* 32;

values, and this risk is heightened where such values are not clearly expressed in a written statement but are discerned through the assessor creating a narrative about that person's life and character, often using the evidence of third parties, into which certain values either fall or do not fall.

When determining the weight to place on the agent's wishes in such cases, it will be important to consider whether the agent is acting in a way which seems incompatible with what they have valued in the past because they cannot, and will never, appreciate those values anymore (such as a person with a neurodegenerative condition or brain injury who has lost rational or emotional connection with those previous values), or whether they continue to hold those values but simply lack the ability to express a choice which furthers them. It would have to be the most extreme of situations to subject someone to significant pain, suffering, or distress in pursuit of values that they are no longer capable of holding or appreciating, even if these would have guided their decision-making if they retained capacity. If, by contrast, they do continue to hold such values, and respecting their wishes will cause them to experience frustration or unhappiness as a result of living or acting in a way which is contrary to those things they value more fundamentally, then this ought also to weigh heavily on the decision-maker.

6.3.3 *The Degree of Incapacity*

One aspect which has not yet been discussed, but which has proved important in past case law, is the degree to which the agent is thought to be incapacitated. As Chapter 5 explained, multiple judgments have suggested that the closer the agent is to meeting the threshold for capacity, the more weight ought to be ascribed to their wishes. This idea reflects the fact that while the law draws a sharp line between those who

D. Parfit, *Reasons and Persons* (Oxford: Oxford University Press, 1986), 204–209; B. A. Rich, 'Prospective Autonomy and Critical Interests: A Narrative Defense of the Moral Authority of Advance Directives' (1997) 6 *Cambridge Quarterly of Healthcare Ethics* 138; H. Kuhse, 'Some Reflections on the Problem of Advance Directives, Personhood, and Personal Identity' (1999) 9.4 *Kennedy Institute of Ethics Journal* 347–364; J. Wall, 'Being and Being Lost' in C. Foster, J. Herring, and I. Doron, *The Law and Ethics of Dementia* (Oxford: Hart Publishing, 2014); C. Korsgard, 'Personal Identity and the Unity of Agency: A Kantian Response to Parfit' (1989) 18(2) *Philosophy & Public Affairs* 101–132; Jaworska, 'Respecting the Margins of Agency', 105–138.

have and those who lack capacity, the realities of decision-making are somewhat more complex. As Emily Jackson captures:

> The reality of the psychological ability to exercise choice is not binary.. . . In addition to the rather obvious fact that a person's capacity will fluctuate over the course of her lifetime, the ability to make decisions, with or without others' help, exists on a spectrum. At one end, there might be someone in a permanent vegetative state, who cannot express a view, while at the other end, someone may appear to be able to take decisions without others' support.[93]

The extent to which a person can be said to be capable of autonomous decision-making depends both on the extent to which a person possesses any particular component (or attribute) of capacity (e.g., understanding, using, weighing etc.), *and* on the number or combination of these different attributes or components. Capacity thus operates not only on a two-dimensional linear spectrum where it can be impaired to a greater or lesser extent (as Jackson or Michael Gunn have depicted it[94]), but the ways in which it may be impaired may also be qualitatively distinct. Ascertaining when a person reaches a 'sufficient' level of these different components to be found to meet the threshold for capacity will thus be difficult, with the result that a number of people may exist on the borderline of capacity.

Any significant medical decision comes with a cargo of more or less complicated information, for example. And the consequences that may flow from it can be various and uncertain. People are rarely, if ever, able to understand *everything* in respect of a particular decision, or able to weigh the information they have been given against salient information to the contrary. Even the most basic treatment decisions involve volumes of potential risks, and while a patient may be able to understand the most substantial or serious of these, they are rarely expected to weigh up each and every risk that could flow from any given treatment; nor to understand the precise biological basis for a treatment and how it works. It is accepted that different people will understand more or less of the information, and at different levels of complexity. An intelligent adult's understanding, for instance, would be greater than that of a child, and that of a trained doctor greater still. However, the level and nature of understanding is not contingent only on the individual's intelligence and

[93] Jackson, 'From "Doctor Knows Best" to Dignity', 247–281, 248.
[94] M. Gunn, 'The Meaning of Incapacity' (1994) 2 *Medical Law Review* 8, 9.

expertise. As Mr Justice Munby points out, there are many other circumstances that may reduce a person's understanding and reasoning – for example, the 'effects of deception, misinformation, physical disability, illness, weakness (physical, mental or moral), tiredness, shock, fatigue, depression, pain or drugs'.[95] Once we accept that all these factors can affect how much information a person is able to take in and process, it is clear that the capacity to understand sits on a spectrum. This is just one way in which their capacity could be thought to be on the borderline: understanding some, but not quite *enough* of the relevant information.

This idea that the closer the agent is to reaching the capacity threshold, the more weight their wishes ought to carry, could reflect one of two important intuitions. The first is that where someone demonstrates some degree of understanding and ability to use information, their wishes ought to carry greater weight than someone who appears to have no meaningful level of understanding of their circumstances, or of the decision being taken. This approach is understandable when the agent suffers from a cognitive impairment. After all, if a person's understanding of the nature and consequences of the decision is better, or his ability to use that information to decide which outcome he prefers is greater, it is more likely that the wishes he expresses will reflect what he authentically wants, and what will result in his welfare being maximised. However, in cases in which the agent evaluates information on the basis of values or beliefs that we think have been caused by mental illness or impairment, this approach has the potential to be dangerous. As the previous discussion has made clear, many people who suffer from anorexia nervosa (and to a lesser extent depression) exhibit relatively high cognitive capacities and score highly in assessments aimed at testing these abilities. Patients suffering from such conditions might therefore be said to exhibit a high degree of capacity or, conversely, that their incapacity is relatively 'borderline'. Yet clearly if one were to give greater weight to their wishes on this basis, the effect would be to ignore (or at least not to attach significance to) the effect that a disorder has on their evaluative judgements. Consequently, if the degree of incapacity is to be relevant to the weight attributed to the agent's wishes, it is of the upmost importance that the changes proposed to the capacity test in Chapter 4 are implemented, to ensure that the effect that a disorder or impairment has on an

[95] *Re SA* (vulnerable adult with capacity: marriage) [2006] 1 FLR 867, [78].

agent's evaluative judgement is properly captured when thinking about the degree or extent of an agent's incapacity.

The second intuition is that the closer the agent is to the threshold, the harder it will be to assess whether they ought to fall just above or below it, and so this uncertainty should be reflected in how we then respond to the capacity assessment. This is a problem in capacity assessments across the board, but it is a particular issue in cases involving disordered valuing, in which an agent might sit on the cusp of capacity for more than one reason. One such reason may be that while it is clear that an agent suffers from a disorder or impairment which is affecting their ability to understand, use, or evaluate information, the extent of the impairment in these abilities is such that it is difficult to tell whether they sit just below or just above the threshold. However, given the challenges we face in concretely defining the line between disorder and non-disorder, a second reason might also be that while we think that the agent is making potentially harmful evaluative judgements, we cannot be sure whether these can be attributable to a disorder, as opposed to merely an unusual value system. *King's College Hospital NHS Foundation Trust v. C & V*[96] is a good example of the latter, in which the evidence was 'equivocal' as to whether the values informing her decision-making were the 'operation of a personality disorder or simply the thought processes of a strong willed, stubborn individual with unpalatable and highly egocentric views'.[97] She was undoubtedly on the borderline, but this owed more to our limits in accurately diagnosing mental disorder than it did to an assessment that her capacity for autonomy was being undermined only to a small degree by that disorder.

The question, then, is whether lack of certainty over whether certain behaviours, beliefs, or evaluative judgements amount to a disorder is a good reason to accord greater weight to the wishes of that person when it comes to determining their best interests. In other words, is it merely the *degree of the person's incapacity* which ought to be relevant, or should any ambiguity surrounding the capacity assessment result in greater weight being given to the wishes of those on the cusp of capacity. In my view, it should. As Chapter 3 explained, the determination that certain behaviours are (or are not) indicative of mental illness relies both on prior, sometimes contentious, value judgements at a societal level about what amounts to psychological dysfunction, and on complex clinical

[96] [2015] EWCOP 80.
[97] Ibid, [94].

judgements about how to apply the diagnostic criteria in given cases. The assessor must form conclusions on the source of the agent's values or beliefs (are they caused by a delusion, or are they just a feature of the agent's long-standing beliefs?), their intensity, and the extent to which these disrupt or interfere with the agent's ordinary functioning. Moreover, even once they have diagnosed a disorder, they must still evaluate what affect this has on the agent's decision-making. Needless to say, such judgements will not always be straightforward, and considerable uncertainty will plague the determination of whether the agent is correctly characterised as having capacity or not. Yet if we are wrong in that assessment, we risk riding roughshod over a person's autonomy, frustrating their authentically held values and beliefs. Given this, it is right to exercise caution, through giving the views of those whose capacity is uncertain, greater weight in the best interests assessment. While the test for capacity must, at least in its current form, be binary – the agent either has capacity or does not – our *confidence* in that capacity assessment ought to be reflected in the best interests assessment.

This discussion is not intended to prescribe exactly how best interests assessors ought to approach different cases; rather, its aim has been to highlight some of the potential considerations which will affect the weight ascribed to the agent's wishes in cases where they wish to do something that exposes them to a risk of significant harm, as well as some of the challenges involved in identifying and applying these. Given this, it is clear that the legislation on best interests cannot be too prescriptive. There is no 'one size fits all' policy that can determine the appropriate degree of weight to be accorded to an agent's wishes in any given case, and it is right to accord assessors considerable discretion to take account of a range of different factors which will all have a bearing on the agent's best interests in these circumstances. This will include the strength and consistency of the views being expressed and how the agent is likely to experience any frustration of them; the likely effect of the decision on the agent's future welfare, including the prospect of them being able to gain fulfilment or enjoyment from their life with or without the intervention proposed; whether fulfilling their present wishes will preclude them from making choices which would further their authentic values, and thus promote their well-being in the future (e.g., because it leads to them being dead, permanently disabled, or incapacitated); and the likelihood of the agent regaining capacity and expressing wishes which differ from those expressed now. It should also reflect the degree of the agent's incapacity, and the level of confidence that the assessor has in that capacity assessment.

But accepting an inevitable role for discretion on the part of the assessor does not mean that this discretion cannot be circumscribed, through greater guidance on the factors which ought to influence the degree of weight given to the agent's expressed wishes in the best interests determination, vis-à-vis other factors. The question, then, is how best to accommodate this within the MCA, in a way which retains the necessary flexibility for assessors to consider a range of factors, while also providing more structure and guidance for assessors called upon to navigate these difficult issues.

6.4 Reforming Section 4 of the MCA

The question of how to reframe section 4 so as to better respect the wishes of the incapacitated individual is not new. As mentioned earlier, this formed part of the Law Commission's review of the MCA and Deprivation of Liberty Safeguards, who, after concluding that a rebuttable presumption would be beyond their remit,[98] went on to propose more modest reforms to section 4 in their Draft Bill. These included a change to the language of section 4(6) in order to give it more 'teeth'. Rather than asking the assessor to 'consider, so far as is reasonably ascertainable' the agent's wishes and feelings, they should instead be required to 'ascertain, so far as is reasonably practicable', the agent's wishes and feelings.[99] The intention was that in most cases, there would be 'a clear duty to ascertain wishes and feelings'.[100] The second proposal was that when making the best interests determination, the assessor 'must give particular weight to any wishes or feelings ascertained'.[101] While they acknowledged that the meaning of 'particular weight' was too 'case-specific to be capable of being defined precisely', they nonetheless felt that 'it would evidently give ascertained wishes and feelings a higher status than all the other factors a decision-maker is required to consider under section 4(6)'.[102]

Neither proposal made it into legislation. The first would certainly seem a positive step forward, placing the onus on the best interests

[98] Law Commission, *Mental Capacity and Deprivation of Liberty* (Law Com. No. 372), 13 March 2017, 14.14.
[99] Ibid, 14.16.
[100] Ibid.
[101] Ibid, 14.17.
[102] Ibid.

assessor to ascertain what the agent's past and present wishes, feelings, values, and beliefs are. More controversial is the second proposal: that the assessor ought to give 'particular weight' to the agent's wishes and feelings in the best interests determination. Such an approach would certainly accord better with article 12(4) of the CRPD, which requires signatories to 'ensure that measures relating to the exercise of legal capacity respect the rights, will and preferences of the person',[103] even if ascribing 'particular weight' to the agent's wishes would still not amount to the 'respect' demanded for full compliance. It might also provide further guidance on how to approach those cases identified earlier in which the agent's expressed wishes appear irreconcilable with those fundamental and authentic values which have guided their life, or in which the agent's wishes reflect inauthentic values. The increased weight given to wishes and feelings was intended to be not only relative to other factors in section 4, but relative to other factors in section 4 (6),[104] with the result that the agent's current wishes and feelings would be weightier than the beliefs and values that would likely influence their decision if they had capacity.

The problem with this proposal is that it seems to give too little weight to the agent's wishes in some contexts, and arguably too greater weight in others. In the absence of significant harm, the agent's wishes should not merely be given 'particular weight'; they ought to be determinative. As the aforesaid discussion makes clear, this reflects the fact that overriding a person's wishes in the treatment and care context invariably encroaches on their liberty or bodily integrity in a way that will cause them some degree of psychological or emotional harm. In other cases, the inability of this provision to differentiate between different kinds of wishes and their relationship with the values or beliefs which motivate them may result in current wishes taking on *too much* significance vis-à-vis the agent's broader value systems. By giving the agent's wishes and feelings a 'higher status' than the values and beliefs that would have influenced their decision if they had capacity, this implies that if they pull in opposite directions, it is the wishes, and not the values, which ought to be given precedence. Yet this will not always necessarily be what is best for the individual. After all, that a set of values would have influenced the agent if they *had* capacity does not necessarily mean they are no longer

[103] UN General Assembly, *Convention on the Rights of Persons with Disabilities: Resolution adopted by the General Assembly*, 24 January 2007, A/RES/61/106, article 12.
[104] Ibid.

important to the agent now that they have *lost* it. The agent may continue to appreciate the fundamental importance of those values or beliefs even if they have lost the cognitive capacities to understand how a given decision will facilitate or frustrate them, and so they may experience the loss or frustration of those values or beliefs, even if their stated wishes do not reflect them. In such cases, it does not make sense to talk of the agent's wishes having a 'higher status' than their values, since those values define what the impact of giving effect to their wishes will be on their well-being, both now and in the future.

It is proposed here that rather than relying on an ambiguous phrase such as giving the agent's wishes 'particular weight' – which offers only minimal guidance on what degree of weight actually ought to be given to an agent's wishes in any given case – section 4 should instead include a list of factors which the assessors must take into account when determining the weight to be ascribed to the agent's wishes (in cases where the presumption does not apply). It is not proposed, therefore, that assessors should have to give any particular, or even higher, degree of weight to the agent's wishes; this must depend on the individual case, and the nature and effect of those wishes. Rather, judges or decision-makers ought to take into account the *same factors* when determining the degree of weight to give to the agent's ascertained wishes and feelings. Such factors might include:

(a) the strength and consistency of the wishes being expressed by P;
(b) whether P's wishes are thought to reflect deeply and authentically held values or beliefs of P;
(c) the possible impact on P of knowledge that their wishes and feelings have not been given effect to, or of intervening against P's will;
(d) the degree of
    (i) P's incapacity and
    (ii) confidence in the assessment of P's capacity;
(e) the likelihood of P regaining capacity and what P's wishes would likely be if they did regain capacity; and
(f) the extent to which giving effect to P's wishes will preclude them from experiencing future enjoyment or well-being in life, which might otherwise be expected for P, including through
    (i) leaving P permanently disabled, incapacitated, or dead, or
    (ii) preventing P from pursuing things they would find valuable in the future.

This might also be supplemented by guidance in the Code of Practice, indicating that proportionately higher weight ought to be given to wishes where a number of these factors are (or are not) present. This could operate similar to the prosecutorial guidelines for Assisted Suicide, which set out factors tending in favour of or against prosecution;[105] here, clearly different factors tend in favour or against giving substantial weight to P's wishes.

The exact wording of these factors would, of course, be subject to drafting amendments. In principle, however, this would provide a framework for assessors to work through the relevant issues when determining what weight the agent's wishes should be given. It would place the onus on assessors to demonstrate that they have taken account of all of these factors, and to provide reasons for why they have chosen to accord greater or lesser weight to them, by reference to the factors listed. It is hoped that this approach would serve to prevent the lack of engagement with the agent's wishes seen in decisions such as *RB*,[106] *KD*,[107] *Neary*,[108] and *RF*.[109]

Such an approach might also help assessors to locate where the challenges lie in determining the agent's best interests in any given case. It might be that it is difficult to establish whether one of these factors is present or absent (e.g., it is hard to know whether a person's wishes really do reflect authentic or deeply held values or beliefs), or it might be that two or more of these factors appear to pull in different directions (e.g., the agent's wish is strongly held, but would preclude them from future enjoyment or well-being). By making it clearer where the challenge lies in a particular case, this will help ensure transparency, allowing for greater scrutiny and challenge of the reasoning (and value judgements) which underpin any given decision.

In some cases, the factors will all (or almost all) pull in the same direction, indicating that either very substantial or very little weight ought to be accorded to the agent's wishes. In *Wye Valley*, for example, Mr B's wishes were expressed with great strength and consistency. They

[105] The Director of Public Prosecutions, 'Suicide: Policy for Prosecutors in Respect of Cases of Encouraging or Assisting Suicide' (October 2014). Available at: www.cps.gov.uk/legal-guidance/suicide-policy-prosecutors-respect-cases-encouraging-or-assisting-suicide. Accessed 7 July 2022.

[106] *RB v. Brighton and Hove City Council* [2014] EWCA Civ 561.

[107] *Hull University Teaching Hospitals NHS Trust v. KD* [2020] EWCOP 35.

[108] *Hillingdon LBC v. Neary* [2011] EWHC 1377 (COP).

[109] *RF* [2015] EWCOP 1.

reflected beliefs which were deeply meaningful to him, and there was substantial evidence that he would experience the frustration of his wishes very keenly. The judge concluded, for example, that he would have to be 'sedated to overcome his resistance and will have to remain sedated for some time afterwards to help him with his inevitable feelings of outrage and distress'.[110] Moreover, his mental health and well-being would be 'further compromised', as

> the loss of his foot will be a continual reminder that his wishes were not respected. Further to that, his religious sentiments will undoubtedly continue and he will believe that the amputation was carried out against the Lord's wishes.[111]

The degree of confidence in his capacity assessment was relatively high, with his incapacity accepted by all parties and medical professionals. Given his chronic schizophrenia, it was unlikely that Mr B would regain capacity, and even if he did, the profound impact that his religious beliefs had played in his life indicated that they may not be simply extinguished by his recovery. The only thing standing against this compelling evidence that his best interests would be served by giving effect to his wishes was the fact that they would, in all likelihood, lead to his imminent death. However, given the evidence that he would find little enjoyment in continued life with an amputated leg, spending much of his remaining life span in rehabilitation and being unable to live in his own accommodation again, giving effect to his wishes was not precluding him from enjoying an otherwise fulfilling life. On the contrary, frustrating them would impose a future on him for which he had 'no appetite'.[112]

Other cases will be less clear cut, with different factors pulling in different directions. In *A Local Authority v. E*, for example,[113] the strength and consistency of E's views, the profound impact that frustrating her wishes would have on her (given that she experienced the forced treatment as abusive) and the relatively high chance (80 per cent) that this traumatic struggle would prove to be in vain, weighed heavily in favour of respecting her wishes. On the other hand, while her wishes may have been influenced in part by the prospect of having to endure a life she found 'pure torment', the judge found them to also reflect disordered

[110] [2015] EWCOP 60, [37].
[111] Ibid.
[112] Ibid, [45].
[113] [2012] EWHC 1639.

valuing associated with her anorexia nervosa, which led her to overvalue the need to avoid food entering her body in a way that compelled her to make certain choices that avoided calorie intake. There was also a 20 per cent chance that she would recover to a quality of life she found acceptable, meaning that giving effect to her wishes would preclude her a chance, at least, of future well-being. Her best interests were thus very finely balanced, and deciding what weight to give her wishes, against a 20 per cent chance of a fulfilling life ahead, was extremely difficult.

It is not suggested here that the proposed framework would provide a straightforward answer to what should happen in complex cases such as this. Nor can this approach ensure consistency of outcome between cases. In such a fact- and person-specific area, there is no 'formula' for how to make such decisions, and the outcome will necessarily depend on the individual and on the decision, with consistency neither possible nor desirable if justice is to be done in each individual case. But what it will do is improve the consistency of the *process* adopted for determining best interests, by asking decision-makers to follow the same procedure as one another. Such an approach reflects existing efforts by Court of Protection judges to discern which factors ought to influence the weight to be accorded to the individual agent's wishes, discussed in Chapter 5, but rather than leaving it to individual judges to pick and choose which factors to consider, these would instead be set out clearly on the face of the statute, ensuring that all judges – but more importantly, all best interests assessors *outside* of the courts – consider the same factors. It is hoped that by setting out a framework through which to evaluate the agent's wishes, doctors and care workers might also feel more confident prioritising them in those cases where the factors *do* lean in favour of placing significant weight on them, since they will have a clearer basis on which to defend the decision if necessary.

Of course, even with these changes, there will inevitably be barriers to effectively implementing these reforms in practice. As Kong and others found, despite there being consensus among legal practitioners and retired judges of the importance of 'putting P at the centre of proceedings', there are nonetheless a number of practical barriers which undermine the effective participation of the agent in court proceedings, such as failures in connecting with or communicating with them.[114] Outside of

[114] C. Kong, R. Stickler, P. Cooper, M. Watkins, and M. Dunn, 'Justifying and Practising Effective Participation in the Court of Protection: An Empirical Study' (2022) 49(4) *Journal of Law and Society* 703–725.

the courtroom, the paucity of time and information available to assessors often makes ascertaining their wishes and values challenging, as does the fact that agents are not always willing to engage productively with professionals. However, these difficulties in ascertaining the agent's wishes does not negate the value in ensuring that appropriate weight is given to those wishes once ascertained.[115]

These proposals for reform aim to ensure that even if a person is deemed to lack capacity, their wishes continue to guide the decisions made about them and are less vulnerable to be overridden on the basis of another's conception of what is best for the person, in the absence of compelling reasons. This would be undermined, however, if doctors could evade them by treating them regardless, and then relying on the defence in section 5. Section 6.5 will therefore briefly set out necessary amendments to that provision, mirroring those already seen in the Northern Ireland Act, to ensure greater consistency between this and the changes to best interests determinations proposed here.

6.5 Amending the Defence to Battery in Section 5 of the MCA

Section 5 provides a defence for anyone acting in connection with the care or treatment of a person, where they reasonably believe the person to lack capacity and where they act according to what they regard as being in the person's best interests. The bar for succeeding under the defence is low: the assessor need only show that they had reasonable grounds for believing that the agent lacked capacity, not that they in fact did believe it. It is also broadly framed, applying to *any* action taken in the agent's best interests where there are any concerns about the agent's capacity, irrespective of whether, for example, the intervention was necessary to prevent serious or immediate harm.

While the relatively unqualified provisions of section 5 have clear advantages for doctors or care workers called upon to make difficult assessments, they do allow the defence to be invoked in a broad set of circumstances, with a risk that it undermines the presumption of capacity and erodes patient autonomy. Notably, the equivalent statutory defence provided for by the recent Northern Ireland MCA is significantly more circumscribed than that in English law. While it also provides a defence for an assessor who reasonably believes that the agent lacks capacity and

[115] Efforts by Kong and others (refer footnote 114) to better facilitate the effective participation of P are also hugely welcome.

that treatment is in their best interests,[116] this is subject to additional safeguards set out elsewhere in the Act.[117] Section 13 qualifies section 9 where the intervention is categorised as 'serious', according to section 63. This will be the case wherever the intervention involves any 'major surgery';[118] causes the agent 'serious pain, serious distress, or serious side-effects';[119] seriously affects the options they have available to them in the future or has a large impact on their day-to-day life;[120] or otherwise has a serious consequence for the agent, be it physical or non-physical.[121] It will also encompass any situation where the agent is deprived of their liberty.[122] In these situations, a formal capacity assessment must be performed[123] and a statement of incapacity made for the agent detailing why it is that the assessor considers them to lack capacity,[124] and what help or support has been given to the agent, without success, to enable them to make the decision in question.[125] The Act further provides that, except in situations of emergency, a nominated person (typically P's carer or a close family member) must be put in place and consulted in determining whether the intervention is in the agent's best interests.[126] If the question of what is in the agent's best interests is finely balanced and the consequences serious, a second opinion must be sought.[127] Only if these extra stipulations are met can the assessor avail themselves of the defence in section 9.[128]

Where the treatment proposed has serious consequences for the agent (which is defined in the same way as 'serious intervention' was defined previously[129]), and their nominated person reasonably objects to it,[130] the agent resists it,[131] or the act amounts to a deprivation of the agent's

[116] Mental Capacity Act (Northern Ireland) 2016, section 9(2).
[117] Ibid, s9(3). The relevant sections are set out in s9(4).
[118] Ibid, s63(1)(a).
[119] Ibid, s63(1)(b).
[120] Ibid, s63(1)(c).
[121] Ibid, s63(1)(d).
[122] Ibid, s63(2)(a).
[123] Under s14(2), this must be conducted by 'a suitably qualified person'.
[124] Ibid, s14(3)(a)–(c).
[125] Ibid, s14(3)(d).
[126] Ibid, s15(3)(a)–(b).
[127] Ibid, s16.
[128] Ibid, s13(2).
[129] Ibid, s21.
[130] Ibid, s19.
[131] Ibid, s20(1)(c)(i).

liberty,[132] the intervention must also satisfy the 'serious harm' condition. For the purposes of these sections, this requires that the assessor reasonably believes that a failure to provide the treatment would create a risk of serious harm to the agent or others;[133] and that the treatment is a proportionate response to the likelihood and severity of that harm.[134] In this sense, the Northern Ireland Act introduces a more complex and nuanced harm threshold for intervention: where the agent resists the treatment, it may only be provided where there is otherwise a risk of serious harm to them and the treatment is proportionate to the likelihood and severity of that harm. More broadly, the Act demands greater steps to be taken by the doctor to avail themselves of the defence, depending on the severity of the consequences of the decision for the agent.

Amending section 5 to contain a provision more akin to that of the Northern Ireland Act would be welcome, ensuring greater consistency between the reforms to section 4 suggested earlier (that would treat the agent's wishes as determinative of their best interests in the absence of significant harm), and when the defence to battery applies. While this would continue to leave assessors some room to manoeuvre in ambiguous cases, it would create a much more limited exception to the general presumption of capacity. There would, once again, be some debate over whether the harm in question is rightly regarded as 'serious'; but this is more easily answered in this context than in relation to best interests, since the question would not be whether the harm *is* significant, but only whether or not the assessor could reasonably have believed it to be significant.

In its review of the MCA, the Law Commission also supported putting in place greater safeguards to limit when section 5 could be relied on by assessors, suggesting that this 'would help to ensure better quality decision-making in relation to people who lack or may lack the requisite capacity'.[135] In particular, they suggested that where the decision was of a particular nature (including serious medical treatment, or treatment known to be against the agent's wishes[136]), the assessor would be unable

[132] Ibid, s24.
[133] Ibid, s22(1)(a).
[134] ibid, ss22(1)(b)(i)–(ii).
[135] Law Commission, 'Mental Capacity and Deprivation of Liberty', Consultation Paper No. 222, 12.47. Available at: www.lawcom.gov.uk/wp-content/uploads/2015/07/cp222_mental_capacity.pdf, 14.35.
[136] Ibid, 14.37.

to rely on the defence *unless* they had provided a written record (or reviewed a written record produced by someone else and believed it to be accurate).[137] This written record must contain the following information:

(1) a description of the steps which have been taken to establish whether the person lacks capacity in relation to the matter in question;
(2) a description of the steps which have been taken to help the person to make the decision or an explanation as to why it was not practicable to take such steps;
(3) an explanation of why it is believed that the person lacks capacity in relation to the matter in question, including:
    (a) identification of the impairment or disturbance in the functioning of the person's brain; and
    (b) an explanation, by reference to section 3 of the Mental Capacity Act, of why the person is unable to make the decision;
(4) a description of the steps which have been taken to establish whether or not it is in the person's best interests for the act to be done;
(5) a description of any ascertained wishes, feelings, beliefs, or values for the purposes of a best interests determination and, if the best interests decision conflicts with the person's ascertained wishes, feelings, beliefs, or values, an explanation of the reason for that decision;
(6) confirmation that any duty to provide an advocate has been complied with; and
(7) confirmation that the act would not be contrary to an advance decision.[138]

While this remains less demanding than the system provided for in Northern Ireland, it would still be a welcome step forward. Although it does not place any restrictions on when or how an assessor can act (e.g., through limiting interventions in the absence of significant harm), it *does* require that the assessor provides clear evidence of the reasons for their decisions, thus improving the transparency of decisions. It also provides a framework for approaching such cases, breaking down the many different steps involved in these assessments. By requiring assessors to write down exactly how the impairment is causing the agent's inability to make a decision, and in what way their decision-making ability is

[137] Ibid, 14.36.
[138] Ibid, 14.38.

impaired, this may also direct their minds to these particular issues, enhancing the specificity of decisions.

While such a requirement might be thought to be onerous for doctors or care workers, all of the mandated steps are already required under the current law. The agent ought to be supported to make a decision by themselves; deemed to lack capacity only if they have an impairment in the functioning of the mind or brain, which renders them incapable to make a decision according to the criteria in the test for capacity; and their wishes and feelings ought to be taken into account when later assessing what is in their best interests. Such changes merely require assessors to document their findings in relation to each of these steps – documentation which, even if not legally required, is already regarded as good medical practice (even if it can be hard to achieve in the current resource-limited settings). In the Code of Practice, for example, it states that

> it is good practice for professionals to carry out a proper assessment of a person's capacity to make particular decisions and to record the findings in the relevant professional records.[139]

Later, meanwhile, when discussing best interests assessments, the Code is explicit that assessors

> should record their decision, how they reached it and the reasons for it in the person's clinical notes. As long as they have recorded objective reasons to show that the decision is in the person's best interests, and the other requirements of section 5 of the Act are met, all healthcare staff taking actions in connection with the particular treatment will be protected from liability.[140]

This documentation is important, as, should the decision later be challenged, this contemporaneous evidence is essential if the court is to be able to assess in any meaningful way whether the defence in section 5 ought to apply or not. In its absence, it is difficult both for the agent to challenge the decision and, as importantly, for the assessor to later justify their actions.

It should be noted, of course, that even absent these kinds of reforms, the fact that the assessor must 'reasonably believe' that they are acting in the best interests of the agent to avail themselves of the defence may indirectly bring the defence in line with the changes proposed earlier.

139 Department for Constitutional Affairs, Mental Capacity Act 2005 Code of Practice (London: TSO, 2007), 4.61.

140 Ibid, 6.17.

This is because, when determining what is in their best interests, they must have regard for the requirements of section 4. These would include, for example, the fact that in the absence of significant harm, the wishes of the agent are assumed to be determinative of their best interests. Arguably, then, if the assessor overrides the agent's wishes in the absence of evidence of harm, their assessment of what is in the agent's best interests could not be said to be 'reasonable', and thus they would not have the protection of the defence.[141] Certainly in *Winspear v. City Hospitals Sunderland NHS Foundation Trust*,[142] a failure to consult the mother of an incapacitated patient before placing a 'do not resuscitate' order in their records, where that consultation was both practicable and appropriate, was sufficient to bar the NHS Trust from relying on section 5 in a claim for a breach of the patient's article 8 rights. Consequently, while the reforms proposed here would certainly be welcome, setting out more clearly what decision-makers will have to do to avail themselves of the section 5 defence, changes to section 4 will have the indirect effect of limiting the remit of section 5.

6.6 Conclusion

This chapter has proposed a series of changes to how best interests are determined under section 4, with a view to ensuring that greater weight is attributed to the wishes of the individual in decisions being made about them. The starting point should be that the assessor making the determination ascertains 'so far is reasonably practicable' the agent's wishes, feelings, beliefs, and values (as advocated by the Law Commission). It shall then be assumed that the agent's ascertainable wishes and feelings will be determinative of their best interests unless giving effect to such wishes would expose the agent to a risk of significant harm. And where giving effect to the agent's ascertainable wishes *would* expose them to a risk of significant harm, the assessor must consider what weight to give to those wishes, taking into account a range of factors set out previously. This ought to be supplemented by amendments to section 5.

[141] This point was argued by counsel Mr Coppel in *ZH v. Commissioner of Police for the Metropolis* [2012] EWHC 604 (QB), [41]. Notably, in the equivalent provision in the Mental Capacity Act (Northern Ireland) 2016, it is explicitly stated that the provisions relating to determining best interests in the Act apply for the 'purposes of determining whether a belief mentioned in subsection (1)(d) is reasonable' (s9(5)).

[142] [2015] EWHC 3250 (QB).

Since many cases that challenge doctors or caregivers and end up in the courts do involve a risk of significant harm, the agent's wishes will often not be determinative of their best interests. This reflects the fact that respecting a person's wishes will not always be empowering for them, particularly where those wishes are motivated by disordered values or beliefs about the world, or where they will preclude the person's ability to exercise autonomy or enjoy well-being in the future. Not all wishes should demand the same weight, and it is important that assessors are provided with a framework through which to evaluate the significance of wishes in different contexts, so they can feel more confident that they are identifying and applying the right factors when deciding whether or not to give effect to those wishes. Empowerment and protection do not always sit in tension with one another, and protecting people from inauthentic and harmful choices is an important part of empowering them not just in one individual decision, but across their life more generally.

Conclusion

This book explores the role that values and value judgements play in assessments of capacity. In doing so, it has attempted to grapple with a fundamental tension that lies at the heart of our capacity legislation. On the one hand, the liberal intuitions that underpin the test for capacity suggest that people ought to be free to make decisions according to their own values and beliefs, no matter how unusual or eccentric these may be. On the other, there *are* certain beliefs or ways of valuing that we intuitively regard as so abnormal, and so harmful, that we think that far from facilitating decisions based on them, people ought instead to be protected from them. We characterise these beliefs, values, or behaviours as 'disordered', yet as the foregoing analysis has shown, the line between the disordered and the eccentric is far from clear cut, being both socially and culturally contingent, and reliant on complex clinical judgements, rather than a matter of objective medical fact.

Thus far, the test for capacity has sought to avoid confronting this tension directly, by adopting a 'value-neutral' test for capacity which is, on the face of the Act, unconcerned with the values or beliefs underpinning any given decision. Provided that the agent's cognitive capacities are intact, it does not matter whether a decision is being motivated by disordered valuing or whether the agent would have reached a different decision were they not acting under the influence of that disorder. Yet the potential for this to give rise to profoundly harmful outcomes is clear, and it is no surprise then that as a result, those called upon to apply the MCA have sought to mitigate this through indirectly (and sometimes rather dubiously) accommodating concerns about the agent's values or beliefs within the question of whether they can 'use or weigh' the relevant information.

This approach may lead to better outcomes than adhering strictly to the statute. But dispensing with value neutrality in this way – through conflating questions about the agent's capacity to weigh information, with the degree of weight they, in fact, attach to information – carries its own risks. The result is that capacity assessments are currently hinging on implicit value-laden assessments about the nature and origins of the agent's values, which are not made explicit and so cannot be subject to the degree of scrutiny appropriate, given the difficulties in ascertaining the origins of given values and their impact on decision-making. Far from preserving liberal dichotomies, then, the failure of the Act to navigate this tension adequately actually risks it being applied *illiberally*.

We cannot shy away from the inherent tension between allowing people freedom to decide according to what matters to them and protecting them from the full effects of a harmful mental disorder. Nor can we analyse the problem away with neat linguistic tricks. Rather a delicate balancing act must be performed, which acknowledges the very real impact that disorder has on the lives of many, while also recognising that the characterisation of behaviours as disordered inevitably involves recourse to contested social norms and complex clinical judgements, which makes such assessments inherently fraught. This balance is best struck by engaging with this issue head-on, examining the way in which disorder or impairment affects the agent's evaluation of the information explicitly so that the value judgements which inevitably underpin the determination of capacity are brought out into the open and subjected to proper scrutiny. Accordingly, this book has proposed a new limb of the test for capacity which would do exactly that, asking whether the agent is unable to make a decision because the values or beliefs by which they evaluate the relevant information have been caused by or altered as a consequence of the person suffering from a disorder, illness, or impairment.

But this tension does not end with the determination of capacity. Once the agent is found to lack capacity, a decision must then be taken in their best interests. Often, this will be served by giving effect to their wishes, since they may continue to hold and appreciate values and beliefs that have guided their life, even if they lack the cognitive capacities to be able to make decisions unaided. But this will not always be the case, and sometimes those wishes may reflect inauthentic values or beliefs prompted by disorder or impairment, which cause them to make choices which entail profound, irreversible, and unnecessary harm to themselves. The law cannot be too prescriptive in setting out when it is right to accede to the agent's wishes in such cases, and assessors must be accorded the discretion to take into account a range of factors which will influence the degree of harm involved in either respecting or frustrating the agent's wishes. Nonetheless, the law could seek to enhance the transparency with which such determinations are made, through making it clearer what factors are feeding into the assessment of the agent's best interests in given cases, and affecting the weight attributed to the agent's wishes. This book has proposed one means of doing this, through including a list of factors to be taken account of in section 4 of the MCA, which includes the authenticity of values or beliefs, to enable assessors to distinguish those situations where deference to idiosyncratic value systems is required, from those where it may not be.

While this book has put forward several tangible proposals for reforming the Mental Capacity Act 2005, there will be some reading it who may feel it to be under-ambitious. One reason for this may be that it focuses only on the impact of disorder or impairment on the formation of the agent's values and beliefs, and not the many other factors which may influence or have the capacity to distort these. As alluded to previously, it is not *only* mental disorder or impairment which might undermine the authenticity of the choices that a person makes, and much academic literature in recent years has focused on the inability of the MCA to capture the numerous and varied ways in which a person's autonomy may be undermined by factors external, rather than internal to the person. The current failure of the Act to do so in part stems from the MCA's reliance on traditional liberal accounts of autonomy, which have been criticised as overly individualistic, failing to give adequate weight to the 'socially embedded'[1] nature of people, and the fact that their identity and sense of self is inevitably influenced by things, and people, around them. As Michael Sandel explains, according to liberal accounts, the autonomous subject is portrayed 'standing always at a certain distance from the interests it has',[2] separate from the values, priorities, and beliefs that he holds. This conceptualisation, of a person choosing between various options to determine the one that best reflects their desires or priorities, ignores the ways in which our choices are influenced by our relationships, social norms, constraints, and influences. As sociologist Paul Wolpe argues, there are all manner of structural factors that may affect a person's decision-making abilities within the healthcare context,

[1] Mackenzie and Stoljar, *Relational Autonomy: Feminist Essays on Autonomy, Agency and Social Self*, 2000.

[2] Sandel, *Liberalism and the Limits of Justice*, 62.

including the influence of prestigious healthcare professionals, coercive influences of families and communities, and class, race, education, cultural, and religious factors.[3] Likewise feminist scholars have noted how the choices open to women are influenced by patriarchal norms, such that decisions which appear to be freely chosen are in fact driven by internalised, learned perspectives.[4] It is therefore not only values that stem from disorder or impairment which affect the way in which people evaluate information, and which may lead to people making inauthentic choices.

It is in response to a perceived failure of traditional liberal accounts to address the influence of social context and embodiment on agency that relational accounts of autonomy have emerged. 'Relational autonomy' is, as Catriona Mackenzie and Natalie Stoljar explain, an 'umbrella term',[5] used to describe all views of autonomy that share the assumption that 'persons are socially embedded and that agents' identities are formed within the context of social relationships and shaped by a complex of intersecting social determinants, such as race, class, gender, and ethnicity'.[6] To better reflect such accounts, the law would have to move beyond considerations merely of the agent's internal reasoning processes (currently its exclusive focus), to instead recognise the way in which factors external to the agent – their social matrix and relationships – may impair their capacity to make decisions. Accordingly, recent literature, notably the work of Camillia Kong,[7] has been concerned with how the law (and the assessors called upon to apply it) might better reflect this relational understanding of autonomy and thus accommodate a broader range of factors which affect an agent's autonomy.

But while these relational accounts are undoubtedly valuable in highlighting the ways in which factors external (as well as internal) to the individual might impair an agent's autonomy and shape the way in which an agent may make decisions, this does not mean that they ought to be captured (and operationalised) within the MCA, as a basis on which (and justification for) intervening in people's decisions. As noted earlier, the difficulty faced by those seeking to accommodate the multitude of

[3] Wolpe, 'The Triumph of Autonomy in American Bioethics'.
[4] See, for example, MacKinnon, *Toward a Feminist Theory of the State.*
[5] Mackenzie and Stoljar, *Relational Autonomy*, 4.
[6] Ibid.
[7] Kong, 'Mental Capacity in Relationship'.

ways in which an agent's autonomy is undermined by their social and cultural matrix within any test for capacity is being able to distinguish those relationships and social interactions which are constitutive of a person's identity and sense of self, and which build the skills of self-respect, self-trust, and self-esteem that, as Catriona MacKenzie argues, are essential to developing a person's agency,[8] from those which serve to impair or undermine it. This is no simple task. Indeed in attempting to capture within the test for capacity the multitude of ways in which a person's autonomy may be impaired through their relationships with others or by societal, gender, or cultural norms, there is a risk that the effect may be to deny or, at the very least, question the autonomy of those who are subject to any form of oppression, thus perpetuating oppressive attitudes by reinforcing beliefs that oppressed minorities are unable to make decisions for themselves. As John Christman writes:

> It is one thing to publicly criticize modes of social practice that denigrate their participants, but it is another to define autonomy in a way to claim that those participants are not fully functioning agents at all.[9]

Moreover, as Mary Donnelly notes, given the concerns about the impact of illness on decision-making autonomy (and the inherent imbalance of power and information between patients and doctors), this could result in many decisions in the healthcare context being handed over to a substitute decision-maker.[10] This, along with the aforementioned concerns, led Christman to warn that:

> It is one thing to claim that social conditions that enable us to develop and maintain the powers of authentic choice and which protect the ongoing interpersonal and social relationships that define ourselves are all part of the background requirements for the development of autonomy... It is another thing, however - and a more dangerous and ultimately problematic move, I have argued - to claim that being autonomous means standing in proper social relations to surrounding others and within social practices and institutions. Taking this position, I have argued, turns the concept of autonomy into an unacceptably perfectionist idea that carries

[8] Mackenzie, 'Relational Autonomy, Normative Authority and Perfectionism', 512, 513.

[9] Christman, 'Relational Autonomy, Liberal Individualism, and the Social Constitution of Selves', 143–164, 158.

[10] M. Donnelly, *Healthcare Decision-Making and the Law: Autonomy, Capacity and the Limits of Liberalism* (Cambridge: Cambridge University Press, 2010).

> with it the danger of exclusion and overarching paternalism that attention to autonomy should well protect against.[11]

Lucy Series has made a similar point, noting that:

> If mental capacity assessments did take into account the deleterious effects of particular relationships this could permit more paternalistic interventions, evoking similar controversies to externalist constitutive approaches to autonomy... which permit coercive interventions on the basis of the properties of oppressive relationships.[12]

Christman and Series are right to be concerned. This book has sought to highlight the tightrope that must already be walked between respect for autonomy and undue paternalism in the context of mental disorder; concluding that while attempts should be made to discern how disorder affects evaluative judgements, the grave difficulties in doing so ought to be recognised and reflected in any best interests assessments that follow. But these difficulties pale in comparison to the challenges involved in discerning how an agent's social or cultural matrix has affected those very same judgements, and whether those influences are constitutive of one's identity or undermining of one's autonomy. Outside of the most extreme of cases of undue influence or coercion (which are, in any event, currently captured by the inherent jurisdiction), it is very difficult to believe that robust determinations of this nature could be made, leading to even more porous and unreliable capacity assessments and ever greater scope for paternalistic interference with individual's choices.[13] Legal capacity performs a vitally important function in delineating the appropriate boundaries of state intervention, but attempting to capture every situation in which a person's autonomy may be undermined within it risks turning capacity law into a tool of oppression rather than a guardian of

[11] Christman, 'Relational Autonomy, Liberal Individualism, and the Social Constitution of Selves', 143–164, 158.

[12] L. Series, 'Relationships, Autonomy and Legal Capacity: Mental Capacity and Support Paradigms' (2015) 40 *International Journal of Law and Psychiatry* 80.

[13] There would also be considerable ambiguity about how to respond to a finding that in best interests determinations, since the fact that an agent's values might be attributable to oppressive norms or relationships does not necessarily mean that choices premised on those values are any less important or meaningful to that individual, or that anyone else is better placed to take those decisions than that individual. A woman's choice to shave her legs might be influenced by entrenched gendered and patriarchal norms, for example, but does not mean that she should be precluded from doing so.

individual liberty. Indeed it was precisely for this reason that the Law Commission sought to limit the MCA to situations in which the inability to make a decision was caused by an impairment in the functioning of the mind or brain in the first place, with this 'diagnostic' element intended to ensure that 'the test is stringent enough *not* to catch large numbers of people who make unusual or unwise decisions',[14] an approach which prompted less 'distress' among consultee responses at the time, given fears about the 'over-extensive use of protective powers'.[15]

The second way in which the book might be felt to be unduly cautious, is that despite its criticisms of the fragile and porous nature of capacity assessments, and its advocacy of the need to reflect this through a softening of the capacity cliff edge, its proposals for reform still assume a continuation of the current binary framework in which the agent either has capacity or they lack it. This binary approach has faced increasing challenge,[16] particularly in the wake of the United Nations Convention on the Rights of Persons with Disabilities (CRPD), article 12, which requires state parties to 'recognise that people with disabilities enjoy legal capacity on an equal basis with others in all aspects of life'.[17] On a literal reading, this precludes any capacity legislation operating a threshold like the MCA, which by its nature differentiates between decisions made with mental capacity and those made without, and imposes substituted decisions only in relation to the latter,[18] leading to calls to abandon a threshold approach entirely and replace it with a system that acknowledges that people's decision-making ability may be impaired to different degrees, requiring different levels of support or intervention. It is this idea which underpins supported decision-making (SDM) schemes, seen in a number of common law jurisdictions across the world, including

14 Law Commission, *Mental Capacity* (HMSO, 1995), para 3.8.

15 Ibid, 3.13.

16 See, for example, Clough, 'The Spaces of Mental Capacity Law'; Martin *et al.*, *Achieving CRPD Compliance*; Richardson 'Mental Disabilities and the Law', 333–354.

17 UN General Assembly, *Convention on the Rights of Persons with Disabilities: Resolution adopted by the General Assembly*, 24 January 2007, A/RES/61/106, article 12.

18 Certainly in its 'General Comment' on article 12, the UN Committee on the Rights of Persons with Disabilities were clear that 'perceived or actual deficits in mental capacity (or decision-making skills) must not be used as justification for denying legal capacity': Committee on the Rights of Persons with Disabilities, *General Comment No 1* (2014) article 12: Equal Recognition before the Law (adopted at the Eleventh session of the Committee, 31 March–11 April 2014, Geneva, CRPD/C/GC/1).

across Canada, parts of Australia, and, most recently, in the Republic of Ireland. In Ireland, for example,[19] there are now three different levels of intervention depending on the agent's degree of capacity: a decision-making assistant, a co-decision-maker, and a decision-making representative. Only in the latter category must the agent lack decision-making capacity.

The central premise of such schemes is that a person should never have a decision taken for them, if they could, with support, take it for themselves. SDM also recognises that even those who might, under a threshold approach, be found to have capacity may still benefit from some support in those decisions. Rather than an all-or-nothing threshold with stark consequences in either direction, it thus recognises different 'grades' of capacity, warranting different levels of support.

As noted in the Introduction, much of the argument put forward in this book lends support for this approach, advocating a move away from a 'cliff-edge' approach to capacity to an approach which better appreciates the uncertain nature of capacity, which inevitably admits of degrees. However, for reasons given there, I have not sought to argue for adopting a supported decision-making scheme in this jurisdiction, at this time. At one level, the reason for this is purely pragmatic: there is unlikely to be the political appetite or the time and resources necessary to implement such changes at present, and so the solutions proposed here are intended to be more politically feasible and workable reforms, that could make a real difference in the near future. However, the reasons are not merely pragmatic or political. Rather a number of issues would also need to be resolved before England and Wales could adopt any such model, which require detailed consideration beyond the scope of this book. For example, what level of 'capacity' is required for each level of intervention, what different 'supporter' roles should be offered, and how does this approach apply in situations where the agent wants mutually exclusive outcomes (not to eat, but to continue to live, for example), and a decision must be made about which to prioritise? Without proper safeguards, such models have the potential to leave vulnerable people open to abuse. Supporters will, particularly in co-decision-making regimes, wield significant power over a person with impaired capacity,

[19] Assisted Decision-Making (Ireland) Act 2015.

as they must be consulted in any decision and are entrusted with 'supporting' that person to form a decision. This gives them substantial scope to influence and pressure the individual, yet because the role of the supporter is more opaque than that of a best interests assessor under the current law, it is much harder to know exactly what influence they might have had over the decision. Any system for England and Wales would thus require substantial safeguards to protect people in such situations, which warrant detailed consideration before any such framework can be advocated for.

Crucially, however, for such a framework to adequately protect and empower those people whose capacity is in doubt, it too needs to navigate the tension between respect for (and deference to) idiosyncratic values, and protection from disorder or impairment. Current SDM frameworks do not provide any basis for distinguishing inauthentic or disordered values or wishes from those authentically held; while the CRPD states simply that the (disabled) person's will and preferences ought to be 'respected', with no attempt made to differentiate between these wills or preferences. In doing so, it arguably falls into the liberal fallacy of assuming all values, no matter where they come from or how the person feels about them, command the same respect and authority. Yet as the foregoing analysis has sought to show, proper respect for the rights and interests of people with disabilities – including mental disabilities – does not demand unbridled deference to their disordered beliefs, but sensitive engagement with the effects of that disability on their capacity to formulate choices that will facilitate their authentically held values in the long term. Any supported decision-making scheme, and any test for capacity on which it relies, must therefore take account of the challenges and suggestions in this book if it is to fulfil the CRPD's core purpose of promoting the rights and dignity of those with disabilities, and we should not be too quick to hand over greater control to the individual, or more opaque powers to the co-decision-maker, until the role that value and value judgements play in assessments of capacity have been made transparent. The suggestions in this book might therefore be seen as a precondition for any shift to an SDM or co-decision-making scheme.

And, of course, there will always be people who, no matter how much support is offered, will not be able to make a decision for themselves. Some degree of substituted decision-making is therefore inevitable – as Ireland recognised when they provided for a 'decision-making representative'[20] for anyone unable to make decisions even with support. While they may lower the threshold for capacity, SDM schemes do not remove it altogether: there will always be a point at which a person cannot decide and someone else must make that decision for them, so the questions still arise of when this point ought to be, how you deal with those on the margins, and how decisions for people incapable of deciding ought to be made (including the role of the agent's values and beliefs in this). Supported decision-making schemes are not a panacea, and the challenges presented by those who sit on the cusp of capacity, identified in this book, are pivotal when considering how such a scheme ought to be successfully implemented in England and Wales.

[20] Ibid.

APPENDICES

Appendix A

Methodology of Empirical Research

The purpose of the empirical research was to gain a better understanding of how the provisions in the MCA are being understood and applied in practice. This is important for two reasons. First, both the provisions on testing for capacity and on assessing best interests are broadly framed, according decision-makers a large margin of discretion when it comes to applying them. Given this, it is important to understand how these provisions are being applied, what factors are affecting the way these assessments are being conducted, and whether or not the application of them is consistent. Secondly, while some information about how the provisions are being applied can be gleaned from the case law, very few cases ever make it to court, and those that do are frequently those that are especially challenging or controversial. The case law does not therefore give an accurate representation of how most decisions are being taken on the ground. Moreover, the circumstances in which most decisions are being made are very different to those present in the majority of Court of Protection cases. While some judgments are made extempore, judges are generally not subject to the same time and resource pressures that doctors and care workers commonly face, which may affect the robustness of both capacity and best interests assessments. Consequently, a series of semi-structured interviews were conducted with medical consultants from a range of specialisms, in order to explore how they conducted capacity and best interests assessments. This section explains the methodology employed for these interviews and how the data that was acquired was then used.

In accordance with the terms of the ethics approval received,[1] named participants were approached by email, having been identified using lists of consultants working in three different NHS trusts: Oxford University Hospitals NHS Foundation Trust, Oxford Health NHS Foundation Trust, and Barts Health NHS Trust (London). In each instance, every consultant working in the given specialism in that trust was emailed, and every person who volunteered to take part in the study and was subsequently available to do

[1] Research Ethics Approval (CUREC 1A), Ref No: R39750/RE001.

so was interviewed (see Appendix C for further details of the study participants). Consequently, the specialisms included in this study are:

(1) Liaison Psychiatry (4 participants)
(2) Old Age Psychiatry (3 participants)
(3) Psychiatry – emergency medicine (1 participant)
(4) Psychiatry – general (1 participant)
(5) Emergency Medicine (3 participants)
(6) Geriatric Medicine (3 participants)
(7) Intensive Care (1 participant)
(8) General Practice (1 participant)

While far greater numbers of participants were approached than agreed to take part in the research, in at least some specialisms (liaison psychiatry, geriatrics, and emergency medicine), there was a high degree of what has been termed by Benjamin Saunders *et al.* 'inductive thematic saturation',[2] with later interviews generating very few new codes or themes. Each interview followed the same format, which began with a series of general questions (Appendix A), asking participants what they thought they were testing for when assessing whether a person has capacity, whether they often came across hard or borderline cases and what it was that made those cases difficult, and what factors they weighed up when deciding what was in the best interests of someone who lacked capacity. They were also asked for their provisional thoughts on recent proposals put forward by the Law Commission.

The participants were then presented with a number of short vignettes in which someone with questionable or uncertain capacity required treatment (Appendix B). The participants were asked to decide in relation to each of the scenarios whether or not they thought the person in question had capacity, what factors or pieces of information were important when making that assessment, and whether there was any other information they would have needed or wanted in order to make that assessment. They were subsequently asked whether, if the person was found to lack capacity, the treatment in question would be in the best interests of the patient, as well as what factors were important when making this assessment, and why they were weighing the factors in that particular way. Depending on the nature of the specialism, some vignettes were omitted from particular interviews. For example, the scenarios of Lucy and Becky, which related to the contraceptive or birthing

[2] B. Saunders *et al.*, 'Saturation in Qualitative Research: Exploring Its Conceptualization and Operationalization' (2018) 52(4) *Quality and Quantity* 1893–1907, 1896.

decisions of young women, were not shown to those specialising in geriatrics. But some specialisms, such as Liaison Psychiatry, were asked to comment on all the vignettes.

The interviews lasted between 40 minutes and 1.5 hours, depending on the number of vignettes considered and the fullness of the answers given. They usually took place at the doctor's place of work, although two were conducted at Merton College, University of Oxford. These were recorded and transcribed, and the transcripts analysed using qualitative analysis software NVivo 10 to classify and organise the data. A thematic analysis was then conducted, which focused on identifying common themes or patterns of meaning that emerged from a number of different sources.[3] This analysis involved coding the transcripts to identify common themes arising in the interviews responses, in particular in relation to two key questions: how doctors understood the test for capacity embedded in the MCA, and what factors were influencing their application of this. These were conceived inductively, using the method set out by Virginia Braun and Victoria Clarke:[4] a line-by-line analysis of the transcripts was conducted picking out key words, phrases, or points. These were then reviewed, to further refine the codes and check for any duplication (where the same or similar content was placed under different codes), and from this, overarching themes or factors were extrapolated. These themes are detailed in Appendix D.

Quotes taken directly from these interviews are used throughout this book. In accordance with the terms of my ethics approval (Appendix E) and the information sheets I provided to participants before they agreed to take part (Appendix F), these have been completely anonymised, with pseudonyms used. Given that a number of the participants work in proximity with one another (including the use of shared offices and shared diarising), exact details of the interviews have not been included so as to preserve anonymity.

This research is qualitative and not quantitative. Given the relatively small sample size (seventeen participants were interviewed in total), the results of this study cannot be extrapolated to the medical body at large, as robust evidence about the way in which capacity assessments are made in general. Moreover, those who took part in the study volunteered to do so, most likely because they regarded the topic as interesting or important in some way, which may have altered both the way they responded to the questions and their level of engagement with the topic. This may also account for the much higher turnout among some specialisms (in particular, psychiatry and geriatrics, who tended to regard capacity as a more pressing issue) than others. For example, across four GP surgeries, only one GP responded.

[3] V. Braun and V. Clarke, 'Using Thematic Analysis in Psychology' (2006) 3(2) Qualitative Research in Psychology 77.

[4] Ibid, 86–93.

Nonetheless, the evidence does demonstrate some common themes or factors which appear to be influencing the decisions of doctors, and some shared concerns amongst the medical profession about the difficulties inherent in making these assessments and the consequences of doing so. It also highlights that even within the relatively small numbers of participants interviewed, there were clear differences of opinion when it came to interpreting and applying the tests. Once these themes had been identified, these were then considered in conjunction with the case law and other research that had been conducted into how the provisions of the MCA were being applied (for example, the results of the House of Lord post-legislative scrutiny of the MCA[5] and the Law Commission's Consultation Analysis[6]) to ascertain whether the issues or patterns raised by doctors in the empirical research had also been identified as operating more broadly. Sometimes, this evidence of how the provisions were being applied in practice provided support for the existence of problems that had already been identified at a theoretical level in the legal or ethical literature (for example, the broad discretion afforded to decision-makers under the best interests provisions, or the lack of attention given to concerns about the authenticity of the person's beliefs). In other places, it unearthed new concerns which had not previously been identified, such as the challenges that circumstances in which decisions must be made present to making robust assessments of capacity.

However, as well as forming the basis for critiquing the current law, the empirical research was also useful when formulating proposals for reform of the law. It allowed me to test reform proposals that had been put forward by others, such as the Law Commission, with interviewees explicitly questioned about possible reforms, in order to evaluate the utility of proposals. It also helped to 'flesh out' ideas for law reform that had been previously raised in the literature, in order to develop more precise proposals for reform. For example, while many commentators have suggested the need to reform the law so as to better ensure that the wishes of the individual are prioritised, there are many different ways that this could be implemented in practice. Having a better understanding of the reasons doctors and care workers have for *not* prioritising the wishes of people therefore helped to formulate a response to this problem, which centred on the need to provide a strong symbolic statement that the person's wishes take precedence, and greater protection from impunity when making empowering decisions.

[5] House of Lords Select Committee on the Mental Capacity Act 2005, '*Mental Capacity Act 2005: Post-Legislative Scrutiny*' (HL Paper 139, 13 March 2014).

[6] Law Commission, 'Mental Capacity and Deprivation of Liberty – Consultation Analysis.' Available at https://s3-eu-west-2.amazonaws.com/lawcom-prod-storage-11jsxou24uy7q/uploads/2017/03/cp222_mental_capacity_responses_analysis.pdf. Accessed 25 September 2018.

Appendix B

General Questions Put to Consultants

(1) When assessing whether a person has capacity, what do you think you are testing for?

(a) *Follow-up questions (depending on the answer):*

(i) What information are they required to understand?
(ii) What exactly do you think that 'use and weigh' is asking? How do you test for it?

(2) Do you often come across cases in which you would regard the person's capacity to be on the cusp or borderline?

(a) What is it that indicates the cusp of capacity?
(b) What sorts of things make a capacity assessment hard?
(c) Is there a particular limb of the capacity test under the MCA, which you are more often uncertain about whether they meet its requirements?
(d) Are there particular conditions where this problem arises more frequently?
(e) Are there particular treatment decisions where this problem arises more frequently?

(3) Where a person is found to lack capacity, what factors do you usually weigh up when deciding what is in their best interests?
(4) How frequently do you perceive a tension arising between what the person lacking capacity wishes and what you consider to be in their best interests?

(a) Are there particular healthcare decisions in which this situation is more likely to arise?

(5) When considering how much weight to give to the patient's views, what factors do you usually consider important when making this assessment?
(6) [Show participant the Law Commission proposals to change section 4 best interests assessment.]

(a) Do you think these changes are going to have an effect on how best interests decisions are made in practice?
(b) Do you think these changes are welcome? Why/why not?

(7) [Explain Law Commission discussion on supported decision-making, in which people who lack capacity would be able to formally appoint a trusted person ("a supporter") to assist with decision-making.]

(a) What are your initial thoughts on whether or not this would be a helpful change?

Appendix C

Vignettes

C.1 Isobel

Isobel is seventy and has been diagnosed as suffering from early-stage dementia. She has a problem with her hip, which, due to stiffness and pain, makes it hard for her to get up the stairs to her bedroom and bathroom. Her family and doctors think it is advisable that she have a hip replacement; however, Isobel strongly objects to this. Although she understands the medical evidence in favour of having the replacement, she is scared of having an anaesthetic. Despite being in otherwise good health, and a low anaesthetic risk, she fears she will never wake up again. The doctors are concerned that if she does not have the hip replacement, Isobel will soon become unable to live in her home and may have to move to a care home. Isobel is deeply opposed to moving from her home but continues to refuse the operation.

Follow-up questions:

(1) Would your answer be different if the operation Isobel required was a heart bypass, which would extend her life significantly rather than a hip replacement?

(2) What about if her reasons for refusal were not a fear of the anaesthesia, but because she does not want to live to an age where she becomes infirm and a burden on her family?

C.2 Lucy

Lucy has a mild learning disability. She is able to carry out basic day-to-day tasks and volunteers once a week in a charity shop, but she struggles with financial and administrative matters and so has to receive assistance with these. She stops taking contraception because she would like to have a baby. Lucy's family is concerned that she does not fully understand the physical and emotional effects of pregnancy. They also think she will not be able to care for a child, which will either have to be raised by them or taken into care, a view supported by the local social services who also think she would not be able to manage. This causes Lucy great emotional distress. Lucy disputes this, saying she has read numerous books on pregnancy and motherhood, and understands the demands it places on her. When questioned by the doctors, she demonstrates a clear knowledge of the basic day-to-day needs of a baby, including feeding, changing nappies, sleep routines and so forth. Doctors suspect, however, that she does not fully appreciate the impact that a baby will have on her life. She says that she wants the chance to experience motherhood and that if she cannot have a baby, she would rather not live at all.

Follow-up questions:

(1) What information would you expect Lucy to be able to understand in order to have capacity to decide whether or not to take contraception?

(2) Do you think her family's wishes on the matter are important here?

C.3 Max

Max suffers from schizophrenia and experiences persecutory delusions. He has a bladder stone, which is causing him some abdominal pain, and he requires an operation to remove it. He understands the medical evidence in favour of having the operation, and the consequences of not having it, but is refusing it because he believes the pain is God's punishment for the sins he has committed during his life. He thinks doctors should not interfere with the actions of God, and that it is only God who will decide his fate. As a devout Christian throughout his life, he believes God will not let him die.

Follow-up question:

(1) If Max did not have schizophrenia but still refused, for the same reasons (i.e., a belief that God will not let him die), would you then think he had capacity?

C.4 Cara

Cara is twenty-six. She has suffered from anorexia nervosa since she was fourteen and has been detained under the Mental Health Act a number of times in those years. She is admitted to hospital after taking an overdose of paracetamol. She says that she does not want to receive any treatment. She explains that her life has, for over ten years, been plagued by her anorexia, and despite trying everything, she cannot get better. She says that she gains no pleasure from her life anymore and wants to be left to die.

C.5 Becky

Becky has been in labour for forty-six hours. She is very insistent that she wants a natural birth and is refusing any painkillers. She is weepy, exhausted, and clearly struggling to cope with the pain. Becky is diagnosed with a placental abruption, and the doctor tells her she requires a caesarean section, and that if she does not have one, she is likely to lose the baby. Becky's mother, Josie, is against her having a C-section. She is a hypnotherapist, who believes strongly that women can avoid pain during childbirth via self-hypnosis, and that natural birthing is best for both mother and child. She encourages Becky to resist any offers of painkillers, telling her to focus on her mental state instead. Becky refuses the C-section. Although she appears to understand the potential consequences, she tells doctors that it is important to her that she gives birth naturally, whatever the consequences.

C.6 Oscar

Oscar is an eighty-five-year-old man. He is brought into hospital having taken a paracetamol overdose. When asked, he says that the suicide attempt had been planned for some time, and that he does not want any treatment, as he would like to end his life. He explains to the doctors that his wife of sixty years died over a year ago, and that, although he is not depressed, he continues to miss her. He tells the doctors that he has had a good life, with a fulfilled career and a happy marriage, but that, without any children or grandchildren, there is nothing left to give meaning to his life and so he believes this is the 'right time to go'.

Appendix D

Participant Information

Practice area	Number of Participants	NHS Trusts	Interview window
Psychiatry	**9**	Oxford University Health, Oxfordshire	March 2017–July 2017
- Liaison psychiatry	4		
- Old-age psychiatry	3	Oxford Health, Oxfordshire	
- Emergency psychiatry	1		
- General psychiatry	1		
Geriatrics	**3**	Oxford University Health, Oxfordshire	March 2017–April 2017
Emergency Medicine	**3**	Oxford University Health, Oxford Barts Health, London	March 2017–July 2017
General Practice	**1**	Oxfordshire	July 2017
Intensive Care	**1**	Oxford University Health, Oxfordshire	March 2017

D.1 Demographic Information

Total Participants	No. of pps at consultant level	Gender distribution	No. of pps known to be BME	Place of work
17	16b	Male: 11 pps Female: 6 pps	1	Oxfordshire: 15 pps London: 2 pps

Appendix E

Themes Deriving from Empirical Research

E.1 Capacity Assessments

The interviews involved both general open-ended questions and a discussion of a series of vignettes. The main themes derived from the empirical data centre on two different questions: the first related to how doctors understood the test for capacity and the second to how they applied the test, and what factors influenced whether or not a person was found to have capacity.

E.1.1 How the Test for Capacity Is Being Understood

When asked what doctors regarded themselves as testing for when they were assessing capacity, the responses largely centred on three common themes:

(1) A legalistic response reiterating the limbs of the test for capacity in section 3 of the Mental Capacity Act 2005.
(2) Whether the person can apply the information to themselves and understand how it would affect them specifically.
(3) Whether the person can make a decision which reflects their values or beliefs.

One issue that frequently arose in the interviews was the precise meaning of the 'use or weigh' limb of the capacity test. The responses indicated four possible meanings were being attributed to this limb:

(1) The person's ability to reason or to provide adequate reasons for deciding in the way that they have.
(2) The person's ability to weigh up the risks and benefits of having the treatment (or the 'pros and cons' of it).
(3) The person's ability to put the information in their own context and appreciate how it applies to them.
(4) The person's ability to understand and appraise the information in light of their values or beliefs.

Further themes that commonly arose in interviews included the following:

(1) Capacity operates on a spectrum (and is not all-or-nothing).
(2) People sit on the cusp of borderline of capacity (albeit different doctors gave different explanations for why a person might be said to be on the 'cusp' of capacity).
(3) The test for capacity was subjective (though, again, doctors focused on different limbs of the test as examples of the test being subjective).

E.1.2 Factors Affecting Capacity Assessments

The factors affecting capacity assessments could broadly be divided into two different categories. The first of these is the factors which affect the person's actual capacity (albeit that they might be accommodated differently as between different doctors in different specialisms). The key factors that commonly arose in interviews were:

(1) Delirium
(2) Pain
(3) Effects of drugs or medication
(4) Capacity fluctuating as between days
(5) Capacity fluctuating within days

The second category is the factors which might affect the conclusion reached about whether or not the person has capacity, but which do not necessarily affect the person's *actual* capacity. These included:

(1) High patient numbers (and in particular the large numbers of older patients).
(2) Staff shortages.
(3) A lack of information about the patient to enable capacity to be robustly assessed, either due to doctors having insufficient time or resources to acquire that information, or due to a lack of engagement on the part of the patient.
(4) An awareness of the outcome of the assessment of capacity – either for the patient themselves (i.e., if found to have capacity, will they be permitted to do something which is seriously harmful to themselves?) or for the other staff members who have to abide by the doctor's decision.
(5) A fear of litigation being brought by or on behalf of the patient.

E.2 Best Interests Assessments

The NVivo analysis suggested that a number of factors were commonly affecting how doctors were making best interests assessments. These often also reflected factors that had been noted in the case law. The most commonly cited of these included:

(1) The invasiveness of the proposed treatment (physically or psychologically)
(2) The outcome of the treatment:
    (a) The prospect of the patient recovering or returning to a 'reasonable' quality of life
    (b) Whether the treatment was life sustaining
    (c) What the perceived risks were of the person refusing the treatment or care intervention
(3) The circumstances of the patient:
    (a) Their degree of incapacity
    (b) Their age
    (c) The distress experienced by the patient of having their wishes overridden
(4) The reasons given by the patient for deciding as they have:
    (a) The perceived authenticity of their reasons
    (b) Whether there was a religious dimension to their reasoning
(5) The decision-maker themselves:
    (a) Their own values and beliefs
    (b) Their age
    (c) Their specialism
    (d) The resources available to the decision-maker
    (e) Their understanding of the legal requirements

Broadly, the empirical evidence suggested the following factors would lend support for greater (or less) weight being placed on the person's wishes.

Factors supporting greater weight being placed on the patients' wishes	Factors supporting less weight being placed on the patients' wishes
The nature of the treatment	
The treatment sought is invasive (e.g., surgery)	The treatment is necessary to save P's life.
There is more time to acquire collateral information about it	It is an emergency situation.
The outcome of the treatment for the patient	
There is no reasonable prospect of recovery or achieving an acceptable quality of life.	There is a reasonable prospect of recovery or achieving an acceptable quality of life.

(*cont.*)

Factors supporting greater weight being placed on the patients' wishes	Factors supporting less weight being placed on the patients' wishes
The risk–benefit analysis of the value of the treatment is finely balanced.	The risk–benefit analysis of the value of the treatment is not finely balanced.
The risks associated with the treatment or care decision are lower.	The risks associated with the treatment or care decision are high.
The circumstances of the patient	
The patient's capacity is closer to meeting the capacity threshold.	The patient's capacity is further from meeting the capacity threshold.
The patient is older.	The patient is younger.
The patient is less vulnerable.	The patient is more vulnerable.
The patient is likely to experience substantial distress as a result of the treatment.	The patient is less likely to be aware of or feel distress at the treatment.
Reasons given by the patient	
The patient's views have been consistently expressed throughout life.	There is a lack of evidence that the patient's views have been consistently held.
The patient's beliefs have a religious dimension.	The beliefs or values are outside of a recognised belief structure.
The decision-maker	
The patient's reasons accord with the decision-maker's beliefs or values.	The patient's reasons do not accord with the decision-maker's beliefs or values.
The decision-maker has a good understanding of their legal obligations.	
The accountability structure for the decision-maker is clear.	

BIBLIOGRAPHY

Books and Articles

J. Ahlin, 'The Impossibility of Reliably Determining the Authenticity of Desires: Implications for Informed Consent' (2017) 21(1) *Medicine, Health Care and Philosophy* 43–50.

B. Amann and H. Grunze, 'Neurochemical Underpinnings in Bipolar Disorder and Epilepsy' (2005) 46(4) *Epilepsia* 26–30.

The Assessment of Decision-Making Capacity: A Guide for Physicians and Other Health Professionals (Oxford: Oxford University Press, 1998), 42–52.

K. Atkins, 'Autonomy and the Subjective Character of Experience' (2000) 17 *Journal of Applied Philosophy* 71.

'Autonomy and Autonomy Competencies: A Practical and Relational Approach' (2006) 7 *Nursing Philosophy* 205, 211.

C. Auckland, '*Barnsley Hospitals NHS Foundation Trust* v *MSP* [2020] EWCOP 26: The Need for Caution When Establishing the Wishes of Incapacitated Patients' (2021) 29(2) *Medical Law Review* 347–358.

'Authenticity and Identity in Adolescent Decision-Making' (2023) *Modern Law Review*. https://doi.org/10.1111/1468-2230.12834.

N. Banner, 'Unreasonable Reasons: Normative Judgements in the Assessment of Mental Capacity' (2012) 18(5) *Journal of Evaluation in Clinical Practice* 1038–1044.

'Can Procedural and Substantive Elements of Decision-Making Be Reconciled in Assessments of Mental Capacity?' (2013) 9(1) *International Journal of Law in Context* 71–86.

J. Baron *et al.*, 'Effect of Assessment Method on the Discrepancy between Judgments of Health Disorders People Have and Do Not Have: A Web Study' (2003) 23(5) *Medical Decision Making* 422–434.

P. Bartlett, *Blackstone's Guide to the Mental Capacity Act 2005*, 2nd ed. (New York: Oxford University Press, 2008).

'The United Nations Convention on the Rights of Persons with Disabilities and Mental Health Law' (2012) 75 *Modern Law Review* 752.

T.L. Beauchamp and J.F. Childress, *The Principles of Biomedical Ethics*, 4th ed. (New York: Oxford University Press, 1994).

P. Benson, 'Feminist Intuitions and the Normative Substance of Autonomy' in J.S. Taylor (ed), *Personal Autonomy: New Essays on Personal Autonomy and Its Role in Contemporary Moral Philosophy* (Cambridge: Cambridge University Press, 2005), 124-142.

B. Berofsky, *Liberation from Self* (New York: Cambridge University Press, 1995).

R. Binstock and S. Post (eds), *Dementia and Aging: Ethics, Values, and Policy Choices* (Baltimore, MD: John Hopkins University Press, 1992).

D. Bolton, 'The Usefulness of Wakefield's Definition for the Diagnostic Manuals' (2007) 6(3) *World Psychiatry* 164–165.

What Is Mental Disorder? An Essay in Philosophy, Science and Values (New York: Oxford University Press, 2008).

'What Is Mental Disorder?' (2009) 8(12) *Psychiatry* 468–470.

'Conceptualisation of Mental Disorder and Its Personal Meanings' (2010) 19(4) *Journal of Mental Health* 328–336.

D. Bolton and N. Banner, 'Does Mental Disorder Involve Loss of Personal Autonomy?' in L. Radoilska (ed), *Autonomy and Mental Disorder* (Oxford: Oxford University Press, 2012), 77–99.

C. Boorse, 'A Rebuttal on Health' in J.M. Humber and R.F. Almeder (eds), *What Is Disease?* (Totowa, NJ: Humana Press, 1997), 1-134.

D. Borsboom. 'Psychometric Perspectives on Diagnostic Systems' (2008) 64 *Journal of Clinical Psychology* 1089-108.

D. Borsboom and A.O.J. Cramer, 'Network Analysis: An Integrative Approach to the Structure of Psychopathology' (2013) 9(1) *Annual Review of Clinical Psychology* 91–121.

T. Bourne *et al.*, 'The Impact of Complaints Procedures on the Welfare, Health and Clinical Practise of 7926 Doctors in the UK: A Cross-Sectional Survey' (2015) 5(1) *BMJ Open*. https://bmjopen.bmj.com/content/5/1/e006687.

N.F. Boyd, H.J. Sutherland, K.Z. Heasman, D.L. Tritchler, and B.J. Cummings, 'Whose Utilities for Decision Analysis?' (1990) 10 *Medical Decision Making* 58–67.

V. Braun and V. Clarke, 'Using Thematic Analysis in Psychology' (2006) 3(2) *Qualitative Research in Psychology* 77.

M. Brazier and J. Miola, 'Bye-bye Bolam: A Medical Litigation Revolution' (2000) 8 *Medical Law Review* 85–114.

P. Brickman, D. Coates, and R. Janoff-Bulman, 'Lottery Winners and Accident Victims: Is Happiness Relative?' (1978) 36 *Journal of Personality and Social Psychology* 917–927.

J. Brierley *et al.*, 'Should Religious Beliefs Be Allowed to Stonewall a Secular Approach to Withdrawing and Withholding Treatment in Children?' (2012) *Journal of Medical Ethics*. https://doi.org/10.1136/medethics-2011-100104.

A. Buchanan and D. Brock, *Deciding for Others: The Ethics of Surrogate Decision Making* (Cambridge: Cambridge University Press, 1989).

D.L. Buick and K.J. Petrie, '"I Know Just How You Feel": The Validity of Healthy Women's Perceptions of Breast Cancer Patients Receiving Treatment' (2002) 32 *Journal of Applied Social Psychology* 110–123.

H. Bursztajn, H.P. Harding, T.G. Gutheil, and A. Brodsky, 'Beyond Cognition: The Role of Disordered Affective States in Impairing Competence to Consent to Treatment' (1991) 19(4) *Bulletin of the American Academy of Psychiatry & the Law* 383–388.

T. Campbell and C. Heginbotham, *Mental Illness: Prejudice, Discrimination and the Law* (Aldershot: Dartmouth, 1991).

H.I. Cannella, M.F. O'Reilly, and G.E. Lancioni, 'Choice and Preference Assessment Research with People with Severe to Profound Developmental Disabilities: A Review of the Literature' (2005) 26 *Research in Developmental Disabilities* 1.

N. Cantor, *Making Medical Decisions for the Profoundly Mentally Disabled* (Cambridge, MA: MIT Press, 2005).

A. Castelnovo *et al.*, 'Post-Bereavement Hallucinatory Experiences: A Critical Overview of Population and Clinical Studies' (2015) 186 *Journal of Affective Disorders* 266–274.

L. Charland, 'Is Mr. Spock Mentally Competent? Competence to Consent and Emotion' (1998) 5 *Philosophy, Psychiatry & Psychology* 67.

'Mental Competence and Value: The Problem of Normativity in the Assessment of Decision-Making Capacity' (2001) 8(2) *Psychology and Law* 135–145.

'Anorexia and the MacCAT-T Test for Mental Competence: Validity, Value, and Emotion' (2006) 13(4) *Philosophy, Psychiatry, & Psychology* 283–287.

J. Christman, 'Autonomy and Personal History' (1991) 21(1) *Canadian Journal of Philosophy* 1–24.

'Relational Autonomy, Liberal Individualism, and the Social Constitution of Selves' (2004) 117(1/2) *Philosophical Studies* 143–164.

The Politics of Persons: Individual Autonomy and Socio-Historical Selves (Cambridge, UK: Cambridge University Press, 2009), 143.

'Autonomy in Moral and Political Philosophy' in Edward N. Zalta (ed), *The Stanford Encyclopedia of Philosophy* (Stanford, CA: Stanford University, Spring 2018 Edition). Available at: https://plato.stanford.edu/archives/spr2018/entries/autonomy-moral/.

B. Clough "People Like That': Realising the Social Model in Mental Capacity Jurisprudence' (2014) 23 *Medical Law Review* 53.

The Spaces of Mental Capacity Law: Moving beyond binaries (Routledge, 2022).

J Coggon, 'Varied and Principled Understandings of Autonomy in English Law: Justifiable Inconsistency or Blinkered Moralism?' (2007) 15 *Health Care Analysis* 235.

J. Coggon and C. Kong, 'From Best Interests to Better Interests? Values, Unwisdom, and Objectivity in Mental Capacity Law' (2021) 80(2) *Cambridge Law Journal* 245–273.

J. Coggon and J. Miola, 'Autonomy, Liberty, and Medical Decision-Making' (2011) 70 (3) *Cambridge Law Journal* 523–543.

L. Cosmides and J. Tooby, 'Toward an Evolutionary Taxonomy of Treatable Conditions' (1999) 108(3) *Journal of Abnormal Psychology* 453–464.

S. Cox, 'Decision-Making and Dementia – How Well Does the Mental Capacity Act Serve People Living with the Condition?' (2015) 2 *Elder Law Journal* 74.

J. Craigie, 'Competence, Practical Rationality and What a Patient Values' (2011) 25(6) *Bioethics* 326–333.

'Introduction: Mental Capacity and Value Neutrality' (2013) 9(1) *International Journal of Law in Context* 1–3.

'A Fine Balance: Reconsidering Patient Autonomy in Light of the UN Convention on the Rights of Persons with Disabilities' (2015) 29 *Bioethics* 398–405.

S. Darwall, 'The Value of Autonomy and Autonomy of the Will' (2006) 116(2) *Ethics* 263.

G. Davidson et al., 'Supported Decision Making: A Review of the International Literature' (2015) 38 *International Journal of Law and Psychiatry* 61, 73.

J. Dawson and G. Schmukler, 'Fusion of Mental Health and Incapacity Legislation' (2006) 1088 *British Journal of Psychiatry* 504–509.

D. DeGrazia, 'Value Theory and the Best Interests Standard' (1995) 9(1) *Bioethics* 50–60.

A Dhanda, 'Legal Capacity in the Disability Rights Convention: Stranglehold of the past or Lodestar for the Future' (2006) 34 *Syracuse Journal of International Law and Commerce* 429.

A. V. Dicey, *An Introduction to the Study of the Law of the Constitution* (Indianapolis: Liberty Classics Edition, 1982).

D. Diekema, 'Parental Refusals of Medical Treatment: The Harm Principle as Threshold for State Intervention' (2004) 25(4) *Theoretical Medicine* 243–264.

M. Donnelly, 'Best Interests, Patient Participation and the Mental Capacity Act 2005' (2009) 17 *Medical Law Review* 1.

Healthcare Decision-Making and the Law: Autonomy, Capacity and the Limits of Liberalism (Cambridge: Cambridge University Press, 2010).

'Determining Best Interests under the Mental Capacity Act 2005' (2011) 19 *Medical Law Review* 304.

'Best Interests in the Mental Capacity Act: Time to Say Goodbye' (2016) 24(3) *Medical Law Review* 318–332.

'Depression and Consent to Treatment: The Limits of a Capacity-Based Approach' in C. Foster and J. Herring (eds), *Depression: Law and Ethics* (Oxford: Oxford University Press, 2017), 200–210.

J. Drescher, 'Out of DSM: Depathologizing Homosexuality' (2015) 5(4) *Behavioral Science (Basel)* 565–575.

R. Dresser, 'Dworkin on Dementia' (1995) 25(6) *Hastings Center Report* 32.

G. Dworkin, *The Theory and Practice of Autonomy* (New York: Cambridge University Press, 1988).

R. Dworkin, 'Autonomy and the Demented Self' (1986) 64 *The Millbank Quarterly* 4.

Life's Dominion: An Argument about Abortion, Euthanasia, and Individual Freedom (New York: Alfred A Knopf Harper Collins, 1993).

'The Nature of Autonomy' (2015) 2 *Nordic Journal of Studies in Educational Policy* 28479, 14.

L. Ekstrom, 'A Coherence Theory of Autonomy' (1993) 53(3) *Philosophy and Phenomenological Research* 599–616.

J. Elster, *Sour Grapes: Studies in the Subversion of Rationality* (Cambridge: Cambridge University Press, 1983).

I. Elzakkers *et al.*, 'Mental Capacity to Consent to Treatment in Anorexia Nervosa: Explorative Study' (2016) 2(2) *British Journal of Psychiatry Open* 147–153.

C. Emmett *et al.*, 'Homeward Bound or Bound for a Home? Assessing the Capacity of Dementia Patients to Make Decisions about Hospital Discharge: Comparing Practice with Legal Standards' (2013) 36(1) *International Journal of Law and Psychiatry* 73–82.

A. Erler and T. Hope, 'Mental Disorder and the Concept of Authenticity' (2014) 21 (3) *Philosophy, Psychiatry and Psychology* 219–232.

J. Fanning, 'Continuities of Risk in the Era of the Mental Capacity Act' (2016) 24 (3) *Medical Law Review* 415–433.

J. Feinberg, *Harm to Self* (Oxford: Oxford University Press, 1986).

Harm to Others: The Moral Limits of the Criminal Law Volume 1 (Oxford Scholarship Online, November 2003).

D. Feldman, 'The Developing Scope of Article 8 of the European Convention on Human Rights' (1997) 3 *European Human Rights Law Review* 265.

'Human Dignity as a Legal Value: Part II' (2000) 61 *Public Law* 61–71.

D.L. Finfgeld, 'Empowerment of Individuals With Enduring Mental Health Problems' (2004) 27(1) *Advances in Nursing Science* 44–52.

C. Foster, *Human Dignity in Bioethics and Law* (Oxford: Hart, 2011).

C. Foster, J Herring, and I Doron, *The Law and Ethics of Dementia* (Hart Publishing, 2014).

M. Foucault, *Madness and Civilization: A History of Insanity in the Age of Reason (Folie et Déraison: Histoire de la folie à l'âge classique)* (Richard Howard (trans.), New York: Vintage, 1965).
H. Frankfurt, *Freedom of the Will and the Concept of a Person*, The Importance of What We Care About edition (Cambridge: Cambridge University Press, 1987).
B. Freedman, 'Competence, Marginal and Otherwise' (1981) A *International Journal of Law and Psychiatry* 53–72.
F. Freyenhagen and T. O'Shea, 'Hidden Substance: Mental Disorder as a Challenge to Normatively Neutral Accounts of Autonomy' (2013) 9 *International Journal of Law in Context* 53.
M. Friedman, 'Autonomy and Social Relationships: Rethinking the Feminist Critique' in D Meyers (ed.), *Feminists Rethink the Self* (Boulder, CO: Westview Press, 1997), 40–61.
K.W.M. Fulford, 'What Is (Mental) Disease?': An Open Letter to Christopher Boorse' (2001) 27 *Journal of Medical Ethics* 80–85.
L. Fuller, 'Consideration and Form' (1941) 41(5) *Columbia Law Review* 799–824.
D. Galligan, *Due Process and Fair Procedures: A Study of Administrative Procedures* (Oxford: Clarendon, 1996).
J. Griffin, Well-Being: Its Meaning, Measurement and Moral Importance (USA: Oxford University Press, 1988).
T. Grisso and P. Appelbaum, 'Appreciating Anorexia: Decisional Capacity and the Role of Values' (2006) 13(4) *Philosophy, Psychiatry and Psychology* 293–297.
M. Gunn, 'The Meaning of Incapacity' (1994) 2 *Medical Law Review* 8.
S. Guze, *Why Psychiatry Is a Branch of Medicine* (New York: Oxford University Press, 1992).
J. Feinberg, Harm to Others: The Moral Limits of the Criminal Law Volume 3 (Oxford Scholarship Online, November 2003).
F. Freyenhagen and T O'Shea, 'Hidden Substance: Mental Disorder as a Challenge to Normatively Neutral Accounts of Autonomy' (2013) 9(1) *International Journal of Law in Context* 53–70.
A. Hall, 'Making Good Choices: Toward a Theory of Well-Being in Medicine' (2016) 37(5) *Theoretical Medicine and Bioethics* 383–400.
J. Halpern and R. Arnold, 'Affective Forecasting: An Unrecognized Challenge in Making Serious Health Decisions' (2008) 23(10) *Journal of General Internal Medicine* 1708–1712.
H.L.A Hart, *Law, Liberty and Morality* (Stanford: Stanford University Press, 1963).
J. Hawkins, 'Why Even a Liberal Can Justify Limited Paternalistic Intervention in Anorexia Nervosa' (2021) 28(2) *Philosophy, Psychiatry & Psychology* 155–158.
'Decision-Making Capacity and Value', in Daniel D. Mosely and Gary Gala (eds), *Philosophy and Psychiatry: Problems, Intersections and New Perspectives* (New York: Routledge, 2016), 204–213.

J. Hawkins and L. Charland, 'Decision-Making Capacity' in *Stanford Encyclopedia of Philosophy* (Stanford, CA: Stanford University, 14th August 2020). Available at: https://stanford.library.sydney.edu.au/entries/decision-capacity/#ChalFourAbilModeValuAuth.

H. Hermann, M. Trachsel, and N. Biller-Andorno, 'Physicians' Personal Values in Determining Medical Decision-Making Capacity: A Survey Study' (2015) 41 *Journal of Medical Ethics* 739–744.

H. Hermann, M. Trachsel, B.S. Elger, and N. Biller-Andorno, "Emotion and Value in the Evaluation of Medical Decision-Making Capacity: A Narrative Review of Arguments" (2016) 7 *Frontiers in Psychology* art.765.

J. Herring, 'Caesarean Sections, Phobias and Foetal Rights' (1997) 56(3) *CLJ* 509–511.

'Losing It? Losing What? The Law and Dementia' (2009) 3 *Child and Family Law Quarterly* 3–29.

'Protecting Vulnerable Adults' (2009) 21 *Child and Family Quarterly* 498.

'Forging a Relational Approach: Best Interests or Human Rights?' (2013) 32 *Medical Law International.* 32.

Caring and the Law (Oxford: Hart Publishing, 2013).

'Peter Skegg and the Question No-One Asks: Why Presume Capacity?' in M. Henaghan and J. Wall (eds), *Law, Ethics, and Medicine: Essays in Honour of Peter Skegg* (New Zealand: Thomson Reuters, 2016), 32–51.

J. Herring and J. Wall, 'Autonomy, Capacity and Vulnerable Adults: Filling the Gaps in the Mental Capacity Act'(2015) 35(4) *Legal Studies* 698–719.

J. Herring *et al.*, 'Elbow Room for Best Practice? Montgomery, Patients' Values, and Balanced Decision-Making in Person-Centred Clinical Care' (2017) 25 (4) *Medical Law Review* 582.

R. Heywood, "Parents and Medical Professionals: Conflict, Cooperation and Best Interests" (2012) 20 *Medical Law Review* 29.

S. Holm, Autonomy, Authenticity, or Best Interest: Everyday Decision-Making and Persons with Dementia' (2001) 4 *Medicine, Health Care & Philosophy* 153.

T. Hope *et al.*, 'Best Interests, Dementia and the Mental Capacity Act 2005' (2009) 35 *Journal of Medical Ethics* 733–738.

'Anorexia Nervosa and the Language of Authenticity' (2011) 40 *Hastings Center Report* 19.

'Agency, Ambivalence and Authenticity: The Many Ways in Which Anorexia Nervosa Can Affect Autonomy" (2013) 9 *International Journal of Law in Context* 20.

A. Horwitz and J. Wakefield, *The Loss of Sadness: How Psychiatry Transformed Normal Sorrow into Depressive Disorder* (USA: Oxford University Press, 2007).

R. Huxtable, 'Autonomy, Best Interests and the Public Interest: Treatment, Non-Treatment and the Values of Medical Law' (2014) 22(4) *Medical Law Review* 459–493.

'From Twilight to Breaking Dawn? Best Interests, Autonomy, and Minimally Conscious Patients: *M v N* [2015] EWCOP 76 (Fam)' (2016) 24(4) *Medical Law Review* 622–631.

R. Huxtable and G. Birchley, 'Seeking Certainty? Judicial Approaches to the (Non-) Treatment of Minimally Conscious Patients' (2017) 25(3) *Medical Law Review* 428–455.

S. E. Hyman, 'The Genetics of Mental Illness: Implications for Practice' (2000) 78 (4) *Bulletin of the World Health Organization* 455–463. Available at: www.scielosp.org/article/bwho/2000.v78n4/455–463/.

M. Jackson and K.W.M Fulford, 'Spiritual Experience and Psychopathology' (1997) 4(1) *Philosophy, Psychiatry & Psychology* 41–65.

P. Jackson, 'Best Interests: The Empty Quarter?' (2013) 1 *Elder Law Journal* 37.

E. Jackson, 'From 'Doctor Knows Best' to Dignity: Placing Adults Who Lack Capacity at the Centre of Decisions about Their Medical Treatment' (2018) 81(2) *Medical Law Review* 247–281.

A. Jaworska, 'Respecting the Margins of Agency: Alzheimer's Patients and the Capacity to Value.' (1999) 28(2) *Philosophy & Public Affairs* 105–138.

R. Johns, 'Who Decides Now? Protecting and Empowering Vulnerable Adults Who Lose the Capacity to Make Decisions for Themselves' (2007) 37 *British Journal of Social Work* 557.

C. Johnston, N. Banner, and A. Fenwick, 'Patient Narrative: An "On-Switch" for Evaluating Best Interests' (2016) 38 *Journal of Social Welfare and Family Law* 249.

M. Jones, A. Dugdale, M. Simpson, *Clerk and Lindsell on Torts* (22nd Edition, Sweet & Maxwell Ltd, 2017), 15-09.

N. Kane, A. Ruck-Keene, G. Owen, and S. Kim, 'Applying Decision-Making Capacity Criteria in Practice: A Content Analysis of Court Judgments' (2021) 16(2) *PLOS ONE* e0246521

N. Kane, A. Ruck Keene, G. Owen, and K. Scott, 'Difficult Capacity Cases – The Experience of Liaison Psychiatrists. An Interview Study across Three Jurisdictions' (2022) 13 *Front Psychiatry.* 946234. https://doi.org/10.3389/fpsyt.2022.946234.

E. Kant, *Groundwork of the Metaphysics of Morals*, Cambridge Texts in the History of Philosophy ed, 2nd ed. (Cambridge University Press, 2012).

J. Katz, 'Can principles Survive in Situations of Critical Care?' in J. Moskop and L. Kopelman (eds), *Can Principles Survive in Situations of Critical Care?* (Dordrecht: D Reidel and Kluwer Academic, 1985), 41–67.

R.E. Kendell, 'What are mental disorders?' in A. M. Freedman, R. Brotman, I. Silverman, and D. Hutson (eds), *Issues in Psychiatric Classification: Science, Practice and Social Policy* (New York: Human Sciences Press, 1986), 23–45.

S. Killmister, 'The Woody Allen Puzzle: How 'Authentic Alienation' Complicates Autonomy' (2015) 49(4) *Noûs* 729–747.

S. Kim, 'The Place of Ability to Value in the Evaluation of Decision-Making Capacity' in Daniel D. Mosely and Gary Gala (eds), *Philosophy and Psychiatry: Problems, Intersections and New Perspectives* (New York: Routledge, 2016), 189–203.

S. Kim, N. Kane, A. Ruck-Keene, and G. Owen, 'Broad Concepts and Messy Realities: Optimising the Application of Mental Capacity Criteria' (2021) 2021 *Journal of Medical Ethics* 1–7.

L.J. Kirmayer, 'Rejoinder to Professor Wakefield. Debate on 'Is the Concept of Disorder Culturally Relative' in S.A. Kirk and S.D. Einbinder (eds), *Controversial Issues in Mental Health* (Boston, MA and London: Allyn & Bacon, 1994), 1–8.

N. Knauer, 'Defining Capacity: Balancing the Competing Interests of Autonomy and Need' (2003) 12 *Temple Political & Civil Rights Law Review* 321.

N. Kohn, J Blumenthal, and A Campbell, 'Supported Decision-Making: A Viable Alternative to Guardianship?' (2013) 117(4) *Penn State Law Review* 1111.

A. Kon, 'When Parents Refuse Treatment for Their Child' (2006) 8(1) *JONA'S Healthcare Law, Ethics, and Regulation* 5–9.

C. Kong, *Mental Capacity in Relationship: Decision-Making, Dialogue and Autonomy* (Cambridge University Press, 2017).

'Constructing Female Sexual and Reproductive Agency in Mental Capacity Law' (2019 66 *International Journal of Law and Psychiatry* 101488.

C. Kong, J. Coggon, M. Dunn, and P. Cooper, 'Judging Values and Participation in Medical Capacity Law' (2019) 8(3) *Laws* 16.

C. Kong, J. Coggon, M. Dunn, and A. Ruck-Keene, 'An Aide Memoire for a Balancing Act? Critiquing the 'Balance Sheet' Approach to Best Interests Decision-Making' (2020) 28(4) *Medical Law Review* 753–780.

C. Kong, R. Stickler, P. Cooper, M. Watkins, and M. Dunn, 'The 'Human Element' in the Social Space of the Courtroom: Framing and Shaping the Deliberative Process in Mental Capacity Law' (2022) 42 *Legal Studies* 715–734.

'Justifying and Practising Effective Participation in the Court of Protection: An Empirical Study,' (2022) 49(4) *Journal of Law and Society* 703–725.

C. Korsgard, 'Personal Identity and the Unity of Agency: A Kantian Response to Parfit' (1989) 18(2) *Philosophy and Public Affairs* 101–132.

H. Kuhse, 'Some Reflections on the Problem of Advance Directives, Personhood, and Personal Identity' (1999) 9(4) *Kennedy Institute of Ethics Journal* 347–364.

W. Kymlicka, *Liberalism, Community, and Culture* (USA: Clarendon Press, 1991).

Law Commission Consultation Paper No. 222, 'Mental Capacity and Deprivation of Liberty' (2015). Available at: www.lawcom.gov.uk/wp-content/uploads/2015/07/cp222_mental_capacity.pdf, 12.44.

G. Laurie, 'Parens Patriae Jurisdiction in the Medico-Legal Context: The Vagaries of Judicial Activism' (1999) 3 *Edinburgh Law Review* 95.

S. Lee, *Law and Morals: Warnock, Gillick, and Beyond* (Oxford: Oxford University Press, 1986).

N. Levy, 'Forced to Be Free? Increasing Patient Autonomy by Constraining It' (2014) 40 *Journal of Management and Entrepreneurship* 293.

S. Lincoln and C. Hooker, 'Neural Structure and Social Dysfunction in Individuals at Clinical High Risk for Psychosis' (2014) 224(3) *Pyschiatry Research: Neuroimaging* 152–158.

G. Loewenstein, 'Hot-Cold Empathy Gaps and Medical Decision Making' (2005) 24(4S) *Health Psychology* S49–S56.

'Projection Bias in Medical Decision-Making' (2005) 25(1) *Medical Decision Making* 96–105.

D. Lush, 'Article 12 of the United Nations Convention on the Rights of Persons with Disabilities' (2011) *Elder Law Journal* 61-68.

'The Academy of European Law's Conference on the Rights of Persons with Disabilities' (2015) 2 *Elder Law Journal* 38-44.

C. Mackenzie, 'Relational Autonomy, Normative Authority and Perfectionism' (2008) 39 *Journal of Social Philosophy* 512.

C. Mackenzie and W. Rogers, 'Autonomy, Vulnerability and Capacity: A Philosophical Appraisal of the Mental Capacity Act' (2013) 9 *International Journal of Law in Context* 37–52.

C. Mackenzie and N. Stoljar, *Relational Autonomy: Feminist Essays on Autonomy, Agency and Social Self* (Oxford University Press, 2000).

R. Mackenzie and J. Watts, "Including Emotionality in Tests of Competence: How Does Neurodiversity Affect Measures of Free Will and Agency in Medical Decision Making?" (2011) 2(3) *AJOB Neuroscience* 27–36.

C. MacKinnon, *Toward a Feminist Theory of the State* (Cambridge: Harvard University Press, 1989).

J. McVey, 'The Experiences of Healthcare Staff in using the Mental Capacity Act (2005) When Working with People with a Learning Disability' (2013). Available at: https://livrepository.liverpool.ac.uk/10673/4/McVeyJul_Jan2013_10673.pdf.

W. Martin, 'The MCA under Scrutiny: Meeting the Challenges of CRPD Compliance' (2015) *Elder Law Journal* 32–37.

A. Mele, *Autonomous Agents: From Self-Control to Autonomy* (New York: Oxford University Press, 2001).

D. Meyers, *Self, Society, and Personal Choice* (New York: Columbia University Press, 1989), 44.

J.S. Mill, *On Liberty* (Cosimo Classics, 2005 [1859]).

Utilitarianism, Oxford Philosophical Text Series edition (Oxford: Oxford University Press, 1998).

D. Molyneux, "And How Is Life Going for You?"—An Account of Subjective Welfare in Medicine (2007) 33(10) *Journal of Medical Ethics*: 568–572.

'Should Healthcare Professionals Respect Autonomy Just Because It Promotes Welfare?' (2009) 35 *Journal of Management and Entrepreneurship* 245.

N. Munro, 'Taking Wishes and Feelings Seriously: The Views of People Lacking Capacity in Court of Protection Decision-Making' (2014) 36(1) *Journal of Social Welfare and Family Law* 59–75.

A. Murrell and L. McCalla, 'Assessing Decision-Making Capacity: The Interpretation and Implementation of the Mental Capacity Act 2005 amongst Social Care Professionals' (2016) 28(1) *Practice: Social Work in Action* 21–36, 28.

J. Nedelsky, "Reconceiving Autonomy: Sources, Thoughts and Possibilities" (1989) 1 *Yale Journal of Law and Feminism* 7–36.

L. Nordernfelt, *On the Nature of Health: An Action-Theoretic Approach* (Dordrecht, The Netherlands: D. Reidel, 1987).

D. Okai, G. Owen, and H. McGuire, 'Mental Capacity in Psychiatric Patients' (2018) 191(4) *The British Journal of Psychiatry* 291–297.

O. O'Neill, *Autonomy and Trust in Bioethics* (Cambridge, Cambridge University Press, 2002).

A. Orb, L. Eisenhauer, and D. Wynaden, 'Ethics in Qualitative Research' (2000) 33 (1) *Journal of Nursing Scholarship* 93–96.

G. Owen *et al.*, 'Mental Capacity to Make Decisions on Treatment in People Admitted to Psychiatric Hospitals: A Cross-Sectional Study' (2008) 337 (7660) *British Medical Journal* 40.

'Temporal Inabilities and Decision-making Capacity in Depression' (2015) 14 *Phenomenology and the Cognitive Sciences* 163.

D. Parfit, *Reasons and Persons* (Oxford: Oxford University Press, 1986).

A. Plumb, 'UN Convention on the Rights of Persons with Disabilities: Out of the Frying Pan and into the Fire? Mental Health Service Users and Survivors Aligning with the Disability Movement' in H. Spandler, J. Anderson, and B. Sapey (eds), *Madness, Distress and the Politics of Disablement* (Bristol: Bristol University Press, 2015).

S. Priebe *et al.*, 'Predictors of Clinical and Social Outcomes Following Involuntary Hospital Admission: A Prospective Observational Study' (2011) 261 *European Archives of Psychiatry and Clinical Neuroscience* 377–386.

J. Pugh, *Autonomy, Rationality, and Contemporary Bioethics* (Oxford: Oxford University Press, 2020).

J. Radden, 'Mental Disorder (Illness)' *The Stanford Encyclopedia of Philosophy* (Stanford, CA: Stanford University, Summer 2023 Edition). https://plato.stanford.edu/archives/sum2023/entries/mental-disorder/.

M. Ratcliffe, *Experiences of Depression: A Study in Phenomenology* (Oxford: Oxford University Press, 2015).

J. Rawls, *Political Liberalism* (New York: Columbia University Press, 1993), 144–150.

V. Raymont, A. Buchanan, A. David *et al.*, 'The Inter-Rater Reliability of Mental Capacity Assessments' (2007) 30(2) *International Journal of Law and Psychiatry* 112–117.

J. Raz, 'The Rule of Law and Its Virtue' (1977) 93 *Law Quarterly Review* 195.

The Morality of Freedom (Oxford: Clarendon Paperbacks Oxford University Press, 1988).

'The Problem of Authority: Revisiting the Service Conception' (2005) 90 *Minnesota Law Review* 1003.

N Rees, 'The Fusion Proposal: A Next Step' in B McSherry and P Weller (eds), *Rethinking Rights-Based Mental Health Laws* (Oxford: Hart Publishing, 2010).

S.P. Reise and N.G. Waller. 'Item Response Theory and Clinical Measurement' (2009) 5 *Annual Review of Clinical Psychology* 27–48.

B.A. Rich, 'Prospective Autonomy and Critical Interests: A Narrative Defense of the Moral Authority of Advance Directives' (1997) 6 *Cambridge Quarterly of Healthcare Ethics* 138.

G. Richardson, 'Balancing Autonomy and Risk: A Failure of Nerve in England and Wales' (2007) 30 *International Journal of Law and Psychiatry* 71.

'Mental Capacity at the Margin: The Interface between Two Acts' (2010) 18 *Medical Law Review* 56–77.

"Mental Disabilities and the Law: From Substitute to Supported Decision Making" (2012) 65(1) *Current Legal Problems* 333–354.

"Mental Capacity in the Shadow of Suicide: What Can the Law Do?" (2013) 9 *International Journal of Law in Context*, 87–105.

J.E. Richters and S.P. Hinshaw, 'The Abduction of Disorder in Psychiatry' (1999) 108(3) *Journal of Abnormal Psychology* 438–445.

A. Ruck Keene *et al.*, *Court of Protection Handbook: A User's Guide* (Legal Action Group, 2014).

A. Ruck Keene and C. Auckland, 'More Presumptions Please? Wishes, Feelings and Best Interests Decision-Making' (2015) 3 *Elder Law Journal* 293.

A. Ruck Keene *et al.*, 'Taking Capacity Seriously? Ten Years of Mental Capacity Disputes before England's Court of Protection' (2019) 62 *International Journal of Law and Psychiatry* 56–76.

A. Ruck Keene, N. Kane, S. Kim, and G. Owen, 'Mental Capacity – Why Look for a Paradigm Shift?' (January 2023) *Medical Law Review* 9 (advanced availability online). Available at: https://academic.oup.com/medlaw/advance-article/doi/10.1093/medlaw/fwac052/6987005.

A. Rudnick, 'Depression and Competence to Refuse Psychiatric Treatment' (2002) 28 *Journal of Medical Ethics* 151–155.

D.L. Sackett, G.W. Torrance, 'The Utility of Different Health States as Perceived by the General Public' (1978) 31 *Journal of Chronic Diseases* 697—704.

M. Sandel, *Liberalism and the Limits of Justice*, 2nd ed. (Cambridge: Cambridge University Press, 1997).

B. Saunders *et al.*, 'Saturation in Qualitative Research: Exploring Its Conceptualization and Operationalization' (2018) 52(4) *Quality and Quantity* 1893–1907.

J. Savulescu, 'Autonomy, the Good Life, and Controversial Choices' in R. Rhodes, L.P. Francis, and A. Silvers (eds), *The Blackwell Guide to Medical Ethics* (Oxford: Blackwell, 2006) 17–37.

G. Scarre, Children and Paternalism (1980) 55(211) *Philosophy* 117–124.

P. Sedgwick, *Psycho Politics* (New York: Harper & Row, 1982).

L. Series, 'Relationships, Autonomy and Legal Capacity: Mental Capacity and Support Paradigms' (2015) 40 *International Journal of Law and Psychiatry* 80.

'The Place of Wishes and Feelings in Best Interests Decisions: Wye Valley NHS Trust v Mr B' (2016) 79(6) *Medical Law Review* 1090–1115.

"The Participation of the Relevant Person in Proceedings in the Court of Protection: A Briefing Paper on International Human Rights Requirements (2015), Version 1.2. Available at: http://sites.cardiff.ac.uk/wccop/files/2014/09/Briefing-on-Personal-Participation-in-the-CoP-v1-2.pdf.

D. Singh and W. Sinnott-Armstrong, 'The DSM-5 Definition of Mental Disorder' (2015) 29(1) *Public Affairs Quarterly* 5–31.

M Sjöstrand and N. Juth, 'Authenticity and Psychiatric Disorder: Does Autonomy of Personal Preferences Matter?' (2014) 17(1) *Medicine, Health Care and Philosophy* 115–122.

C. Sutcliffe, A. Burns D. Challis *et al.*, 'Depressed Mood, Cognitive Impairment, and Survival in Older People Admitted to Care Homes in England' (2007) 15(8) *American Journal of Geriatric Psychiatry* 708–715.

T. Szasz, *The Myth of Mental Illness* (London: Paladin, 1972).

The Medicalization of Everyday Life (New York: Syracuse University Press, 2007).

P Szawarski, 'Classic Cases Revisited: The Suicide of Kerrie Wooltorton' (2013) 14 (3) *The Intensive Care Society* 211–214. Available at http://journals.sagepub.com/doi/pdf/10.1177/175114371301400307.

G. Szmukler and F. Holloway, 'Reform of the Mental Health Act: Health or Safety?' (2000) 177 *British Journal of Psychiatry* 196.

J. Tan, 'Competence to Refuse Treatment in Anorexia Nervosa' (2013) 26(6) *International Journal of Law and Psychiatry* 697–707.

J. Tan, A. Stewart, R. Fitzpatrick, and R.A. Hope, 'Competence to Make Treatment Decisions in Anorexia Nervosa: Thinking Processes and Values' (2006) 13 (4) *Philosophy, Psychiatry & Psychology* p267–282.

H. Taylor, 'What Are "Best Interests"? A Critical Evaluation of "Best Interests" Decision-Making in Clinical Practice' (2016) 24 *Medical Law Review* 176.

E. Fuller Torrey *et al.*, 'Neurochemical Markers for Schizophrenia, Bipolar Disorder, and Major Depression in Postmortem Brains' (2005) 57(3) *Biological Psychiatry* 252–260.

P.A. Ubel *et al.*, 'Do Nonpatients Underestimate the Quality of Life Associated with Chronic Health Conditions Because of a Focusing Illusion?' (2001) 21 (3) *Medical Decision Making* 190–9.

P.A. Ubel, G. Loewenstein, N. Schwarz, and D. Smith, 'Misimagining the Unimaginable: The Disability Paradox and Health Care Decision Making' (2005) 24(4S) *Health Psychology* S57–62.

R. Veatch, 'Doctor Does Not Know Best: Why in the New Century Physicians Must Stop Trying to Benefit Patients' (2000) 25(6) *Journal of Medicine and Philosophy* 701–721.

L.C. Vogel *et al.*, 'Long-Term Outcomes and Life Satisfaction of Adults Who Had Pediatric Spinal Cord Injuries' (1998) 79 *Archives of Physical Medicine and Rehabilitation* 1496.

J. Wakefield, 'The Concept of Mental Disorder: On the Boundary between Biological Facts and Social Values' (1992) 47(3) *American Psychologist* 373–388.

'The Biostatistical Theory versus the Harmful Dysfunction Analysis, Part 1: Is Part-Dysfunction a Sufficient Condition for Medical Disorder?' (2014) 39 *Journal of Medicine and Philosophy* 648–682.

S. Waldfogel and S. Meadows, 'Religious Issues in the Capacity Evaluation' (1996) 18 *General Hospital Psychiatry* 173–182.

J. Wall, 'Being and Being Lost' in C. Foster, J. Herring, and I. Doron (eds), *The Law and Ethics of Dementia* (Oxford: Hart Publishing, 2014), 327–337.

'Being Yourself: Authentic Decision-Making and Depression' in C. Foster and J. Herring (eds), *Depression: Law and Ethics* (Oxford: Oxford University Press, 2017), 134–144.

G. Watson, 'Free Agency' (1975) 72(8) *The Journal of Philosophy* 205–220.

J.V.M. Welie and S.P.K. Welie, 'Patient Decision-Making Competence: Outlines of a Conceptual Analysis' (2001) 4(2) *Medicine, Healthcare and Philosophy* 127–138.

T. Williamson *et al.*, 'Listening to the Lady in the Bed: The Mental Capacity Act 2005 in Practice for Older People' (2012) 3 *Elder Law Journal* 185.

B. Winick, 'The Rights to Refuse Mental Health Treatment: A Therapeutic Jurisprudence Analysis' (1994) 17 *International Journal of Law and Psychiatry* 99.

P. Wolpe, 'The Triumph of Autonomy in American Bioethics: A Sociological View' in R. de Vries and H. Subedi (eds), *Bioethics and Society: Constructing the Ethical Enterprise* (Upper Saddle River, NJ: Prentice Hall, 1988).

A. Yildiz-Yesiloglu and D. Pauler Ankerst, Neurochemical Alterations of the Brain in Bipolar Disorder and Their Implications for Pathophysiology: A Systematic Review of the In Vivo Proton Magnetic Resonance Spectroscopy Findings' (2006) 30(6) *Progress in Neuro-Psychopharmacology and Biological Psychiatry* 969–995.

Reports and Guidance

Alzheimer's Society, *Fix Dementia Care: Hospitals* (January 2016). Available at: www.alzheimers.org.uk/sites/default/files/migrate/downloads/fix_dementia_care_-_hospitals.pdf. Accessed 3 June 2016.

American Psychiatric Association, *Diagnostic and Statistical Manual of Mental Disorders*, 5th ed. (Arlington, VA: American Psychiatric Publishing, 2013).

Chief Medical Officer, *Making Amends: A Consultation Paper Setting out Proposals for Reforming the Approach to Clinical Negligence in the NHS* (London, UK: Department of Health, 30 June 2003).

Committee on the Rights of Persons with Disabilities, *General Comment No 1* (2014) Article 12: Equal Recognition Before the Law (adopted at the Eleventh session of the Committee, 31 March–11 April 2014, Geneva, CRPD/C/GC/1).

Department for Constitutional Affairs, *Mental Capacity Act 2005 Code of Practice* (London: TSO, 2007).

Department of Health and Social Care, *Modernising the Mental Health Act: Increasing Choice, Reducing Compulsion: Final Report of the Independent Review of the Mental Health Act 1983* (London: TSO, 2018).

Department of Health and Social Services and Public Safety, Northern Ireland, Department of Justice, *Draft Mental Capacity Bill (Nl): Consultation Document*. DHSSNI 'DOJ, 2014. Available at: www.health-ni.gov.uk/sites/default/files/consultations/dhssps/mental-capacity-consultation-document.pdf. Accessed 8 October 2016.

Department of Health, *Independence, Choice and Risk: A Guide to Best Practice in Supported Decision Making* (London: Department of Health, 2007).

No Voice Unheard, No Right Ignored – A Consultation for People with Learning Disabilities, Autism and Mental Health Conditions (Department of Health, UK Government, HMSO, 2015) Cm 9007.

The Director of Public Prosecutions, 'Suicide: Policy for Prosecutors in Respect of Cases of Encouraging or Assisting Suicide' (October 2014). Available at: www.cps.gov.uk/legal-guidance/suicide-policy-prosecutors-respect-cases-encouraging-or-assisting-suicide. Accessed 10 October 2017.

Explanatory Notes to the Mental Capacity Act, [37]. Available at: www.legislation.gov.uk/ukpga/2005/9/notes/division/6/1/2/4.

Fourth Programme of Law Reform (1989) Law Commission No. 185 Cm 800.

Government Response to the Scrutiny Committee's Report on the Draft Mental Incapacity Bill (London, February 2004) Cm 6121.

House of Lords Select Committee on the Mental Capacity Act 2005, *Mental Capacity Act 2005: Post-Legislative Scrutiny* (HL Paper 139, 13/3/14) (also House of Lords Debate on the Select Committee Report, UK).

ICD-10: International Statistical Classification of Diseases and Related Health Problems, tenth revision, 2nd ed. (Geneva: World Health Organization, 2003).

K. Keywood *et al.*, *Best Practice? Healthcare Decision-Making by, with and for Adults with Learning Disabilities* (Manchester: National Development Team, 1999).

L. Lakey, *Counting the Cost: Caring for People with Dementia in Hospital Wards* (London: Alzheimer's Society, 2009). Available at: www.alzheimers.org.uk/sites/default/files/2018–05/Counting_the_cost_report.pdf. Accessed 20 August 2017.

Law Commission Consultation Paper, *Mental Incapacitated Adults and Decision-Making: A New Jurisdiction*, Law Com No. 128 (HMSO, 1993).

Mental Incapacity, Law Com No. 231 (Edinburgh: HMSO, 1995).

Mentally *Incapacitated Adults and Decision-Making: An Overview*, Law Com Consultation Paper No. 119 (Switzerland: HMSO, 1991).

Law Commission, *Mental Capacity and Deprivation of Liberty – Consultation Analysis* (2017). Available at: https://s3-eu-west-2.amazonaws.com/lawcom-prod-storage-11jsxou24uy7q/uploads/2017/03/cp222_mental_capacity_responses_analysis.pdf. Accessed 25 September 2018.

Mental Capacity and Deprivation of Liberty (Law Com No. 372) (HMSO, 13 March 2017).

Law Commission's Consultation Paper No. 222, *Mental Capacity and Deprivation of Liberty* (The Law Commission of England and Wales, HMSO, 2015).

W. Martin *et al.*, *Achieving CRPD Compliance: Is the Mental Capacity Act of England and Wales Compatible with the UN Convention on the Rights of Persons with Disabilities? If Not, What Next?* (Colchester: University of Essex, 2014) Essex Autonomy Project, 22 September 2014.

Three Jurisdictions Report: Towards Compliance with CRPD Art. 12 in Capacity/Incapacity Legislation across the UK (Colchester: University of Essex, 2016). Essex Autonomy Project. Available at: https://autonomy.essex.ac.uk/wp-content/uploads/2017/01/EAP-3J-Final-Report-2016.pdf. Accessed 20 September 2018.

S. McManus *et al.*, *Adult Psychiatric Morbidity in England, 2007: Results of a Household Survey* (England: The NHS Information Centre for Health and Social Care, 2009).

National Mental Capacity Forum, *Fourth Report of the National Mental Capacity Forum* (HM Government, August 2020). Available at: https://assets.publishing.service.gov.uk/government/uploads/system/uploads/attachment_data/file/908360/nmcf-chair_s-fourth-annual-report-2019–20.pdf. Accessed 8 January 2021.

NHS England, *Dementia Assessment and Referral Data Collection – April 2018* (2018). Available at: www.england.nhs.uk/statistics/wp-content/uploads/sites/2/2018/07/Dementia-Press-Notice-April-2018-PDF-195KB.pdf. Accessed 1 July 2019.

Northern Ireland Assembly Ad Hoc Joint Committee on the Mental Capacity Bill, 'Report on the Mental Capacity Bill' (Report: NIA 252/11-16) (25 January 2016).

Report of the Joint Committee on the Draft Mental Incapacity Bill (HL 189-1, HC 1083–1 (London, UK: TSO, 2003).

Report on Incapable Adults, Scottish Law Commission Report No. 151 (1995).

The Royal College of Emergency Medicine, *Best Practice Guidelines: The Mental Capacity Act in Emergency Medicine Practice* (February 2017). Available at: https://rcem.ac.uk/wp-content/uploads/2021/10/RCEM_Mental_Capacity_Act_in_EM_Practice_Feb2017.pdf. Accessed 5 February 2024.

Social Care Institute for Excellence, *Mental Capacity Assessment Tool Guidance* (UK, August 2015). Available at: https://www.advancedassessments.co.uk/resources/Mental-Capacity-Assessment-Tool.pdf.

V. Williams *et al.*, *Making Best Interests Decisions: People and Processes* (London: Mental Health Foundation, 2012). Available at: www.mentalhealth.org.uk/publications/bids-report. Accessed 15 April 2016.

World Health Organization. *The ICD-10 Classification of Mental and Behavioural Disorders: Clinical Descriptions and Diagnostic Guidelines.* (Geneva: World Health Organization, 1992).

INDEX

CAMBRIDGE BIOETHICS AND LAW

Books in the Series

Marcus Radetzki, Marian Radetzki and Niklas Juth *Genes and Insurance: Ethical, Legal and Economic Issues*

Ruth Macklin *Double Standards in Medical Research in Developing Countries*

Donna Dickenson *Property in the Body: Feminist Perspectives*

Matti Häyry, Ruth Chadwick, Vilhjálmur Árnason and Gardar Árnason *The Ethics and Governance of Human Genetic Databases: European Perspectives*

J. K. Mason *The Troubled Pregnancy: Legal Wrongs and Rights in Reproduction*

Daniel Sperling *Posthumous Interests: Legal and Ethical Perspectives*

Keith Syrett *Law, Legitimacy and the Rationing of Health Care: A Contextual and Comparative Perspective*

Alasdair Maclean *Autonomy, Informed Consent and Medical Law: A Relational Change*

Heather Widdows and Caroline Mullen *The Governance of Genetic Information: Who Decides?*

David Price *Human Tissue in Transplantation and Research: A Model Legal and Ethical Donation Framework*

Matti Häyry *Rationality and the Genetic Challenge: Making People Better?*

Mary Donnelly *Healthcare Decision-Making and the Law: Autonomy, Capacity and the Limits of Liberalism*

Anne-Maree Farrell, David Price and Muireann Quigley *Organ Shortage: Ethics, Law and Pragmatism*

Sara Fovargue *Xenotransplantation and Risk: Regulating a Developing Biotechnology*

John Coggon *What Makes Health Public? A Critical Evaluation of Moral, Legal, and Political Claims in Public Health*

Mark Taylor *Genetic Data and the Law: A Critical Perspective on Privacy Protection*

Anne-Maree Farrell *The Politics of Blood: Ethics, Innovation and the Regulation of Risk*

Stephen W. Smith *End-of-Life Decisions in Medical Care: Principles and Policies for Regulating the Dying Process*

Michael Parker *Ethical Problems and Genetics Practice*

William W. Lowrance *Privacy, Confidentiality, and Health Research*

Kerry Lynn Macintosh *Human Cloning: Four Fallacies and Their Legal Consequence*

Heather Widdows *The Connected Self: The Ethics and Governance of the Genetic Individual*

Amel Alghrani, Rebecca Bennett and Suzanne Ost *Bioethics, Medicine and the Criminal Law Volume I: The Criminal Law and Bioethical Conflict: Walking the Tightrope*

Danielle Griffiths and Andrew Sanders *Bioethics, Medicine and the Criminal Law Volume II: Medicine, Crime and Society*

Margaret Brazier and Suzanne Ost *Bioethics, Medicine and the Criminal Law Volume III: Medicine and Bioethics in the Theatre of the Criminal Process*

Sigrid Sterckx, Kasper Raus and Freddy Mortier *Continuous Sedation at the End of Life: Ethical, Clinical and Legal Perspectives*

A. M. Viens, John Coggon and Anthony S. Kessel *Criminal Law, Philosophy and Public Health Practice*

Ruth Chadwick, Mairi Levitt and Darren Shickle *The Right to Know and the Right Not to Know: Genetic Privacy and Responsibility*

Eleanor D. Kinney *The Affordable Care Act and Medicare in Comparative Context*

Katri Lõhmus *Caring Autonomy: European Human Rights Law and the Challenge of Individualism*

Catherine Stanton and Hannah Quirk *Criminalising Contagion: Legal and Ethical Challenges of Disease Transmission and the Criminal Law*

Sharona Hoffman *Electronic Health Records and Medical Big Data: Law and Policy*

Barbara Prainsack and Alena Buyx *Solidarity in Biomedicine and Beyond*

Camillia Kong *Mental Capacity in Relationship: Decision-Making, Dialogue, and Autonomy*

Oliver Quick *Regulating Patient Safety: The End of Professional Dominance?*

Thana Cristina de Campos *The Global Health Crisis: Ethical Responsibilities*

Jonathan Ives, Michael Dunn and Alan Cribb *Empirical Bioethics: Theoretical and Practical Perspectives*

Alan Merry and Warren Brookbanks Merry and McCall Smith's Errors, Medicine and the Law (second edition)

Donna Dickenson *Property in the Body: Feminist Perspectives* (second edition)

Rosie Harding *Duties to Care: Dementia, Relationality and Law*

Ruud ter Meulen *Solidarity and Justice in Health and Social Care*

David Albert Jones, Chris Gastmans and Calum MacKellar *Euthanasia and Assisted Suicide: Lessons from Belgium*

Muireann Quigley *Self-Ownership, Property Rights, and the Human Body: A Legal Perspective*

Françoise Baylis and Alice Dreger *Bioethics in Action*

John Keown Euthanasia, Ethics and Public Policy: An Argument against Legislation (second edition)

Amel Alghrani *Regulating Assisted Reproductive Technologies: New Horizons*

Britta van Beers, Sigrid Sterckx and Donna Dickenson *Personalised Medicine, Individual Choice and the Common Good*

David G. Kirchhoffer and Bernadette J. Richards *Beyond Autonomy: Limits and Alternatives to Informed Consent in Research Ethics and Law*

Markus Wolfensberger and Anthony Wrigley *Trust in Medicine: Its Nature, Justification, Significance, and Decline*

Catriona A. W. McMillan *The Human Embryo in vitro: Breaking the Legal Stalemate*

Benjamin Peter White and , Lindy Willmott (editors) *International Perspectives on End-of-Life Law Reform: Politics, Persuasion and Persistence*

Carolyn Adams, Judy Allen and Felicity Flack *Sharing Linked Data for Health Research: Toward Better Decision Making*

Emily Postan *Embodied Narratives: Protecting Identity Interests through Ethical Governance of Bioinformation*

Jaime Lindsey *Reimagining the Court of Protection: Access to Justice in Mental Capacity Law*

Marcelo Corrales Compagnucci, Michael Lowery Wilson, Mark Fenwick, Nikolaus Forgó, Till Bärnighausen *AI in eHealth: Human Autonomy, Data Governance and Privacy in Healthcare*

Steph Jowett *Consent for Medical Treatment of Trans and Gender Diverse Youth*

Julia Duffy *Mental Capacity, Dignity and the Power of International Human Rights*

For EU product safety concerns, contact us at Calle de José Abascal, 56–1°, 28003 Madrid, Spain or eugpsr@cambridge.org.

www.ingramcontent.com/pod-product-compliance
Ingram Content Group UK Ltd.
Pitfield, Milton Keynes, MK11 3LW, UK
UKHW020113040726
472853UK00010B/534
* 9 7 8 1 0 0 9 4 8 2 0 6 6 *